PERVERSION OF JUSTICE

PERVER

OF J

THE JEFFREY EPSTEIN STORY

SION
USTICE

JULIE K. BROWN

DEY ST.
An Imprint of WILLIAM MORROW

DEY ST.

PERVERSION OF JUSTICE. Copyright © 2021 by Julie K. Brown.
All rights reserved. Printed in the United States of America.
No part of this book may be used or reproduced in any manner
whatsoever without written permission except in the case of brief
quotations embodied in critical articles and reviews. For information, address
HarperCollins Publishers, 195 Broadway, New York, NY 10007.

HarperCollins books may be purchased for educational, business,
or sales promotional use. For information, please email the
Special Markets Department at SPsales@harpercollins.com.

FIRST EDITION

Designed by Renata De Oliveira

Library of Congress Cataloging-in-Publication Data

Names: Brown, Julie K., 1961– author.
Title: Perversion of justice : the Jeffrey Epstein story / Julie K. Brown.
Description: First edition. | New York, NY : Dey Street, [2021] | Includes
    bibliographical references.
Identifiers: LCCN 2021012257 (print) | LCCN 2021012258 (ebook) | ISBN
    9780063000582 (hardcover) | ISBN 9780063000599 (paperback) | ISBN
    9780063063174 (hardcover) | ISBN 9780063000605 (ebook) | ISBN
    9780063000612 (audio) | ISBN 9780063000629 (audio)
Subjects: LCSH: Epstein, Jeffrey, 1953–2019. | Human trafficking—United
    States—Case studies. | Sex crimes—United States—Case studies. |
    Criminal justice, Administration of—Corrupt practices—United
    States—Case studies. | Capitalists and financiers—United States—
    Case studies.
Classification: LCC HQ285.E67 B76 2021 (print) | LCC HQ285.E67 (ebook) |
    DDC 306.3/620973—dc23
LC record available at https://lccn.loc.gov/2021012257
LC ebook record available at https://lccn.loc.gov/2021012258

ISBN 978-0-06-300058-2 (hardcover)
ISBN 978-0-06-320545-1 (international edition)

21 22 23 24 25 LSC 10 9 8 7 6 5 4 3 2 1

THIS BOOK IS DEDICATED TO ALL OF
JEFFREY EPSTEIN'S SURVIVORS,

especially
MICHELLE LICATA,
COURTNEY WILD,
VIRGINIA GIUFFRE, AND
JENA-LISA JONES.

with special thanks to
MICHAEL REITER

and the late
JOE RECAREY.

CONTENTS

AUTHOR'S NOTE

Unless otherwise noted, all the information contained in this book is from my own reporting and interviews or court or government records. The names of some of the victims in this story have been changed to protect their privacy.

PREFACE

In September 2006, Detective Joe Recarey handed state prosecutors in South Florida a textbook underage sex case he thought would be a no-brainer to prosecute.

For at least six years, multimillionaire financier Jeffrey Edward Epstein, fifty-three, and others working for him had been luring middle school and high school girls to his waterfront mansion in Palm Beach, Florida, by offering to pay them for massages. The girls, mostly thirteen to sixteen years old, arrived at all hours of the day and night, whereupon they were sexually abused in acts ranging from inappropriate touching to rape. Afterward, Epstein paid them two to three hundred dollars each, then offered to give them even more money if the teenagers brought their friends, creating a revolving door of fresh young girls to fill his pedophile obsession.

Epstein was wealthy enough to buy anything he wanted, including prostitutes. But he didn't want experienced women; his preferred prey were waiflike prepubescent girls from troubled backgrounds who needed money and had little or no sexual experience.

These were girls he thought no one would believe, and Epstein and his accomplices would do everything in their power to silence them.

Palm Beach police nevertheless did their due diligence, interviewing about three dozen girls and building a solid criminal case. They compiled thick files of evidence to support the girls' accounts, including phone records and messages, documents, plane manifests, and witnesses' statements.

Epstein hired the flamboyant Harvard lawyer Alan Dershowitz, who met with Barry Krischer, the Palm Beach state attorney responsible for prosecuting the case. Soon, criminal prosecutors were no longer scrutinizing Epstein; they were excoriating his underage victims.

Over the course of a year, everything that Recarey believed about justice was shaken to its core. Krischer, seemingly dazzled by Dershowitz's fame, would turn his back on the victims and the police working the case; Epstein and the private investigators hired by his lawyers stalked and threatened the girls and their families, tearing their lives apart. Ultimately, the FBI would take over the investigation. The man who would oversee the federal case was a young, rising star in the Republican Party who had ambitions to become a U.S. Supreme Court justice. Rene Alexander Acosta, thirty-seven, was sworn in as U.S. attorney in Miami in October 2006, just as the FBI began to suspect that Epstein's crimes went well beyond South Florida.

Epstein had given liberally to Democratic candidates and causes, but he knew that if he wanted the Republicans then in the White House in his corner, he needed someone with clout in Washington. His legal dream team included Kenneth Starr, the former independent counsel who had employed his skills of moral outrage and prosecutorial kill to make the case for President Bill Clinton's 1998 impeachment.

Citing a "solemn intent to ensure fairness and integrity in the administration of justice," Starr asked the Justice Department to essentially quash the federal case that prosecutors in Miami were mounting against Epstein.

Despite their opposite political alliances, Starr and Epstein had some things in common: both were adept at cultivating power and had an arsenal of tricks at their disposal to outwit people to whatever ends met their goals.

Sure enough, in 2008, Epstein and his high-priced lawyers wrangled an unusual plea bargain from federal prosecutors, one that defied some of our nation's most basic legal principles.

Acosta would later contend that he agreed to give Epstein federal immunity from sex trafficking charges based on the unlikely success that prosecutors felt they would have at trial.

Even with the little bit that I knew about the case in 2016, this never made sense to me. After all, immunity is a benefit granted in exchange for something else of value to prosecutors. What, if anything, did federal authorities get for giving Epstein and his co-conspirators—both named and unnamed—immunity?

Over the past decade, much had been written about this case by countless journalists. But little of it offered real insight into how someone so evil was able to manipulate so many people—from the offices of Wall Street to the corridors of the Department of Justice.

By 2016, the Jeffrey Epstein case seemed to be just a footnote in history.

I felt the story needed a more rigorous analysis, and so I set out to unpack the case and take a fresh look. I wanted to learn how and why such a prolific child sex predator could get away with his crimes.

I learned that there were plenty of people who knew what Epstein was doing, not only in Palm Beach, but in New York and on his private island, as he flaunted his young conquests at dinner parties and events he attended with well-heeled, socially and politically connected people, some of whom worked in the media, led billion-dollar companies, and had Nobel Prizes on their résumés.

Even when it later became clear that Epstein had been exploiting and abusing girls, his friends, professional acquaintances, and those who wanted the benefit of his checkbook continued to associate with him.

In liberal circles, political analysts who studied the case often focused on Epstein's connection to Donald Trump, while conservatives tried to link the scandal to Bill Clinton.

The truth is there were powerful people on both sides of the political rails—as well as people in the worlds of finance, academia, and science—who were involved with Epstein or, at the very least, complicit with what he was doing.

I also learned that Epstein likely conducted video surveillance in every home he owned. As insurance, he probably had tapes and photographs of important visitors—mainly men—in compromising situations. Whether that was true or not, even the possibility that he had blackmail material was enough motive for many powerful people to do everything possible to cover up Epstein's crimes.

THE JEFFREY EPSTEIN STORY EPITOMIZES OUR NATION'S LOPSIDED system of justice, and how victims of sexual assault, especially those who are young and poor, are discarded, shamed, and mistreated by the very people who are supposed to protect them.

Epstein got away with his crimes because nearly every element of society allowed him to get away with them. Professional, legal, and moral ethics were set aside for a broken system of values that places corporate profits, personal wealth, political connections, and celebrity above some of the most sacred tenets of our faiths, our teachings, and our democracy.

When I became a journalist, I learned that the most rewarding part of my work was in righting injustices for those who could not fight for themselves.

Few people seemed to recognize that Epstein not only beat the system—but he was probably still hunting, terrorizing, and abusing young women and girls.

I would face many obstacles on my path to the truth. I would be attacked by the legal forces who failed their solemn oaths, by the defense attorneys who profited off Epstein's crimes—and by some of those within my own industry who thought that what I was doing was nothing more than a rehash of an old story.

In my lifetime, there has never been a more urgent need for journalism, or a more important time to play a role in giving voice to those who have none.

I believe that at this moment in history, when world events test our resilience, and when propaganda, conspiracies, and lies threaten to undermine all that our nation holds dear, it will be journalists who hold the corrupt and powerful to account. As journalists, we cannot put aside this important mission, even if we think the story has already been told.

Because this was one story that wasn't finished.

Julie K. Brown
March 1, 2021

INTRODUCTION

In February 2017, just weeks before newly elected President Donald J. Trump was to give his first State of the Union address, I was holed up in my apartment in Hollywood, Florida, gathering string for the most grueling job application process of my career.

My assignment was to pick three stories from the previous week and quickly spin out prospective investigative projects from each of the three stories. With Trump now in the White House, there was a frenzy of national media coverage, and no shortage of topics to choose from: the deportation of immigrants; the president's daily threats to dismantle Obamacare; and Trump's first military act as president, a controversial raid in Yemen that claimed the life of a U.S. Navy SEAL.

I had been working for the *Miami Herald* for more than a decade and, with my children now almost grown, I was excited about the possibility of change. I was applying for a job with the storied *Washington Post*, which was hiring a handful of journalists for a newly created investigations team, called the Rapid Response Team.

The team was uncannily suited for me. As part of the *Herald*'s investigative team for several years, I had carved out a niche in being able to take breaking news stories about big events, dig into the backgrounds of the people involved, and quickly churn out deeply researched stories.

My investigative work at the paper had earned several honors, including a George Polk Award and a Robert F. Kennedy Journalism Award, both among the most prestigious awards in journalism.

The recognition I received led me to begin a series of conversations with the *Washington Post*, starting in 2014. The *Post* is affectionately referred to as the *Miami Herald North*, because so many reporters at the *Herald* have gone on to work there. But now it was 2017—three years later—and I was still trying to get hired.

The editors' comments, however, were ever encouraging; I was told that it was "a process" and each time I went through it, I would likely get closer to being tapped.

I was more excited about the prospect of working at the paper now because it had been purchased by Amazon owner Jeff Bezos and was flush with money. I hoped it would offer me the kind of stability that I never felt I had at the *Herald*, where layoffs, pay cuts, and unpaid leaves were an annual ritual. As a single parent with two children, there was never a time during my journalism career when I didn't worry that I would lose my job, or that I would have to supplement my income by getting a part-time job. I was finally, in 2016, earning almost the same amount as when I was hired at the *Herald* a decade earlier. This was because I had been through so many pay cuts and furloughs that my salary kept going down, rather than up.

The *Post* was also doing the kind of dogged journalism that I loved. I was a fast, competitive reporter who preferred to report investigative developments as they happened rather than unfurling a long, tedious piece that readers often don't have the time to read. One of the biggest challenges of an investigative journalist is to make dense information and data compelling enough to hold people's attention until the end. I did this (or tried to) by focusing on the people behind the headlines.

So, in February 2017, I spent several weeks putting together what I hoped would be a successful application package for the *Post*. Not only did I pitch a story about Bill Owens, the heartbroken father of the fallen U.S. Navy SEAL, but ten days after submitting my proposal, I actually landed the piece for the *Miami Herald*: an exclusive interview with the father, a former Fort Lauderdale police officer who had refused to meet Donald Trump when the president arrived to pay his respects to the family at Dover Air Force Base.

When I first met Mr. Owens, he wasn't ready to talk about the loss of his son, Ryan. I respected that, and even though I could have written some of the things I learned the first night I met him, I didn't tell anyone except my editor that I had met with Owens and his wife.

I gave Mr. Owens my business card and told him I wanted to write his story when he was ready to tell it.

Then I set out to learn everything I could about being a Navy SEAL. I don't know why, but I had a feeling I would hear from Mr. Owens again.

By then, I had already submitted my package to the *Post* in which I pitched the Navy SEAL story and two additional story ideas, including one about past allegations of domestic abuse against Trump's new nominee for labor secretary, Andrew Puzder.

I crossed my fingers and told myself that if I didn't get the job, it wasn't meant to be, that God had other plans for me.

The SEAL story ran in the *Herald* in late February 2017 and drew international attention. The interview was made even more controversial by Owens's remarks that the president was trying to block an investigation into what had happened in the raid that claimed his son's life.

The days rolled by, and I buried my head in other work. On March 2, the *Post*'s chief investigative editor, Jeff Leen, told me I was still very much in the running, and I would be contacted soon.

Finally, in late April, I got the word that I had been passed over. "It was a very hard decision," Leen told me.

It was a blow, but I reminded myself that it was all part of the "process."

I'd been rejected plenty of times during my forty-year career. But this one really hit me hard. I was more depressed than I had been in many years. So I did what I always do when I'm dealt a hard blow: I jog, I hug my children, and I get back to work.

Thankfully, by that time, I was already nibbling on another project.

In October 2016, I had decided I needed to take a break from Florida prisons—a beat I had been covering for four years. The grind of writing about such a dark place for so long was wearing on me. So I picked another subject that was cheery and uplifting: sex trafficking.

During my years interviewing countless women in Florida's prisons, I knew that trafficking was an epidemic and that Florida is ground zero for sex traffickers, particularly traffickers recruiting victims from Latin America.

But when I searched "sex trafficking" and "Florida" on the internet, the name "Jeffrey Epstein" kept popping up again and again.

I knew the broad strokes of the case: how a supremely wealthy money manager with political connections wrestled an incredible immunity agreement out of the federal government—despite having molested, raped, and sexually abused dozens of girls.

Then, in the midst of my traumatic *Washington Post* experience, Puzder, Trump's labor secretary nominee, was forced to abandon the nomination after it came out that his wife had accused him of abuse and he had employed an undocumented immigrant as his housekeeper.

Trump nominated Acosta for the post. The forty-eight-year-old law school dean "will be a tremendous secretary of labor," Trump announced. Acosta was hailed in news stories as a "brilliant and creative leader," and, as a Cuban American and a Republican, would be the first and only Hispanic cabinet member in Trump's administration.

I was keenly aware at that moment that there was something else in Acosta's background that, in my mind, could sink his nomination.

The man who gave Jeffrey Epstein that controversial plea bargain was Alex Acosta.

So, I followed with interest Acosta's nomination hearing, expecting that he would be grilled over that deal.

I was astonished that Epstein's name barely came up, and that the questions Acosta was asked showed that the senators didn't understand the gravity of what Acosta had done. He sailed through the nomination process and was sworn in as labor secretary.

At night, when my mind tended to wander, mostly into work issues, I kept thinking about Epstein's victims. I wondered what they thought—all these years later—about the prosecutor who had let their predator off the hook. I knew they were now in their late twenties and early thirties. Maybe they had something to say about Acosta running a massive government agency with oversight of human trafficking and child labor laws.

The next day, I suggested to my boss, investigations editor Casey Frank, that I should try to find the women and talk to them.

I was already deep into public records about the Epstein case when I got a call from Jeff Leen informing me that I was, inexplicably, back in the running for a job with the *Washington Post*'s Rapid Response Team. I was surprised and elated.

I flew to Washington and met a long list of editors at the paper during a grueling day of interviews. I finally got an audience with the executive editor, Marty Baron. I was in awe and felt hopeful.

But after several more weeks of agony, the job went to the gifted Beth Reinhard, a former *Miami Herald* reporter who went on the following year to deservedly win a Pulitzer Prize.

I guess God did have other plans for me.

Sometimes I think about how, if I had landed that job at the *Washington Post*, Alexander Acosta might now be a Supreme Court justice—and Jeffrey Epstein might still be jetting around the world abusing children and young women.

chapter 1

JOE

The old police report was typed, single-spaced. Case Number 1-05-000368 was categorized as a closed sexual battery case. There were eighteen girls, ranging in age from fourteen to eighteen, listed as possible victims. All of their names were blacked out. There were witnesses, too, their names also blacked out. The evidence was difficult to discern, except through the trained eye of a police detective.

I had probably read thousands of police reports in my long journey through journalism. When you're covering a story, the police report often forms the backbone of your work, and you can count yourself lucky when you get a cop who knows how to write, does so legibly, and sneaks in scraps of life that make your story more vivid, helping readers understand the human part of tragedy—a teddy bear found in the back seat of a wrecked car; a yellowed photograph in a dead man's wallet; the words of a father, mother, or son upon learning they had lost a loved one. A writer treasures the smallest of details. They don't come often, so when you are given them, they are gold.

The Jeffrey Epstein police report was not one of those golden police reports. At 109 pages, the tome included probable-cause affidavits, arrest warrants, and nearly fifty separate reports, most of them written by Joe Recarey, then a thirtysomething police detective who had risen through the ranks of the Palm Beach Police Department.

The gregarious Queens-born detective had moved to Florida with his family at the age of thirteen, but never lost his New York swagger and his love for the Yankees. He began his law enforcement career in the Palm Beach state attorney's office in the mailroom. The scrawny nineteen-year-old then graduated to become a process server who had the thankless job of serving cops with subpoenas to appear in court.

"That's where I got my start in law enforcement," Recarey said. "I did the mail for the investigations team at the state attorney's office. That's where I got my love for investigations."

After five years, Recarey left the state attorney's office to attend the police academy. In 1991, he was hired as a patrolman by the Town of Palm Beach, Florida. In just three years, he was promoted to detective.

Recarey wasn't book educated. He didn't have a college degree like many of the officers who came before or after him on the force. In some ways, he was an odd fit on an island populated by some of the most affluent people in the world, including more pro sports team owners than anywhere in the country. Howard Stern, Jimmy Buffett, Rod Stewart, and Jon Bon Jovi all have (or had) winter estates in Palm Beach.

But Joe had a knack for putting people at ease and he was brilliant at his job. He was a sharp dresser and smoked a pack of cigarettes a day. He was charming and polite, with a boyish grin and prankster sense of humor.

"He used to impersonate me, and he was good at it," his chief,

Michael Reiter, said. "Talking to Joe was like talking to your cousin across the kitchen table. He was the salt-of-the-earth kind of cop."

At the time Recarey took over the Jeffrey Epstein case, he was divorced, and had started dating Jennifer, who worked in the police department's administration. He had two children from a previous marriage, a daughter who was eight and a six-year-old son.

Recarey knew at the outset that the Epstein case was more complex than the usual crimes he had handled during his career. What he didn't know was how the case would haunt him for the rest of his life.

Reading his police report was like reading a story with half the words in another language, or trying to put together a puzzle with half the pieces missing. The names of sexual assault victims and minors are routinely blacked out in police reports to protect victims' identities, so this report was typical.

But I nevertheless was able to piece together the basics of the crime: the suspect, Jeffrey Epstein, was an uber-wealthy financial adviser who sexually abused dozens of teenage girls in Palm Beach, offering them money for massages and manipulating them into believing he cared so much about them that he would pay for their college or art schools, or help them become the next Victoria's Secret supermodel.

He was able to persuade many of them to work for him by recruiting new victims, similar to a sexual pyramid scheme.

A cultlike figure, Epstein convinced his targets that he would provide for them—as long as they obeyed him and did as they were ordered. Those who followed his rules were richly rewarded, not only with money but with clothes and cars, trips on his private jet to exotic places, and adventures that many of them probably never would have dreamed possible. As some of them grew older, he also hooked them up with prospective husbands in the worlds of finance, tech, and industry.

Those who remained most loyal he continued to support, and

women came to depend on him, often because they had no one else in their lives. Without him, they felt lost and alone.

Most of the girls he preyed upon in Palm Beach came from broken families. A few were homeless. One slept under a highway overpass; another was a witness in the murder of her own stepbrother. Often they had been raised by single mothers, or they had parents who were alcoholics, drug addicts, or simply struggling to keep roofs over their heads. A few of the girls attended schools for troubled teenagers or lived in foster homes.

Epstein promised to rescue them, but at a cost: not only were they expected to perform for him sexually, but in some cases, they were pressured to have sex with other men old enough to be their grandfathers.

It's difficult to know how and when Epstein's scheme began. What is known is that in 1998, Epstein's then girlfriend, the British socialite Ghislaine Maxwell, began visiting colleges, art schools, spas, fitness centers, and resorts in and around Palm Beach County, under the guise that she wanted to hire young and pretty masseuses or "assistants" to come to Epstein's home and work for him.

Epstein's houseman, Juan Alessi, was ordered to drive Maxwell from resort to resort for her to hand out business cards and recruit massage therapists for Epstein. Alessi was skeptical of her motives, especially when the girls who began coming to the house looked as young as Alessi's daughter.

By 2005, the operation was in full swing. Girls from in and around West Palm Beach arrived two, three, four, or more times a day to Epstein's cotton-candy-pink waterfront mansion on the island of Palm Beach. He lived at 358 El Brillo Way, on a dead-end street lined with multimillion-dollar homes hidden behind high hedges, stone walls, and iron gates.

The estate fronted a private cove that opens to the wider Intercoastal Waterway separating Palm Beach from the mainland of Palm Beach County.

The Mediterranean-style villa was built in the 1950s, in a historic neighborhood where some of the homes date back to the 1920s. It had a second-floor wraparound balcony, a swimming pool, and separate maids' quarters.

Epstein purchased the property for $2.5 million in 1990, and set about refurbishing it with the finest furnishings and unusual pieces of art, per his rather eclectic taste. His walls were covered with photographs of naked girls and women who were his conquests. One girl recalled seeing a large black-and-white photo of a penis.

His garage was filled with SUVs, exotic cars, and motorcycles, and he employed a chef who offered the girls snacks every time they visited. For the most part, neighbors were weekenders, retirees, or snowbirds who kept to themselves and minded their own business.

But if one of them got curious and started asking questions, Epstein was known on at least one occasion to send a girl over to the man of the house to keep him happy—and get him to keep his wife quiet.

Among the resorts Maxwell visited was Canopy Beach Resort in Riviera Beach. A young woman who worked there was friends with a waitress named Haley Robson, and they both began working as recruiters for Epstein in 2004.

It was Robson who introduced the first victim reported to police in 2005.

Identified in the report as Jane Doe 1, the girl was fourteen years old, with long, wavy brown hair streaked with blond. She and her twin sister lived in nearby Royal Palm Beach, and went back and forth between their divorced parents.

Jane Doe 1 told police that she was brought to the house to give an old man a massage.

But it was next to impossible for me to decipher exactly what happened because the police report was so redacted.

I soon realized it was not going to be easy finding Jane Doe 1 and the other Jane Does whose names were scrubbed from the police report.

ON MARCH 14, 2005, PALM BEACH POLICE DETECTIVE MICHELE PAGAN took a phone call from a woman who was so distraught and nervous that she didn't want to give her name.

"My fourteen-year-old stepdaughter possibly has been molested in Palm Beach by a rich man," the woman said, explaining that she learned about the incident secondhand from another mother.

"The mother overheard a conversation between her daughter and a boy about how my stepdaughter had met a forty-five-year-old man and had sex with him and got paid for it," the woman told Pagan.

Jane Doe 1 was in her first year at Royal Palm Beach High School, a sprawling suburban secondary school that had lost four of its students to violence in the past four years, including one who was shot dead in a drug deal and another who had been planning a Columbine-style shooting on its campus.[1]

By the time police got involved, word had gotten around the school that Jane Doe 1 and other girls were having sex with a rich man on Palm Beach island. One of Jane's friends began calling her a whore and a prostitute, and Jane socked the girl in the face. That's when the principal got involved. Jane's purse was searched, and inside, the principal found three hundred dollars. Jane's parents were contacted, and in the month following the discovery of the money, Jane Doe 1's life spiraled out of control.

Both she and her sister were taking drugs, drinking, and partying, according to police and court documents. Jane Doe 1 ran away from home several times. Finally, both sisters were sent to a school for troubled kids. Jane Doe 1 was a full-time resident of the facility at the time that Pagan began the Epstein investigation.

At first, Jane denied everything, telling police that she had only accompanied Haley to Epstein's mansion so that Haley could collect money from him.

But little by little, the details spilled out.

JANE DOE 1'S SEVENTEEN-YEAR-OLD BOYFRIEND WAS HALEY ROBSON'S cousin, and he introduced the two girls.

Robson worked at an Olive Garden in Wellington. She told Jane that she also worked part-time for a wealthy man who lived in a mansion in Palm Beach. The daughter of a retired police detective, Robson said she resisted Epstein's efforts to fondle her with a vibrator during a massage.

"I know you're not comfortable, but I'll pay you two hundred dollars if you bring me some girls," Epstein told Robson afterward, adding, "the younger the better."

Robson had a confidence that Jane Doe 1 admired. She also had a lot of cash. She told Jane that she, too, could earn two to three hundred dollars for giving her boss a massage.

One Sunday, Robson picked Jane Doe 1 up at her home. They drove from Royal Palm Beach toward West Palm Beach, then crossed a bridge onto Palm Beach island, where the narrow streets were lined with homes larger than Jane had ever seen. Before arriving at the house, Haley told Jane to make sure that if her boss, "Jeff," asked, she was to say that she was eighteen years old.

Robson parked at the end of a road, got out, and led Jane up the driveway, to the side entrance, just off the patio.

"I'm here for Jeff," Robson informed the security guard, who allowed them to enter. Shortly thereafter, a silver-haired man with a long face and bushy eyebrows entered the kitchen, along with a young woman who appeared to be about Haley's age. His name was Jeffrey. The young woman's name, police would later learn, was Emmy Tayler. At the time, Tayler arranged Epstein's massage schedule and also worked as Maxwell's assistant. After the introductions,

Tayler led Jane Doe 1 up a spiral staircase from the kitchen to a master bedroom and bath. Jane told police she became anxious as Tayler put up a folding massage table and laid out a bunch of oils. "Jeff will be up in a minute," she told Jane.

"There was a big bathroom. I mean it was humongous," Jane told police. "Like a zillion people could be in that shower . . . and there was the big couch in there, it was pink and green. Hot pink and green. And a table with a phone on it. And during the massage he made a phone call but I don't remember what he said. He just said, like, four words and then hung up."

She figured she could be in and out of there with her money after a quick massage, but as Epstein ended the call, he firmly ordered her to take off all her clothes.

Suddenly, she realized she was all alone, and that no one except Haley knew where she was. Robson was nowhere to be seen. She feared what this creepy man was going to do to her. She nervously disrobed, leaving only her bra and panties on.

"I didn't know what to do because I was the only one up there, so I just took off my shirt and I was in a bra, and when he came in, and had a towel over him, he was like, 'No, take off everything.' And he said, 'Now you can get on my back.' "

Jane Doe 1 told police Epstein directed her to straddle him as he laid on his stomach. He instructed her to rub his back by moving her hands in a circular fashion, clockwise.

He then told her to climb down, and he rolled over and dropped his towel, exposing himself. He began stroking his penis with one hand, while reaching over with his other hand to fondle her breasts under her bra. He placed a vibrator between her legs. She was disgusted by his hairy back and thought that he must have been on steroids because his body was muscular but his penis was egg-shaped and small.

As she told Pagan the story, Jane Doe 1 wept and pressed her finger hard against her thigh, recalling how Epstein admired her body and told her how she was sexually arousing him.

"It was disgusting, and I couldn't even look," she said.

Epstein asked her how she knew Haley, how old she was, what grade she was in, and what school she went to. She lied, telling him she was an eighteen-year-old senior at Wellington High School.

It was not clear how long she was in the room, but after he ejaculated, he ordered her to get dressed and gave her three hundred dollars. He told her to leave her name and phone number with his assistant. And then he went into the shower.

Robson collected two hundred dollars as a finder's fee and the two of them left the mansion.

"If we do this every Saturday, we will be rich," Robson told Jane Doe 1, giddy with excitement.

They then went shopping.

Robson bought a purse.

But Jane Doe couldn't bring herself to spend the money.

PAGAN HAD REQUESTED A TRANSFER FROM THE DETECTIVE BUREAU well before she was assigned the Epstein case, and when the request was granted, Joe Recarey inherited the investigation. While a female detective was probably more ideal, there was no other woman in the investigations bureau, so when Pagan left, Recarey was assigned to head the probe.

The questioning that Recarey conducted with the victims at times reflected the awkwardness of a father stumbling as he explains the facts of life to his daughter. The video interviews were included in discs from the case file I obtained from the state attorney's office. The recordings are grainy and the victims' faces are blurred. More so, they are excruciating to watch. The girls were uncomfortable, and many of them cried. At least initially, they did not want to say what had happened to them—and some of them tried to deny everything. They were ashamed and clearly afraid that their parents would find out.

Most of all, they were scared because they all knew how powerful Epstein was. They were certain he would never be arrested. And they were terrified he would come after them.

"Jeffrey's going to get me. You guys know that, right?" one victim told Recarey. "He's going to figure this out. I'm not safe now."

Recarey, in a fatherly tone, tried to reassure them that they would indeed be safe and that Epstein would be arrested, telling them: "It doesn't matter how much money you have or how many connections you have, if you commit a crime then you will be punished. That's the way our justice system works."

chapter 2

FINDING JANE DOE

One of the many mysteries of the Epstein case is how he got away with such flagrant sex crimes at a time when the FBI was cracking down on child exploitation and putting away men for decades for far lesser sex crimes.

In 2006, the Justice Department under President George W. Bush had launched a task force focused on sex crimes against children. Hundreds of arrests and prosecutions happened during these years. Although the effort focused largely on child pornography, combating human trafficking was also one of its aims, even though I later came to learn that trafficking, at least back then, was seen by law enforcement as a largely foreign phenomenon perpetrated mostly by black and brown people who came from other countries.

The Justice Department didn't seem to fathom that sex trafficking could be a pervasive crime committed by well-to-do and powerful people in the United States. Or that pornography—especially child pornography—was fast becoming a multibillion-dollar worldwide industry.

I knew from covering women in prison that there were organizations across the United States that were trafficking women and children, but that law enforcement sources—at least in Florida—didn't seem to be going after those who were making millions here in the Sunshine State. In hindsight, maybe that was because those "traffickers" were their neighbors, bosses, community leaders, lawyers, politicians, friends, and relatives.

In 2004, Alexander Acosta became the point person in the Justice Department's battle against human trafficking. Acosta—then the assistant U.S. attorney general in the Civil Rights Division in Washington, wrote a piece in an interactive web forum called "Ask the White House," in which he talked about sex trafficking.

"When I talk about human trafficking," Acosta wrote, "I often use a photograph to make clear how evil human trafficking is."

The photograph was from one of the Department of Justice's cases, and he said he kept that photograph in his office.[1]

The picture was of a small room, barely large enough to hold a twin bed. A fourteen-year-old Mexican girl had been held captive in the room and forced to have sex with up to thirty men a day, day after day. By the bed, he said, was a small nightstand, and also in the photo was a teddy bear.

"She told us later that she kept this teddy bear because it reminded her of her childhood. She was barely 14 but she recognized that her childhood had been lost already," Acosta wrote.

"Where do you find traffickers?" someone wrote in the interactive forum. "Are they just pathetic, soul-less monsters?"

Acosta responded: "In a word, yes. These are individuals who engage in modern day slavery. They prey on young, innocent, poor, and the most vulnerable. They beat them, they rape them, they abuse them, and sometimes they kill them and they do this for profit."

Acosta had visited India and witnessed children on the streets of

Mumbai, many of them using sex as a way to survive. He attributed the proliferation of human trafficking to organized crime elements working in Southeast Asia and the Pacific, Central and Latin America, and eastern Europe. Most of the victims are promised better lives only to become prisoners of sex traffickers.

Acosta's empathy for refugees fleeing their home countries for America was genuine.

Acosta's parents had immigrated with their families to Miami from Havana, Cuba, when they were teenagers. His father worked as a salesman and his mother became a paralegal. An only child, Acosta learned Spanish from his maternal grandmother, who took care of him while his parents worked. His parents invested everything they earned to send him to the private Gulliver Preparatory School and later Harvard University.

Childhood friends recalled that Acosta could quote texts in Latin, was hawkish, and had a large insect collection.

"He was not a child you had to push. He always wanted to push himself," his mother, Delia, told the *Miami Herald* in a 2004 interview.[2]

Acosta skipped his senior year of high school to enter Harvard a year early.

The family thought he would become a doctor like his grandfather in Cuba, but in his sophomore year, he changed his major from premed to economics. Upon graduation, he worked in international banking at Shearson Lehman before returning to Harvard and earning his law degree.[3]

Acosta said he was impressed by the ability of people in the legal field who were able to make precedent-setting decisions that stood the test of time.

As head of the Justice Department's Civil Rights Division, Acosta wrote more than 125 opinions, according to a biography posted on the website of the Florida International University law school, where he would later serve as dean.

While at the Justice Department, he was credited with spearheading the reopening of the investigation into the death of Emmett Till, a fourteen-year-old black youth who was abducted, beaten, and lynched in Mississippi in 1955.

"The Emmett Till case stands at the heart of the American civil rights movement," Acosta said in a press release issued in May 2004.

But Acosta's tenure with the Justice Department was tarnished by scandal. A DOJ internal probe, concluded in 2008, found that Acosta and others in the department politicized the Civil Rights Division by purging career civil service attorneys in favor of conservative lawyers. Acosta had married Jan Williams, a Justice Department lawyer who was a liaison to the White House. Williams was singled out in the probe for her aggressive tactics in the scheme to hire based on political patronage.[4]

Acosta claimed he wasn't aware of the effort, but evidence showed that he should have known about some of the illegal activities of his staff.[5]

By the time of the report, Acosta and Williams had moved on.

In 2005, Acosta was appointed as interim U.S. attorney in the Southern District of Florida, which comprises ten counties in the southeastern part of the state, from Fort Pierce to Key West. The district is based in Miami, which had a notorious reputation as the oceanfront mecca of cocaine cowboys, arms dealers, and terrorists. His appointment firmly placed Acosta on the national stage. As a Cuban American and rising star in Republican politics, Acosta got right to work, gaining prominence by prosecuting Washington lobbyist Jack Abramoff in a South Florida–based fraud case, as well as the founders of the Cali cocaine cartel.

In October 2006, Acosta was officially sworn in by his mentor, Samuel Alito, who had just been appointed to the U.S. Supreme Court.

When I began my research on Epstein in October 2016, I was trying to find a "new" angle in order to convince my editor to take another look at the case.

There was a timely peg, I pointed out, involving the Republican nominee for president, Donald J. Trump, who had been accused by a number of women of inappropriate sexual contact. One of the women had filed a lawsuit claiming that Trump and Epstein had raped her when she was thirteen.

I looked deeper. I learned that in the eight years since Epstein's criminal case was closed, dozens of civil lawsuits had been filed against him by victims. There was Jane Doe 1, Jane Doe 2, Jane Doe 3, and almost two dozen more. Some of the victims were identified only by their initials. In fact, there were so many lawsuits and so many Jane Does, I discovered that occasionally even their own lawyers would get the cases mixed up.

But there was one case that stood out from all the others. It was filed in July 2008, the same year that Epstein pled guilty to minor solicitation charges in state court as part of his controversial deal.

Two lawyers had been aggressively litigating the case for almost a decade—and it was still open in federal court in the Southern District of Florida.

It was brought by two of Epstein's victims—not against Epstein, but against the federal government. The women were suing to void Epstein's 2008 plea deal and force federal prosecutors to take another look in hopes that Epstein would be properly charged and prosecuted.

Epstein had long ago returned to his jet-setting life after serving just thirteen months in a Palm Beach County jail. He was released in 2009, and by 2016 seemed to have dropped off the public radar.

The lawsuit seemed to be a long shot. The very idea that the Justice Department would admit that it erred and return a man to prison who had already served a jail sentence (albeit a light one) seemed unfathomable. The fact that the case was dragging on for so long meant that it wasn't going anywhere. In fact, it had almost been vacated at one point by the judge because the parties involved in the case paused for nearly a year to allow the victims to file civil claims against Epstein.

As I contemplated whether there was something new to write about Jeffrey Epstein, and whether it was worth my time, I decided it couldn't hurt to place public records requests for the FBI files, even though I knew getting them also was unlikely.

As I waited, I turned to new projects.

There were other stories early in 2017, including the story of Esteban Santiago, a former member of the National Guard who pulled out a semiautomatic pistol in the Fort Lauderdale–Hollywood International Airport on January 6, killing five people and injuring six others.

That particular day, I was about two miles from the airport, in a dentist's office waiting room while my twenty-one-year-old daughter was in the chair, about to have her wisdom teeth removed.

Jay Ducassi, the *Herald*'s metro editor at the time, knew I lived near the airport and called me.

I looked at my daughter, then I looked at the dentist, and I said, "Will she be okay to take an Uber home?"

I hopped in El Chapo, my kids' affectionate nickname for my beat-up 2003 PT Cruiser convertible, which my father had bought in Mexico. I got to the airport so fast that I briefly thought I was in the wrong place because there were no news vans, cameras, or reporters even there yet.

I spent almost fifteen hours at the airport that day, and then followed up in the next few days with a deeper look at the troubled soldier, who I learned had committed the rampage after suffering a mental breakdown upon his return from Iraq, where he had lost two of his fellow reservists in a roadside bombing.

I also had subsequent installments to a series of reports I had written about corruption and suspicious inmate deaths in Florida prisons.

My boss, the *Herald*'s investigations editor, Casey Frank, was squarely focused on my prison coverage, but I was tiring of it. I had worked on almost nothing else for the last three and a half years. It was a struggle between us, one that reared its head often.

The Epstein story never really left my mind.

"I have been looking into this Epstein case," I finally told Casey. "You know, the guy who signed off on that plea deal was Acosta."

I referred Casey to a story written by *Politico* reporter Josh Gerstein, which predicted that Acosta would face scrutiny at his Senate confirmation hearing for cutting such a deal for a child molester.[6]

"He was. Which we reported," Casey said, adding that another new story was in the works by some of my colleagues at the *Herald*.

"I pulled a lot of stuff on the story because I was doing some research for a possible piece on sex trafficking. I have all the documents. Didn't see it mentioned in our story on Acosta, but I didn't read it carefully, apparently," I wrote in an email to Casey. As far as I was concerned, the matter was far from closed.

ACOSTA WAS CONFIRMED WITH LITTLE MENTION OF THE SCANDAL. WHEN I suggested that we reach out to some of Epstein's victims, Casey agreed, somewhat reluctantly, that it was worth a try to see if they would talk after all these years.

I instinctively knew that the story was unlike anything I had done before. There were powerful, influential men and women involved, a multimillionaire who got away with a horrible crime. Private investigators who stalked Epstein's victims and their families. High-profile lawyers who would sue us in a second, if they could. I wasn't afraid, as the *Herald* had undertaken controversial stories before. But I thought it might be prudent to let our executive editor, Mindy Marqués, know what I was working on.

I walked into her office. She and I have children the same age, and we both liked shoes, so besides the pressing news of the day, we could always chat about kids and shoes. I told her I was working on a new project. She had never heard of Epstein and was unfamiliar with the case history. While the *Herald* had covered the basics of the story over the years, it was not usually front-page material, largely because the crime happened in Palm Beach County and we were struggling, like all local newspapers, with limited staff and slashed budgets, to cover the stories in our own backyard of Miami.

I explained what I aimed to accomplish—and theorized that there could be a backlash from Epstein and his lawyers. I also wanted her to know that it was a project that was going to take patience because I had to first find, and then persuade, the victims to speak to me. Writing it would also be a challenge, since it was a story that was dark and sexually explicit.

Mindy had climbed her way up in the newspaper business during a time when it was pretty much a boys club. With some exceptions, female editors mostly worked in the editorial or lifestyle sections, and those who managed to break the glass ceiling often didn't last long in their jobs. Mindy had begun her career twenty-five years earlier as a summer intern for the *Herald*, covering community news. She was then hired as a reporter, writing stories about corruption in Hialeah, the second-largest city in Miami-Dade County. She advanced to deputy metro editor, then left the paper to work at *People* magazine as the Miami bureau chief, covering Latin America. Five years later, she returned to the *Herald*, where she eventually became executive editor, vice president, and, later, publisher.

"This is going to be a tough one," I recall telling her. "I thought I should warn you."

She listened quietly. She asked a few questions. I told her why I believed the story was important, about how these girls had never found justice.

Then she said, "Go for it."

FROM MARCH 2017 THROUGH THE SUMMER OF THAT YEAR, I ROTATED between prison stories and working on finding Epstein's victims. I began to sense that Casey wasn't thrilled with the idea of my doing an Epstein project, in part because he kept giving me more prison stories to do. I did a few to keep him happy and shoved others aside.

I began working from home so I couldn't be distracted.

Casey was (and still is) one of the best editors at the *Herald*, but we didn't always see eye to eye. I learned that it was best to just say, "Okay, sure, I'll do it," because, like most editors, he could be passive-aggressive and stubborn. We clashed at times. This is mostly because we are both passionate about our work.

Like Mindy, Casey was pretty much a *Herald* lifer, starting as a reporter and graduating to become an editor in the Broward County bureau, then front page editor, Sunday editor, and investigations editor. Few people had weathered the ups and downs of the newspaper business like Casey had. He knew the *Herald*'s tough culture probably better than anyone, and he was loyal to its leaders almost to a fault.

Editors aren't always very good humans. I can say that because at one point in my career, I, too, was an editor, and I wasn't always the best human. Editors have to force headstrong reporters like me to look at things from the boss's perspective—and to do it the editor's way and on his or her time line—and that isn't easy (and sometimes impossible) to do gently. As an editor, you have to walk the line between holding a gun to a reporter's head and patiently steering them to the finish line.

There were only a few people who knew and understood how challenging the Epstein investigation was. One was Casey, and the other was Emily.

Emily Michot has been a photographer at the *Herald* since 1994, when she began as an intern in the paper's Broward bureau. I didn't get a chance to work with her often, but at the time of this project, she was the only female photographer at the paper. Besides being incredibly talented, Emily is able to see details about people or subjects that others do not see. One of the best interviews we did together was of an elderly woman who had been imprisoned for life for killing her husband, who had been beating her for years. The time in prison had taken a toll on her body. She was now in her eighties, in a wheelchair, and her hands were covered with sores. She couldn't get medication to help ease her pain, so Emily took a photograph of her hands that we used for the story, brutal visual evidence of how women in Florida prisons are neglected and mistreated.

We also sent that photograph to the Florida Department of Corrections. A few weeks later, I got a letter from that woman saying she had finally received ointment for her hands.

Many of those women had been physically and sexually abused, so Emily and I had experience interviewing women who had suffered through trauma and violence because we had put together three documentaries featuring the voices of women in prison as part of a series on Lowell Correctional Institution called "Beyond Punishment."

Emily began working with me that October as we mapped out a way to tell the Epstein story in words, photographs, and video. We had learned, from the work we did on women in prison, that no one could possibly tell the Epstein story better than the victims themselves.

We still, however, didn't know if any of the victims would talk— and we wondered how they would react to being contacted a decade or more after they had been molested as teenagers.

I created a war room in the spare bedroom of my apartment. I started filling boxes with public records.

I also decided very early on that I wanted to start the case from scratch, the way a cold-case detective opens an old file and begins to examine every piece of evidence in hopes of finding clues that others had not noticed or seen the significance of before. I purposefully avoided reading previous reporting about the case because I wanted the story to evolve organically, based solely on the records I obtained or from my own original interviews and reporting.

I remembered the sage words of a former editor at the *Philadelphia Daily News*, Jack Morrison, who had been my guiding light at the start of my career. One of the assignments I was given was the disappearance of John F. Kennedy Jr.'s plane off the coast of Martha's Vineyard in July 1999. Every media organization in the world was gathered on the tiny island that summer weekend. I was one reporter from a small but feisty tabloid in Philadelphia—up against the world's most esteemed journalism institutions. What the hell was I going to do or get that nobody else could?

Jack told me something important that would stay with me the rest of my career:

"When you see a pack of journalists, go the other way."

So I never went to any of the press briefings, which were held almost hourly. Instead, I went to the local library. I spoke to local historians and I wrote about how the Indian tribe on the island had been scouring the sandy coast's most ancient Indian lands for remnants of Kennedy's small plane.

"It was there, in the shadow of the Aquinnah Cliffs, where Kennedy's family had a home, that those same Indians who had fought his family over rights to their land were now praying for a lost son swallowed by the sea," I wrote.

There were plenty of journalists writing stories about the plane crash. But the story about the Kennedy family's contentious history on the island was one that no one else had written.

FINDING THE GIRLS AND TELLING THEIR STORY, TO ME, WAS GOING IN A direction different from other journalists who covered the case over the years. I knew that the women had gone on with their lives and many of them probably had never told a soul what had happened to them. They might not want to be found.

In reading the case files, I was able to obtain a few snippets about the girls: maybe their birth date or last name, portions of their address, or the name of a family member. I learned that a good many of them had married and no longer used their maiden names.

There were rare occasions that I got lucky, when the redaction police accidentally forgot to black out a name. "The redaction police" was the nickname I gave to the faceless members of the criminal justice system who, armed with bucketloads of black Magic Markers, manage to scrub perfectly good police reports and court documents. I had no intention of using the girls' names without their permission, but I hoped I would find several of them who were willing to talk.

Slowly, using pieces of information I found in court records and the redacted police reports, I managed to put together a list of victims. I didn't have many names, but I had enough to start.

Then, using those names, I was able to go on their Facebook and other social media pages and uncover other victims' names. For example, if I knew the initials of one victim were R.L., I looked on one of the other girls' Facebook pages and saw she had a friend whose initials were R.L.

Because Epstein targeted girls who had a certain look, this was a creepy process at times. They all seemed to be blond, blue-eyed, petite, beautiful—and most of them grew up in West Palm Beach.

My list kept growing, and by October 2017, some eight months after my search began, I had identified about sixty possible victims, and had tracked down addresses for most of them. I was contemplating the best way to reach out to them when Harvey Weinstein happened.

The #MeToo movement exploded with a series of stories in *The New Yorker* and the *New York Times* about more than a dozen women who had accused Hollywood mogul Weinstein of widespread sexual harassment, abuse, and rape over decades as one of the entertainment industry's most powerful men. The stories, which later shared a Pulitzer Prize, also led to a sea change in attitudes about the sexual abuse and harassment of women. As a result, there was a major cultural shift in the way the public and the media treated cases of sexual assault, particularly those involving perpetrators who were wealthy and powerful.

Suddenly, Casey was keen on my story. Emily and I quietly celebrated the shift in his support for the project. While some editors may have seen threads of similarities with the Weinstein story, Casey and I saw important differences: Epstein's victims in Florida were not Hollywood actresses; they were girls from poor and troubled backgrounds who were betrayed by the very people in the criminal justice system who were supposed to protect them.

But as I read the stories about Weinstein, and I watched Olympic gymnastics champions testify in court about how they were sexually abused by a Michigan State University doctor, I also recognized a cover-up similar to that in the Epstein case and people who, by their silence, were complicit in the abuse.

Weinstein had surrounded himself with what the *New York Times* aptly called his "Complicity Machine"—enablers and loyalists who protected him, including people in media, entertainment, and politics. Like Weinstein, Epstein was a man of great financial resources and political connections.

Weinstein's victims were now also talking.

I was hopeful that this new movement would prompt Epstein's victims to finally open up as well.

chapter 3

THE POLICE PROBE

The girls arrived, sometimes by car, some by taxi, at all hours of the day and night. They were told the most basic of details: that they would be paid for giving a very rich old man a massage, that he might ask them to do it in their underwear or naked, and that if he asked their age, they should tell him they were eighteen.

In September 2005, Detective Joe Recarey was beginning to connect the dots of what appeared to be a well-organized sex scheme, led by an influential man who employed a handful of others to help him.

By then, Jane Doe 1 had moved to live with her mother in Georgia. But she had already given police the names of other girls at Royal Palm Beach High School who were possible victims. Members of the Palm Beach Police Department's Burglary Strike Force, a unit that handled surveillance for all serious crimes, had been watching Epstein's mansion for several weeks, and other officers had been assigned to follow Haley Robson, one of Epstein's recruiters.

On September 24, 2005, Palm Beach's sanitation department was brought on the case.

Tony Higgins, supervisor of the department, met with police and agreed to set up a plan to search Epstein's garbage. The garbagemen were instructed to pick up Epstein's trash bags on designated days, place them in the well in the rear of the garbage truck, then drive to another location to offload. The police then placed the trash bags in larger black bags, which were transported to the police station, where they could be inspected.

Over the next several weeks and months, the garbage pickups continued, yielding a cache of phone messages and notes with girls' names and phone numbers like: "For a good time call Beth and Alice." The numbers were collected and categorized, and Recarey prepared subpoenas for Cingular Wireless and Bell South Telecommunications to obtain subscriber information.

Police found mail addressed to a woman named Nadia Marcinkova; call records from prominent New York publicist Peggy Siegal; messages from famous men like Harvey Weinstein, Donald Trump, and David Copperfield; notepaper embossed with the name of Ghislaine Maxwell, Epstein's onetime girlfriend who seemed to spend a lot of time at his Palm Beach mansion.

But there were snags: The first subpoena for phone records was written incorrectly, with the phone numbers juxtaposed. Another subpoena had to be prepared. Surveillance tapes and audio interviews of witnesses occasionally got jammed or were damaged because of the department's outdated equipment.

Still the searches were yielding good leads, mostly in the form of notes from girls confirming their visits, such as "Linda can come at 4, she will bring Adriana," or "Sandy can't come at 4 because she has soccer practice." Most of the messages were dated and had phone numbers on them, but when Recarey reached out, not all the girls wanted to cooperate.

Recarey contacted the Palm Beach State Attorney's Office to

arrange for assistance in interviewing Robson, who lived in Palm Beach County, outside of Recarey's jurisdiction in the Town of Palm Beach. An investigator from the state attorney's office was assigned to accompany Recarey to Robson's house.

Robson, who was studying journalism at Palm Beach Community College, agreed to allow them to take her to the Palm Beach police station to be interviewed. Unlike some of the other girls who were still underage, Robson was nineteen, therefore the police didn't need her parents' permission to talk to her. Her father, as a retired police detective, probably would not have approved. Recarey placed a tape recorder in the unmarked police cruiser and turned it on as they spoke to Robson on the way to the station.

She matter-of-factly described how she was introduced to Epstein when she was seventeen and began working for him as a recruiter.

She said he wanted all very young girls, and she explained how he had once gotten angry when she brought him a twenty-three-year-old. The youngest girl she introduced to him was fourteen, she said, naming a total of six girls whom she had brought to his mansion.

She said she tried to find girls whom she knew needed money, and she claimed she was clear about the fact that they might have to do the massages in the nude and that some "touching" might be involved, according to the police report.

"Every girl I brought knew what to expect," Robson told Recarey.

In Jane Doe 1's case, she said another girl came with them. One of Epstein's female assistants would contact Robson every time Epstein had scheduled a visit to his Palm Beach home and ask her to bring him girls.

"Jeff likes to have his fun with girls," Robson admitted in an interview with police I obtained from the case files.

She claimed she had stopped working for Epstein after her parents found out she had been visiting the old bachelor.

Recarey advised her she had possibly implicated herself in a crime and asked her whether she was willing to cooperate with the case. Robson waived her rights and agreed to help in hopes that she wouldn't be arrested.

"I'm like a little Heidi Fleiss," police recorded her as saying on the ride home, referring to the Hollywood madam who ran a high-end prostitution ring for celebrity clients in California in the 1990s.

Robson, however, backed down on her promise of cooperation, Recarey later testified in a 2010 deposition.

I met Robson early on in my investigation. We spoke at a little restaurant in Delray Beach. It was clear she had suffered a lot of guilt over what she had done and, at the end of the conversation, she agreed to meet with Emily and me to talk on camera about Epstein.

We needed a place to do the interview, and I convinced Casey to let us rent a hotel suite in Palm Beach for the interview. I texted and called to confirm the interview with Haley several times to make sure she was still on board. She assured me she was.

But on the day of the interview, I couldn't reach her. I called and texted, as Emily and I sat in the hotel room waiting. And waiting. She didn't answer, and after two hours, we packed up and left.

I tried her several more times over the next few days with no response. Finally, she reached out about two weeks later, telling me she had been sick and in the hospital with a serious case of the flu. I tried several times after that to reschedule the interview, but Robson ignored my calls. I was back to square one.

RECAREY FACED A SIMILAR RESISTANCE FROM EPSTEIN'S VICTIMS. Some of the girls who were initially cooperative and shared information would, upon reflection, change their minds and go silent. A few practically slammed doors in his face. Two of them told him they were in love with Epstein and would never betray him.

To Recarey, this was a sign of how successful Epstein had been in convincing his victims he cared about them, when in reality Epstein cared only about control and satisfying his sexual appetite.

One of the girls whom Robson brought to Epstein lived in Loxahatchee, a dusty, rural enclave twenty miles west of Palm Beach, but worlds away from the tract houses, chain restaurants, and golf courses of suburban life in South Florida.

"All that happened is that I went there with Haley, sat in his kitchen with the chef, and nothing happened," the victim told Recarey.

Recarey knew she was holding back, possibly because her parents were there, so he left his business card and moved on to the next girl on his list.

He and other detectives traveled throughout September 2005, visiting girls in Royal Palm Beach, West Palm Beach, and Loxahatchee, speaking to some of those whom Robson had recruited, as well as tracking others whose names and phone numbers were found in Epstein's trash. A decision was made to send two detectives to every interview, because there was a concern that if Epstein found out about the probe, he might try to set Recarey up with a girl who would claim the detective acted inappropriately during a one-on-one interview.

One day, as Recarey was interviewing a potential victim, she received a phone call. It went into voice mail, and while Recarey was there, she played it for him.

It was Epstein's assistant, Sarah Kellen. She asked the girl to call her back because, she said, she wanted to know whether she was being questioned by police.

"Did you tell anyone that we were talking to you?" Recarey asked.

"Well, I inadvertently told a friend I know," the girl said.

It became apparent to Recarey that the word was spreading among Epstein's victims that police were asking questions. It would be only a matter of time before Epstein found out about the probe, if he hadn't already.

By October, Recarey had interviewed almost a dozen victims, but still didn't have enough to charge Epstein with anything other than lewd and lascivious acts on a child under sixteen, a second-degree felony. Up until then, none of the acts described rose to the level of sexual battery.

But that would soon change.

THE FRIEND THAT THE GIRL HAD CONFIDED IN ABOUT THE POLICE investigation was now a student at a local university. Recarey went to the school the next day and pulled her out of class.

The girl, identified as Jane Doe 4, admitted she knew about the police probe and agreed to give a sworn, taped statement. She described Epstein as a pervert who kept pushing her to go further and further sexually, each time she came to give him a massage. She kept telling him she was uncomfortable because she had a boyfriend, yet he kept pushing her boundaries. She told Recarey that Robson had brought her to the estate two years earlier, when she was sixteen. Recently, Epstein had rented a car for her, a Nissan Sentra, to make it easier for her to come and visit him. She was still driving that car, and led the detectives out to the parking lot to show them the vehicle. Recarey wrote down the license plate number and later confirmed that the car had indeed been rented by Epstein.

It was a good lead. Recarey knew he had to work quickly to get a search warrant.

"Do I think all the victims were truthful in their initial interviews? No," Recarey told me. "They were afraid. They were afraid of how powerful he was, so that was my initial hurdle I had to jump over. I had to get them to trust me."

The girls often downplayed or distorted the number of times they'd visited Epstein and the number of other girls they brought.

Some of the girls were molested and never returned to his house again. Others came back and brought their friends, and still other girls, like Robson, became recruiters.

But the story, once it spilled out, was always the same.

JANE DOE 103 SAID SHE WAS WORKING IN THE WELLINGTON MALL WHEN one of her friends told her about Epstein, and how she could earn two hundred dollars if she gave him a massage while naked.

Jane Doe 103 thought about it and agreed to go the following day.

Her friend brought her to Epstein's house, into the kitchen, where she was greeted by Sarah Kellen. Kellen then led her upstairs to the master bedroom and bath area that all the other girls described. His method was almost exactly the same: asking her to undress, telling her to get on top of him, then turning over, exposing himself while fondling her and masturbating.

Jane Doe 103 suddenly began sobbing hysterically on the phone, telling Recarey she had been to Epstein's house hundreds of times and earned thousands of dollars over a two-year period. Kellen had come to call it "work," arranging Epstein's schedule by calling Doe 103 and asking her the times each day that she wanted to come to work.

But sometimes Epstein would call her directly on her cell phone to arrange encounters.

She told Recarey that Epstein went from touching her inappropriately to performing oral sex on her, and then digitally penetrating her, and directing her to have sex with one of his young assistants, Nadia Marcinkova, while he watched and masturbated. Each time, he pushed her toward more deviant behavior than before and paid her more money. On the phone with Recarey, she started crying so hard that she couldn't continue. Recarey let her calm down, and then arranged to meet her the following day in Jacksonville, where she was now living.

He and another detective traveled to Jacksonville, where they met with Doe 103 and one of her friends, whom she brought along for moral support. In a sworn taped statement, Doe 103 described her two years with Epstein, and how she became so much a part of his sex life that he asked her to come live with him as an emancipated minor. There were times she went to parties and dinners with him, meeting some of his famous friends, including the magician David Copperfield. And in a lawsuit she filed years later, she said that when she turned seventeen, he invited her to stay with him at his home in Manhattan, paying for airfare and theater tickets and a chauffeur as gifts for her birthday.

Their sexual activity continued to escalate, as Epstein made more demands, and paid her more money. He also persuaded her to do more explicit things with Marcinkova. Initially she refused, but Epstein then offered her an additional two hundred dollars if she would do these sex acts for just five minutes, and after she complied, they became part of the routine.

He then introduced toys in their encounters, and bought her lingerie, jewelry, flowers, art books, and purses. Each time he asked for something new, more money and gifts followed.

Epstein took photographs of her naked, including several of her with Marcinkova naked in a bathtub.

When she was still in high school, he delivered a bucket of flowers to her when she was in a play.

But Doe 103 said she did set boundaries—making it clear to Epstein that she did not want to have intercourse with him, no matter how much he offered to pay her.

One day, during one of their trysts with Marcinkova, Epstein suddenly turned Jane Doe 103 on her stomach over the massage table and inserted his penis inside of her, while holding her head against the table, forcibly, as she told him to stop.

Epstein pulled out and apologized, then paid her one thousand dollars.

"There were times that I was so sore when I left that I couldn't walk," she told Recarey.

Epstein learned that she wanted to be a model. He offered to help connect her with the right people to advance her career. She was a good student and wanted to attend New York University or Columbia, and Epstein took an interest in her academics, helping her with her college application and offering to pay for her tuition, all to keep her ensnared in his web.

She also shared with Recarey the names of other girls she knew who had been having sex with Epstein.

The following day, Recarey and another detective went to Orlando to interview another girl, Amy, who had been identified as a victim. She was visibly nervous, Recarey noted in his report. Amy said she had only visited Epstein a few times, starting in March 2005. She said she provided a fully clothed massage and that nothing inappropriate had happened. Her answers to his questions seemed almost scripted, he noted in his report.

"I sensed hesitancy in her answers, so I asked her if she had been contacted by anyone from Epstein's house," Recarey wrote.

"Well, two days ago, a guy who said he worked for Epstein called me. He told me his name was Paul and he wanted to know if the cops had contacted me," Amy said.

Epstein had now graduated from having his assistants contact victims to hiring private investigators to intimidate them.

Recarey returned to Palm Beach and began writing his application for a search warrant.

He had only been on the case for one month and had covered a lot of ground, identifying more than a dozen underage victims, one of whom said Epstein had raped her.

But Recarey knew that Epstein was gathering his forces.

chapter 4

EPPY

Jeffrey Epstein led a relatively private life up until a glowing profile of him appeared in *New York* magazine in 2002. Titled "Jeffrey Epstein: International Moneyman of Mystery," the story followed a globe-trotting adventure Epstein had taken a month earlier with former president Bill Clinton, actor Kevin Spacey, and comedian Chris Tucker on the financier's customized Boeing 727 jet.[1]

CALL IT "THE THREE AMIGOS' " MOST EXCELLENT AFRICAN ADVEN-TURE, read a headline in the *New York Post* that September, touting the jaunt more as a boys' safari than the humanitarian trip Clinton would later portray it as. The trip took them to Ghana, Nigeria, Mozambique, and South Africa, where Clinton was to join Nelson Mandela in an AIDS-prevention event.[2]

The *New York* article solidified Epstein's status as a billionaire money manager who was so selective that he would only accept clients who could invest one billion dollars or more. The story likened him to an elusive financial Wizard of Oz—aloof, yet mesmerizing in his ability to cultivate an exclusive circle of friends, including some of the most brilliant minds in science, academics, philanthropy, and business.

"Here's the thing about Epstein," the *New York* writer, Landon Thomas Jr., wrote effusively. "As some collect butterflies, he collects beautiful minds."[3]

The story, however, was arguably most memorable for a single quote that has been repeated hundreds and perhaps thousands of times in the past few years.

"I've known Jeff for fifteen years. Terrific guy," said Donald Trump, fifteen years before he would be elected president. "He's a lot of fun to be with. It is even said that he likes beautiful women almost as much as I do, and many of them are on the younger side. No doubt about it—Jeffrey enjoys his social life."[4]

Thomas profiled Epstein again, this time for the *New York Times*, in 2008. Thomas visited Epstein's private island, which he described as a "palm-fringed Xanadu" overlooking the Caribbean.[5] Thomas interviewed him over a lunch of crab and steak as Epstein compared himself to Gulliver in *Gulliver's Travels*.

"Gulliver's playfulness had unintentional consequences," Epstein told Thomas. "That is what happens with wealth. There are unexpected burdens as well as benefits."[6]

Thomas became friends with Epstein and solicited a thirty-thousand-dollar charitable donation from the millionaire in 2017 for a Harlem cultural center. Thomas's editor, David Enrich, found out about the donation after Thomas declined to do another story about Epstein, citing their friendship. Thomas was banned from writing about Epstein again and later left the paper.[7]

IT WAS CLEAR EPSTEIN WAS MANIPULATIVE AND WELL CONNECTED, but on a deeper level, I wondered about the roots of his obsession with girls. Was there something in his childhood that engendered in him a compulsion to manipulate and dominate those whom he considered of lesser intellect—and to compete with those whose intellect he admired? One thing that most people do agree on was that Jeffrey Epstein was brilliant.

But also he had the mind and inflated ego of a mad scientist. He dreamed of ways to improve the human race and regaled scientists with his knowledge about esoteric topics like artificial intelligence, eugenics, and cryonics.

I began researching his family history through archives collected in databases, such as Ancestry.com, and by combing U.S. census and military records, as well as New York birth, death, and marriage records.

EPSTEIN'S RISE FROM A MIDDLE-CLASS CONEY ISLAND KID TO HAVING a seat at the table with some of the greatest minds in America was not something I was going to entirely grasp in the course of my effort to expose his crimes. But I did enough digging to know that Epstein's ancestors, like many Jewish families who emigrated to America at the turn of the century, experienced incredible hatred and bloodshed in the aftermath of Germany's takeover of Europe during World War II.

Epstein's paternal grandfather, Julius, was born about 1884 in Bialystok, a part of Poland that had been annexed by Russia in an 1804 treaty that ended Napoleon Bonaparte's Coalition Wars across Europe. As a result, the anti-Polish and anti-Jewish repression that grew under the Russian empire led many to flee the war-torn city. Julius and his parents, Morris and Sarah Epstein, were among those who emigrated to the United States in about 1900.

Julius settled in Brooklyn, and in 1916, he married Bessie Fisher, who had immigrated from Austria with her family when she was about three years old.

Jeffrey Epstein's maternal grandparents were also Jewish refugees who escaped war, famine, and anti-Semitism in Russian-occupied Poland in the early 1900s. His mother's parents, Max Stolofsky and Lena Berlin, immigrated from small Jewish villages in Lithuania, that were later occupied by Germany. Lena's ancestors lived in Moletai, one of the oldest villages in Lithuania. On August 29, 1941, about 80 percent of the town's population, including many of Lena Berlin's extended family, were murdered by German firing squads. Her father was from Kopciowo, which was also invaded by the Germans in 1941. The Jews from that town were taken to a ghetto outside of Lazdijai, where they were executed.

Epstein's grandparents settled in different parts of Brooklyn, which in 1890 was listed as the fourth largest city in America prior to becoming one of New York City's five boroughs at the turn of the century.

During the Great Depression, Julius Epstein took advantage of New Deal programs instituted by Franklin D. Roosevelt in the president's quest to provide jobs and security to end the worst downturn in the history of the industrialized world. Despite only having an eighth-grade education, Julius used those programs to launch his own demolition company that prospered under the Works Progress Administration, a federal program that employed unskilled labor to demolish and build new infrastructure across the country, including New York.

Wrecking companies started razing buildings and demolishing entire blocks of homes in some of New York City's more blighted neighborhoods. But a lot of questions were being asked about those demolitions, especially the historic buildings that were destroyed. In 1939, Congress began an investigation into the WPA, examining where and how the program's federal monies were being spent, particularly in New York, where the costs of the program had skyrocketed.

Julius Epstein submitted an affidavit to the committee, dated May 29, 1939, in which he detailed how private contractors would demolish the buildings for a fraction of the cost that the WPA was paying the city, and then the city of New York would seize and resell the building's materials, suggesting that state officials were taking kickbacks for the salvage and that developers were buying up the properties at a fraction of their value.[8]

As an example of possible wrongdoing, Julius alleged that the WPA was paying the costs for the demolition while city officials were pocketing millions of dollars from selling the salvage. In April 1939, Epstein said the city was selling salvaged bricks for $3 per thousand. He offered the city a $10,000 advance for brick, covering a rate of $4 per thousand. The city refused his offer and continued to sell the salvaged bricks for $3 per thousand to private contractors who turned around and sold them for $5 or more per thousand, pocketing the profit, he said.

"I would like to add that they are not only taking down buildings which are part of the slum districts," Julius said in the affidavit, "but they are taking down buildings in Central Park West, Manhattan, Clinton Avenue, Brooklyn and a brewery in Ridgewood, all of which locations are not considered slum districts. The buildings which have been torn down . . . are buildings that belong to banks, trust companies and out of town owners."[9]

JULIUS AND BESSIE HAD TWO SONS: SEYMOUR, WHO WAS BORN IN 1916, and Arnold, who was born in 1923. The family moved to 421 Crown Street in Crown Heights, one of the city's premier areas, an upper-middle-class, predominately Jewish neighborhood.

Seymour worked with his father and lived in a rented apartment with his parents until he was twenty-four, when he enlisted in the U.S. Army and was sent to Camp Upton in Suffolk County, New York, where Japanese Americans were interned during World War II.

It's not clear whether Seymour served on the front, but records show he disembarked from a naval ship in Baltimore in 1944. He returned to Brooklyn, but didn't marry until nine years later, at the age of thirty-six. His wife, Pauline "Paula," was thirty-four.

Seymour worked for the New York Department of Parks and Recreation as a groundskeeper, and his wife was a homemaker who later worked for an insurance company.

Jeffrey Edward Epstein was born on January 20, 1953, in Brooklyn. His brother, Mark, was born a year later. They lived in Coney Island, a modest middle-class neighborhood.

As a kid, Jeffrey was chubby, with curly hair; he was smart and often helped his classmates with their work. He was able to skip third grade at P.S. 188 and then skipped eighth grade at Mark Twain Junior High School for the Gifted and Talented, a middle school that admitted students based on a tryout of their skills in a range of academic and performance areas, including music and science.

In a short autobiography he wrote for prosecutors in 2006, Epstein said that in his youth, the family played a game called Concentration that helped develop his interest in math and numbers.

In the 1960s, the family lived in Sea Gate, a gated community adjacent to Coney Island, surrounded on three sides by water and private beaches. Epstein's family lived in a multi-unit apartment house with a large wraparound porch that was across the street from Sea Gate's oldest synagogue, Kneses Israel. The insulated seaside community was mostly populated with Russian, Hasidic, and other Jewish families. There were no schools in the neighborhood, so students had to leave "the Gate," as it was known, to go to public school.

JEFFREY ATTENDED LAFAYETTE HIGH SCHOOL WITH STUDENTS FROM mostly blue-collar Italian families. During the summer of 1967, when he was fourteen, he attended arts camp at Interlochen School in Michigan, where he practiced and learned piano.

A former high school classmate, Beverly Donatelli, recalls that he was a kindhearted boy who was considered a prodigy on the piano and at mathematics. He was nicknamed "Eppy" and while a bit shy, he made friends easily, friends recalled. He graduated high school in 1969, when he was sixteen.[10]

He applied to and was accepted at the Cooper Union college in the East Village, where he took advanced math classes and earned money by tutoring other students.

He dropped out of Cooper Union to attend New York University.

Thomas Volscho, a sociology professor at the City University of New York, College of Staten Island, who researched Epstein's background for the *Daily Beast*, verified that Epstein was enrolled in NYU from September 1971 to June 1974, but did not graduate.[11]

In 1974, Epstein was hired as a mathematics teacher at the Dalton School, one of the most prestigious prep schools in New York, catering to children of the wealthy. Though he had no college degree, he was nevertheless hired by headmaster Donald Barr, the father of William Barr, who would become U.S. attorney general under presidents George H. W. Bush and Donald Trump.

Headmaster Barr left under a cloud in early 1974, but by that time, Epstein had already been given a teaching position.[12]

Former teachers at the school said Barr was an eccentric but strict taskmaster who liked hiring people, such as Epstein, who were unconventional choices. Barr himself didn't exactly fit the mold of headmaster of a top private school. In 1973, he published a science fiction novel, *Space Relations*, about a planet of wealthy aliens who kidnap humans and force them into sex slavery. It was an odd topic to write about for someone in his position, and the questions that were later raised about Epstein's sex trafficking led to a plethora of conspiracy theories about whether Donald Barr knew about Epstein's sexual proclivities.[13]

"As a teacher, Jeffrey was commended for being lively, interesting, and uniquely gifted in presenting the material in a way which challenged the students," according to his bio.

But not everyone remembers him that way. Peter Branch, an interim headmaster at the school after Barr resigned, told the *New York Times* that he had concerns about Epstein's teaching style, and some former female students said he made them uncomfortable. One unnamed woman said he tried to spend time with her outside of school, and his behavior was alarming enough that she and another student reported it to former headmaster Gardner Dunnan. Dunnan would later be accused of inappropriate behavior himself after a fourteen-year-old girl whom he asked to move in with him later claimed in a lawsuit that he sexually assaulted her.[14]

"Epstein was a little creepy by the girls," alumna Karin Williams told the *Times*. "I won't say the girls didn't like him. But they thought he was odd."

Williams also said he was the only man she ever met who had a full-length fur coat, which was considered out of place for someone who was a teacher at a school with a conservative dress code.

"In retrospect, you could see how maybe he was looking for young nymphs," said alumna Heidi Knecht-Seegers. Others theorized that Epstein's experience at Dalton may have given him the idea to use schools as hunting grounds for young victims.[15]

DALTON ALSO GAVE EPSTEIN THE CONNECTIONS THAT WOULD LEAD HIM into the upper echelons of New York's financial world. Among those he met was Alan "Ace" Greenberg, an executive at the Wall Street brokerage firm Bear Stearns, who took him under his wing.

At a parent-teacher conference in 1976, Epstein so impressed a student's father that he recommended him to Greenberg, the son of an Oklahoma City women's clothing store owner who rose to become Bear Stearns' CEO. Greenberg, who died in 2014, liked to hire men whom he called "PSDs"—poor, smart, and desperate to be rich.

Greenberg's daughter, Lynne Koeppel, recalled that her late father recognized that Epstein had potential, not only as a trader but as someone who could bring in clients and investors.

"He was very smart and he knew how to woo people, how to schmooze. He's personable and makes good company," she said.[16]

SO IN 1976, AT THE END OF THE SCHOOL YEAR, EPSTEIN WENT TO WORK at Bear Stearns and quickly became adept at cultivating a number of affluent clients.

One of his former bosses, Michael Tennenbaum, a senior executive, later told the *Wall Street Journal* that Epstein lied about his credentials on his résumé, claiming that he had a degree from Stanford University. When confronted with the lie, Epstein apologized, saying that he padded his résumé to get a teaching post. Epstein was given another chance and after four years, made limited partner at the firm. He was asked to leave in 1981 amid allegations that he had given shares to people who were not his clients.[17]

ALL THE WHILE, HOWEVER, EPSTEIN WAS LEVERAGING HIS NEW YORK profile and his financial contacts to aggrandize himself. In July 1980, while he was still a trader, he was named "Bachelor of the Month" by *Cosmopolitan* magazine. Then just twenty-seven, with no college degree, he described himself as a financial strategist who only took on clients who earned more than one billion dollars a year.

"If you're a cute Texas girl, write this New York dynamo . . ." the article said.[18]

BY THE 1990S, EPSTEIN HAD BUILT A VAST FORTUNE AND BEGAN TO USE his resources to prey on young girls at arts schools in New York and elsewhere.

His first known underage victim was recruited at his former summer arts camp in northern Michigan, Interlochen. Epstein donated money for scholarships and built a lodge on campus, where events were held for the camp's alumni, including people like Felicity Huff-man and musicians Norah Jones, Jewel, and Josh Groban.

Both Epstein and Maxwell stayed at the lodge from time to time. In 1994, he and Maxwell befriended a thirteen-year-old girl who was studying to be a singer. The girl's mother said in an interview with the *Daily Mail* in 2011 that Epstein targeted her daughter, who looked much younger than her actual years.[19]

"Everyone thought she was nine or ten," said her mother. The girl had just lost her father, a classical music conductor, so she was still grieving and vulnerable.

The camp maintains that they've never received a complaint about Epstein, and the woman, who is now living in California, has not spoken publicly.

In a sworn deposition, Epstein's former butler, Alessi, mentioned that the girl often visited Epstein's Florida mansion and in later years, her name appears on the flight logs of his plane.

"She came to the house as a friend, I think," Alessi said during a statement he gave to police and the state attorney's office in 2005.

In January 2020, a lawsuit was filed by a woman who told a similar story about meeting Epstein at Interlochen. She alleges that she was thirteen when she met Epstein and Maxwell while she was studying at the camp. The woman said she was sitting alone on a bench between classes when Epstein and Maxwell approached her, telling her that they were arts patrons who wanted to give talented young artists like her scholarships. They asked questions about her family and background and she told them that she lived with her mother in Florida. Epstein asked for her number, and she gave it to him even though she felt uncomfortable, the lawsuit said.

Epstein began a series of conversations with the girl's mother about how he helped young talent and ultimately invited the girl and her mother to visit him at his Palm Beach mansion. He sent his driver to pick them up.

Over the next several months, Epstein and Maxwell tried to groom the thirteen-year-old girl. He told her to call him her "godfather," and Maxwell befriended her like an older sister, the suit claims.

They took her to the movies, went shopping, and invited her to spend more and more time at the estate. Soon, the sexual comments started. For instance, Maxwell told her that having sex with ex-boyfriends was easy "because once you slept with them they've been grandfathered in and you could go back and fuck them whenever you wanted," the lawsuit claimed.

They began selecting clothes for her, insisting she wear cotton panties. After each visit, they sent her home with two to three hundred dollars to give her mother since "she is having a hard time and struggling as a widow," the lawsuit said.

Epstein began to pay for the girl's music lessons, and when she resisted his sexual overtures, he and Maxwell would scold her for being ungrateful.

Once, Epstein took the girl to Mar-a-Lago, where he introduced her to Donald Trump. She was fourteen at the time and recalls that upon meeting Trump, Epstein elbowed him and said: "This is a good one, right?"

Trump smiled and nodded in agreement, the suit says.

She was assaulted for several years and, as with his other victims, Epstein would push her to perform more aggressive sex acts each time she saw him. She began to travel with him to his home in New York and his sprawling, secluded ranch in New Mexico.

When she turned sixteen, she moved with her mother to an apartment that Epstein owned on Sixty-fifth Street and Second Avenue in New York City. He paid for her to attend an exclusive private school in Manhattan.

In 1999, when she was eighteen, she finally left him and moved away to start a new life. For a while, Epstein repeatedly called and berated her for not appreciating him.

But soon, the calls stopped. By then Epstein had moved on to new, younger prey.

JOURNALIST VICKY WARD PROBABLY CAME THE CLOSEST TO EXPOSING Epstein's secret life in a March 2003 *Vanity Fair* profile, "The Talented Mr. Epstein," in which she described Epstein as a complicated man who had no boundaries.[20]

Then fifty, the gray-haired money manager had a goliath-sized ego that was only surpassed by the ostentatiousness of the seven-story mansion he lived in on Manhattan's Upper East Side. He bought the town house, which was once a school, from his billion-dollar client Les Wexner, owner of L Brands and Victoria's Secret stores. It has long been considered the largest private residence in the city: a twenty-one-thousand-square-foot fortress with heated sidewalks that span the entire block of Seventy-first Street between Fifth and Madison Avenues.

The mansion was filled with gilded antique furniture, mosque-sized Persian rugs, sculptures of African warriors, giant paintings, and walls lined with rows of individually framed glass eyeballs that had been made in England for injured soldiers.[21]

It was dark and ominous, much like Epstein himself, who designated one room as the "leather room" and another as the "dungeon."

There was a room full of security screens showing footage from cameras placed all over the house, including the bathrooms.

His friends included newspaper publisher Mort Zuckerman, Hyatt Hotel CEO Tom Pritzker, Revlon chairman Ron Perelman, real estate tycoon Leon Black, and other towering business executives. There were also Harvard academics like Henry Rosovsky; Larry Summers, then president of Harvard; and lawyer Alan Dershowitz, who would later become one of his most vocal and aggressive defenders.[22]

Epstein's "admirers," Ward said, also included former senator

George Mitchell and a bevy of scientists, some of them Nobel Prize winners; and royalty like Prince Andrew, whom Epstein called "Andy."

WARD'S RESEARCH, HOWEVER, TOOK AN UNEXPECTED TURN AFTER SHE discovered two young women—sisters—who claimed that Epstein had tried to sexually assault them. One of them, Annie Farmer, was just sixteen at the time.

Ward managed to get the two sisters and their mother on the record and, along with other details about Epstein's eccentric lifestyle, tried to draw a portrait of a successful man who had a sinister and potentially criminal side.

But when Epstein learned about Ward's reporting, he denied the allegations and called her editor, Graydon Carter. Carter in turn scrubbed the piece of any hint of illicit activity with young women. Carter would later claim that the allegations weren't corroborated and didn't meet *Vanity Fair*'s journalistic standards.

But Ward alleges that Carter was threatened by Epstein, who had a history of killing stories in the media that were negative about him. Epstein had a mob-boss-like way of intimidating people who crossed him, and in Carter's case, the warning came in the form of a bullet that was found outside his front door.[23]

Years later, when Epstein was under federal investigation in Florida, writer John Connolly attempted to write another piece for *Vanity Fair*. He had flown to Florida to interview some of Epstein's female employees when Carter called him and told him that he had found a cat's head in his front yard.

Carter was rattled, and Connolly didn't blame him. They decided to quash the story.

Ward, who had been pregnant with twins at the time she wrote Epstein's profile, was scared as well. She said the twins were born prematurely, and afterward, she remembered that Epstein had earlier asked her in which hospital she had chosen to give birth.

"I was so afraid that somehow with all his connections to the academic and medical community, that he was coming for my little ones that I put security on them in the NICU," she later wrote in a follow-up piece in the *Daily Beast* in 2015.[24]

IT'S HARD TO KNOW WHEN FORBIDDEN AND ILLEGAL SEX ACTS WITH minors became Epstein's obsession—whether it was something he developed as a child or young man, or whether it was just another twisted privilege he felt entitled to because of his great wealth and the illustrious people he had in his pocket.

One thing is clear: Eppy believed that there was no one who couldn't be scared off—or bought.

chapter 5

THE MIAMI HERALD

The *Miami Herald*, which was first published in 1903, has a long, proud journalism tradition, not only in Florida but around the nation, as a legacy newspaper that fights above its punching weight. It has broken major stories of national and international significance. It was the flagship newspaper for Knight-Ridder, once the largest and most progressive newspaper chain in the nation. At its height, the *Herald* employed more than five hundred staffers in bureaus around the world, including Beijing, Jerusalem, London, and Buenos Aires. It also had a sizable staff at its sister paper, the Spanish-language *El Nuevo Herald*, which has been a voice for Miami's Latin community for four decades.

Over the course of its history, the *Herald* has won twenty-two Pulitzer Prizes, and became known in the profession as a model in graphics design, color photography, and exemplary writing. It launched the careers of writers such as Leonard Pitts Jr., Dave Barry,

Carl Hiaasen, and Edna Buchanan, to name a few, and served as an important stepping-stone in the careers of countless journalists now at the *Washington Post* and the *New York Times*.

The newspaper's coverage of crime in Miami, especially during the "Cocaine Cowboy" era of the 1980s, spawned many books and documentaries. Its famed newsroom overlooking Biscayne Bay was the setting for the 1985 movie *The Mean Season*, a thriller about a reporter stalked by a serial killer, and the 1981 legal drama *Absence of Malice*, about a journalist who commits multiple ethical lapses that implicate a Florida businessman in the disappearance of a local labor leader.

Twice, the *Herald* was named one of *Time* magazine's top newspapers of the decade, in the 1970s and '80s, and along the way, sometimes embarrassed the big boys at the *Times* and *Post* with major scoops. It was the *Miami Herald* that exposed Oliver North and broke the Iran-Contra story, winning a Pulitzer for its coverage of the Reagan administration scandal. The paper also broke the Gary Hart *Monkey Business* story, knocking the Democratic front-runner from the presidential race when it was discovered he was having an extramarital affair. The newspaper covered Hurricane Andrew, the McDuffie race riots, and the Mariel boatlifts, cataclysmic events that happened in the newspaper's own backyard but impacted the nation.

While hurt by the effects of the internet on advertising, like newspapers everywhere, the *Herald* was still a robust journalism machine the year I was hired in 2005, from the *Philadelphia Daily News*, which was also owned by Knight-Ridder.

The *Daily News* was already feeling the loss of advertising, but Miami's hot real estate market reduced the hit to the *Herald*. I didn't really want to leave Philadelphia, but layoffs in Philly seemed inevitable and I felt I had gone as far as I could go in my career at the *Daily News*. At the time, I was divorcing my husband of eleven years, a police officer who had decided to move to Florida because the state had a shortage of cops.

I didn't want our children, who were then in elementary school, to be far away from their father. My parents had retired to Naples, so I envisioned I would have a good support system to help me transition to a new job, a new state, and a new life. I was ready for a change myself, and applied to the *St. Petersburg Times* and the *Tampa Bay Tribune* as well as the *Herald*.

I was offered a position at the *Herald* as an enterprise editor in its Broward County bureau, located on the westernmost side of the county, a good forty-five minutes from downtown Miami. The office was actually closer to the alligators in the Everglades than to Miami.

So I did all the things you're not supposed to do at the same time: I got a divorce, I moved to a new city, and I started a new job. All with two kids in grade school.

The kids and I moved into a cookie-cutter house in a nice development on a lake in Weston, a sophisticated enclave populated mostly by transplants and retirees who all came from somewhere other than Florida. It was a typical suburb, but nothing like the suburbs I grew up in outside of Philadelphia.

There is a true culture shock when one moves from the Northeast or probably anywhere in the country to Miami. Nobody can describe Florida and Miami better than Dave Barry and Carl Hiaasen, so I'm not going to even begin to try. South Florida in many ways is the opposite of Philadelphia, so transient that as soon as my kids made friends, their families would move away. There's no real public transit system, so you're left on your own to get from point A to point B without getting killed by drivers who don't have licenses. People come to South Florida to escape, to retire, and to die, and before dying, they spend a lot of time lying in the sun and drinking alcohol.

I call Florida the state of Haves and Have Nots. The Haves are all those people who live in waterfront palaces, drive fast expensive cars, break the law, and get VIP treatment everywhere they go; while they donate to charitable causes, they would rather not mix with those who benefit from that charity, the Have Nots.

The Have Nots are behind the wheels of Toyotas, Mazdas, and Ford pickup trucks, stuck in traffic, at a complete standstill, while all the Haves, who can afford the tolls charged for the high-speed lanes, soar past them in their BMWs and Maseratis.

Florida's wackiness, however, does kind of grow on you, and as a journalist, especially, it's a gold mine, providing a never-ending stream of stories that often garner worldwide attention, and sometimes ridicule. There's always a Florida man or a Florida woman somewhere doing something that gives new meaning to stupidity.

Because of this, a lot of people who are native Floridians don't brag about being from Florida; they usually say they are from somewhere else. The only real Floridians, after all, are the Native Americans—the Seminole and Miccosukee tribes—who were decimated by European settlers who arrived here in the 1600s.

When most people think of Florida, they think of beaches, Disney World, orange juice, or fishing. There are some truly magical, beautiful places across the Sunshine State. The Everglades are a tropical natural wonderland, and the Florida Reef is the only living coral reef in the continental United States. Central Florida is largely agricultural, but has crystal-clear rivers, natural springs, hammocks, and wetlands. One could get lost in nature here, and many people do, finding a slice of paradise in the middle of nowhere, living in a trailer on a patch of land, choosing to abandon most modern conveniences for a quieter life.

Unlike Philadelphia or New York, the Florida sports fan is elusive, because most sports fans who move here still root for their hometown teams. The year I moved to Florida, the Miami Heat made it to the NBA finals. I would go to a bar to watch the game and have to ask the bartender to put it on the overhead television. When I took my kids to a Marlins-Phillies game, there were more Phillies fans in the stands than Marlins fans. I know everyone tells me that this is a huge football town. But the Miami Dolphins have been a losing team for almost the entire time I've lived in Florida. I keep hoping, along with the rest of South Florida, that they put together a winning season.

This made for a bit of a journalism culture shock as well. In Philly, if the team won, the story was always on the front page the next day for one simple reason: it sold papers. In Miami, I would sit through the morning news meetings and sports would be the poor stepchild in the room.

I WAS PRETTY BATTLE TESTED AT THE *HERALD* BY THE TIME I GOT involved in the Epstein story. The editor who hired me, Patricia Andrews, told me always to watch my back, because the *Herald* was a tough place to work. I know I did feel pretty chewed up, between the pay cuts, the furloughs, and the inability of our parent company to find a path back to a more profitable journalism model. To that end, we were constantly experimenting with different ways to present and package the news, which meant we were on a never-ending training merry-go-round. It felt like just after we mastered one particular computer program, that system would be tossed out for some "new and improved" interface. Journalists aren't fast learners when it comes to technology, or at least us veterans aren't. In fact, my desktop computer in the newsroom was so ancient that I put in almost daily calls to our computer help desk. It was unfathomable to me that a company that relies on computers to produce its content was so far behind that I had to wait twenty minutes or more to download a single lawsuit.

As an editor, I helped less-seasoned journalists develop in-depth stories on their beats. Some people were born to be editors, but I was not one of them. I was too hard-charging of a reporter to have the patience of a good editor. I think I've become kinder and gentler in time, mostly because I feel a little less scared that I'm going to be jobless and out on the street tomorrow.

But knowing that editors were expendable, and that the paper still needed content, I volunteered to return to reporting during a round of painful layoffs in 2009. Everyone was getting a 10 percent pay cut, but because I had volunteered to return to reporting, I was rewarded for my team spirit with a 15 percent pay cut. I had just moved into a house, which I was renting for twenty-five hundred dollars a month. I was supporting two children in a rental market that was among the most expensive in the nation. I remember screaming in the hallway outside the *Herald*'s human resources department the day they told me my pay was cut. I actually pleaded with Human Resources in agony, telling them that I had two kids to support, begging them to please just give me the 10 percent cut that everyone else had received. I looked around the newsroom, filled with reporters who had spouses to help shoulder the burden, or reporters who were married with no children. I know they were hurting, too. But I felt unfairly singled out. I didn't have any savings. Besides, I had put down all I had on the first and last months' rent and the security deposit on the house.

I consoled myself by remembering that I still had my waitressing chops from my early years in journalism in case I needed them.

I THINK YOU EITHER LIKE DIGGING AND DOING RESEARCH—OR YOU don't. I always likened being an investigative reporter to being a police detective. Part of me wanted to solve mysteries that even the real crime detectives couldn't.

One of my first assignments when I returned to reporting was the murder of the heir to the storied Fontainebleau hotel fortune. Ben Novack Jr. was found bludgeoned to death in a hotel in Rye Brook, Westchester County, New York, in July 2009. His father, Ben Novack Sr., had founded the iconic Fontainebleau in Miami in 1954. It was legendary in the 1950s and '60s as a hangout for mobsters, royalty, and crooners, such as Frank Sinatra and Sammy Davis Jr.

Ben Novack Jr., or Benji, as he was called, formed a convention planning business after his late father lost the hotel to bankruptcy in 1977. He and his wife, Narcy, were holding a convention at the Hilton in Rye Brook at the time his body was found half naked, with his eyes gouged out, in his penthouse suite in July 2009.

The first thing I saw upon taking up the story was that Benji's mother, Bernice, an elegant woman in her late eighties, had been found dead just three months earlier. The medical examiner had ruled her death an accident, the result of a fall in her Fort Lauderdale home, but her autopsy was still being kept under wraps, which I felt was suspicious.

If she had died of a fall, it was the bloodiest fall in history. There was blood spattered from inside her car, through the garage, the kitchen, and the downstairs bathroom. Her body was found in the mudroom, off the garage. The medical examiner's theory was that she fell in the kitchen, then stumbled into the bathroom, went into the garage to try to drive herself to the hospital, then returned to the house in an attempt to call an ambulance, then collapsed and died.

It sounded ridiculous. I was convinced that she too had been murdered.

But no one believed me—not the police and not my editors, who rolled their eyes at me and buried some of my stories. The Fort Lauderdale police, who investigated her death, got so annoyed with me for pestering them with questions about what they did (and didn't do) that they called my editors to complain.

A few years before Ben and Bernice's deaths, Benji and Narcy were in the midst of a bitter divorce. Narcy hired a team of henchmen to pistol whip and threaten her husband after she had tied him up in their bedroom as part of a sex game. The hired guns packed up all Narcy's belongings and emptied Benji's safe, and Narcy disappeared. It was Bernice who found Benji bound and gagged half naked in his bedroom.

Fort Lauderdale police perhaps weren't paying much attention to the series of stories that I was writing laying out how Bernice may have been murdered, but police in Rye Brook, New York, were.

In July 2010, one year after Benji's murder, his wife, Narcy, her brother, Cristobal Veliz, and three other hit men were indicted for the murders of Benji and Bernice Novack. One of the hit men confessed to beating Bernice repeatedly with a monkey wrench.

Investigating the Novack murders taught me a lot about good and bad criminal investigations. That would help me when I turned a few years later to a new beat, covering one of the most barbaric and corrupt systems in the state of Florida: prisons.

I visited prisons from Florida's Panhandle to the Everglades, vividly documenting the inhumane treatment of inmates. There was Randall Jordan-Aparo, a twenty-seven-year-old prisoner at Franklin Correctional Institution, who was serving time for writing bad checks. He suffered from a rare blood disorder and had complained for weeks that it was flaring up. He was having difficulty breathing, but instead of treating him, the nurses scoffed. Aparo cursed at the nurses for not treating him, and corrections officers then punished him for his behavior by gassing him so much that he died in his cell from the fumes.

Then there was Darren Rainey, who suffered from mental illness. Corrections officers, frustrated that he didn't obey their commands, locked him in a 180-degree shower where he screamed for more than an hour before collapsing dead, his skin peeling from his body.

Taking on the state's largest bureaucracy wasn't easy, and I was often concerned for my safety because dozens of corrections officers were fired or forced to resign as a result of my stories. A few of them were even arrested. More than once, I was awakened by prowlers outside my windows in the middle of the night. I knew what some of the officers were capable of, and they didn't have to do their own dirty work. All they had to do was pay an inmate to find some unsavory character on the outside to do it.

For four years, I covered nothing but Florida prisons and inmate deaths. Each case seemed worse than the last. There were a lot of reforms that happened as a result of my coverage.

But Florida's prisons are still among the worst in the nation, and each year, the death tally of those behind bars rises.

The fact that Jeffrey Epstein was spared the cruel and usual punishment that so many of the inmates in Florida's prisons suffered wasn't lost on me. Had he been sent to state prison, he would have entered as a convicted child molester. These criminals are on the lowest tier of the prison hierarchy, and most child molesters don't live long in Florida prisons and jails. They are raped and tortured so badly that they often commit suicide, are found dead of drug overdoses, or simply have "an accident."

But Epstein's incarceration in the Palm Beach County jail would be brief, and what little time he actually spent behind bars would be like a visit to a country club compared to being in a Florida state prison.

chapter 6

DEAD ENDS

There seemed to be only two people who were willing to risk their careers to go after Jeffrey Epstein.

And to my surprise, neither of them had ever given a public interview.

One was Joe Recarey, and the other was former Palm Beach police chief Michael Reiter.

Reiter, sixty-three, was a native of Pittsburgh who had retired from the department in 2009 and launched his own company, Michael Reiter and Associates, which offers security, crisis management, and investigations for well-to-do corporate executives and their families, mostly in Palm Beach.

Recarey, fifty, had retired in 2013. He was now working in security and human resource management for a large restaurant chain.

I reached out to Reiter first, feeling pretty confident that I would be the one to get him to talk after all these years.

"My goal would be to do a thorough analysis of the case and drill down on the justice system and those who let this case get swept under the rug. From what I read, you were not one of those people," I wrote in an email to him in 2017.

The former chief was out of state when I reached out, but he responded quickly. It was clear he had done a cursory background check on me; he knew my investigative work with the Florida prisons and told me that that was one of the reasons he even returned my email.

Many journalists had contacted Reiter over the years. A soft-spoken gentleman who is painfully careful with his words, Reiter still took his role as an officer of the law very seriously. Both he and Recarey secretly hoped that justice would be served someday in the Epstein case. To that end, Reiter had spoken with some reporters off the record over the years, pointing them to angles of the story that he felt were important and, in his mind, had not been adequately covered. He would eventually tell me that he and Recarey had been frustrated by media coverage of the case, and Reiter, especially, was wary of speaking to another journalist who would, as he put it, "start working on the Epstein story only to end up being transferred to the paper's real estate department."

Though he didn't mention any journalists by name, he said he had worked in an off-the-record capacity to help steer both reporters and writers in certain directions, only to never hear from them again or to be disappointed that they had not dug deep enough into the story. He felt that the media coverage, for the most part, had failed to connect the dots of the case, and he was convinced that Epstein or the powers around him had killed a number of stories that attempted to accomplish that over the years.

Reiter wasn't the only one who told me this. Two lawyers involved in the case said that they also had tried to get the *New York Times*, the *Washington Post*, and ABC News to do in-depth pieces about the case to no avail.

Both Recarey and Reiter were understandably skeptical that I, as a reporter for a local newspaper, would get any further. It would take me *months* to get Reiter and Recarey to even sit down and talk to me about the case. At first, Reiter did what he always did with reporters who called: he referred me to a transcript of a nine-hour deposition he had given in the case in 2009. The deposition was part of a spate of civil lawsuits that were filed against Epstein in the years following his plea bargain.

He and Recarey were deposed by Palm Beach lawyer Spencer Kuvin, who represented a number of victims, including Jane Doe 1, who was seeking civil damages from Epstein.

Reiter did not want to speak about the Epstein case publicly because he still held out some hope that federal prosecutors would one day take another look at the case—or that new evidence would emerge to force authorities to reopen the investigation. He and Recarey believed that in the event this happened, they would be called upon to testify and any public comments they made over the years could possibly be used to taint their credibility.

I couldn't find much that had been written publicly about either of their 2009 depositions. But each of them was more than four hundred pages long and exhaustive. If you've never read a deposition, trust me, it is one of the most tedious court documents you could ever suffer through.

These were the first of many reports that I would have to read in the eighteen months I worked on the Epstein project. I was beginning to understand why so many journalists had passed or had been dissuaded from doing more on the story.

I soon realized that every court document needed to be read and analyzed in the context of other court records and lawsuits produced during the past decade. For example, there were details that I would find that didn't make sense alone, but if I put the details together with something I discovered in another document, the information suddenly became significant.

Finally, I heard from the FBI, denying my records request for the

Epstein files. I wasn't surprised. But I discovered that Dan Novack, a New York lawyer working for the celebrity gossip website Radar Online, had filed a court motion to force the FBI to release the files. As the months went by, and I lost track of his effort, he actually gained a victory of sorts when the FBI began turning over some of the records to him in large batches in the fall of 2017. I didn't realize that my additional request triggered the FBI to place all the records online, in what it calls its "vault," a portal of publicly released FBI case files. But for some reason, Radar Online wasn't publishing anything about the records. The site is owned by American Media Inc. (AMI), publisher of the *National Enquirer*. Its CEO, David Pecker, was friends with Donald Trump, and a year earlier, in 2016, AMI had paid Playboy model Karen McDougal $150,000 for exclusive rights to her claim that she had an affair with Trump while he was married. Instead of publishing the story, however, AMI killed it to protect Trump, a pattern that came to be called "Catch and Kill."[1]

Novack couldn't explain why Radar passed on publishing Epstein's FBI records, but I was glad they did, and in the daily chaos of the Trump White House, no other media noticed.

It's not that the files were enlightening material. Pages and pages were completely redacted, and others were filled with codes that were indecipherable. But because I had read the lawsuits and was plodding through the court and public files, there were tidbits in the FBI files that fit with other facts I had gathered.

For example, there was an FBI report that hinted that Epstein was working in some cooperative capacity as an informant with the FBI. The reference was vaguely worded, but I remembered that the U.S. Attorney's Office referenced something similar in the tangle of civil lawsuits filed over the years. It didn't make sense at the time, but now I was able to put some pieces together. Did Epstein become an intelligence asset, and was that the reason he got a sweet deal from the government? I didn't know yet, but it was something new that I needed to pursue.

I was not as successful getting details from the gaggle of attorneys who had represented Epstein's victims over the years.

I was most intrigued by Brad Edwards—one of the two lawyers who had the tenacity to sue the federal government for giving Epstein the deal in the first place.

Edwards was reluctant to speak to me, and the other lawyer on the case, a former federal judge in Utah, Paul Cassell, referred me back to Edwards.

Like Reiter, Edwards pointed me to the court files, specifically, his motion for summary judgment filed about a year earlier. He also gave me a long list of exhibits and advised me to read them all and to get back to him after I did so.

THE EDWARDS-CASSELL LAWSUIT, KNOWN AS THE CVRA (CRIME VICTIMS' Rights Act) case, contained more than five hundred docket entries, with some of those entries encompassing dozens of exhibits and hundreds of pages. At first, I thought I could do what I always did with stories about court cases, which is to read the main case components: the complaint, the motion for summary judgment, and a few others that stood out.

But again, I had come to accept that there were no shortcuts to this project.

BY THEN, I HAD DOWNSIZED TO A TINY APARTMENT IN HOLLYWOOD, Florida, a 2.5-mile stretch of beach that is the opposite of what most people think of when they think of Miami. It remains one of the few vestiges of old Florida, with mom-and-pop motels from the 1950s and '60s with names like the Marlin, the Silver Spray, and the Walkabout. They snake along a brick-paved walkway along the beach, called the "Broadwalk"—lined mostly with pizzerias, ice cream parlors, and souvenir shops. In recent years, time has been sneaking up on the eclectic, sleepy beach town, but I found a peace here that gave me the creative space and escape I needed to cope with some of the darker places I had to go to cover people like murderers, violent prison guards, corrupt bureaucrats, and child sex traffickers.

My kids were away from home now, one in college and the other living with my ex-husband in North Carolina. My eighty-year-old mother, who had arrived on my doorstep earlier in the year vowing to divorce my stepfather after forty-five years of marriage, thought better of that decision—I guess after living with me for a while—and went back to him.

I filled my closet-sized spare bedroom with Epstein's civil cases and public records, organizing them in separate boxes and lining them up on the bed. I created files for each victim.

There were times I would wake up in the middle of the night thinking about the story, unable to go back to sleep, so I would pull open one of the case files, or a deposition, and read it until I drifted off again.

I was still trying to figure out how to approach Epstein's survivors when an idea occurred to me. When my mother had visited, I thought it would help to get her a mental-health checkup, so I brought her in to visit my therapist, whom I had not seen in a long time. I realized, however, that I, too, needed some therapy to deal with my mother. My counselor, Sloane Veshinski, asked what else was going on in my life. I confessed I was back again with my on-and-off boyfriend, which wasn't really a good thing, but I needed a distraction from the story I was investigating. Being with my ex-boyfriend was a little like putting on a warm sweater. He was a spoiled party boy trapped in the body of a fiftysomething man. Now mostly retired, he had been in my life for about fifteen years—almost the entire time I'd lived in Florida. The Sunshine State is a dating wilderness that's scarier than Florida's bloodiest prisons. My single friends and I tried to keep a sense of humor about our dating adventures. We would give nicknames to the men we dated because it was easier to remember them by funny names than to keep track of their real ones. One guy I dated I came to call "Chief" because he had very briefly played for the Kansas City Chiefs football team, and another I called "The Boss," because, like me, he was a big Bruce Springsteen fan.

My on-again, off-again man was named Mr. Big—not because he was anything like the Mr. Big in *Sex and the City*, but because he was very tall. We had incredible chemistry, but he was a bad habit that I knew I had to break, someday, but now was not the time.

My sister, Terry, would often bemoan how tough I was in my career but what a marshmallow I was in my love life. When I fell in love, I fell hard. I sought guidance from Sloane about Mr. Big, but your favorite sweater is hard to give up, holes and all.

My new project was taking over my waking and sleeping thoughts. Sloane and I discussed coping mechanisms, and she also counseled me about how to approach the victims so that I would not retraumatize them after so many years, an issue that was also troubling me.

I reached out to other therapists, and later, to Kenneth Lanning, a former FBI agent who worked for twenty years in the behavioral science unit studying child sexual abuse. Lanning helped open my eyes to how sex predators groom and manipulate vulnerable people, especially children and teenagers. It was vital for me to understand not only the trauma that the victims went through, but the reasons that many of them kept returning to Epstein after they had been abused.

I found that the prosecutors in the case didn't seem to understand the psychology behind childhood sexual abuse. Because some of the girls had returned and others had even fallen in love with Epstein, the state and federal prosecutors, for the most part, had dismissed them as willing partners, or even prostitutes.

"What society wants is a victim who is a sweet, adorable, innocent angel that God sent from heaven—and an offender who is this evil horrible sexual predator, a 'dirty old man in a wrinkled raincoat,' that's what we prefer, but that's not reality," Lanning said.

The Epstein case, he explained, was complicated by the fact that the girls, the victims, didn't fit into the comfortable mold that the criminal justice system prefers.

"The prosecutors who were looking at the case were saying 'that's not what she said, she changed her story' and the children, they look like adults. But they are mentally and emotionally immature, so it is normal for them to give differing accounts of the trauma they experienced. In fact, it would have been abnormal for them to tell the same story with the same exact details every single time. The child's brain doesn't work that way unless they are coached."

What I learned from the therapists and others I spoke to helped me realize something important: the women didn't have to tell me the sensitive details about what Epstein did to them. The plea agreement named thirty-four girls as victims. There was no longer any dispute that he had sexually abused them. Even though their names weren't public, the fact that there were thirty-four listed in the court record meant that federal prosecutors had confirmed that Epstein abused these girls. And in accepting the plea agreement, Epstein also had acknowledged, to some degree, his guilt. He just didn't think what he did was a big deal, and apparently, neither did prosecutors.

ONE SATURDAY, I PUT TOGETHER A LIST OF VICTIMS WHO STILL LIVED IN the Palm Beach area, mapped out where they were, printed out the maps, and drove up to Palm Beach County to knock on their doors. They weren't responding to my phone calls, and neither were their lawyers. So much time had passed and many of them had moved on with their lives, got married, started careers, or, more sadly, fallen into drug addiction, depression, or domestic abuse. One had essentially opened a house of prostitution.

I knocked on a few doors that Saturday. In one case, a woman's father answered the door. I quickly left before giving him a chance to ask what I wanted. I went onto the next address and pulled into the driveway. Then I thought, *What do I say if her husband answers the door and asks what I want?*

I needed more time to think and plan.

I decided on the fly to drive up to Central Florida, on the north side of Lake Okeechobee, where it appeared one of the women owned a piece of property. It was hours away, but I finally had bought myself a decent, comfortable used car, a 2013 Nissan Altima. I had nothing else to do that weekend, so I began driving.

I had seen some parts of Central Florida during my tenure at the *Miami Herald*. But as I drove deeper and deeper into the north-central part of the state, I was astonished at how rural Florida was. So isolated, in fact, that my GPS lost its signal. I was driving by pastures that were so endless that I pondered, briefly, what it must be like to live in such a desolate place with nothing but the land and sky for miles. There were no houses, no buildings, no gas stations, no trees, only grass and cattle.

It dawned on me that I had told no one where I was going that day. If my car broke down, I could die from dehydration and no one would be able to find me. I got a brief bar on my phone and I called my daughter, just to tell her, kind of, where I was, even though I had only a rough idea.

I finally arrived at my destination, or what I thought was my destination. It was a weed-choked dirt road, well off the main highway. As soon as I pulled my car onto the path, I realized I had made a big mistake. My car was not the kind of vehicle that could maneuver this rocky, uneven terrain. I gripped the steering wheel tight, sweating, as the underbelly of my car scraped the road. There was no place to turn around.

I was scared, but consoled myself by the fact that I saw two homes off in the distance, so if I wrecked my car, or flattened my tires, at least there were some signs of civilization.

I finally reached the end of the road and found a gate with a "No Trespassing" sign. I got out of my car to inspect the damage, but I really couldn't know if anything had ruptured the undercarriage. I ventured over to the gate and saw an abandoned old trailer on the property, which was overgrown. No one had lived here for a long time.

Another dead end. I made the long drive home pondering my next move.

Then I remembered how I had written a letter to the father of the Navy SEAL asking him for an interview.

That Monday, I began a new approach.

I addressed nearly sixty letters, with names compiled from the spreadsheet I had put together.

"For the past few months, I have been investigating Epstein's case. As you know, a lot has been written about him in the media. Most of the stories have raised more questions than they answer. And no story has analyzed exactly why and how the criminal justice system failed to render justice to his victims," I wrote.

I explained how I believed that Epstein and prosecutors had benefited from the silence of his victims.

"One of the reasons Epstein walks free today is because his victims, for the most part, have been voiceless and faceless . . . which enabled prosecutors to 'blame the victims' and write them off as strippers, prostitutes, drug addicts, and gold-diggers, when in fact, many of them were lost teenagers. . . ."

I pointed out that Epstein, despite having to register as a sex offender, had been trying to lower his sex offender status in New York so that he would have fewer restrictions. It was quite possible, I suggested, that he might be out preying on other victims. I told them I had done a lot of research on the case, and I had learned that prosecutors had found ways to minimize public scrutiny while exploiting the weaknesses of many of the survivors.

"The only thing missing is your voice. I hope to hear from you," I wrote at the end.

About a week later, my phone rang. It was Michelle Licata, otherwise known in the case file as Jane Doe 2. She lived in a small town outside of Nashville.

I immediately called Emily.

"Emily, get your gear together, we're going to Nashville."

chapter 7

THE FIRST DEAL

The social bonds between the monied people of Palm Beach and the merchants of the county's justice system cannot be overstated. In 2006, the cocktail party, country club, and charity ball circuits were still dominated by dyed-in-the-wool islanders who had wintered on this 7.8-square-mile stretch of paradise for generations. But there was a new aristocracy of young, ambitious socialites, stockbrokers, and lawyers who visited only on weekends, looking to make marital and business connections they could leverage in New York, Washington, or Los Angeles. The average age in Palm Beach was still about seventy, but the children of the septuagenarians were religiously breaking the old-guard tradition that your name should appear in print just three times: when you're born, when you get married, and when you die. Publicity, and being seen with the right people at parties, was now as in style as the Palm Beach cheese puff.

Epstein wasn't a social butterfly, but he made the right connections. One of them was C. Gerald "Gerry" Goldsmith, a founder of the Palm Beach National Bank and board chairman of First Bank of the Palm Beaches. A former town councilman, Goldsmith was involved in a financial scandal in the Bahamas in the 1970s in which he was accused of diverting millions of dollars for political payoffs.[1]

He managed to escape prosecution and, with his questionable business dealings now a blip in his past, Goldsmith was able to start fresh. He built a new business and political empire in Palm Beach that included a failed 2009 bid to become mayor.

In a 2009 deposition, Chief Reiter said that before the Epstein case ever became public, Goldsmith, who wielded a lot of power as chairman of the town's police pension board, pressured him to back off of Epstein.

Goldsmith admitted he had been friends with the financier for years and downplayed the seriousness of Epstein's crimes, telling Reiter, "This really isn't necessary. It's really very minor," Reiter recalled.

"He said the victims had lifestyles that don't make them, shouldn't make them, believable to the police department," Reiter said. It wasn't the last time Reiter said he heard from Goldsmith or a number of other people in the Palm Beach social circuit.

MESSAGE PADS SEIZED FROM EPSTEIN'S MANSION SHOWED THAT ON October 1, 2005, Goldsmith called Epstein and left a message with one of his assistants for Epstein to call him back.

But less than three weeks later, on October 20, 2005, when Recarey and about a dozen officers arrived at Epstein's Palm Beach mansion to serve a search warrant, it was clear that Epstein had been expecting them.

The warrant had been signed only two days earlier by Palm Beach County Judge Laura Johnson. Johnson, a former assistant state prosecutor, had her own family ties to the county's justice system: she was the daughter-in-law of a commanding former state attorney who also had served as a Florida state senator and circuit court judge. It wasn't until much later that I fully began to understand the incestuous nature of Palm Beach's political and social ecosystem.

IT'S NOT CLEAR HOW OR WHEN EPSTEIN WAS TOLD ABOUT THE SEARCH warrant, but he was adept from the beginning of the case at marshaling the weaknesses of the criminal justice system for his benefit.

When Recarey and his team arrived at his mansion shortly after 8:00 A.M. that Thursday, six computer hard drives in the house had been hastily removed, leaving dangling wires attached to monitors in several areas of the house.

"All the wires were still there, as if someone had pulled them just before we arrived," Recarey told Reiter in his report about the search.

Epstein, who was not home at the time, had managed to arrange for one of his assistants to pull the computers, and several other key pieces of evidence were missing. Many of the victims described how Epstein had nude photographs displayed around his house. At least one girl told them that his assistant took a nude photograph of her in a shower. They did find some photographs of nude girls in one of Epstein's closets, but most of the framed images described by the victims were gone.

Police also found surveillance cameras had been disconnected, and the video recordings and other electronic storage data were gone.

Recarey would later learn that Epstein's lawyers had the computers, and presumably the videos, but by that time, the veteran police detective was getting pushback on the case from the Palm Beach state attorney's office.

Perhaps the most incriminating piece of evidence they found during the search was a single piece of paper in a desk in Epstein's master bedroom: a high school transcript for Jane Doe 103, the girl who told Recarey that Epstein had raped her. They also found a receipt showing that he had sent her a bucket of roses.

"The house was sanitized, but it wasn't *that* sanitized," Recarey said. "Besides the report card, we could see that the bedroom, the bathroom, everything was exactly as the girls had described it, right down to the lime-green couch."

BARRY KRISCHER HAD BEEN PALM BEACH STATE ATTORNEY FOR fourteen years by the time Jeffrey Epstein's case landed on his desk. A Brooklyn-born lawyer, Krischer had toiled for years as a prosecutor in the state attorney's office in the 1980s, first as an assistant state attorney, then chief assistant, and later, he left the office to go into private practice, working as a lawyer for the county's powerful police union—a strategic connection that would help him in his pursuit to be elected state attorney and possibly higher office in the future.

Krischer had handled controversial cases before, including the 2006 prosecution of conservative radio personality Rush Limbaugh, accused of doctor-shopping for prescription painkillers. Like Epstein, Limbaugh was able to work out a non-prosecution agreement following three years of legal wrangling with Krischer's office. Limbaugh's lawyer, Roy Black, helped broker a settlement, under which Limbaugh, who lived in a forty-eight-million-dollar oceanfront Palm Beach mansion, would be cleared of fraud charges and avoid trial as long as he complied with an agreement to continue drug treatment.

Epstein was friends with Harvard lawyer Alan Dershowitz, having met him at a party on Martha's Vineyard years earlier. Dershowitz, a pit bull known for taking on high-profile clients such as O. J. Simpson, Claus von Bülow, and Mike Tyson, met with Krischer first. As the case became more serious, Epstein added Limbaugh's attorney Roy Black and a former Palm Beach assistant state attorney, Guy Fronstin, to his arsenal.

IN JULY 2017, I PLOWED THROUGH THE CONTENTS OF THE STATE attorney's file on Epstein. I was struck by how much of the file was padded with copies of two of the victims' social media pages. I couldn't help thinking that it seemed a waste of paper to include so many copies of the same pages. It was as if someone was trying to make the case file thicker than it actually was. These were pages from Myspace, the precursor to Facebook. They weren't much different from social media pages of teenagers today, talking about boys, dating, school, problems with their parents, parties, drinking, and smoking pot. There was profanity and explicit sexual language, but a lot of it read to me as typical teenage bravado.

It was odd that so much of the file contained nothing more than the social media scribbles of a few victims, when there were at least fifteen other girls who had made almost identical claims of sexual assault or inappropriate touching against Epstein.

There were some court documents, a couple of depositions, and letters to and from Epstein's lawyers. The search warrants and redacted police report were repeated at least six times over, creating more reams of unnecessary paper. When these were sifted out, including all the Myspace pages, the state attorney's entire case file on Epstein and his seventeen victims could fit into one file folder.

There was not a single email to or from any of the state prosecutors involved in the case.

There was also nothing about Epstein's missing computers, and no indication that anyone had tried to subpoena them.

Having covered criminal cases for two decades, I realized that the story here was not what was *in* the case file, but what was *not* in the file. There was almost nothing in the file about Epstein. Normally, when there is a criminal investigation into a suspect, a file will include a background check on the individual. In this case, there were extensive background checks on the victims, and even their parents—but nothing on Epstein or, for that matter, on any of the other people accused of helping him. There was no information on his assistants Emmy Tayler, Sarah Kellen, or Nadia Marcinkova; there appeared to have been no effort to talk to Ghislaine Maxwell, Epstein's ex-girlfriend, whose name was also on the message pads found in Epstein's trash.

Thinking there was something I may have missed (or that had been unintentionally left out), I submitted another public records request asking for the documents again. This time, I specified more details about the emails, saying that I wanted all letters and emails in their system that mentioned the words "Epstein" and/or "Dershowitz." Normally, when agencies receive these kinds of requests, they engage someone in their computer department to do a search. I received negative results.

David Aronberg, now the Palm Beach state attorney, correctly pointed out that he was not in office when the Epstein criminal case was closed in 2008. But there are still too many questions about missing documents, and he hasn't seen fit to investigate why or have the political will to help the public understand the case. (Following public pressure, he later placed the entire Epstein case file on the Palm Beach state attorney's website.)

I suspected that the file was sanitized, or large swaths of materials were destroyed. Florida does have records retention laws that allow officials to get rid of paper files after a certain period of time. But, in this case, the lawyers representing Epstein's victims had requested this same file years before, at a time before any records should have been deleted or trashed. The lawyers, too, were suspicious that the state attorney's office under Krischer had thinned out important information. (Krischer did not respond to my numerous requests for comment.)

BOTH RECAREY AND REITER CONFIDED TO ME THAT THEY WERE concerned that Epstein's attorneys had been provided with confidential information to undermine the police probe. By 2006, Reiter moved the case files to a more secure server that only he and Recarey could access.

Recarey diligently lined up witnesses and other physical evidence to support the victims' statements. He had hundreds of pages of phone records, showing that Epstein's assistants had called the various victims; and he had recovered dozens more copies of phone message pads from Epstein's home that listed the names and phone numbers for countless girls—not all of them in Palm Beach.

Some of those messages lined up exactly to the dates, times, and circumstances surrounding the events described by his victims. Police even found a note on Epstein's own embossed stationery that said: "Haley called, she is bringing [Jane Doe 1] on Saturday."

The message pads also contained a who's who of influential people calling Epstein: Donald Trump, Les Wexner, former J.P. Morgan banker Jes Staley, real estate mogul Mort Zuckerman, former Maine senator George Mitchell, and Hollywood producer Harvey Weinstein.

RECAREY WAS ALREADY SUSPICIOUS AFTER THE COMPUTER FIASCO, but the relationship between Recarey and the prosecutor's office, which had previously been solid, was now on shaky ground.

Recarey became even more skeptical when Krischer seemed to endorse a private polygraph test Epstein's lawyers arranged for their client.

Recarey, who was a polygraph examiner at the time, knew this was not standard procedure and offered to observe. The offer was rejected.

"Barry, he is taking the test unsupervised," Recarey said he told Krischer. "Do you understand that they can ask him anything? They could ask him 'do you like a ham and cheese sandwich?' and he can say, 'yes I do,' and it would show truthful because he likes ham and cheese sandwiches. These are not the questions that law enforcement would ask."

The test concluded that "no deception was found," and was cited by Krischer as another reason not to charge Epstein, even though lie detector tests are inadmissible in court.

Recarey was never shown the test, or what questions Epstein was asked, and there is no documentation about the test in the state attorney's case file.

But what aggravated Recarey the most was how enamored Krischer seemed to be with Dershowitz.

"Dershowitz flew down to Florida and met with Krischer privately, and the shenanigans that happened afterwards I don't think I've ever seen or ever heard of anywhere else," Recarey said.

Krischer would later describe Dershowitz as "overly aggressive" and claim that the Harvard lawyer threatened to destroy the girls if Krischer took the case to trial.

Dershowitz denied this, but nevertheless mounted a campaign to discredit the victims, sending state prosecutors piles of documents obtained by private investigators hired by Epstein. Nothing was off limits, including investigating the girls' families and talking to their teachers, ex-boyfriends, and coaches.

Dershowitz pointed to one of the victims' Myspace pages as a "troublesome and telling illustration of her character."

Dershowitz enclosed some samples.

"You will note that she, herself, has chosen to go by the name 'Pimp Juice' and the site goes on to detail, including photos, her apparent fascination with marijuana. This will come as no surprise to you as I'm sure you are already aware of her recent Palm Beach arrest for both possession of marijuana and possession of drug paraphernalia," Dershowitz wrote.

Recarey, in his usual no-bullshit way, told prosecutors that Dershowitz was out of line.

KRISCHER'S HAND-PICKED PROSECUTOR, LANNA BELOHLAVEK, HAD LED the sex crimes division in the state attorney's office and had experience with child sex abuse cases, yet she, too, began to refer to the victims as if they were prostitutes, Recarey said.

Under Florida law, it is illegal to have sex with anyone seventeen or younger, regardless of whether they consent, or whether the perpetrator is unaware they are underage.

"How can you not believe them, when you haven't even interviewed them?" Recarey asked Belohlavek.

"Look, we have pictures of a girl holding a beer in her hand," Belohlavek said, referring to the girl's Myspace page. "She is underage and she is drinking. They are talking about smoking pot and drinking and sex. This is problematic," Belohlavek said.

"Tell me what teenager doesn't drink!" Recarey replied, exasperated. "Does that mean she wasn't a victim because she took a sip of a beer? Based on these criteria, basically, what you're telling me is the only victim of a sexual battery could be a nun."

Belohlavek was also concerned that, under state law at the time, minors as young as fourteen could be prosecuted for prostitution, meaning the girls could be charged.

From then on, Recarey felt that Krischer and Belohlavek were slow-walking the case.

Privately, Recarey and Reiter were baffled by the change in Krischer's approach to the case.

"He went from 'let's get him' to 'why do you want to subpoena those records?' " Recarey recalled.

ON JANUARY 4, 2006, A FORMER HOUSEMAN FOR EPSTEIN APPEARED AT the state attorney's office in Palm Beach to give a taped sworn statement in the case. Alfredo Rodriguez had worked for Epstein for about six months, from November 2004 to May 2005—a key period of time involving the assaults that police were investigating.

Rodriguez described Epstein as a demanding boss. He ordered his staff to stay out of his sight and not to look at him when they waited on him. Rodriguez said Epstein had many visitors, most of them young masseuses who he said appeared to be of high school age.

While he was nervous, Rodriguez was cooperative. He said the girls who were coming to Epstein's house came at all hours of the day and, as time went on, they appeared to be younger and younger.

As evidence, he told them he had kept a journal of his work, including the names of visitors to Epstein's mansion.

Rodriguez called himself a "human ATM" because Epstein required him to have two thousand dollars in cash on hand at all times so that he could pay the girls, even when Epstein wasn't there. He was also instructed to buy them electronic equipment, jewelry, and almost anything else they wanted.

Rodriguez said once the girls arrived, he would let them into the kitchen and offer them something to eat and drink.

"They ate just like my daughter who is also in high school," he said. "They would eat tons of cereal and drink milk all the time."

After the girls left, he would go upstairs to clean the master bedroom and bath, often finding sex toys scattered on the floor.

Recarey asked Rodriguez whether he would turn over his journal. They made plans to meet a few days later at a shopping plaza in Boca Raton.

Rodriguez turned over a green folder containing documents with phone numbers and names, along with a rental receipt for a car that Epstein had rented for one of the girls.

A STRATEGIC ADDITION TO EPSTEIN'S DEFENSE TEAM ABOUT THIS TIME was Palm Beach criminal lawyer Jack Goldberger. Goldberger, a former public defender, didn't have the same kind of high-profile name recognition as the other lawyers on Epstein's team, but he did get some attention early in his career when he defended a Vietnam veteran who got into trouble for keeping a pint-sized pet monkey he brought back from Thailand in his Palm Beach home without a permit. "Groucho," the veteran's toothless, four-pound gibbon, was part of the man's family, but state wildlife officials threatened to seize his furry friend. The *Miami Herald* covered the case when it went to trial in 1983, garnering national attention.[2]

Goldberger successfully defended the vet, who was allowed to keep Groucho as long as he agreed to keep him in a cage.

But Epstein didn't pick Goldberger for his skills at defending small creatures. Goldberger's law partner, Jason Weiss, was married to Daliah Weiss, who just happened to be the other assistant state attorney Krischer had assigned to the Epstein case. Weiss was considered a tough prosecutor who was chief of the state attorney's Special Victims Unit. Recarey felt that Weiss was more serious about prosecuting Epstein and he began working more closely with her after Krischer and Belohlavek indicated they didn't want to move forward with charges. By hiring Goldberger, Epstein saw to it that Weiss had to step down from the case because of the potential conflict her husband's involvement posed.

WEISS LEFT THE CASE IN MAY 2006, BUT BY THEN SHE HAD ALREADY been privy to most of the evidence police had collected. There was no mention of her recusal in the state attorney's case files, and Recarey found out about her departure thirdhand, well after Goldberger was hired by Epstein. It was just another aspect of the case that made him question whether the state attorney's office had been compromised.

ONE DAY, AS RECAREY WAS TRACKING DOWN VICTIMS, HE GOT A CALL from another of Epstein's attorneys, Guy Fronstin. Recarey had been pursuing an interview with Epstein and Fronstin finally had an answer.

"I'm sorry, but Mr. Epstein isn't going to be available for an interview," Fronstin said in the voice message. "We've spoken to Ms. Belohlavek and we've told her that Mr. Epstein has a passion for massages."

It was an odd thing to say in a message, so Recarey called Belohlavek to find out what was going on.

She was evasive, insisting that she had not discussed anything significant with Fronstin.

Several days later, Fronstin called Recarey again on his work-issued cell phone.

"Mr. Epstein wants me to tell you a few things," Fronstin said cryptically.

"He wants me to relay that he is very passionate about massages. In fact, he has donated over one hundred thousand dollars to the Ballet of Florida for massages," he said, referring to Ballet Florida, a dance company and school in West Palm Beach.

"The massages are therapeutic and spiritually sound for him and that is why he has had many, many massages. He also wants me to tell you that he is appreciative of the way the case has not been leaked to the press."

"It's important to protect the innocent if the allegations are not substantiated," Recarey agreed.

But by February 2006, Recarey and his team, which included an intelligence analyst, sergeant, and police captain, had built a strong case against Epstein. They had seventeen victims who were willing to testify, as well as two witnesses who worked for Epstein and backed up the girls' stories. There were also phone records, message pads, the high school transcript, and the note written on Epstein's stationery. In their surveillance of Epstein's mansion, police had taken photographs of girls coming and going, and they had also snapped shots of license plates that were traced to some of the victims. Recarey was still getting names of more girls and, as the months wore on, it seemed that the list of victims would never end.

Recarey had also received plane logs for Epstein's private jet, showing that he was in Palm Beach during the time period his victims said they were assaulted.

In March, one of Epstein's victims received an ominous call.

"Those who help Jeffrey will be compensated and those who hurt him will be dealt with," said the woman, identified later as a nineteen-year-old recruiter for Epstein.

The girl was petrified but didn't want to pursue witness intimidation charges.

"She knew details that I had only told you," she told Recarey. "How did she know what I told you?"

Now Recarey was angry.

And Belohlavek wasn't returning his phone messages.

THE MORE EVIDENCE THAT RECAREY COLLECTED, THE MORE UNWILLING prosecutors were to move forward.

"I had dealt with Lanna [Belohlavek] over the years, and we were always good until this case," Recarey said. "Now, mind you, these people, we were allies, and all of a sudden we became adversaries overnight. I worked at the state attorney's office for five years. A lot of these people I knew a long time.

"I worked with these prosecutors on other cases. They stood behind you, and they were willing to go to bat with you and fight this case in court."

Recarey said by the time he finished the investigation, he had thirty-four victims, including several who said they had been raped. He prepared warrants for the arrest of Epstein, Sarah Kellen, and Robson.

BUT THEN KRISCHER DID SOMETHING UNUSUAL.

He decided to put the case before a state grand jury. In Florida, state attorneys have wide discretion over whether to bring charges, and grand juries are only usually reserved for capital murder cases. So Krischer seemed to be raising questions about whether the case merited charges, leaving it to a grand jury to decide. Probably more strategic for Epstein, however, was that placing it in front of a grand jury also limited media scrutiny because the panel's proceedings are kept secret.

The grand jury was scheduled to convene the following week. Normally prosecutors work together with police to help prepare witnesses before testifying, but Recarey wasn't given any instructions about which victims should appear and at what time.

He left messages for Belohlavek all day on April 13 and 14, and again on April 17—three days before the grand jury was to convene.

Finally, he went personally to the state attorney's office and knocked on Belohlavek's door.

"Oh, I was just going to return your phone call," she told the detective sweetly. "We made an offer to the defense. One count of aggravated assault with intent to commit a felony, five years' probation with adjudication withheld." The deal meant that Epstein would only be charged with assaulting one girl, Jane Doe 1, and he would not face any sex charges and serve no time in jail.

"What about all the other victims?" Recarey asked as Belohlavek's cell phone rang and went to voice mail.

The call was from Fronstin. Belohlavek listened to the message on speakerphone so Recarey could hear.

"I spoke with Mr. Epstein and he has agreed to the deal. So please call off the grand jury," Fronstin said.

Recarey was stunned. He wasn't even aware the prosecutors were negotiating a plea.

"I'm going to have to talk to the chief," he said.

Recarey left the state attorney's office and drove straight to police headquarters. When Reiter learned about the deal, he picked up the phone and called Krischer, yelling.

By then, both Reiter and Recarey were getting calls from the parents of some of the victims, complaining that their repeated phone calls to Krischer's office had not been returned. They wanted to know what was going on with the case, which had dragged on for almost a year. Their daughters had received subpoenas to testify before the grand jury in less than a week, yet no one had contacted them to confirm and prepare them.

That afternoon, Tim Valentine, an investigator in the state attorney's office, called Recarey to officially notify him that the grand jury had been canceled. He wanted Recarey to call all the victims who had been served with subpoenas to appear.

"Call them yourself. This was the state attorney's decision, not ours," he said, and hung up.

Reiter sent a confidential letter to Krischer. Enclosed were the probable cause affidavits and the arrest warrants.

"After giving this much thought and consideration, I must urge you to examine the unusual course that your office's handling of this matter has taken and consider if good and sufficient reason exists to require your disqualification from the prosecution of these cases," Reiter wrote.

Krischer didn't want to sign off on warrants, but pressure was mounting for him to do something. The media also was now digging deeper into the story.

A FEW WEEKS LATER, EPSTEIN CHANGED HIS MIND AND REJECTED THE state's deal. The grand jury was back on again.

"I was told, 'We're going to the grand jury,' then 'No, we're not having a grand jury,' then 'Yes, we are, but we have to push it back, here's a new date, no, push it back,'" Recarey recalled. "It was crazy. I finally just filed my arrest warrants directly with the warrants division. Then that went back and forth. They kept giving me my warrants back."

Finally, a grand jury date was set, giving Recarey and the victims two days' notice.

"Some of the victims were local and some were not. The ones who could go went, but the ones who couldn't didn't go." Among those who were unable to testify that day was one of his most solid witnesses: Jane Doe 103, who had college exams.

Recarey knew full well that the grand jury schedule set by prosecutors—and by Epstein's lawyers—was designed to fail, and, in an interview, he told me how and why he believed that they were throwing the case.

It was part political, he said, because Epstein was a million-dollar donor to the Democratic Party, which controls Palm Beach. Krischer was reminded that Clinton was friends with Epstein, and there were a lot of other political heavyweights also tied to Epstein, including George Mitchell. If Epstein's secrets got out in a big way, it would hurt the party. Krischer was a powerful force in Palm Beach politics, and it was up to him to contain the case.

"He was protecting the system," Recarey said.

There is no written code, no playbook, and no briefcase full of money passed under the table to wield influence in Florida politics. This is not unique to one party over another. The divide is not Republican versus Democrat; it's the rich and powerful versus everyone else.

"It's more like, if your bread is buttered by the rich, 'if you go after Epstein, we are going to break from you and you won't get our support,' that's how it works," explained Jose Lambiet, a former longtime columnist for the *Palm Beach Post* who covered the Epstein case.

"Epstein was a major danger. It's clear the Palm Beach establishment will protect the cash cows, and he was a major cash cow to the Democratic Party."

Lambiet, now a licensed private investigator, admits that he and the *Post*'s editors failed to fully understand the seriousness of Epstein's crimes.

"I thought he was the run-of-the-mill, garden-variety pervert. I personally misread the story at the beginning and nobody at the *Post* was pushing for us to see it the right way," Lambiet said.

He recalls Krischer and his spokesman, Mike Edmundson, telling him back then that the girls amounted to nothing more than prostitutes.

Recarey saw the chain of events as a politically expedient effort by Krischer, who had higher career aspirations.

"It is the state attorney's job to get the jury on the same page. These girls were children in Florida, they were under eighteen, and it was illegal. Why wouldn't any of the prosecutors stand up and say that to the grand jury?"

chapter 8

MUSIC CITY

There are few people I adore more in the *Miami Herald* newsroom than Monika Leal. Simply calling her a librarian doesn't do her justice. She knows more about Florida history, and more about Miami, than most people who have lived in South Florida all their lives. In another life, Monika would probably have been an amazing investigative reporter, and in truth, she knows how to gather information better than most journalists. She can unearth almost anything, and has an immense patience, especially with frantic reporters. There have been times, well past normal working hours, or long before dawn, when a story was breaking and I couldn't get access to some government website, so I would write her a panicked email—and within minutes, she would send me the link, the password, or other information I couldn't find on my own. She has supported me in ways big and small throughout my decade-long career at the *Herald*. I'm always surprised that she seems to know exactly what I'm working on and what I've written, given that she assists dozens of other staff members daily. As at most newspapers these days, she has watched her staff of researchers dwindle until now she is the last one standing, and I'm sure she manages tasks that I can't even fathom.

In my search for Epstein's victims, Monika was my sounding board, helping me on numerous occasions when I couldn't find a girl whom I thought was important to my story. She helped with the research on Epstein's companies and on his charities, and she just listened to me on days when I discussed my doubts about taking on the story at all. Librarians are the unsung heroes of journalism, the fact-finders and fact-checkers behind the scenes who often don't get the credit they deserve. We fail to truly appreciate them.

In the fall of 2017, despite Monika's support and assistance, I was beginning to think my search for victims who would be willing to speak to me about Epstein had reached the end of the road. I had already spent months gathering a list, and had written dozens of letters. I wrote to some of the victims via Facebook. A few of them did respond, but their messages didn't give me much hope. Some of them were angry with me for contacting them at all. I was polite, and I understood.

Jane Doe 1—the first girl to come forward in Palm Beach— had just gotten married about the time that I began my search. She lived in the Midwest and she and her husband had started their own business. She was probably one of the most stunning women I have ever seen, and her wedding photos made her look like a princess in a fairy tale. It was nothing less than miraculous that she seemed to have come out of the Jeffrey ordeal whole. I knew from the court files about her fractured family life and the hell that Epstein and his lawyers put her and her family through.

There were other women who had gone on to careers in real estate and health care; one became an elementary school teacher. Another, recruited by Epstein when she was thirteen, went on to become a successful actress. I was happy for all of them.

Another, Leigh Skye Patrick, wasn't so lucky. By the time I found her, she was already gone.

Skye had been addicted to opioids for years, and finally succumbed to her drug demons on May 30, 2017. She left behind a three-year-old boy, and I was moved by how her twin sister, Selby, had adopted her nephew, despite the fact that she was grieving the death of her fiancé, who had also died of an opioid overdose that year.

Selby didn't want to talk to me. At the time, she believed that her sister's relationship with Epstein had nothing to do with her sister's addictions. She reasoned that her twin had been addicted long before Epstein came into her life.

I knew Selby was probably dealing with a lot of pain, and I didn't want to cause her any more agony. But I reached out to her one more time without success before my series ran because I thought her sister's story was an important one to tell. I could see that Skye had been arrested twelve times in the fourteen years since she met Epstein, mostly on drug charges. Her life certainly wasn't made easier by her association with Jeffrey Epstein.

And I later learned that Skye had wanted to tell her story.

In 2015, two years before her death, she gave an interview to London's *Daily Mail* that, for some reason, the paper declined to publish at the time.

IN THE INTERVIEW, WHICH WAS PUBLISHED IN JULY 2019, SKYE SAID that she was sixteen and in rehab, trying to overcome drug and alcohol addiction when she was introduced to Epstein in 2003. A classmate of hers at Wellington Christian School convinced her to go to a mansion in Palm Beach for a house party, and they drove seventeen miles to Epstein's waterfront estate. When they arrived, Skye became immediately alarmed because the only people she saw there were Epstein and one of his female assistants.

"When we got there, my friend left in a hurry and there I was, alone in that big mansion. There was no party going on," she said in the *Mail* interview.[1]

"The woman took me to a large bathroom and Jeffrey was already there with only a towel around his waist," she recalled.

"I remember he had a black-and-white photo of a dick on the wall. I thought the whole thing was creepy."

He asked her to take off her shirt, and then her bra.

"He was getting aggressive about what he wanted, and I got really uncomfortable so I grabbed my shirt and left. . . . I was a scared sixteen-year-old. I ran out because he was so creepy. He scared the life out of me."[2]

She returned again but didn't want to talk about what happened. In the years following her encounters with Epstein, she descended into a hell she could not escape. She lost custody of her son and was in and out of halfway houses and rehab facilities.

At the time she gave the *Mail* interview, she said she was still angry.

In 2008, she was one of thirty-four women listed by federal prosecutors as a victim, and she eventually received a fifty-thousand-dollar settlement from Epstein. But she was like many of the girls who received settlements, unfortunately, who used the money to numb their pain with drugs and alcohol.

Two years after her interview with the *Mail*, her naked body was found in room 212 of a flophouse motel in Greenacres, Florida.

At the time, the motel had been targeted by law enforcement as a headquarters for drugs and prostitution, and the rooms were infested with cockroaches. The walls and floors were dirty, filled with peeling paint chips. The rooms stank of cigarettes, and the bedsheets were stained. Guests who reviewed the place claimed they sometimes slept with a hammer or a knife under their pillows.

The motel's brochure reads: "We blend the warmth and charm of old Florida with the convenience and service the modern-day traveler expects."

Skye was so badly bruised, with abrasions and open wounds, that when her frail and battered body was found, the sheriff's department treated her death as a possible homicide. The deputy who found her described her in his report as a beautiful lost young soul.

"She has reddish-brown hair and light-brown eyes," wrote Detective Joe Noyes of the Palm Beach County Sheriff's Office. "There was a blue flower on her left forearm; a symbol, possibly Chinese, on her left front hip; a tattoo on her right wrist that said 'exit.' I took 53 photographs of the scene for documentation. I bagged each hand and secured the wrists with tape. I wrote my case number and initials on each wrist. The decedent was placed in a black homicide body bag which was sealed with red tag No. 1686210."

The investigation showed that a man had rented the room, and when they spoke to him, he said he had had sex with her and when he left, she was fine. The implication was that she had been paid and then used the money to buy drugs.

Her cause of death was later determined to be drug and alcohol intoxication.

I was thinking of Skye and all the other victims on my trip to interview the first woman willing to talk to me about her ordeal with Epstein. I flew into Nashville a day ahead of Emily. In the years since her encounter with Epstein, Michelle Licata had moved with her family from Florida to a small village in Coffee County, Tennessee, outside Nashville. They ran a cozy mom-and-pop lunch spot, the Coffee Café, known for its decadent cinnamon rolls and fat cheeseburgers. A single mother with a little boy, Michelle had gotten as far away from Epstein as she could. But no matter how much distance she put between herself and him, fear, trauma, and shame seemed to follow her wherever she went.

Michelle worked long shifts at her parents' restaurant, and then she left at the end of the afternoon, weary, to take care of her son. We still weren't even 100 percent sure she would be able to sit for an interview, as her lawyer had advised against it. She had also received a settlement nearly a decade earlier. It wasn't clear whether she was even allowed to talk, since she didn't know whether she had signed a nondisclosure agreement.

I WAS EXCITED ABOUT TRAVELING TO NASHVILLE, EVEN IF ONLY FOR A brief visit. I rarely took vacations. There was plenty of traveling I wanted to do, but didn't have the means or the time. About the only way I got to see any of the country was when I was on a work assignment.

A friend of mine who lived outside Nashville picked me up at the airport that evening. It was a blustery cold November night, a shock to my system that only someone who has brined themselves in Florida's sunshine truly understands. But I was so buoyed by the fact that I had an interview that I forgot about my chattering teeth and cold feet.

I had rented a two-bedroom Airbnb in East Nashville. When we arrived, the house was pitch-dark. My friend Linda and her boyfriend, Steve, helped me to the door, and I was so happy to have found a cute little house with a pretty backyard. Emily and I are always trying to do our trips on the cheap, terrified that we would get grilled about our expenses. There were many times we paid for things out of pocket, and I was terrible at keeping track of all my receipts, so it was more than once that I returned from a business trip with pennies left in my bank account.

Emily and I always tried our best to book budget hotels—but they often turned out to be dumps, like so-called "business-friendly" hotels that didn't have internet or family roadside motels swarming with bedbugs.

I did find out the next morning in Nashville why the place was so reasonable—the property backed up directly to the railroad tracks, so we were awakened bright and early by the sound of a train whistle blowing outside our bedroom windows.

Still, it wasn't a red-light district like some places we had stayed in, and it was so nice to be somewhere else, particularly in such a great city. I was alone the first night and the house was much too quiet. I wrapped myself in layers and took an Uber into downtown Nashville for dinner.

I bathed myself in the sound of blues and the smell of southern barbecue that night. I was in awe of all the music coming out of every nook of the city. It was a momentary escape from the Epstein case and I kept wishing that my kids were with me. I knew my daughter, especially, would love Nashville. She played five instruments in high school, wore Pink Floyd Converse sneakers, and played Bob Dylan songs on her guitar, occasionally with a band on the beach. I made a mental note that when this project was over I would bring her to Nashville.

It was getting late and my feet were numb by the time I took an Uber back to the little house in East Nashville.

Emily arrived early the next morning, hauling her usual massive cargo of suitcases filled with photo and video equipment. I was always trying to help her, but she had a certain way of organizing her gear and always refused. It was awkward for me when we went on assignment, because she had so much to lug around, and here I was, with nothing but my purse and a notebook. She treated this reality as if it was her cross to bear, and claimed that she was absolutely used to it. But I still felt guilty and would often try grabbing things haphazardly, as she scolded me for my feeble attempts to lug heavy video and camera gear while wearing a skirt and high heels.

It was a good forty-five minutes to Manchester, the small town where Michelle lived. The drive was magnificent. The rolling Tennessee hills were carpeted with the beautiful colors of fall that don't exist in South Florida. Emily and I talked about missing the beauty of autumn. She was an air force brat who had moved around a lot growing up, but had spent her middle and high school years in Eastport and Presque Isle, Maine, a place as provincial as the town I grew up in, but with mannerly people with practical wardrobes filled with fishermen's sweaters and L.L.Bean boots.

WHEN WE ARRIVED IN MANCHESTER, I WAS STRUCK BY HOW MUCH slower Michelle's life must seem now than when she lived in the urban sprawl of West Palm Beach a decade earlier. Manchester is a fourteen-square-mile village nestled along the Little Duck River amid shaded dirt back roads of God's country. The town has native American stone ruins dating back two thousand years, and travel guides describe Manchester as "sprinkled with sour mash and Tennessee whiskey." It's the county seat of Coffee County, and probably best known for hosting the international Bonnaroo Music & Arts Festival each June on a seven-hundred-acre farm outside the town center. During the festival, Manchester's population swells from ten thousand permanent residents to upward of seventy thousand, making it one of the largest outdoor events in North America.

The narrow square buildings, pre–World War II storefronts, and antiques shops took me back to the postage-stamp-sized borough where I grew up, in Sellersville, Pennsylvania, a one-square-mile town, population four thousand. Our version of Bonnaroo was the local carnival in a parking lot behind the fire station. Our hangouts in the 1970s were the Sellersville Cinema, the Dairy Queen, and a chrome-and-neon 1950s-style diner named Emil's. Most everyone worked at the hulking factory down the street from my house known as "The Gauge."

The Ametek company's Sellersville manufacturing plant was built in 1904, providing air pressure and temperature sensing instruments for the military during World Wars I and II. After the wars, the Sellersville division provided circuitry for commercial aircraft and automotive companies. The Gauge has long since closed, succumbing to the march of high-tech industry and computerization. I moved out on my own at sixteen, after spending years being taunted by kids in the neighborhood whose parents disapproved of my mother's status as a divorced single mother with three children. We spent a lot of time running around the neighborhood unsupervised because Mom worked as a full-time secretary during the day and as a waitress at night. Halloween was particularly scary, not because of the ghosts and goblins, but because the kids in the neighborhood would throw big mud bombs at our house all night.

As a young girl, I was always writing stories. In hindsight, I think they helped me cope with not having a father around, a mother who was often working, and the bullying I endured on the school playground.

I used to keep my stories in shoeboxes in my closet.

I remember when I was in fourth grade, I wrote an essay that the teacher was so convinced I had plagiarized, she made me stay in at recess and write another one.

I sat at my desk all alone, the teacher just waiting for me to break down and confess, I suppose. Instead, I pulled out a dictionary, opened it up to a random page, and found a big magical word that rolled off my tongue. I read the definition and wrote a new essay around the word and others that I randomly picked from that dictionary. I don't know why I wrote like this back then; maybe I was just drawn to beautiful words.

"To make the perfect composition in words is more than to make the best building or machine, or the best statue or picture. It shall be the glory of the greatest masters to make perfect compositions in words," Walt Whitman wrote. I would later embroider that paragraph and frame it.

After this punitive exercise, the teacher apologized to my mother for doubting I had written the original essay.

Right about that time, I submitted an essay to the VFW for a contest they ran every year for Memorial Day. The topic that year was "Why I Am Proud to Be an American."

It was a long shot because I was told that no student at Sellersville

Elementary had ever won the contest; the winner was almost always from St. Agnes, a private Catholic school where some of the more well-to-do families sent their kids.

Everyone was shocked, including me, when I won and was crowned Miss Poppy Queen at the Memorial Day parade that year.

At Pennridge High School, I was editor for the *Penndulum*, the school newspaper. I was having a lot of problems at home, however, and struggling to keep up with my schoolwork. Because of this, the paper's adviser fired me as editor, which I remember to this day as one of the most devastating things that happened to me in high school.

At sixteen, I left home and became an emancipated minor. This enabled me to live away from home in a walk-up apartment I shared with some friends who had already graduated from high school. I also spent a lot of time with two other older friends, Candace and John Croft, who lived on a farm on the outskirts of town. Candace became a mother figure in my life. The two of them told me a lot of colorful stories about the 1960s, about civil rights protests and sit-ins they had participated in against the war in Vietnam. I also met a group of writers and artists. We all used to sit for hours discussing music and poetry—as they smoked joints and I drank beer, joking about how we managed to solve all the world's problems in one night.

At the time, I worked a bunch of low-paying jobs, first in a lamp-shade factory, then as a clerk in a bell factory, to pay rent.

I finally decided that I wanted to do something worthwhile with my life. So I applied and was accepted into the journalism program at Temple University in Philadelphia in 1984.

Two years later, I left Sellersville and never looked back.

chapter 9

BLOOD MONEY

Michelle Licata and her mother, Lisa Moreland, greeted Emily and me at the restaurant that morning, not knowing what to expect. I had spoken to Michelle on the phone several times ahead of my trip, trying to ease her mind, but nothing really prepares someone for an on-camera interview about the worst thing that ever happened to you.

I asked Michelle before we met if she could pull out some old photo albums from when she was in high school. There were pictures of her at summer camp, and others of her with her family at holidays and birthday parties. The youngest of seven brothers and sisters, Michelle was working a part-time job at Publix supermarket in West Palm Beach in 2004 while both her parents worked long hours at a local Home Depot. Michelle was a straight-A student and cheerleader at Royal Palm Beach High School who loved to write poetry.

Michelle's memories of her adolescence recalled a time of innocence, when selfishness and immaturity were normal, and there was little fear that someone armed with an AR-15 would march into your school and kill you and all your friends.

"The best way to describe me back then is I was in a fairy-tale world full of unicorns, butterflies, and rainbows, and I wanted to be in that world. I didn't want to know that people could hurt other people. I didn't want to hear the bad parts of life," she told me.

She began writing in ninth grade. A friend of hers wrote songs, and she had a notebook they would take turns passing back and forth. Her poems were the lyrics of everyday life: boys, nature, her sisters and brothers, teachers and school.

"It was all the things that was going on in my life at the time," she said.

She loved movies and went to a different one every Friday night with her best friend. Cell phones were a new phenomenon, and texts back then cost ten cents each, so few of her peers could afford them.

"I think the world wasn't so exposed. Because of the internet and the Facebook and all of these things coming out now, everybody knows everything about everyone. Back then, you had a little bit of privacy. You had to memorize your friends' phone numbers. You had to actually use that muscle memory in your brain. Now everyone just pushes a button—they don't know anybody's number anymore," she said.

"Computers were different, too. You had to use a dial-up mechanism and it took so long and sometimes didn't connect, it was crazy how things changed so fast."

During the interview, her mother left the café to try to find more family photo albums.

Emily and I could sense that Michelle was uncomfortable talking about Epstein in front of her mom, and I suggested that perhaps, if she was able, she could talk about him with her mother gone. I reminded her again, as I had previously, that she did not have to share details of her assault.

Emily has a way of focusing a camera so that subjects don't feel the lens upon them. She stepped away from the equipment, and I fell so deeply into my thoughts and worry for Michelle that I forgot Emily was there, too.

We paused to let Michelle think, letting the silence be a moment for her to breathe. When she finally spoke, she forcefully pressed a finger hard against the side of her leg and fumbled like a frightened child trying to find the right words.

"I don't even like anyone looking at me when I talk about it," she said, with tears welling up in her eyes. She turned her eyes away from the camera.

"I'm so ashamed, and so angry, I don't know where to start . . ."

IT WAS RIGHT BEFORE CHRISTMAS WHEN A FRIEND OF HERS SENT HER A note in class. Michelle was sixteen and still in braces.

"Do you want to make some extra money for the holidays?"

"That would be great, because I'd like to get everybody something for Christmas," she replied. "What do I have to do?"

"You just have to massage some old guys."

Michelle, who had a friend whose mother was a masseuse, pictured the spa where her friend's mother worked, where she herself had once gotten a massage.

"Don't you have to have a license? Don't you have to be a professional to do that?" Michelle asked.

"No," the girl said.

"Okay, when do you want me to do it?"

"I will pick you up from work one day. But if you tell anybody about this, I will beat your ass."

"Like, why would I say anything?" Michelle wrote, a bit flustered by the threat. She then crumpled up the note.

A few days later, her friend picked her up and drove her to Palm Beach island. Michelle was surprised when they drove onto a street with nothing but mansions. Up until then, she thought that she was going to a spa or a nursing home to give some old men massages.

She and her friend entered through the gate, went to the side door, and were led into the kitchen. A blond woman greeted them and told Michelle to write down her name and number on a piece of paper.

"Come with me," the woman then said, leading Michelle toward a hidden side door off the kitchen.

"I followed her and remembered there was a staircase, like, a spiral almost, it just went straight then curved back. There were pictures of girls, naked girls, all along the wall right in front of me. And we went past a hallway into a large bedroom.

"She said, 'Okay, now Jeffrey, he's going to be coming in, he'll be on the phone, you just give him a massage and then he will tell you what to do.' "

The room was freezing and dark. As she walked in, there was just a table and, next to the table, a vanity with a mirror. On that table, there were three hundred-dollar bills.

THE DOOR TO THE CAFÉ SQUEAKED OPEN, AND MICHELLE'S MOTHER walked in, holding the photo albums. Michelle stopped, looking nervously at her mother, who walked over and opened one of the books.

Michelle turned white.

"Look at this one, when you and Cody were in the hospital," Lisa said, pointing.

"Mom, yes, okay," Michelle stammered. "Um, Mom, do you want to go in the back while I relive this story?"

Lisa, who had gone through years of anxiety of her own over the trauma her daughter had been through, nodded her head and disappeared into the kitchen.

Michelle took another deep breath.

"So where did I leave off?"

"Yes, the room . . . the room . . ."

EPSTEIN CAME INTO THE ROOM, JUST AS HIS ASSISTANT HAD SAID. HE was clad only in a towel and was on the phone. He lay on the table on his stomach.

Michelle looked at the white-haired man with bushy eyebrows. She felt uncomfortable and queasy, as he pointed to a bottle of lotion and motioned for her to begin. She quickly realized, fumbling in the dim lighting, that this was not a typical massage session.

"I can't remember what his conversations were on the phone, because at this point, I was alone, I was nervous, and thinking, Whoa, I don't know where I am. This is not anything like I thought it was supposed to be."

He instructed her to rub his feet, then his legs.

"I kept one eye on the timer, and I just kept watching it, hoping it would be all over," she recalled.

When she was about halfway through the hour, she began to breathe a bit easier, as he continued to talk on the phone.

"Okay, this is going to be okay," she told herself.

Then he flipped over and dropped his towel, exposing himself.

"That's when he said, 'You can go ahead and take off your shirt and pants, but you can stay in your underwear.' "

She nervously obeyed, feeling too frightened to say no.

"He then wanted to just look at me like a piece of meat," she said. "He was telling me, 'Just turn around a little bit. Let me look at you! You're so beautiful! Do you have a boyfriend?' "

She trained her eyes back on the timer.

"He was hitting on me, which I didn't know at the time. It was just really creepy."

He pulled her close to him and unsnapped her bra, then began assaulting her.

Up until then, the only sexual encounters that Michelle had had were with boys her own age. She had never even been naked in front of a boy before.

"He was looking at me up and down and talking to me in the

most vulgar way. Back then, even with guys my age, I was still wearing my T-shirt, and here this guy is just stripping me down to the core."

He began touching her under her underwear while masturbating.

In what felt like an eternity, the timer finally went off. She didn't know whether he had finished, but then he jumped up and wrapped the towel around him.

"There's two hundred dollars on the table for you and another hundred for your friend. I'd like to see you again," he said.

She didn't know that her friend was being paid to bring her there. Michelle felt betrayed.

"I grabbed the money and I thought, That was so not worth it."

ON THE WAY HOME, HER FRIEND REALIZED HOW UPSET SHE WAS AND asked her what had happened.

Michelle told her how he had assaulted her.

"Oh, that's okay, he tried to do that with my other friend, too."

"What? Are you kidding me?" Michelle replied.

"Yes, it's okay."

Michelle was stunned. She put on her dark sunglasses to cover up her watery eyes.

"As we drove home, I was just in tears," she recalled, choking back sobs as she spoke. "I was looking out the window so she couldn't see me crying. I was just thinking . . . nobody is going to want to be with me ever again . . . for the rest of my life."

She said she prayed that no one would ever find out.

But she was distraught and couldn't hide it from her best friend, whom she told the next day. She made her promise not to tell anyone.

"I sat there on the floor with her and we cried together. And she gave me a hug and told me it was okay, and it was just . . . really, really, really bad. I didn't tell anyone but her for a year—until the police showed up at my house."

ON DECEMBER 12, 2005, ALMOST A YEAR AFTER SHE HAD BEEN molested by Epstein, Michelle sat down with Detective Joe Recarey for an interview. Michelle's name and phone number had been found among the message pads seized in the raid on Epstein's mansion three months earlier.

The worst part, however, was not telling the police what had happened; it was telling her family.

"I remember telling my mom," she said, her voice cracking at the memory.

"I told her, 'I just don't want you to think of me as not your little girl anymore. Don't think of me other than what you already know of me . . . but I have to tell you something . . .'"

She paused, wiping her face.

"I didn't want my family to look at me in a different way. I didn't want them to think I was a whore . . . I was so worried that they would be mad at me."

WITHIN MONTHS AFTER THE ASSAULT, MICHELLE STOPPED STUDYING and began locking herself in her room. She grew angrier each day. When her family asked her what was wrong, she screamed, "I DON'T KNOW!" and ran back to her room.

"I started sleeping with everybody, and people were calling me a slut. I wanted to treat guys the way I thought guys treated girls; that they were objects, that girls were nothing," she said. "I wanted to treat boys like that. I wanted to make them hurt. The ones who liked me, who were nice, I didn't like. The ones who were jerks, who were mean, those were the ones I wanted to be with."

She started failing her classes, staying out until 4:00 A.M. partying, sneaking in and out of the house and waking up hungover. Her mother and stepfather were both working so much that they didn't notice.

"I was punching holes in walls, bruising my knuckles, locking myself in my room, crying."

She went to Home Depot and bought a dead-bolt lock and installed it on her bedroom door.

"I wanted to keep everyone out."

Then, in a small, childlike voice, she said: "What I really wanted was my parents to come and ask me what was wrong. My brothers kept calling me a crybaby. But I was crying because I was so hurt all the time."

She began cutting her wrists, and breaking things around the house. The depth of her anger surprised even her. Once, she was so furious that she lifted a kitchen countertop off a cabinet.

When her parents asked her why she was behaving so erratically, she didn't know what to tell them. It seemed to them it was just typical teenage angst.

"Later on, I had visions of his face; I was so terrified of ever having to see him again."

Her brothers mocked her anger, labeling her fits as her "ostrich dance," when she clenched her fists and stomped her feet.

By then, she was drinking heavily and taking Xanax to dull the pain. Once, she fell asleep at a gas station.

"I took a knife and cut myself, and I saw blood, and my whole head felt calm. Finally. Something stopped me from being so angry. I just wanted to fucking die."

AFTER MICHELLE TOLD DETECTIVE RECAREY WHAT HAD HAPPENED, paranoia set in. Once, when a man approached her in a parking lot and started asking her where he could get drugs, she felt sure that she was being followed by someone associated with Epstein.

She started taking different routes to work.

"Even to this day, I still look to see if cars are following me."

Her darkest hour came when police found her half clothed in the middle of the night stumbling around a shopping center parking lot. She was mumbling incoherently, high on drugs, when they asked where she lived.

"Right here," she said, pointing to the pavement. "I lost my mind."

SHE HAD NOT HEARD ANYTHING ABOUT THE POLICE INVESTIGATION FOR almost a year. Then, suddenly, one day, she saw on television that Epstein had pleaded guilty to a prostitution charge.

"I was just shocked. I had no idea."

No one, including the FBI or prosecutors, had reached out to her, so she thought they were still working on the case and felt hopeful that Epstein would be put away for a long time.

Instead, she realized he had gotten away with his crimes.

"It was like we are a pawn in a chess game to them. The higher-ups get to do whatever they want. They can ruin lives if they want. Who are we? We are nobody."

SHE HIRED A LAWYER, AND, AS ONE OF THE ORIGINAL THIRTY-FOUR victims identified by police, was eligible to receive a financial settlement from Epstein. Under the terms of the arrangement, a lawyer was selected to represent the victims, with his fees paid by Epstein. The settlements weren't capped, but if the victims did not accept the amounts that Epstein's attorneys put on the table, they would be forced to sue him and confront their predator in court. Most of the girls were now over eighteen, and many of them had never told their parents what happened. They were afraid that if they sued, they would be exposed. Epstein was aware of this.

This seemed suspicious to Michelle. So she hired another lawyer, not paid by Epstein. At a mediation, Epstein's lawyers gave her an offer she would have to accept or reject immediately. She was troubled when her attorney informed her she couldn't talk to her parents about the settlement first.

By then, Epstein's lawyers had already sent a message that they intended to destroy her and her family.

At a deposition during the civil case, they grilled her about every boy she had ever slept with, her dysfunctional family life, her relationships with her brothers and her parents.

"The way the lawyer used his words, it was like he was attacking me and my life and the way I was before Jeffrey and after Jeffrey. They were trying to say 'She is a slut, she is doing this for the money, she's not a cute little girl.' They wanted to make me look bad."

Epstein's lawyers threatened to depose her parents and brothers, and Michelle had been adamant about protecting her brothers.

"They wanted to pressure me by going after my family. They were trying to say this must have happened because your dad wasn't in your life, or your brothers were fighting all the time."

They obtained some of her own doctor's psychological reports and learned details about her childhood.

Epstein's legal team also hired their own psychologist to evaluate her.

"I had to talk about myself to numerous people over and over. They were just in my life inside and out. Did you have an abortion? Did you take drugs?

"And I said, 'You're going to come at me like that when you represent a guy who is raping hundreds of girls? How do you sleep at night?' "

As a trial neared, Michelle realized that she would have to face Epstein in a courtroom, and the thought terrified her.

"His lawyer scared the crap out of me, and I just didn't want anybody to find out or know my name. So I said, 'No, I'm done.' "

THE MONEY, HOWEVER, ONLY EXACERBATED HER PROBLEMS.

"I came from a home where I had to buy my own school supplies in high school. I worked all through high school just to buy my own clothes. So, after I got the money, I wanted to know what it felt like to not have a job and what it felt like to get new clothes and shoes. My brothers would say, 'She's rubbing it in our faces.'

"But I bought every one of my siblings something from it, just like what I did for Christmas—which is why I went to Jeffrey's to begin with."

She helped one brother pay his rent and bought gifts for the others. Then she met the wrong guy, one who was glad to help himself to her money. She had bought a house and new furniture, but was spiraling deeper and deeper into opioid addiction.

She had drug-fueled nightmares about Epstein. She installed a video surveillance system at her house and adopted two pit bulls to protect her, convinced that Epstein or someone he hired would kill her.

In a desperate effort to get clean and escape her abusive boyfriend, she moved to North Carolina to live with her biological father.

Her father, a devout Christian, told her to let it all go, that the money wasn't ever hers to begin with.

"He said it was blood money. It wasn't my money. But I feel like I had to go through what I went through to get to the other side of it."

She was victimized by every aspect of the system and almost every person she loved and trusted. Epstein tried to destroy her, but by then, she had something more important to live for: a three-year-old son.

MICHELLE TALKED ABOUT THE FORMER FEDERAL PROSECUTOR, ALEX

Acosta, and how she didn't understand how, as a father of daughters, he could have let Epstein get away with abusing so many girls and women. And how, after he allowed the sealing of Epstein's plea bargain, he and so many other lawyers involved in the case just seemed to go on with their lives and careers.

"I feel like I'm being super brave right now," she said at the end of the interview. "This took a lot for me. I didn't know if I should. But I really want to stand up. I think women really get a bad rap. 'Girls are whores and sluts. Girls and women can't be president,' they say. It's like we are second class to men. This is pretty horrific what this guy did, and people need to know what really happened here."

THE INTERVIEW HAD LASTED THREE HOURS. WE WERE ALL EXHAUSTED.
In the car, headed back to the airport, Emily and I were quiet, lost in our thoughts. It was unusual for us not to talk about our interviews afterward, to plan how to illustrate them, or to discuss what portions of them were most important. This time, we were in shocked silence.

I was also worried about Michelle. I knew it had taken courage to talk about what she had been through, and I was aware of the responsibility that was now on my shoulders to tell her story in a way that was respectful of her and her family. I made a mental note to call her when we got to the airport to check in, but I didn't have to wait that long.

My cell phone rang, and I wondered if Michelle had changed her mind about going public or had misgivings about how raw and honest she had been in front of someone she had never met before.

"I just want to tell you that I have not felt this good in years," she said, sounding serene. "I feel such a relief, like a big boulder was just lifted off my shoulders. Thank you so much."

I thanked her for trusting us and I told her we would stay in touch.

Then I ended the call and cried.

chapter 10

MIKE

At work, I'm generally all business, and when I'm on deadline or focused, I'm not always a pleasant person to be around. In fact, I'm told I can be quite scary.

I've never been very good at small talk, or pretending to be interested in anything other than the project I'm buried in.

This is not on purpose. In my early days at the *Herald,* I was dedicated to only two things: my work and my children. I was juggling two young kids and all the pressures that come with being a single mom: soccer practice, guitar lessons, math homework, doctor visits, sick days, and later, the daily crises of teenagers. I hired a student teacher to be home with my kids in the evenings when they were in elementary school because I was working ten to fifteen hours a day and often didn't get home until well past nine. I would get up at dawn to make them breakfast and lunch and dinner for later in the day, do the laundry, take them to school—all between reading the news and getting a jump on whatever story was breaking that I had to follow when I got into the office. This schedule didn't change much as my kids grew older; their problems just became more complicated. The weekend soccer mom in me looked forward to watching my kids play, but sitting on the sidelines, I often worried over the bills and how I was going to pay for college. My paycheck never went far enough. As the years went on, my paycheck got smaller and I could no longer afford the rent on our house. But I didn't want to uproot my kids from their friends and schools. I was constantly bouncing checks and being charged overdraft fees. My bills were always late, and my debts piled up. My ex-husband, who had been paying me a little child support, was on work disability. He figured out a way to spend more time with the kids, which I welcomed, but it meant that I would have to pay *him* child support.

I drowned myself in my work, determined to be so versatile and indispensable I would be the last to be laid off. I almost never turned down even the most mundane assignment. I told myself that the best writers were those who could make a good story out of anything. I tried to learn something about almost every beat at every paper I worked at and to cover them so well that I would be able to slide easily into any beat or assignment. A lot of other reporters didn't like this about me. It wasn't that I was trying to bigfoot them; it was more that I was just trying to survive.

Consequently, I wasn't friends with many people in the *Herald* newsroom. I just didn't have time.

I was one of those people who came to work and went straight to my computer, never looking up except to go to the bathroom. I ate at my desk, working through lunch and dinner. If I was in the middle of writing a story on deadline and another reporter would come up to talk to me, the look on my face was usually enough to make them scamper away.

Emily and I would later joke that if a bomb went off in the newsroom, I would probably still be there, writing the story through the smoke and flames, typing as much detail as I could about the sound of the bomb, the smell of the smoke, and how many bodies were sprawled on the floor around me.

Not much of that changed while I was working on the Epstein project. Emily knew as soon as she walked up to me whether it was a good day or a bad day. On a good day, I would stop what I was doing, reluctantly, and talk about the documentary she was putting together to accompany the Epstein story. On a bad day, I would growl, and she would smile sweetly and walk away.

Emily is probably the only person at the *Herald* who "gets" me, and she might know me better than I know myself. We laughed about all the trouble I could have gotten into had she not used her clear thinking to keep me on the straight and narrow. When I was sent on the road without her, we crossed our fingers I wouldn't get arrested for trespassing or arguing with a cop.

I was always encouraging Emily to ignore whatever rule the powers that be set up to keep us journalists and photographers from getting the truth.

Here's a typical Julie-Emily conversation, as we arrived at an assignment:

ME TO EMILY: "Just park here, right in front of the building."

EMILY: "We're not allowed to park here, there's a sign that says 'no parking.'"

ME: "Come on, Emily, the cops aren't writing tickets right now."

EMILY: "But they might tow my car!"

ME: "They won't tow your car. I'll put a note on the windshield."

EMILY: "Yeah, right. It's not your car. I'm not parking here."

ME: "They really won't care, they have a lot of things going on and aren't worried about us."

EMILY: "Get out of my car. I'll go park."

WE HAD LOGGED HUNDREDS OF MILES ACROSS THE STATE OF FLORIDA visiting prisons. We learned a lot about each other during those long drives. In some ways, I think I was as good for her as she was for me.

She calmed my anxieties, and I coaxed out her inner badass.

We were also both mothers. A great deal of our drive and fly time was spent talking about our children, who were on the verge of becoming adults, going to college, having their first boyfriends and girlfriends—and all the tribulations that go with growing up. Her husband, Walt, had recently retired after working as a photographer for the *Herald* for thirty-three years. I loved hearing stories about Walt and how he was *not* adjusting to retirement. Whenever a big story broke, he would pace and grit his teeth because he couldn't be on the street in the middle of the media madness.

At work, Emily sometimes got understandably flustered by the paper's lack of staff, equipment, and planning. She rarely pushed back, however, and sometimes management took advantage of her inability to say no.

"Don't they know that you are the great visual journalist Emily Michot?" I would tell her as she was on her way out the door to shoot a kids' carnival.

"I don't . . . think . . . they . . . do," she would answer, throwing up her hands.

IN THE MIDDLE OF MY RESEARCH, REITER SUGGESTED THAT I READ A 2016 book cowritten by James Patterson and John Connelly about the Epstein case, *Filthy Rich*. Perhaps as a result of my fourth-grade teacher's belief that I hadn't written my own essay, I have long had a policy to not read other people's work on a subject that I am writing about. I didn't want someone else's words or findings to color what I was doing—and I felt that this was even more important for the Epstein case because so much had been written about it.

I told Reiter that I would read the book after I finished writing my stories.

Also, I wanted to hear from Reiter firsthand about what went wrong in the Epstein case.

I had hoped my interview with Michelle would convince Reiter and Recarey that I was trying to examine the story in a way that others had been unable to. The key to accomplishing my goal was getting them to talk on the record for the first time.

They continued to be a difficult sell. At one point, Reiter asked me to just submit questions to him that he would answer in writing. I told him that for a story of this nature, this would not be ethical. I knew I was stretching it—and he wasn't buying it. He then asked me for a copy of the journalism code of ethics.

As long as Reiter wouldn't talk, Recarey wouldn't, either. Recarey provided me with a written statement instead.

Then Reiter began expressing concern that he might place himself in legal jeopardy by speaking to me because some of the powerful people involved could sue him.

"Assertively pursuing this case has caused problems for me and my family that you will never know," he wrote.

I reminded him that I had been reading all the lawsuits, and I was familiar with the various legal maneuvers that Epstein and his attorneys used to manipulate the case. I pointed out that I had identified many of the victims, had interviewed one on the record, and had several others who were on the verge of doing the same.

He kept insisting that the *Herald*, like other media he had observed, would back away from the story.

Around and around we went.

I finally asked Casey if he would assure Reiter that the *Herald* wasn't going to be intimidated by the onslaught of powerful people who might try to derail the project. Casey agreed to intervene.

I still don't know the details of that conversation, but Reiter told me later that Casey spoke highly of me and assured him that we were going to tell the story no matter what. Casey had by then read some of the court files, too, and also felt that there had been a horrible miscarriage of justice, a cover-up of epic proportions.

"You know, someone, somewhere who has a lot of power and money will call your publisher and tell him or her to kill the story," Reiter told Casey.

"We won't kill the story," Casey assured him.

"What would happen, though, if you were told to kill the story?" Reiter persisted.

"Then I would resign," Casey answered.

Reiter would later tell me the reasons he and Joe cooperated with me: they could see I was willing to do the painstaking work to understand the case; I had a good body of work that showed that I was capable of doing it; and he said: "We had a gut feeling that you had the grit and tenacity to see this through, and I felt it was a good gamble that Casey did, too."

My first interview with Reiter and Recarey happened on February 5, 2018. I remember the date because it was two days after one of the best days of my life: when the Philadelphia Eagles won the Super Bowl.

I emailed Reiter the next day, firming up our interview time. I was still basking in the win, and couldn't help but mention it to him. He was a Pittsburgh Steelers fan, but told me that he had been rooting for the Eagles, too. I hoped the sports talk would help make him more comfortable, as I observed this tactic usually seemed to work with male reporters interviewing male subjects. But I had no such luck.

At 1:00 P.M. the following day, I was sitting in Reiter's wood-paneled office. Behind his desk, in a case, were all of his badges, from the time he was a patrolman until he retired as chief.

Both of the ex-cops were cagey. There would be no cameras allowed. I would be permitted to take notes, as our interview would be "on the record," but I wasn't allowed to record it. Instead, Reiter would record it, then have it transcribed and sent to me. He was worried that if I recorded the interview, the recording might end up being stolen and his voice would end up on *Inside Edition*. Now he was making me paranoid.

He had already sent me in writing a list of salient points that he wanted to make so that this travesty would, hopefully, never happen again.

He spoke into the recorder:

"Present for the purposes of transcription are Julie, the only female in the room, and Joe, the other male in the room, and Mike, this is my voice," the interview began.

"Why don't you guys just start talking? I mean, obviously there are certain things that you really want to get out there and that you feel are important that people should know," I said, clumsily trying to break the ice.

"When I used to teach case preparation on court presentation classes in the police academy, the first thing I would tell the police officers is when in a deposition a lawyer says, 'Well, just tell me about this. Just tell me your story,' is to never answer that.

"I'd prefer you just ask me questions," he said stiffly.

This is going to be a very long and circuitous interview, I thought.

REITER GREW UP IN THE SMALL WESTERN PENNSYLVANIA TOWN OF Irwin, Westmoreland County, graduating from Norwin High School in 1975. Both his father and uncle were pilots who served in World War II, and his uncle went on to be elected town mayor. His uncle had been shot down over Hungary and was a prisoner of war until the war ended. His father was a bombardier-navigator who was among the first American bombers during World War II to land at Soviet airfields to refuel and rearm, enabling the Allies to reach distant German targets.

Reiter's father and uncle were larger-than-life role models, instilling in him the importance of service, duty, and patriotism. After high school, Reiter attended Penn State University, majoring in meteorology. But in his second semester, he took a criminal justice course and was hooked.

He began his career at the North Huntingdon Police Department, working an unpaid internship, then as a campus cop at the University of Pittsburgh directing traffic for a year. In 1981, he noticed a recruitment ad for police officers in Palm Beach. Moving to a warmer climate appealed to him after so many harsh winters, so he applied and got the job. He worked his way up, holding every rank and working almost every assignment in the department. At the same time, he earned a master of science in leadership, attended the FBI National Academy and Harvard's Kennedy School Program for Senior Executives in Government, and, later, completed a crisis management program at Harvard. He was also active in the community, serving on many boards, nonprofits, and civic associations.

For Joe and Mike, the Epstein case was the one that they couldn't let go, and that's saying something, considering they had handled many complicated and high-profile cases. One of Reiter's first major cases as an investigator was the drug overdose death of David Kennedy, twenty-eight, the third son of Ethel and Robert F. Kennedy, who died in a Palm Beach hotel in 1984. Reiter spent two years tracking down the cocaine traffickers who provided Kennedy the lethal dose.

Reiter became chief of the department in 2001.

He insists that the Epstein case had nothing to do with his leaving the force, but I would later learn that the pressure that came to bear on both Reiter and Recarey—not just from Epstein but from political forces within Palm Beach—was powerful.

Recarey had worked the Organized Crime, Vice, and Narcotics Unit and was a member of the Palm Beach State Attorney's Public Integrity and Sexual Predator Units. At the time of the Epstein probe, he had been lauded as the Palm Beach Bar Association's Officer of the Year and the *Palm Beach Post*'s Distinguished Law Officer of the Year.

And yet, when it came to Jeffrey Epstein, the sting of failure was unshakable.

THE FIRST TIME THAT RECAREY BECAME AWARE OF JEFFREY EPSTEIN was when Epstein reported that someone had stolen thousands of dollars in cash and a handgun from his home in October 2003. The cash was taken over the course of a month from a briefcase Epstein had kept in his office, and Epstein told police that he had purchased a spy camera and installed it in his office to catch the culprit, who he suspected was among his staff.

Recarey was one of the investigators who handled the video equipment. According to the police report, Epstein was able to pull up the surveillance video on his computer and learned that the thief was his former butler, Juan Alessi. By then, Alessi no longer worked for Epstein, but had been sneaking into his mansion before dawn over the course of several weeks, swiping wads of cash that Epstein kept in white envelopes in his briefcase. Investigators tracked down Alessi, who admitted he went to Epstein's mansion to steal a gun that he knew Epstein kept in his office. He told police that he intended to use the gun to kill himself because he had been depressed. He claimed that he couldn't find Epstein's gun, however, and took the cash instead.

In the end, Alessi agreed to pay back the money, and Epstein decided not to prosecute.

But as a result of the case, Epstein learned that the Palm Beach Police Department was not equipped to view his video, so Epstein donated thirty-six thousand dollars for a forensic video analysis system.

This wasn't unusual. The residents of the wealthy enclave often made donations to the police department to help pay for crime-fighting efforts.

A year earlier, in April 2002, Epstein had made an unsolicited donation to the Palm Beach Police Scholarship Fund, which benefited the higher education needs of children of police officers. In both cases, Reiter sent Epstein a letter of thanks. He invited Epstein to the police station to demonstrate the video equipment that had been purchased. It was the first time that Reiter met him, and they spoke only briefly in his office after Epstein declined to attend the demonstration.

Then, in the summer of 2004, Epstein reached out to a police captain, Elmer Gudger, who had helped with the investigation into Epstein's earlier theft. He asked Gudger whether the police needed any additional equipment. Reiter subsequently had a discussion with Epstein about the possibility of donating ninety thousand dollars for a firearms training simulator. Several months passed before Epstein donated the money, on December 15, 2004.

What neither Reiter nor Recarey knew at the time was that just two weeks before that second hefty donation, Palm Beach police were summoned to Epstein's mansion on a report that there was a suspicious vehicle in his driveway.

On November 28, 2004, a Sunday, at about 7:00 P.M., Epstein's then houseman, Rodriguez, greeted the two officers dispatched to Epstein's mansion to investigate. According to the police report, officers approached the vehicle, still parked in the driveway, and the driver, a seventeen-year-old girl, identified herself. Rodriguez, recognizing the girl, quickly told the cops that he had forgotten that she was coming to pick up an envelope that Epstein had left for her. He then went inside, came out with a thick envelope, and gave it to the girl.

"The envelope appeared to have money in it, in my opinion," the officer wrote in his report. Rodriguez was suddenly very nervous. The girl's cell phone rang, and she picked it up.

"I can't talk, I can't talk. I'm at school. I gotta go," she answered, still sitting in her car.

"Who were you talking to?" one of the officers asked.

"My mom," she said.

"How do you know Mr. Epstein?" the officer asked suspiciously.

"I work at Abercrombie & Fitch in the Wellington Mall and I met him through a girlfriend I know from work. He lets us come over anytime to use the house and the pool," she said, then quickly started the car and drove off.

The officers turned their attention back to Rodriguez.

"What was in that envelope?" they asked. "Was it drugs?"

"Money," the houseman quickly replied, nervously.

"What kind of job does the girl perform?" the officer asked skeptically.

"She is a massage therapist," Rodriguez said.

"Which muscle does she massage?" the cop asked.

Rodriguez laughed and said, "Off the record, Epstein has many girls come over for that. There's always a different young girl at the pool or inside with him when he is here."

In fact, police had received a number of other complaints about young women coming and going from Epstein's mansion. They tried to reach out to the girl in the car that day, but she did not return their calls. So they began to watch Epstein's house.

But the women who came and went all appeared to be women eighteen or older, mostly college students.

Two weeks later, Epstein donated money for the firearms simulator. Reiter assigned someone to start looking into purchasing the equipment. But shortly thereafter, he learned about the investigation into Epstein and put a hold on the purchase. As time went on with the case, Reiter began to suspect that Epstein's altruistic endeavors were aimed more at influencing the police than they were at helping them.

Reiter was smart enough not to return the money immediately. He didn't want to alert Epstein or jeopardize their investigation.

He shared his concerns with the town manager, who agreed to hang on to the donation for the time being.

Throughout 2005, Epstein and his representatives spoke with Gudger, Major Michael Mason, and the chief regarding the donation. Reiter pretended to go along with the idea that the money was being accepted and the department was appreciative of his generosity.

"His enthusiasm in making contact and in finalizing the donation was somewhat suspicious, different in manner than when he made previous donations and suggested that he may have become aware of the investigation at that time," Reiter wrote later in a report.

Epstein then offered to donate even more money to the police department. Reiter was uncomfortable about the continued pressure, but in order to not tip his hand, Reiter discussed with Epstein a donation for an automated identification system that would cost about $130,000.

Epstein, however, said he wanted to do something that would provide "direct benefit" to police officers, and suggested instead that he give them the services of a chiropractor for one year. Reiter told him he would give it some thought and contact him later.

chapter 11

FOLLOW THE MONEY

An eccentric bachelor, Epstein was obsessive about his privacy, rarely ate out, and seldom attended cocktail parties or nightclubs.

Socially awkward and a germophobe, Epstein drank Evian and never touched drugs, alcohol, or tobacco. He practiced yoga and had a private chef accompany him around the world making him tofu concoctions. He only drank one brand of Colombian coffee and ate seven-grain bread he purchased from Zabar's in New York. He worked out religiously and took long walks. He preferred light meals of fruit and vegetables and was allergic to garlic.

He shunned suits in favor of jeans and tracksuits.

He enjoyed small social gatherings or salons in which he surrounded himself with intellectuals with whom he could converse about human dynamics and mathematical options-trading models.

Friends said he had the mind of a physicist and the ability to apply complex formulas and computer algorithms to evaluate financial data and trends.

Epstein didn't need to use flamboyant charisma or to showboat his smarts to build his international network of influential people; he did that the old-fashioned way—with his money.

One of his specialties was helping the super wealthy—as well as himself—to avoid paying taxes. Yet he was never in the Forbes 400 list of the wealthiest Americans, largely because the magazine was never able to determine the true size of his fortune.

And that was by design, as Epstein was able to amass his fortune by breaking the law time and time again.

Perhaps the most lucrative financial feat he designed was a five-hundred-million-dollar scheme in the 1990s, which, at the time (pre–Bernie Madoff), was considered the largest Ponzi scam in U.S. history. His then partner, Steven Hoffenberg, served eighteen years in federal prison for the crime and later claimed that Epstein was the mastermind behind the complicated financial alchemy they used to swindle investors.

Hoffenberg, seventy-four, prefers to characterize the scam as an "accounting estimation problem," but concedes that a lot of people lost boatloads of money.

Hoffenberg states that the idea for the scam started in the late 1980s, when Epstein was broke and sleeping on his lawyer's couch.

"He was always living above his means, and he was always spending more money than he earned," Hoffenberg says, in explaining why Epstein was cash-strapped at the time.[1]

So Epstein came up with an idea: selling investors phony bonds. Hoffenberg's company, Towers Financial, was a debt-collection agency with sales of ninety-five million dollars a year. Epstein concocted a plan to take over struggling Pan Am Airways by financing a raid through Towers's purchase of two Illinois insurance companies. Epstein, who didn't have a broker's license, lured investors to purchase bonds by assuring them that they were safe because they were backed by the millions of dollars in debts that the company was collecting.[2]

They would even show investors a stack of medical bills to prove they were collecting huge sums of money, Hoffenberg says.

In reality, they were fake invoices created with names plucked from the New York City phone book.

Hoffenberg says the whole scam, down to the office they had set up and the actors they hired (who were actually doing crossword puzzles at their desks), was all a ruse to fool investors who visited the company's offices at the Villard Houses in midtown Manhattan.[3]

It was Epstein, Hoffenberg claims, who designed an added level of sophistication to the con by creating long legal documents that would pass the scrutiny of securities lawyers and government regulators.

But Hoffenberg, too, was taken for a ride by Epstein.

"Epstein got under your skin," Hoffenberg now says. "He figured you out right away and he was able to embellish and say to you what you wanted to hear."

To help bankroll Epstein and Hoffenberg's lavish lifestyles, they began to fraudulently drain money from the company, labeling the transfers from the insurance companies as consultants' fees. The Pan Am bid failed, and they launched another unsuccessful corporate raid, of Emery Air Freight, again swindling more investors by generating phony financial documents.

Their suspicious dealings eventually attracted the attention of Illinois state regulators and finally the feds. Epstein was known by authorities to be involved, court records would later show, and Hoffenberg testified to the grand jury that Epstein was the mastermind. Yet Epstein somehow escaped unscathed.[4]

Hoffenberg pleaded guilty to mail fraud, tax evasion, and obstruction of justice in 1995. Since his release from federal prison in 2013, Hoffenberg has filed several lawsuits against Epstein to try to recover some of the money that investors lost. The lawsuits were dropped, however, and to this day, no one knows where the bulk of the money went, except perhaps into Epstein's pocket.

Epstein's brother, Mark, who lives in New York, said that his brother was a math whiz who mastered Wall Street at a time when it was "the wild, wild West." Mark said Jeffrey would often mention how easy it was to manipulate investors. "He said if the general public knew what was taking place on Wall Street, there would be a revolution. People would be appalled at how corrupt it was."

PERHAPS EPSTEIN'S LARGEST CONQUEST, HOWEVER, WAS LES WEXNER, founder and CEO of L Brands, the company that owns the Limited stores and Victoria's Secret. Wexner and Epstein met in the 1980s, when Epstein was still with Bear Stearns. Wexner immediately took a liking to the charming yet eccentric financier who boasted about how much money he was able to earn for his clients. Wexner's fortunes were soaring during a time when his stores were benefiting from a boom in retail shopping malls. In 1985, Wexner made the Forbes list of the four hundred richest people in America, with his worth valued at over one billion dollars. Over the years, that would grow to over seven billion dollars.[5]

Robert Morosky, the former vice chairman of the Limited, told the *New York Times* that most people were mystified about why Wexner trusted his fortune to a college dropout.

"I tried to find out how did [Epstein] get from a high school math teacher to a private investment adviser," Morosky said. "There was just nothing there."[6]

The relationship with Wexner blossomed to the point where Wexner ceded Epstein almost complete control over his finances, even giving him power of attorney. Wexner installed him as a trustee of his charity, the Wexner Foundation, in place of Wexner's own mother.[7]

Epstein managed Wexner's taxes and a portion of his company's stock. He conducted real estate transactions, ran his charities, and was given authority to borrow money and sign contracts on the retail mogul's behalf.

Epstein was more than a financial adviser, however. He oversaw the construction of Wexner's 316-foot superyacht, the *Limitless*; bought Wexner's corporate plane and the massive mansion Wexner owned in Manhattan; drafted the prenuptial agreement between Wexner and his wife, Abigail, whom he married in 1993; and purchased and moved himself into a $3.5 million home on Wexner's sprawling compound in New Albany, Ohio.[8]

Epstein often worked as Wexner's hatchet man, firing or suing contractors and staff, and intervening in family disputes. Epstein took a cut of Wexner's fortune, and it made him a very wealthy man.

Wexner told journalist Vicky Ward in 2003 that he valued Epstein's ability to know when and how to pick a battle.

"Many times, people confuse winning and losing," Wexner said. "Jeffrey has the unusual quality of knowing when he is winning. Whether in conversations or negotiations, he always stands back and lets the other person determine the style and manner of the conversation or negotiation. And then he responds in their style. Jeffrey sees it in chivalrous terms. He does not pick a fight, but if there is a fight, he will let you choose the weapon."[9]

Later, Wexner faced intense scrutiny over his long association with Epstein and accused him of bilking him out of "vast sums" of money. But Wexner never reported the theft to authorities, and it's still not clear how much money Epstein absconded with.

Indeed, Epstein's name would become a scarlet letter for Wexner—and many other powerful men who associated with the financier.

Wexner has denied he knew anything about Epstein's deviant sexual practices—or participated in them. But one of Epstein's victims, a seventeen-year-old runaway named Virginia Roberts Giuffre, alleges that she was ordered by Epstein and Maxwell to have sex with a number of prominent men, including Prince Andrew, Dershowitz—and Wexner. All three men have vociferously denied they ever met Giuffre.

Wexner, eighty-three, was a longtime Republican donor who also supported Israel and Jewish causes. Epstein cultivated Republican connections, but the bulk of his generosity went to Democratic candidates and their charities.

Bill Clinton likely met Epstein during his reelection campaign in 1995, when, during a swing through Florida, Clinton attended a private dinner in Palm Beach hosted by Revlon chairman Ron Perelman and his wife. It was organized by Arnold Paul Prosperi, a college friend of Clinton's. The *Palm Beach Post* called it a three-hour dinner with "a very select group of people" who contributed as much as one hundred thousand dollars per person to the Democratic National Committee. Only fifteen people were on the guest list, including actor Don Johnson, singer Jimmy Buffett, and Epstein.[10]

How close Epstein was to the former president is not known, but Clinton has downplayed the friendship.

The former president did make more than two dozen trips on Epstein's private jet in 2002 and 2003, visiting Europe, Africa, and Asia. Clinton has claimed that the jaunts were part of humanitarian efforts connected to the former president's foundation.

One letter contained in the court records is from a former Epstein lawyer, Gerald Lefcourt, who noted that Epstein had spent a month with Clinton on the trip to Africa as part of the Clinton Global Initiative.

Clinton claims that he took only four trips on Epstein's plane, and it's possible that he grouped various legs of his trips into single expeditions. Epstein's flight logs, however, show he took at least six trips. In addition to the African excursion, logs show that Clinton also jetted with Epstein in 2002 from Miami to New York; from New York to London; from Japan to Hong Kong, and then to China and Singapore; from Morocco to the Azores, then to New York. In

2003, Clinton flew to Brussels, Norway, Hong Kong, and China as part of another AIDS-prevention effort.

Epstein often bragged about his connections to Clinton and other important people in an effort to impress and perhaps intimidate his victims. He told one girl who flew with him on his jet that she was sitting in his "good friend" Bill Clinton's seat, according to a 2019 lawsuit filed by the victim, Jane Doe 15, who said she met Epstein in 2004 on a school trip to New York City.

She described how Epstein's plane had a bedroom with carpeted floors that were actually fitted with mattresslike cushioning. Epstein told her he installed the foam mattress floors so that his girls could sleep beside his bed.

Other victims reported seeing framed photographs of Epstein with Clinton and other important people at his various residences. In 2019, the *Daily Mail* published a photo of a painting in Epstein's home depicting Bill Clinton wearing Monica Lewinsky's infamous sapphire-blue dress.

The artist, Petrina Ryan-Kleid, recalled that the piece was part of a set of satirized political figures, including one of George W. Bush, that was sold at the Tribeca Ball in 2012. She was never told who the buyer was.[11]

ON NEW YEAR'S DAY 1998, PRESIDENT BILL CLINTON AND FIRST LADY Hillary Clinton, aboard Air Force One, arrived at the Cyril E. King Airport at about five P.M. They were driven by motorcade to "a private residence" that is not listed on the president's official schedule. His itinerary noted that he had the day and evening off.

Later that night, three U.S. Customs agents who were providing security for President Clinton were involved in a violent boat crash in the U.S. Virgin Islands. Officials said the thirty-seven-foot speedboat was ending its patrol at about eight thirty that evening when it hit a reef in waters off the coast of St. Thomas. One of the agents, Manuel

Zurita, died in the hospital from his injuries five days later.[12] Two other agents were seriously injured. The Associated Press reported that the agents were an advance security team sent to monitor the flight path of Air Force One as it arrived at Cyril E. King Airport on St. Thomas. At the time of the crash, Clinton and his family had already left the airport by motorcade for a four-day vacation somewhere in the Virgin Islands. The AP report did not say where.

At the time, Epstein was a frequent visitor to a nearby island, Little St. James, which was owned by Arch Cummin, a Palm Beach financier. Cummin can't recall how he met Epstein, but said that the mysterious moneyman expressed interest in buying the island in 1997, so Cummin let Epstein use the property because he seemed like a serious buyer.

Cummin's housekeeper on the island did complain a couple of times about all the young women who accompanied Epstein on his visits.

One time, Cummin recalled, he was notified that a team of federal agents had come onto the island and demanded to inspect the compound.

"They went around and looked at everything and then left," Cummin said. He couldn't recall exactly when it happened or whether the visitors were Customs agents or from some other agency.

Epstein didn't officially buy the property until several months after the fatal crash. But locals who I later spoke to on the island have long whispered about the crash, and wondered why the agents who were assigned to work Clinton's detail on New Year's were motoring so fast in a rocky, treacherous area not far off the coast of what would later come to be known as Epstein's "Pedophile Island."

chapter 12

FOREVER CHANGED

Joe Recarey arrived to testify before the Epstein grand jury at the Palm Beach County courthouse shortly before 9:00 A.M. on July 19, 2006. He was dressed in a suit and tie and had a thick binder full of reports and notes under his arm. He had been studying the case file for weeks and was prepared to recite details about each of the underage victims and all the evidence that he had corroborating their stories.

When he arrived at room 4A, the first thing he noticed was the man sitting right outside the door: Jack Goldberger, Epstein's lawyer.

"It was the strangest thing, because they allowed a defense attorney to sit outside the grand jury room to watch who came in. He sat outside, just watching," Recarey recalled. He explained that usually prosecutors don't allow defendants and their lawyers to sit outside the grand jury room because of concerns that it would intimidate witnesses.

Later, Recarey learned that prosecutor Lanna Belohlavek had not only allowed Epstein's lawyers to sit outside the hearing room; she had also invited Epstein to testify and present evidence before the grand jury.

"You and your client are invited to appear before the Grand Jury," Belohlavek wrote in her February 9 letter to Epstein's attorney Guy Fronstin. "The invitation is extended to provide an opportunity for your client to present any personal testimony you may think is proper. You should understand, however, that anything your client testifies to may be used against him in a subsequent criminal prosecution."

She further invited the defense attorneys to submit physical evidence, opening up the door for them to give the grand jury printouts of the girls' Myspace pages.

Recarey took the witness stand, not knowing what Belohlavek intended to present. There had been no practice preparation, and Joe wondered how she was going to make the case, given that she had not interviewed any victims.

Belohlavek asked softball questions.

"She gave me the impression that she was not giving the grand jury the entire picture of what transpired. It made it appear that she was trying to downplay his crimes. That was my impression, based on what she asked me," Recarey recalled.

"I could only answer questions; I wasn't permitted to volunteer any information, and it was clear from her questions that the grand jury had not been given the whole story."

Recarey said he knows of only one victim who was called to testify. It appeared as if Belohlavek was resting the entire case on one girl who was molested by Epstein. She didn't tell the grand jury that Epstein had raped at least a half dozen others, or that there were more than two dozen other victims.

"The severity of the crime didn't account for what she was presenting to the jury. Jurors can only weigh on what they are presented.

If they are only telling you a portion of the story, they are only going to charge on a portion of the story," Recarey said.

On Monday, July 26, 2006, Epstein was indicted on a single charge of solicitation of prostitution, a second-degree misdemeanor, which meant that Epstein would likely serve no time in jail. There were no charges involving minors, no assault charges, and no sex charges. It was a whitewash. Epstein turned himself in and was released on bail.

By then, Recarey and Reiter already suspected that the state attorney, for whatever reason, was throwing the case and simply using the grand jury as a mechanism to legitimize their decision not to prosecute Epstein.

"I saw how enamored prosecutors were with the defense team, and that bothered me," Recarey said of his decision to go to the FBI.

The fact that evidence had disappeared—chiefly Epstein's computers—and that the state attorney's office didn't see fit to issue subpoenas for them, also rankled Recarey.

"The amount of evidence that disappeared, was destroyed or covered up in this case is mind boggling," the detective told me.

Recarey began discussing the case with Ann Marie Villafaña, an assistant prosecutor who had worked in the major crimes division of the U.S. Attorney's Office in Miami and later transferred to the district office in West Palm Beach, where she specialized in child exploitation cases. She was also coordinator for Project Safe Childhood, a federal initiative to combat child abuse and trafficking.

Recarey told Villafaña that Epstein had hired private investigators to tail him and Reiter, and in his view, how Krischer had sabotaged the criminal investigation.

IT WAS POURING A TROPICAL RAIN THE DAY IN SEPTEMBER 2006 WHEN FBI agents appeared at the Town of Palm Beach Police Department with a large truck. They produced a subpoena for all the police records on Epstein, and Recarey turned over everything, including his own notes.

"The FBI was on board. They couldn't understand why the state would not pursue more serious charges," Recarey said.

He felt relieved that someone was finally going to help him put Epstein away.

AFTER EPSTEIN'S INDICTMENT, THE STORY BECAME NATIONAL NEWS. Epstein hired publicists in New York, Los Angeles, and Florida to help "get his side of the story out." The *New York Post* quoted one of Epstein's New York lawyers, Gerald Lefcourt, as saying Epstein was only being targeted "because of the craziness of the police chief," and Jack Goldberger, Epstein's Palm Beach attorney, told the *Palm Beach Post* that police were tarnishing the reputation of an upstanding citizen by trying to expand a run-of-the-mill prostitution offense into a salacious major crime based on the stories of girls who were liars and opportunists.

"It was just a childish performance by the Palm Beach Police Department," Goldberger told the newspaper.[1]

THE CHARACTER ASSASSINATION AGAINST REITER AND RECAREY mounted as Epstein's lawyers went beyond reasonable efforts to defend their client. They obtained Reiter's entire police personnel file, and began to track down people who knew him from childhood. Even one of his grade-school teachers called Reiter's brother to tell him that private investigators had tried to talk to her about him. Other people he knew in law enforcement also warned him that they were getting calls from Epstein's camp.

Reiter found himself not only defending his long, unblemished career but also his personal life.

They dug into his divorce, which had been amicable, and accused the chief of being anti-Semitic because he was persecuting Epstein, who was Jewish.

Recarey was also targeted, as Epstein's lawyers drafted a complaint to Florida's Department of Law Enforcement's compliance unit in an effort to go after his badge. In the letter, they complained that Recarey had misrepresented the facts in the case and that he had leaked police reports to the media, which was not true.

For months, Epstein's private investigators had been following Recarey. It could have been comical, almost straight out of a movie, had Reiter and Recarey not suspected what Epstein was capable of. They knew that Epstein was trying to smear them in order to discredit their case—and it was working. Furthermore, Epstein made it clear, through his emissaries, that his victims had better keep their mouths shut or they would regret it. Some of them were afraid for their lives.

Recarey, in the police report, noted how Jane Doe 1's father had called him to report that a man had been at his house photographing his family and chasing after visitors who came and went from the house. Recarey traced the license plate number of the car, which was registered to a private investigator who worked for Epstein.

Recarey wasn't worried about himself, but he was worried about his children.

"For a police officer to throw out his trash and everyone has a mountain of trash in their cans and mine is empty, when the night before it had been full, you have to start to watch what is happening and see similar patterns of cars and people."

He knew he was being tailed. He was getting hang-up calls from untraceable numbers in the middle of the night.

Spencer Kuvin, Jane Doe 1's lawyer, recalls the first time he met with Recarey at a Starbucks in West Palm Beach. Recarey was sitting near the door with his back to the window.

"He kept saying that he was being watched and followed and he kept looking over his shoulder. It was very creepy."

Recarey wasn't paranoid; he really was being followed.

"I began to take different routes to visit my children," he said. "I switched cars. If I turned right, Epstein's investigators would turn right. At some point it became like a cat-and-mouse game. It wore on me. I was worried about my family's safety."

IN THE SPRING OF 2018, I CONTINUED TO PRY DETAILS OF THE EPSTEIN case from Recarey and Reiter. The two of them were finally becoming more comfortable talking to me, and I began to confide more in them about the various angles I was developing for what Emily and I envisioned would be a three-part series with a documentary featuring interviews with the victims. But I still was unable to convince Mike and Joe to go on camera.

Finally, in late April, Reiter agreed to be part of our documentary.

"I think that I have to be 'all in' on this in hopes that your efforts may have a chance to right the wrongs in this case," he wrote me in an email.

I was elated, but still not able to convince Recarey to go on camera. Joe did, however, agree to sit with Emily and me for another interview.

Recarey was waiting outside his office building in Palm Beach as Emily began unloading her car with her usual cargo of camera equipment. I had still secretly hoped I could talk Recarey into doing the interview on video, but when he saw all her gear, he just shook his head and laughed, a gentle reminder that he wasn't going to fall for our not-so-subtle cajolery.

Sitting inside a stark basement conference room, I couldn't help but think that he had to miss being a police detective, similar to the way Emily's husband, Walt, was still glued to the computerized version of the old-fashioned police scanner.

While Recarey was firm about the video, he did let us take a few photographs of him. He was very uncomfortable and stiff, and it took him having a smoke break, along with some more of our coaxing, to get him to relax.

The interview lasted about two hours. He spoke a lot about the victims and how difficult the case was for him, given the unsuccessful outcome.

After the interview, I continued to talk to Recarey throughout the following month, holding out hope that we could get him to participate in the documentary.

Then in May, I got an email from Reiter telling me that Joe had stopped breathing in the middle of the night and was hospitalized in a coma. He had suffered irreversible organ damage and his prospects for survival didn't look good.

A few days later, Joe was gone.

My heart ached because I wanted so much for him to find justice for these women and, more than anything, for him to see his work had not been in vain.

Recarey's wife, Jennifer, said that Joe thought of Epstein's victims as if they could have been his own daughter.

"In his mind, this could be her in a couple of years. Joe was always advocating for the underdog, and he hated Epstein's lawyers going after the girls. That just infuriated him and fueled him even more to find justice for them."

I searched for my last email from him.

In it, we were talking about meeting for another interview.

His mind was on something he had heard on the radio. It was a song by the country singer Vince Gill, called "Forever Changed."

"I thought of the victims when I heard this," Joe wrote. "Here's the opening lyrics: 'You put your hands where they don't belong, and now her innocence is dead and gone . . . Because of you, she's forever changed.' "

Later, I would often listen to that song, especially on my morning runs, thinking about Joe, and about Mike, and how they were among the only people who, from the start, never stopped fighting for Epstein's victims.

chapter 13

OPERATION LEAP YEAR

Ann Marie Villafaña had never heard of Jeffrey Epstein.

But after doing some homework, she knew she was up against a wealthy, politically connected man who had a history of taking a scorched-earth approach to his adversaries. Like Recarey, she suspected that Epstein and his defense team had manipulated Barry Krischer, and she knew it was possible that he would put the same pressure to bear on the U.S. Attorney's Office.

She wanted to make sure that that didn't happen. So she asked for a meeting with her top bosses: Alex Acosta, the Miami U.S. attorney, and Jeff Sloman, who was in charge of Miami's criminal division. She told them she knew that the case was going to require a lot of time and resources and that it was possible they would face political pressure as a result of the investigation. They told her they weren't concerned about the pressure; after all, they had prosecuted high-profile, politically connected people before, such as lobbyist Jack Abramoff.

THE FBI CHRISTENED THE EPSTEIN PROBE "OPERATION LEAP YEAR" because at the time they took over the state's criminal case in 2006, there were twenty-nine victims. In October, shortly after reviewing the police and state attorney's files, the FBI began carving out federal grand jury subpoenas in New York and Florida. FBI records show that the feds were not only looking into Epstein's Palm Beach sex operation, but also investigating whether he was abusing girls in other cities where he lived. They were also poking into his finances, which had always been a mystery, and exploring the possibility of seizing some of his assets under a category they labeled in their reports as "general forfeiture matters." Agents traveled to all the places where Epstein had homes—New York; Santa Fe, New Mexico; and St. Thomas in the U.S. Virgin Islands—in order to interview possible witnesses and victims.

At the same time, Epstein was regrouping his legal team, hiring new attorneys who had experience and political connections to the White House, then occupied by George W. Bush. Epstein had already dropped Fronstin, but kept Roy Black and Gerald Lefcourt, a prominent New York criminal attorney with a reputation for taking on tough cases. He added former Miami U.S. attorney and Acosta predecessor Guy Lewis; Lilly Ann Sanchez, who had just left her federal prosecutor's post as deputy chief of the Palm Beach criminal division; and Jay Lefkowitz, an adviser to President George W. Bush and an attorney with the influential law firm of Kirkland & Ellis, where Acosta had worked early in his career. Epstein also brought on Kenneth Starr, the former Clinton-Whitewater prosecutor, who was also with Kirkland. Both Starr and Lefkowitz were members of the conservative Federalist Society, which produced six Supreme Court justices, including Acosta's mentor, Samuel Alito.

Dershowitz took a back seat, but only temporarily.

On the government side, besides Acosta, Sloman, and Villafaña, there was Matthew Menchel, who would head the criminal division of the Miami U.S. Attorney's Office after Sloman was promoted to chief deputy, and Andrew Lourie, who would become a high-level Justice Department official in the Bush administration.

The agents on the FBI case were Timothy Slater, Jason Richards, and Nesbitt Kuyrkendall, who worked out of the bureau's West Palm Beach office.

Just as Epstein had learned early on about the Palm Beach police probe, he also learned quickly that the feds had opened their investigation. And as with the state case, Epstein employed defense lawyers with ties to the U.S. Attorney's Office. Lewis, who had served in the U.S. Attorney's Office for a decade, was close friends with Lourie; Sanchez was Menchel's deputy in the U.S. Attorney's Office—and had dated him.

THE FBI FILES SHOW THAT IN 2006, AS AGENTS WERE LEARNING MORE about Epstein's sex operation, federal prosecutors in Florida were working on two platforms: one, to build evidence that would eventually inform the draft of a fifty-three-page federal indictment; and the other, to negotiate a settlement before the case became a national scandal that threatened to upset the political goals of Epstein's friends on both sides of the aisle. While George W. Bush was in the White House, in November 2006, Democrats took back control of both houses of Congress. A sex scandal involving a powerful Democratic donor connected to former president Clinton could derail the party's plan to win back the White House, particularly since Clinton's wife, Hillary, was at the time the Democratic front-runner to be the party's candidate in 2008. Bush was ineligible to run because of term limits, so it was the first election since 1952 in which neither party would have an incumbent president or vice president on the ticket.

In 2006, as Epstein was under FBI investigation, the financier donated twenty-five thousand dollars to the Clinton Foundation.

But Epstein was smart enough to spread his money around, having donated in previous years to Republicans George H. W. Bush and Bob Dole, the former Senate majority leader.

In fall of 2007, George W. Bush's Justice Department was in turmoil. The attorney general, Alberto R. Gonzales, had resigned amid accusations that he had hired and fired prosecutors for political reasons. Bush picked a former federal judge, Michael Mukasey, to succeed Gonzales and help bring stability to the department.[1]

A law-and-order conservative, Mukasey had been nominated to the bench by former president Ronald Reagan and was best known for presiding over the detention hearing in New York of terrorist Jose Padilla, the so-called "dirty bomber" who was later prosecuted in Miami in 2007 for planning a radiological bomb attack against the United States and aiding terrorists overseas.

Adding Lefkowitz to his defense arsenal guaranteed Epstein a direct connection to the new attorney general. Lefkowitz was close friends with Mukasey, and both were Orthodox congregants of Kehilath Jeshurun synagogue on Manhattan's Upper East Side. It was rumored that it was Lefkowitz who suggested Mukasey for the Justice Department slot, so Lefkowitz's influence was not lost on Epstein—or on Acosta. Lefkowitz was someone who could help Acosta's career, and Epstein was a master of the Achilles' heel.

Even those within the DOJ admitted that there were deep-pocketed, influential defendants at the time who received preferential treatment based on who was representing them. Kenneth Starr, meanwhile, leaned on Alice S. Fisher, the U.S. assistant attorney general in charge of the Criminal Division, to drop the case, records and emails show. Fisher, however, has denied she was involved or took any action on Starr's request.

BOTH REITER AND RECAREY SAID THAT AT THE TIME THE CASE WAS transferred to the FBI, they felt confident leaving it in Villafaña's hands.

As one of the few female prosecutors in the Miami U.S. Attorney's Office, Villafaña had to work almost twice as hard to prove herself. She was passionate about her work and well regarded.

Epstein's lawyers realized how aggressively Villafaña was going after their client—so they went over her head.

This was easy for people like Guy Lewis and Lily Sanchez, who had friendships in the department. Sanchez merely picked up the phone, called Lourie, and set up a meeting. Lourie didn't think there was anything wrong with this, later telling federal investigators that it was "good for us" to learn the defense's strategy and that part of the process was for the defense team to believe "they were heard."

Villafaña objected to the meeting and others that were held between prosecutors and defense attorneys. She reasoned that Epstein's attorneys were smart enough to hide their cards, and Lourie and Menchel weren't careful about revealing aspects of the government's strategy.

THROUGHOUT MY INVESTIGATION, SOURCES SHARED THAT VILLAFAÑA was well intentioned and probably the only voice in her office who expressed empathy for Epstein's victims. There were sources, however, who felt otherwise—that she had caved when she had a duty not to. I heard, also, from a well-placed source, that if she had filed charges against Epstein, she would be fired or risk losing her law license. As if Epstein wanted to send her a message, his attorneys filed at least one complaint against her with DOJ's Office of Professional Responsibility, the agency charged with investigating federal prosecutors. The results of those investigations are rarely made public.

Public records, however, show she was under pressure by her bosses to make the Epstein case go away.

"I bent over backwards to keep in mind the effect that the agreement would have on Mr. Epstein," Villafaña wrote in a letter to Epstein's lawyers during the course of the negotiations for his plea deal.

She threatened several times to go forward with filing charges. But her bosses, Menchel and Lourie, undermined her at every turn, records and emails show.

Villafaña was repeatedly scolded for taking an aggressive stand on charging Epstein. She became angry when Menchel told her that he had proposed a plea bargain with Sanchez—his ex-girlfriend—without discussing it with Villafaña. He then questioned Villafaña's professionalism when she demanded that she be consulted about her own case. At the time, she was preparing a fifty-three-count federal indictment.

"You were never given authorization by anyone to seek an indictment in this case," Menchel wrote.

Still, Villafaña's emails show she went to great lengths to keep a lid on the case.

She suggested ways to keep the media, the public, and the victims from learning about it by sentencing Epstein in Miami, rather than Palm Beach, where publicity would have garnered more attention. Later, she also coached state prosecutors how to frame the case for the judge, telling them to "not highlight" how many underage girls Epstein had sexually abused. Keeping the judge in the dark was another victory for Epstein.

As the negotiations continued, FBI agents built their criminal case. In early 2007, agents received information that Epstein had been involved with a sixteen-year-old girl who traveled frequently with him to his homes and other locales around the world. They reached out to Virginia Giuffre, who was then living in Australia with her husband. Agents Slater and Kuyrkendall made plans to interview her by phone.

But a few days before the agents could reach her, Giuffre received two phone calls—the first from Ghislaine Maxwell, and the second from Epstein and his lawyer. Giuffre said she had not heard from Epstein or Maxwell in five years. She believed she had finally freed herself from their grip.

Giuffre recalled that Maxwell asked her whether she had been contacted by anyone from the police or FBI.

"Have you reported us to anyone?" Virginia said Maxwell asked.

"No, I'm living a simple life here and I don't want to be a part of that," Giuffre responded.

"Okay, good. You stay like that, you stay quiet," Virginia said Maxwell told her.

The very next day, Epstein called, with his lawyer on the line. He asked the same questions about whether she had told anybody about her time with him.

"Where is this all coming from?" Giuffre asked. "What's going on?"

"Oh, nothing to worry about," Epstein said. "We just don't want you to talk to anyone, that's all. Do you understand?"

ONLY DAYS LATER, THE FBI CALLED. IT WAS AGENT SLATER.

"Straight off the bat the guy says to me, 'Have you given Jeffrey Epstein a blow job? Did you have a shower with Jeffrey Epstein? Did you bring girls over to Jeffrey Epstein?' And I'm like, 'I don't even know who you are, I'm on the phone with you. Unless you can come here and show me some official documentation that says you're with the FBI, then I am not saying a word to you,' " Virginia recalled telling Slater.

At the time, Giuffre was pregnant with her second child and it occurred to her that the caller could have been someone working for Epstein, not the FBI. She was so terrified that she and her husband left their house and went to stay with her mother-in-law until the birth of their baby.

"I was worried he would come after me or my family," Virginia said. "Epstein always told me that he had the police in his pocket, that he owned them, that he gave them regular payments—and that if I ever said anything to anyone, the police were going to report right back to him and then God knows what would happen to me or my family."

Slater would later provide his account of the conversation in a report.

"I provided her with the phone number of the FBI Field Office in Miami, Florida, and told her she could hang up and verify the number. . . . [Ms. Giuffre] said that was not necessary."

He confirmed that he began asking questions, and noted in his report that "she quickly became uncomfortable," and told him, "Let this be in my past."

"She asked that I not bother her with this again," Slater wrote, and then he gave her his contact information in case she changed her mind. It would take Virginia four years to change her mind.

BUT THE FBI HAD OTHER WITNESSES. THEY INTERVIEWED RODRIGUEZ, Epstein's former house manager, and he told them everything he had told Recarey, much of it backing up the fact that he was helping Epstein with the girls, cleaning up after their trysts, and acting as a "human ATM" who paid them after every "massage."

Villafaña drafted an eighty-two-page prosecution memo, a document that outlines the legal basis for the criminal charges. She proposed an indictment charging Epstein with a litany of federal crimes involving the sex trafficking of minors, and she detailed all the evidence that investigators had gathered to support the charges.

She immediately faced pushback from Lourie as he questioned the credibility of the witnesses and whether her legal arguments would be successful.

He sent the prosecution memo to Menchel, along with an email.

"It's a major case because the target is one of the richest men in the country," Lourie wrote in an email that was later included in a Justice Department investigation about the case. "He has a stable of attorneys, including Dershowitz, Black, Lefcourt, Lewis, and Sanchez . . . the state intentionally torpedoed it in the grand jury so it was brought to us."

Lourie and Menchel dragged their feet.

Meanwhile, the agents were getting resistance from other victims besides Giuffre. The girls were frightened. Epstein's intimidation tactics were working.

After interviewing just a handful of the victims, Villafaña and the FBI agents assigned to the case began having reservations about whether it was practical to take it to trial.

"No victims expressed a strong opinion that Epstein be prosecuted," Kuyrkendall would later write in a report. Among the obstacles they faced was that some of the girls remained loyal to Epstein, who had hired lawyers to represent them. He also lawyered up the female assistants he employed to help him recruit and abuse the victims. He hired lawyers for his butlers, his pilots, and his drivers.

IN MAY 2007, LOURIE RECOMMENDED CHARGING EPSTEIN BY COMPLAINT and then waiting to see if he was willing to accept a pre-indictment plea deal to lesser charges. This tactic would give prosecutors more leverage over a deal than if they just indicted him. After the indictment a judge would have to approve a dismissal of any charges in favor of a plea.

Throughout June, Menchel and Lourie met with defense attorneys to discuss the case, according to the Justice Department report. Villafaña was being stonewalled, and wrote to Lourie, Menchel, and Sloman, complaining that she had not received a response to her latest indictment package.

But by then Menchel and Lourie, with Acosta's approval, had

proposed a deal that would hand the case back to Krischer, the state prosecutor in Palm Beach.

LAWYERS REPRESENTING THE VICTIMS SAID THAT FEDERAL PROSECUTORS didn't seem to understand how to build a sensitive case involving someone who had power and money.

"The prosecutors didn't need two dozen girls to testify; all they needed was one or two," said lawyer Spencer Kuvin.

Kuvin said the FBI only interviewed one of his clients, and there were two other victims who would have helped their case.

"What these girls were really looking for was for the criminal justice system to do what it was supposed to do," Kuvin said. "Every one of my clients wanted Epstein to go to jail."

Some of the victims were even intimidated by the FBI agents and prosecutors, who at times seemed to treat the girls as if they had done something wrong. Prosecutors did little to help ease victims' anxieties, pointing out that testifying against Epstein would be difficult on them and their families, who would likely be pulled into the spotlight in the event of such a high-profile prosecution. Ultimately, most of the victims were never formally interviewed by the FBI or federal prosecutors. And some of those who were interviewed were too uncomfortable to share all the details of Epstein's abuse.

"We knew the whole story had not been told," said Adam Horowitz, another one of the civil attorneys representing victims. "We knew there were many more victims and girls who had not yet contacted a lawyer."

"It was clear that prosecutors were uninformed about how to deal with victims of sex crimes," said Marci Hamilton, a law professor at the University of Pennsylvania and an expert on crimes against children. "They clearly had no awareness about sex trafficking, how it starts and how it flourishes. Epstein was not engaging in individual sex abuse; he was creating an entire system." The FBI agents tailored their questions so narrowly that it seemed as if they didn't want to know how deep the crimes were, and who was involved.

"The FBI agents told them, 'We just want the facts. We don't want hearsay and opinions,'" Kuvin said.

Jessica Arbour, a young lawyer who was hired by victims' lawyer Jeffrey Herman to help with the case, said she spent most of her time fielding calls from the victims at all hours of the day and night. At the time, she was around the same age as the victims, and tried to act as a bridge between them and the legal system.

The girls were very distrustful of the FBI, she said, because they showed up without any warning, knocking on their doors and questioning them in front of their parents and spouses. In some cases, the girls couldn't even tell whether the agents were working for the government or whether they had been sent by Epstein.

"Epstein basically manipulated them so much that they didn't know who to believe," Arbour said. "It was a bizarre human experiment in the use of the justice system to harass and intimidate victims. On a day-to-day basis these girls were terrified for their lives."

chapter 14

THE SWEETHEART DEAL

It was now almost eight months since Epstein's arrest in Palm Beach County on solicitation charges, and rumors were circulating that there was a plea bargain in the offing.

FBI records show that a tentative date of May 15, 2007, had been set for Epstein's indictment, and the agency engaged its gang and criminal enterprise team to help assist with the case, as they began to look at possible money laundering charges to bolster their case.

A subpoena was issued to two of Epstein's companies, demanding tax records and W-2s from all his employees, as well as a list of his corporate directors, board members, and shareholders.

Villafaña stood firm, saying that an indictment was drafted, and if both sides couldn't agree to a deal, she intended to file charges. But the May date came and went.

In July, Lefcourt and Dershowitz wrote another treatise on behalf of their client. This one was twenty-three pages long, and it was addressed to Villafaña's bosses, Sloman and Lourie.

The letter was stuffed with federal statutes and common definitions to explain the dense language of some of the statutes. They salted the letter with complicated case law and even hired a linguist to help translate state statutes. The linguist was Steven Pinker, a psychology professor at Harvard, whose expertise in language was yet another masterful touch by Epstein, who was friends with Pinker.

More notably, however, the lawyers also went to great lengths to emphasize Epstein's Horatio Alger–like success story, describing their egotistical client as a generous self-made soul who had devoted a good deal of his money and time to noble causes.

They wrote about the two-year-old son of one of Epstein's employees who was diagnosed with retinal blastoma, and how Epstein gave the employee unlimited time off and put him in contact with a noted eye researcher at Washington University. The letter said that Epstein further paid for the private schooling of the child, along with his five siblings.

Four pages of the letter were devoted to all the good deeds that Epstein had done in his fifty-plus years, sponsoring athletic wellness programs, community building projects, and peace missions; helping poor children; investing in scientific discoveries and research; even hiring masseuses for ballet dancers.

They talked about Epstein's business, professional, and personal ties, noting that one of them was Clinton. They quoted the former president from a magazine story in which he described Epstein as "a committed philanthropist," adding that Epstein had taken a monthlong trip to Africa with Clinton. Epstein, they added, was part of the original group that conceived of the Clinton Global Initiative.

They talked about all his business and financial connections to

Florida, including being a founder of First Bank of the Palm Beaches, a member of the Breakers Club, and the owner of a Palm Beach mansion, two jets, twelve automobiles, and a boat.

"Those who know Mr. Epstein will describe him admittedly as quirky but certainly not immoral; and overall as kind, generous and warm-hearted," they wrote.

Those "warm-hearted" ways the lawyers described so tenderly rang hollow just a few weeks later when FBI agents learned that, in a fit of rage, Epstein had slapped his longtime girlfriend Nadia Marcinkova in the face while on his private jet. He had been headed to New York on August 21, 2007, but abruptly ordered his pilot to turn the plane around after he was tipped off that the FBI was waiting at Teterboro Airport in New Jersey with a subpoena and target letter for Marcinkova.

Instead, he ordered his crew to head to his island off St. Thomas, and during an argument, he struck Marcinkova in the face, FBI and court records show.

The incident happened after FBI agents, earlier that day, went to the New York home of his personal assistant in New York, Lesley Groff, for the purpose of serving her with a federal grand jury subpoena. Groff let them in, then immediately excused herself, saying she had to go upstairs and check on her sleeping child. According to the FBI report, she went upstairs and called Epstein. Epstein, on his plane, warned her to stay quiet, telling her that she would regret it if she turned over anything to the FBI or testified for the grand jury.

"Mr. Epstein applied pressure to keep Ms. Groff from complying with the grand jury subpoena that the agents had served upon her. In particular, Mr. Epstein warned Ms. Groff against turning over documents and electronic evidence responsive to the subpoena and pressured her to delay her appearance before the grand jury in the Southern District of Florida," the FBI report said.

THROUGHOUT THE LATE SUMMER AND FALL OF 2007, A FLURRY OF letters was exchanged between Epstein's camp and federal prosecutors. Acosta was copied on many of them, and often the letters referred to meetings that had been held between the parties.

Plea agreements were drafted and redrafted, as Epstein's lawyers dictated the terms, only to have their client nix them and have to start over.

Epstein's private investigators were instructed to look for dirt on every prosecutor, digging up anything they could find, no matter how insignificant, in an effort to disqualify one of them. They learned that one of the prosecutors, for example, had had his home burglarized, and they tried to have him removed from the case because he had testified in court against the burglar.

ON OCTOBER 23, 2007, AS FEDERAL PROSECUTORS IN PALM BEACH were in the midst of negotiations with Epstein's lawyers, a senior prosecutor in their office was quietly laying out plans to leave the U.S. Attorney's Office after eleven years.

On that date, Assistant U.S. Attorney Bruce Reinhart opened a limited liability company in Florida that established what would become his new criminal defense practice. His address, according to Florida corporate records: 250 South Australian Avenue, Suite 1400, which was the same office as Epstein's lead criminal defense attorney, Jack Goldberger. By the end of the year, Reinhart had resigned his post in the U.S. Attorney's Office, and on January 2, 2008, he was hired to represent several of Epstein's accomplices who would, like Epstein, later receive federal immunity.

Paul Cassell, one of the victims' lawyers, filed a complaint against Reinhart with the Justice Department's Office of Professional Responsibility, but there's no record whether it was ever investigated.

In a sworn affidavit, Reinhart denied he did anything unethical or improper. He claimed, under the penalty of perjury, that he was not part of the team involved in Epstein's investigation and therefore, was not privy to any confidential information about the case. But his former bosses in the U.S. Attorney's Office, in a 2013 federal court pleading, said that Reinhart "learned confidential, non-public information about the Epstein matter."

Reinhart, whose wife, Carolyn Bell, was also an assistant federal prosecutor in Palm Beach in 2007, was appointed to a federal magistrate post in May 2018. That same week, his wife was appointed by then Florida governor Rick Scott to the Palm Beach circuit court bench.

IN THE SUMMER AND FALL OF 2007, ACOSTA WAS NEGOTIATING DIRECTLY with Epstein's lawyers, emails show.

Each reiteration of the plea seemed to be more watered down than the last, records show.

"I have been spending some quality time with Title 18 [the criminal code] looking for misdemeanors," Villafaña wrote to Lefkowitz.

Drafts of the plea deal were passed back and forth, some of them sent to Villafaña's personal email. She gave Lefkowitz her personal cell phone number and invited him to call her over the weekend after giving him another offer and asking him for suggestions.

About the only interesting part of these drafts, some of which became part of the public record, was that they barely mentioned Epstein's missing computers, the ones that were removed in advance of the police search warrant.

It's not clear why the feds didn't ever get their hands on them.

One of the drafts read: "Epstein and his counsel agree that the computers that are currently under [redacted] will be safeguarded in their current condition by Epstein's counsel . . . until the terms and conditions of the agreement are fulfilled."

ON SEPTEMBER 19, 2007, A TENTATIVE ACCORD WAS REACHED. Goldberger called Barry Krischer to coordinate Epstein's arraignment in state court in Palm Beach. He told the state attorney to contact Acosta directly to discuss the particulars.

"Barry, here is Acosta's phone number. Let me know what he has to say because Jay Lefkowitz has to follow up with a call to him to finalize," Goldberger wrote to Krischer.

But one day later, the deal had disintegrated—yet again.

"Our plea negotiations are not going very well, and I have given the defense a deadline of tomorrow afternoon to provide me with a signed agreement," Villafaña wrote to Krischer on September 20. "If we cannot reach such an agreement, then I will need to indict the case on Tuesday. . . . I think Mr. Epstein is having second thoughts about spending time in jail and paying damages to the girls."

The issue of paying restitution to his victims had been discussed throughout the negotiations, but there was no consensus as to how it was going to be administered through the Justice Department.

Then there was the issue of Acosta's wanting Epstein to register as a sex offender, a designation that would follow him for the rest of his life, requiring him to take certain steps each time he traveled to a new state.

Lefkowitz, in an email to Acosta, told the U.S. attorney that Krischer and Belohlavek had assured him that his client wouldn't have to register as a sex offender, writing: "Registration is a life sentence . . . a punishment harsher than what Mr. Epstein deserves."

BY SEPTEMBER 24, A NEW NON-PROSECUTION DOCUMENT WAS DRAFTED that enumerated five criminal counts Epstein violated under federal law, most of them involving underage girls whom he recruited through interstate and foreign commerce to engage in commercial sex acts.

Federal prosecutors, however, agreed to defer prosecution on those federal charges in exchange for Epstein pleading guilty to the weak charge that the state grand jury had indicted him on: one count of solicitation of prostitution. The feds, however, asked the state to draw up an additional charge: solicitation *of minors* to engage in prostitution, a registerable offense.

Epstein's lawyers knew that their client wouldn't agree to being a registered sex offender. But they convinced Epstein that they would later be able to downgrade or even remove his sex registration requirement, telling him that until then, they would come up with ways for him to circumvent the strictest requirements of sex offender laws in the multiple jurisdictions where Epstein owned homes.

His lawyers were also successful in getting prosecutors to insert a little-noticed provision in the deal giving immunity to any potential criminal accomplices, "including but not limited to" four women who worked for Epstein: Kellen, Groff, Marcinkova, and another assistant, Adriana Ross. Curiously, Ghislaine Maxwell was not listed, but the agreement's vague wording seemed to leave the door open for others to be covered by the global agreement.

Despite signing the agreement, Epstein ordered Lefkowitz to continue to haggle over the restitution portion of the deal and to eliminate the sex offender requirement.

Sloman and Villafaña kept insisting they were legally bound to notify the victims about the plea deal under the federal Crime Victims' Rights Act. But every time prosecutors prepared the letters, Lefkowitz or another one of Epstein's attorneys would strenuously object, warning prosecutors that doing so would jeopardize their deal. It was clear, for some reason, that Epstein had the upper hand because prosecutors never enforced Epstein's signature and, at each step of the continuing negotiations, they backed down.

Finally, on October 12, with the deal still at an impasse, Acosta drove up to West Palm Beach to meet personally with Lefkowitz at the Marriott Hotel off Okeechobee Road. Acosta had a speaking engagement at noon with the Palm Beach Bar Association, but with the Epstein negotiations still unresolved, Acosta wanted to find a way to dispose of the case once and for all.

In preparation for the meeting, Lefkowitz wrote a six-page letter to Acosta, whom he addressed as "Alex," mentioning the "serious disagreements" Epstein's team still had with Villafaña about some of the provisions in the agreement.

Lefkowitz, later memorializing what Acosta had promised at the Marriott meeting, wrote: "I wanted to thank you for the commitment you made to me during our Oct. 12 meeting in which you promised genuine finality with regard to this matter, and assured me your office would not intervene with the state attorney's office regarding this matter; or contact any of the individuals, potential witnesses, or potential civil claimants and their respective counsel. . . ."

ACOSTA SIGNED OFF ON NEARLY ALL OF EPSTEIN'S DEMANDS.

But Epstein still believed he could make the charges go away.

Next up was Kenneth Starr.

chapter 15

DANCING WITH WOLVES

Brad Edwards was among a crop of freshly minted cogs in a 150-member legal stable at Rothstein, Rosenfeldt and Adler, one of the most prestigious law firms in South Florida.

In 2008, Edwards was representing a small group of Epstein's victims who had brought individual civil lawsuits against the multimillionaire. But Edwards, who had a solo practice in Hollywood, Florida, was outgunned by Epstein's vast legal arsenal, and had hoped that by joining Rothstein's firm, he could gain more muscle. Soon, he had seven of Epstein's victims—but, unbeknownst to him, the firm was under scrutiny by federal authorities. The following year, the firm imploded when Scott Rothstein, the flamboyant senior partner, was arrested for operating a massive Ponzi scheme. Edwards would later learn that Rothstein used him and a lot of other lawyers at the firm as unwitting pawns to sell legal settlements to unsuspecting investors for profit.

Edwards found himself back out on his own and waging a lop-sided battle against Epstein's fat war chest.

EDWARDS WAS TALL, YOUNG, AND CONFIDENT, WITH A BROOKS BROTHERS law firm look. A former all-star tennis player at Florida State and state prosecutor, he was outgoing and hungry to be successful. Edwards had plowed through the records that were part of the yearlong police investigation. After several months of long hours reviewing interviews that the police detectives conducted in the case, he was exasperated.

There was something very wrong with the way the case had been handled.

EDWARDS WASN'T PARTICULARLY ENCOURAGING WHEN I REACHED OUT to him in July 2017 and explained my project. I had already tracked down about two dozen victims, but was still having difficulty getting anyone to talk. I hoped he, and a number of other victims' lawyers I had reached out to, would help connect me with them.

But Edwards had been burned by the media at least once before. In 2015, Edwards had traveled with Giuffre, whom he was representing at the time, to New York for an interview with ABC News. Giuffre, dressed in a new white suit, was interviewed at the Ritz Carlton Hotel in New York, telling her story on camera for the first time, to reporter Amy Robach.

But the story never saw the light of day. ABC claimed that "not all of the reporting met our standards to air," and while the story was shelved at the time, it remained one they claimed they continued to probe with the intention to air. But in reality, a number of influential people, including Dershowitz and representatives of Prince Andrew, objected to the story, and ABC killed it.

I didn't really, at the time, believe that any media network would have succumbed to pressure to ignore or drop such an important story.

I just told myself that decisions are made every day about which stories to dedicate news resources to. I was, however, naïve, and wrong.

I would later learn that NBC News had discouraged journalist Ronan Farrow from reporting the Harvey Weinstein story, forcing him to take the story to *The New Yorker*, which published the piece. The story subsequently shared a Pulitzer Prize with the *New York Times* for exposing the Hollywood movie mogul's sexual abuse of women.

So I learned that there are news organizations that protect powerful people, especially when it comes to sexual harassment and abuse. The words of victims, especially those whose lives are lived on the margins, don't matter as much as the words of the man in the boardroom with major dollars at stake. Transparency and accountability, values journalists are supposed to fight for, apparently were easy to push aside. This was a bitter truth for me to accept, as I watched how men like *Today* show co-anchor Matt Lauer, *CBS This Morning* anchor Charlie Rose, Weinstein, and others accused of sexual improprieties were protected. It was horrifying that so many people, including those in my own industry, looked the other way when it came to predators, rapists, and abusers.

EDWARDS AND I MET FOR THE FIRST TIME AT HIS LAW OFFICES IN FORT Lauderdale on August 8, 2017. His building, along Andrews Avenue, was on the edge of an up-and-coming area of the city, in the midst of a transformation from its "old Florida" beginnings. Edwards's office was in a decaying warehouse district blossoming into a magnet for young urban professionals, with gleaming new high-rise condos on one side of the street and dilapidated pawnshops (soon to be trendy vegan cafés) on the other. His building embraced its modern industrial architecture, with high open ceilings and exposed pipes, ducts, and beams. The firm itself occupied a maze of very small, cubicle-like offices, with dim lighting and a craft-beer-bar vibe, even though three of its partners were old enough to have millennial-aged children.

Edwards, who was in his early forties, was among the youngest in the firm, which was then Farmer, Jaffe, Weissing, Edwards, Fistos & Lehrman—all of the name partners Rothstein law firm alums.

I already knew that Edwards was a shrewd lawyer from reading some of the case files and depositions. I remember reviewing one particular civil case, involving eleven of Epstein's victims, all of whom had their own lawyers. The women were listed as Jane Does, and all had initially filed separate civil lawsuits that were eventually consolidated into one case.

Epstein's civil lawyers, Robert Deweese Critton Jr., Michael Tein, and James Pike, were ruthless, and the legal maneuvers had become incredibly ugly. Magistrate Judge Linnea R. Johnson presided over the case, and it astonished me how much room she gave those civil lawyers to torture Epstein's victims.

The worst was that she allowed Epstein's lawyers to depose one of the girls' parents and question them about their religious beliefs on abortion. The victim, who had undergone several abortions, had never told her devout Catholic parents about the abortions, and the depositions of her and her parents are among the most painful I've ever read.

But Edwards aggressively fought for his victims, not allowing them to be bullied by Epstein's lawyers.

One of Edwards's first smart moves among many was to ask the court to appoint a receiver to control and account for Epstein's assets. By that time, twenty-five victims had filed lawsuits against Epstein, seeking damages. Edwards claimed that Epstein was fraudulently transferring money to overseas locations in order to insulate his fortune from being captured in civil litigation.

Another brilliant gambit was to compel Epstein and his lawyers to produce all materials relating to the 2006–08 criminal case. This would include exchange of discovery in both the state case and the federal probe of Epstein's crimes. This meant all documents, evidence, and correspondence that prosecutors collected in his criminal case would become part of the civil litigation against Epstein.

Neither Epstein nor federal prosecutors wanted the victims to learn what evidence they had collected. So this move triggered Epstein's criminal lawyers to also join the civil cases.

Now the civil cases weren't just about damages; they were about exposing the depth of Epstein's crimes and the lengths to which the government went to cover them up.

Epstein was now facing a perilous attack in the civil courts, largely because of Edwards.

AT THE TIME OF OUR MEETING, HOWEVER, EDWARDS WASN'T READY TO empty his playbook. I knew that and, at the time, I really only wanted him to allow me to interview some of his clients, telling him that my goal was to write a story from their point of view. By the time I met him in person, I had already interviewed a number of other lawyers connected to the case who had brought civil claims against Epstein.

But Edwards was protective of his clients, and I understood why.

He talked a lot about his long, sordid war with Epstein, a well-armed adversary with formidable connections and a bottomless bank account. His description of his decade-long war with Epstein made me think about the movie *The Silence of the Lambs*—Epstein as a Hannibal Lecter character who deploys his brilliant mind and devious psychological games to extract traumatic childhood memories from his victims, then taking twisted pleasure in manipulating their vulnerabilities to violate and control them.

Edwards was the Clarice Starling of the story, delving into the psyche of a madman, chasing the villain's trail all over the world in hopes of finally conquering a predatory monster without falling into the psychological traps he had set for him—sort of like the odd severed head in a jar from the movie.

Edwards's story, at times, was hard to believe: how Epstein had thrown his money around like bait, so much of it that he could get his lawyers, private investigators, and his female recruiters to do anything he wanted. He suspected that Epstein tried to bribe or extort almost everyone involved in the case, offering them lucrative jobs or warning them that there were events in their pasts that would be exposed if they continued to pursue him.

Worst of all, neither the state nor federal prosecutors ever put a stop to his intimidation tactics, thereby sabotaging their own cases—especially their ability to gain the confidence and trust of the victims who could form the backbone of a strong criminal prosecution.

Edwards worried about the safety of his own family, as he chased tips about Epstein's sex trafficking from California to Bratislava, Slovakia. Epstein's bodyguard, Igor, more than once warned Edwards to back off. As evidence of Epstein's power, Igor claimed that when his boss was jailed in 2008, Igor was instructed to take a CIA class in Washington where his chief role as a student was to get CIA communications slipped to him to pass to Epstein in jail. Edwards didn't know whether to believe Igor or not. He considered the possibility that Epstein just wanted Igor to scare him.

There were other cloak-and-dagger anecdotes, including a shadowy story he mentioned about an unnamed couple in Manhattan connected to Epstein who ran a child-grooming service for pedophiles.

Edwards insisted that despite all the intrigue, he had never found a direct connection to anyone in government or the justice system who put a stop to Epstein's prosecution as part of some elaborate extortion plot or conspiracy.

Still, he acknowledged that there remained many people, mainly powerful men, whom he theorized Epstein had blackmail material on.

"I think Jeffrey Epstein's main philosophy is that if you know the right people and you have enough money, you can get away with anything," Edwards said.

EDWARDS REMEMBERS VIVIDLY THE DAY HE MET COURTNEY WILD IN 2008, and the story she told him about how she had been sexually assaulted by Epstein when she was fourteen.

Edwards thought that his role would be to help represent her when she was questioned by the FBI, and possibly later, if she testified against Epstein during what they both expected would be an upcoming criminal trial.

She was led to believe that the FBI had compiled a strong case against Epstein and that a criminal indictment was imminent. She was a good witness because she had been with Epstein for five years and knew many of the other victims as well as Epstein's assistants. She also knew how his operation worked because she herself had helped recruit perhaps a hundred victims.

Courtney was street smart and not easily rattled. She was expecting the case to be tough and was ready to stand up to Epstein and his lawyers.

But she was disturbed by the fact that, after she provided the feds with extensive information about Epstein's crimes, neither the FBI nor federal prosecutors were returning her calls.

Courtney was alarmed that Epstein was sending private investigators to harass her at the bagel shop where she worked and that prosecutors were ignoring her concerns. She was starting to feel worried that with Epstein still free, her life could be in danger.

"Look," she told Edwards. "I just want the government to talk to me. I'm a victim, and I want to make sure I'm protected because this guy is really scary, and I want to make sure he is being prosecuted. I want to know what's going on, what is the timing? What can I expect?"

By then, Courtney was nineteen, but she was struggling with trauma and was taking drugs to ease her anxiety.

Edwards offered to reach out to the lead federal prosecutor, Villafaña.

"I was sure it wasn't going to be a big deal," Edwards recalled. "Courtney came to me only to help her make sure the government would communicate with her."

Edwards called Villafaña the following day. The conversation was cordial, but Edwards sensed that she was unusually guarded, even for a federal prosecutor.

"I can't share any information with you," she told Edwards. "But I will listen to all the information that you bring me."

"My client has been molested many times as a minor by this guy, and she knows he has molested a hundred little girls," Edwards told her.

"We know how big this case is," Villafaña told him. "You're not telling us any information so far that we don't already know."

"I'll help you in any way I can," Edwards offered. "In fact, I'm supposed to meet with another friend of my client's very soon and she may give you more information."

Villafaña knew the name of this victim as well.

"There's a problem with her," she said. "She's been represented by an Epstein-paid lawyer and we know the statements she gave us are not true. She has not helped our case at all."

"Well, I'm going to meet with her," Edwards said. "And let her tell me what happened."

Over the course of the following weeks, Edwards persuaded the second client to cooperate with authorities. Yet he was becoming increasingly uneasy about the behavior of the federal prosecutors.

"There was something very strange here," Edwards told Emily and me in a subsequent videotaped interview. "We were offering a lot of information to the assistant U.S. attorney handling a massive prosecution on a case that couldn't be any easier to prove and instead we are getting resistance."

He sensed that Villafaña wanted to tell him more but was sworn to silence by her bosses at the U.S. Attorney's Office.

"I started getting the inclination that for some reason, the defendant and the government were working together against the victims, although I knew that kind of conspiracy theory was so far-fetched that I didn't want to believe it."

chapter 16

COURTNEY

Emily's and my work on prisons helped us cut through the red tape in the Florida Department of Corrections and expedite an interview with Courtney, who was fighting Epstein, his powerful team of lawyers—and the federal government—from a state prison cell.

It's never easy to get to any of Florida's prisons, as most of them are in rural outposts, far from an airport. Emily and I got permission to visit Courtney on January 29, 2018, which meant flying into Tallahassee, renting a car, and driving forty miles to Quincy, Florida, in the Panhandle, then back to Tallahassee the same day.

I had never been to Gadsden Correctional Institution, but the fifteen hundred women housed at Gadsden had to endure the same harsh treatment as all women in Florida prisons.

The *Herald* has written much about the violent abuse and unsanitary conditions at Gadsden, a twenty-two-year-old facility that is among a handful of state prisons run by private prison companies.

Gadsden was a country club compared to Lowell, which isn't saying much because in the months before we were there, inmates at Gadsden were living without hot water and heat, and were forced to walk through bathrooms flooded with human waste. They were on water rations because the septic tanks were jammed.

By the time I met Courtney, she had led two very different lives: one before Jeffrey and one after Jeffrey.

Before Jeffrey, she was captain of the cheerleading squad and first trumpet in the band at Lake Worth Middle School. Despite a history of family problems, she managed to get straight As and excelled at writing.

After Jeffrey, Courtney dropped out of school, became one of his teenaged recruiters, began taking drugs, and then worked as a stripper before landing in jail for selling drugs at a local Walmart.

Courtney's mother, Eva Ford, was the sole supporter of the family, which included her older brother, Justin. They lived in a trailer park on the outskirts of West Palm Beach, and her mother worked two waitressing jobs to try to keep food on the table. They lived in a single-wide two-bedroom mobile home with a monthly rent of six hundred dollars. Ford, however, also had her own drug problems, including a crack-cocaine habit that led her to be evicted from her trailer, leaving the family homeless.

Now thirty, with a son in grade school, Courtney was clean. Her son was living with her mother, who had also been sober for fifteen years. There was little opportunity for Courtney to see her son because Gadsden was on the other side of the state, almost as far from Palm Beach as one can be and still be in Florida.

It was a chilly fifty-seven degrees that morning in northwest Florida when Emily and I made the trip to Gadsden. Neither Emily nor I remember the drive—but we do remember the interview as if it were yesterday.

Courtney looked similar to all the other girls in Epstein's orbit. She had light brown hair, large blue eyes; she was fair-skinned and petite. At our first meeting, she was pale and a bit frail, dressed in her baggy blue prison uniform—looking nothing like the fighter that she would soon become.

Like some of the other Epstein victims I spoke to, she was skeptical of our motives. But Edwards had encouraged her to talk to us, and she was willing to do almost anything for Brad, as he had been working her case pro bono for more than a decade. He believed in her, when almost no one else did.

So she agreed to speak for the first time, not as the anonymous, voiceless Jane Doe in the Crime Victims' Rights lawsuit, but as a sexual assault survivor turned crime victims' rights fighter named Courtney Elizabeth Wild.

Courtney had been fighting for justice for years by the time I met her—first enduring endless interviews with the FBI and federal prosecutors, then facing Epstein and his lawyers in civil court, and then, indirectly, facing Epstein himself when the financier joined in the Crime Victims' Rights lawsuit in another effort to silence his victims. Edwards may have been Courtney's proxy, but he could not have successfully battled Epstein without her.

Courtney was unemotional but guarded, and she spoke matter-of-factly. It was hard to believe that she had faced a life-altering fifteen-year ordeal; it was more like she had been mentally preparing for a prize fight.

AT FOURTEEN, COURTNEY HAD SOMEHOW OVERCOME OBSTACLES THAT would have led a weaker girl down a fatal path long before she had met someone like Epstein.

I had interviewed her mother prior to visiting Courtney in prison, and Eva was brutally honest about her failings. She had divorced Courtney's father when Courtney was two. Shortly thereafter, the Hernando County Sheriff's Department opened an investigation into whether her father had sexually abused Courtney as a toddler.

The case was eventually dropped, but over the years, records show that Florida's Department of Children and Families investigated a number of child abuse complaints against Courtney's parents.

Her family history showed that her mother worked from eight thirty in the morning at one restaurant, returned home at midday, then went back to waitressing at another restaurant in the evenings. In a good week, Eva would earn four hundred dollars in tips. She would pick up odds and ends that other people would put out on the curb with their trash and, on weekends, go to a local flea market, pay for a table, and sell the junk for extra money.

"Christmastime I had to work ungodly hours," Eva recalled. "We never spent Christmas together as a family, but we would celebrate ahead of time and pretend it was Christmas. I would say, 'You know, we are going to drive to Key West and camp out,' or 'Let's go to Rapids Water Park all day and eat pizza.'"

It reminded me of how my own mother always waited until late on Christmas Eve to buy our tree, knowing that she could often get it for free. Like Eva, my mother worked multiple jobs and often bought us clothes on old-fashioned layaway plans, at thrift stores, and at church bazaars. And like Courtney, I understood what it was like coming home to an empty house, and the temptations of being an unsupervised teenager with a lot of free time on my hands.

"It is a sacrifice you do as a parent. There is always a way to make money—it's just a question of whether you are willing to work hard to do it," Eva said.

In elementary school, Courtney was invited to go on a trip to Washington, D.C., but the cost was five hundred dollars, and her mother just couldn't afford it. Eva recalled that she asked Courtney's teacher whether she could do a payment plan for the trip.

"The teacher just looked at me and said: 'Courtney is going on this trip,' and I said, 'I don't have the money to give you,' and she said, 'Courtney won an essay contest, and she is the one carrying the wreath for the unknown soldier.'"

In middle school, Courtney continued to achieve. She never got anything less than an A.

Around that time, Eva's father fell in the nursing home where he was living in Rhode Island. Eva felt she needed to tend to him, but she didn't have the money to go to Rhode Island, so she took up an offer from a friend of hers who needed someone to take care of her father in New York for the summer. She offered to pay Eva to care for him, giving Eva the ability to visit her father during her time off.

Eva took the job, and went to New York and Rhode Island that summer, leaving her son, who was still a teenager, in charge of her younger teenage daughter.

"My son was pretty much the head honcho taking care of things. Courtney wasn't listening to him. They fought a lot. It was a lot for her," Eva recalled.

Courtney became rebellious during that time and started coming home at all hours of the night. Eva came home later that summer to find her daughter was no longer a little girl. Once Courtney came home with a nose ring, and Eva admits she was so angry that she smacked her daughter. Someone saw them fighting and called the police.

Eva recalls that the drugs began as a way to cope with the fears and pressures of not knowing whether her next waitressing shift would produce enough tips to buy a week's worth of groceries.

"I wasn't there for her emotionally and she kind of slipped through the cracks," Eva said. "Have I forgiven myself? Probably not."

EVA SOON LOST THE ABILITY TO PAY RENT AND SHE AND HER HUSBAND moved into an efficiency apartment, leaving Courtney and her brother to fend for themselves.

Her brother moved in with a girlfriend, and Courtney went to stay with the family of a school friend who also lived in the same trailer park.

The friend became a sister to Courtney, and the two would regularly hang out, drinking alcohol and smoking pot.

Courtney began skipping school and going to more parties in the summer of 2002. At one of them, a girl asked her if they wanted to make two hundred dollars each to give an older man a massage. The girl, who was the same age as Courtney, assured them that it was legitimate, but warned them that they might have to take their clothes off.

Courtney recalled that she was uncomfortable, and said no.

"I wasn't raised like that and I just didn't want to do it," she said.

Courtney's friend, however, agreed to go, and came home with two crisp hundred-dollar bills.

"Once I saw the money, I wanted to do it, too," Courtney admitted. "I was pretty much homeless. I didn't have any of my own things, and I was going from middle school to high school, which was a transition in itself. I didn't have any of the things I needed for school."

She went with her friend the first time and was so nervous she barely remembered the long drive from her trailer park to Palm Beach island, about forty minutes away. She was greeted at the mansion by Sarah Kellen, who would become her point of contact with Epstein for the next four years.

Courtney soon became one of Epstein's top recruiters.

"I was kind of self-medicating, drinking and smoking weed just to have a good time, [and] so I didn't have to deal with any of what I was doing. That's another reason the money came in handy. I was able to buy everything I needed that I didn't have, and I was basically able to do whatever I wanted because I didn't need to ask anybody for anything.

"That was at fourteen years old . . . it was so crazy," Courtney said.

She was under the impression that Epstein was a wealthy brain surgeon. He had told several of the girls that he was a doctor, and led others to believe that he had powerful contacts in the modeling world who could make their dreams come true.

Courtney didn't pay much attention to how Epstein earned his money, but she was mesmerized by his luxurious lifestyle. His waterfront estate was worlds away from the trailer park where Courtney grew up.

One visit turned into two visits, which turned into four visits, which turned to more.

I asked her how many times, as a teenager, she was sexually abused by Epstein, and by other women in his mansion.

"So many times that I can't even count," she said.

"In the beginning when we went, he said, 'You can take your clothes off, but you don't have to take them all off. Just take your bra off, you can keep your panties on.' And that made me feel a little more comfortable. But then, for some reason, I was persuaded to take off everything. And he just kept pressuring me to do more.

"I can't remember the exact time he raped me, or what went through my head, other than, none of it made sense. I remember leaving his house, and I had so much shame, guilt, and a dirty feeling. I guess in my mind, because I had the money, I tried to cover up my feelings in order to survive."

Like other girls who were brought to his house, she learned that she could avoid being abused herself by offering him new, younger girls to divert his attention from her. She started bringing him victims morning, noon, and night.

She dropped out of school and began working for him regularly, earning enough money to get a small apartment by the time she was sixteen. For a while, she lived with an older boyfriend in an efficiency on Dixie Highway, a seedy strip in Lake Worth lined with run-down art deco motels with fifty-dollar-a-night rooms that smelled of cigarettes.

Her boyfriend was a drug addict whom she supplied with money to support his habit. Epstein was now paying her four hundred dollars per girl.

"I made the money and gave it to him for about a year and a half," she said.

About six months after they broke up, her boyfriend moved back with his mother, then took a gun from a bedroom, walked into the room where his mother was standing, said, "I'm sorry, Mom," then went into the backyard and shot himself in the head.

This was, sadly, a familiar story.

I had already read about another one of Epstein's victims who, after having a fight with her boyfriend, chased him out to the dirt road in front of her parents' trailer, where he put a gun to his head and pulled the trigger, killing himself.

These were the people who made up these girls' lives, and Epstein knew it. He used their troubled existence and his wealth as leverage to give them hope that, if they did what he asked, they would be able to escape their cycle of misery.

"Jeffrey was our saving grace," Courtney would tell me in a subsequent interview. "He helped us during a traumatic time. It's taken me a long time to not feel that way. But guess what? I wasn't homeless. I had an apartment. So for a long, long time, I didn't think of myself as a victim."

She told her mother that she was working at a restaurant, but her mother worried that something else was going on.

"I knew how hard I worked. And she was making a lot of money, so I wondered," Eva said.

Courtney fell into a pattern, compartmentalizing the trauma that she was suffering.

"It was just where I would massage him for thirty minutes and then go downstairs and wait for the [other] girls to come down. Once that happened, when I didn't have to do the sex anymore, I kind of lost sight of what I was really doing.

"It was never enough. If I had a girl to bring him breakfast, lunch, and dinner, then that's how many times I would go a day. He wanted as many girls as I could bring him."

By the time she was seventeen, Epstein no longer wanted Courtney sexually. She was too old for him, and she no longer hung around with girls who were thirteen, fourteen, and fifteen. She began to have trouble finding girls of that age to bring him.

"He would get angry with me, and it became a headache to deal with him," she said.

She began dancing at a strip club, earning more money than she had been working for Epstein, so she went to see Epstein less and less.

She was saving money, but the men in her life were addicts, and it wasn't long before she graduated to hard drugs. Her first arrests were for petty theft, and by the time she was twenty, she had a long rap sheet.

"I didn't want to live unless I was impaired," she explained. "It was this unbearable hurt and pain that I just didn't want to feel."

By August 2007, when the FBI finally knocked on her door, Courtney had been arrested ten times on charges ranging from petty theft to possession of cocaine. She had a new boyfriend and was trying to get clean.

"I started to take things seriously, and stopped dancing and got two jobs," she said.

The FBI questioned her on August 14, 2007.

"I was being treated like I had done something wrong, and I was scared," she recalled.

She confessed that she had brought at least twenty-five to thirty girls to Epstein's house over the four years she was working for him. In reality, it was a lot more.

She told the FBI the times that she had sex with him when she was underage, and how he pressured her to have sex with other girls and young women, including Marcinkova.

"He would get angry with me if I didn't have a girl to bring him," she told the agents.

"His preference was short, little white girls," she said. "One time one of the girls brought him a black girl and he got angry and told her to get the girl out because he did not want black girls or girls with tattoos."

Soon, Epstein began to call and ask her questions about what the FBI wanted to know.

"I didn't know who to talk to or not talk to. I remember I just began calling a bunch of attorneys."

She told Edwards that all she wanted was for Epstein to go to jail so he couldn't hurt any other girls.

Two weeks later, she learned that Epstein had taken a plea deal.

"I can remember finding out," Courtney recalled.

To her, it was a betrayal.

"All I know is that the federal government has tried to cover up everything that Jeffrey Epstein has done," Courtney said. "As far as justice for me, and all his other victims, that was taken away as soon as they made that agreement."

Courtney recalled that Villafaña, with tears in her eyes, had promised to prosecute Epstein.

"They put us in the dark. We had no voice. I can't even express it in words . . ."

She had had a long time in prison to think about what had happened. With eight months left in her sentence, she had successfully navigated rehab. She found comfort in reading and in God. The Weinstein case was on the news, as well as coverage of the Olympic gymnasts who had been molested by their doctor.

Courtney, however, found no solace in the cultural awakening over sexual abuse that was happening across the country.

"Jeffrey Epstein preyed on girls who were homeless and were addicted to drugs. He didn't victimize girls who were Olympic stars and Hollywood actresses. He victimized people he thought nobody would ever listen to, and he was right."

EMILY AND I DROVE BACK TO TALLAHASSEE THAT AFTERNOON. WE WERE exhausted but wired at the same time. We had dinner at a little Indian restaurant in a strip mall I had been to on a previous trip to

Tallahassee. Then we drove over to the local movie theater. We'd both been so busy with our families and work that we hadn't seen a movie in years.

One of the films offered that evening was by Steven Spielberg.

It detailed how the *Washington Post* had exposed the Pentagon Papers scandal—one of the biggest government cover-ups in history. It seemed fitting.

chapter 17

VIRGINIA

On February 14, 2018, a nineteen-year-old student armed with a semiautomatic rifle walked into Marjory Stoneman Douglas High School in Parkland, Florida, and killed seventeen people, mostly students, and injured seventeen others in one of the worst school shootings in U.S. history.

I was home, with bronchitis, reading Epstein lawsuits in bed when I heard the news that afternoon. I didn't have much of a voice, but I called Casey as soon as I heard and offered to do whatever was needed.

The next several days were spent working on that story. I wrote a seventy-inch piece for Sunday's paper, and continued to dig into various angles to the tragedy.

In the coming days and weeks, the story would take over the attention of the nation.

At the end of March, I was able to return to the Epstein project. Virginia Roberts Giuffre, the Epstein victim who now lived in Australia, was scheduled to be in Florida to meet with her attorney, Sigrid McCawley, of Boies Schiller Flexner, one of the best-known law firms in the nation.

David Boies, the firm's founder—together with McCawley—had represented Virginia in a civil lawsuit she had brought in 2016 against Epstein's former girlfriend Ghislaine Maxwell, whom she had accused of recruiting and abusing her. The trial for the lawsuit was much anticipated, as it was said to reveal, for the first time, new evidence of Epstein's sex trafficking operation, as well as the names of other prominent men and women who were possibly involved. By this time, Epstein had already settled dozens of civil lawsuits with his victims and had been out of jail for seven years.

Giuffre, however, was determined to see that both Epstein and Maxwell be sent to prison.

But there was never a trial, as the case was settled for an undisclosed sum in early 2017. Nearly every part of the lawsuit had been sealed by the federal judge, meaning that—unless someone challenged the judge's decision—nobody would ever learn the names of the prominent people involved, or the scope of Epstein and Maxwell's operation.

Boies and McCawley knew what evidence was contained in the lawsuit, but were prohibited from revealing anything that was sealed.

On February 23, 2018, I met with Boies and McCawley at the firm's offices in Boca Raton to discuss my project. We had already had discussions about interviewing Virginia, who would be visiting Florida in March.

I also wanted to know how the lawyers felt about the *Miami Herald* going to court to try to unseal the Maxwell case file, now that it was closed. I was concerned that Virginia might want to keep certain details sealed, as it was a sex case. But to my surprise, Boies said that they were as eager to reveal the truth as I was. I mentally laid out plans to try to convince the bean counters at our parent company McClatchy's offices in California to go to court to unseal the documents. It would be a costly endeavor, so I had to show my bosses why it was important.

DAVID BOIES IS ONE OF THE MOST POWERFUL LAWYERS IN AMERICA. HE had taken on cases that made him the darling of liberals and the media, representing Al Gore during the 2000 presidential recount in *Bush v. Gore*, defending the First Amendment as part of a libel suit brought against CBS News by General William C. Westmoreland, and filing a lawsuit that ultimately gave gays and lesbians the right to marry in California.

By the time I met him, in early 2018, however, his prestige as a superstar litigator had been sullied by a number of legal solecisms. Some critics called them public relations disasters.

It turned out that Boies, who was counsel for the *New York Times*, was also representing Harvey Weinstein, the focus of two back-to-back investigations.

In his piece for *The New Yorker*, journalist Ronan Farrow revealed that Boies had hired a firm run by Israeli intelligence operatives to intimidate and silence the movie mogul's victims and to thwart publication of Farrow's story, as well as another by the *New York Times*.

The *Times*, upon learning of Boies's involvement, promptly fired him, and the fallout led to a media storm, as it came on the heels of revelations that Boies was also connected to Theranos, a Silicon Valley blood-testing company that had perpetuated a massive investment fraud.

Boies had been a stockholder and a member of Theranos's board of directors at the same time that his firm represented the company. *Wall Street Journal* reporter John Carreyrou had been writing stories exposing how the company's owner, Elizabeth Holmes, had conned millions of dollars from investors for a technology that didn't work. Boies sent a legal team to discredit the company whistleblowers, then turned the law firm's legal muscle against the *Journal*, threatening to sue the paper for its coverage.

Boies admits he made errors in judgment, but the bad publicity continued to haunt him in 2018, with the publication of Carreyrou's bestselling book about Theranos, *Bad Blood*.

BOIES, SEVENTY-NINE, GREW UP IN A RURAL ILLINOIS FARM TOWN AND has a gentlemanly midwestern niceness about him that belies his reputation as a ferocious courtroom foe. In early 2018, despite the controversies, he was still being courted by major corporations and taking on high-profile causes. At the time I met him, he was working on a case involving priceless paintings that were looted by the Nazis during the Holocaust.

The great-grandson of a Jewish woman who surrendered her Camille Pissarro painting during the war had been battling a Spanish museum to return the family heirloom, and Boies was working on behalf of the woman's family.

The museum, which valued the work at more than thirty million dollars, maintained it had acquired it from a German industrialist and knew little about its history. Boies was preparing for trial in Los Angeles later that year.

It was clear he had a full plate, but I had spoken at length with his public relations spokeswoman, Dawn Schneider, explaining the story I intended to do about Epstein. I knew that he and McCawley also represented another victim named Sarah Ransome, and I hoped to interview her as well.

McCawley, a super-smart lawyer and mother of four children, had just returned from maternity leave when she became the lead attorney in the Maxwell case.

Though McCawley's background was mostly in corporate law, the forty-two-year-old attorney had worked in a shelter for abused women during law school at the University of Florida, and was later chair of ChildNet, a nonprofit based in Fort Lauderdale that provides aid for abused, abandoned, and neglected children.

Boies wisely recognized that McCawley's background and her resilience as a lawyer would help them build a case against Maxwell and, by extension, Epstein.

Giuffre, now in her thirties, was suing Maxwell for defamation, after the British socialite issued a number of public statements branding Virginia a liar. Giuffre alleged, as part of the suit, that Maxwell recruited her into Epstein's sex trafficking operation and groomed her to be a sex slave for Epstein, Maxwell, and other prominent men, including Alan Dershowitz and Prince Andrew.

While the case was at its heart a defamation claim, it would require McCawley to produce evidence that Giuffre's sex abuse allegations against Epstein and Maxwell were true. To this end, McCawley deposed a number of witnesses, including several of Epstein's employees.

Every part of the case tested McCawley's mettle, as she faced criticism from both Maxwell's lawyers and others in the legal community who warned her that going up against Epstein and his powerful lawyers was going to limit her career opportunities.

"I never worked so hard or cared so much about a case," McCawley said. "The fight was so incredibly fierce."

Dershowitz was hoping that he would be able to leverage some of the testimony and evidence produced during the case to exonerate himself. Part of his strategy involved not just going after Virginia but attacking her lawyers. He would file bar complaints against both Boies and McCawley, alleging a number of ethical improprieties that were ruled to be without merit.

"The bullying got to such a level that it affected my law license," McCawley recalled. "It was beyond a low blow; it was meant to distract from the case—and it did."

During this time, McCawley filed an application for a vacancy on the federal bench, but was rejected. She was later told that Epstein's lawyers played a role in her not getting a judgeship.

But she would have the last laugh when the case was settled in Virginia's favor for about five million dollars.

"The best thing they could have done was to get rid of me," McCawley now says, looking back.

VIRGINIA HAD SPOKEN PUBLICLY IN 2011. HER INTERVIEWS WITH SHARON Churcher of London's *Daily Mail* focused primarily on her allegations that she had been ordered by Epstein and Maxwell to have sex with Prince Andrew when she was seventeen. Virginia had not been interviewed by journalists in the United States because her agreement with the British tabloid was an exclusive, which meant she was paid for the piece and agreed not to speak to other media.

I WAS SO SICK ON THE DAY IN MARCH 2018 WHEN EMILY AND I MET Virginia that I coughed my way through the entire interview. Edwards and McCawley were both there, as was a young woman named Jena-Lisa Jones who had just contacted Edwards to see if he could represent her. She had been to Epstein's mansion one time, when she was fifteen, brought by a friend of a friend. She had never spoken to anyone about the ordeal. So unlike Virginia, she was still very raw with her emotions. Though she was in her early thirties, she looked at least ten years younger. I'm sure when she met Epstein she looked like she was eleven.

I won't say that her story was like all the others, because I've come to learn that each survivor's trauma is often as fresh as it was the day it happened, and each woman's healing journey is their own. Jena-Lisa had lived a tough life, and she had never been able to forgive herself for what happened. The absolute hardest part for me about doing this project was watching how these women, so many years later, still harbored so much shame.

But I was struck by the contrast between the two women I spoke to that day. While nearly the same age, one was still lost and almost as childlike as the day she was abused, and the other had grown into a determined survivor who would stop at nothing to put Epstein and all those who had harmed her in jail.

"I'm not going to stop until all these girls get justice," Virginia told us at the end of that first interview.

BORN AUGUST 9, 1983, IN SACRAMENTO, CALIFORNIA, VIRGINIA—WHOSE nickname is Jenna—spent her early years in California with her parents, Lynn Trude Cabell and Sky William Roberts. Both had previously been married, and she had two stepbrothers, Sky, who is younger, and Daniel, who is two years older.

Her father was a maintenance man who worked at various apartment and condo buildings in California.

"He was kind of a jack of all trades," Virginia recalled. Both her parents believed in corporal punishment, and she was hit when she misbehaved from the time she was very young.

When she was in grade school, the family moved across the country to Loxahatchee, Florida, where they lived in a single-story home on a two-acre property surrounded by plots of land that stretched for miles. They had horses, chickens, and goats. Their house was on a pond, and she often went swimming and rode horseback along the dirt roads.

"My mother used to dress me in dresses with my hair in bows. I look really embarrassing in the school photos."

LOXAHATCHEE TAKES ITS NAME FROM THE SEMINOLE INDIAN WORD meaning "turtle creek," and residents often lived nonconformist lives on vast horse farms and landscape nurseries. Many lived in trailers set in the middle of heavily wooded properties, some with barbed-wire gates and posted signs that read "No Trespassing," "Keep OUT," or "Beware of Dog."

Virginia attended Loxahatchee Groves Elementary School at a time when the closest gas station was five miles away and the local grocery store was ten miles away. There was one fruit stand and a nudist camp, along with Ku Klux Klan members who held a rally with a cross-burning in 1980.[1]

She recalls being carefree and happy until the age of seven, when she was first sexually abused by someone she describes as a family friend.

"It started as a bedtime ritual and then it graduated to cuddles and . . ." Her voice trailed off. It's difficult for her to talk about, even now. She won't identify the person who abused her, but said it went on for a long time.

Her horse, Brumby, was her best friend and companion at a time when she was routinely being molested. She began to reject the abuse as she got older, but when she resisted, she was given pills to sedate her so she wouldn't fight back.

"It turned my entire life around," she recalled of the abuse. "Everything changed. I went from being a very happy child to a completely different person. If you look at my school photographs, you can see the drastic change in my eyes from kindergarten to second grade."

Back then, kids had a lot of freedom to run around until past dark. There were no cell phones, so Virginia was able to stay out later and later to avoid going home.

"I began to hang out with older kids. They were all smoking pot, and I fell into this group of misfits."

She ran away frequently, crashing from one friend's home to another.

"At one point, my parents put alarms on the windows to try to keep me in," she said. "I thought I would try a MacGyver," she said, referring to a 1980s TV show about a secret agent who used his Boy Scout–like skills to get himself out of life-and-death situations. "I put foil between the red wire to see if it bounced back, to deactivate the alarm, but it didn't work," she said, laughing.

Virginia's rebellious nature likely came from her maternal grandmother, Shelly Louise Walters, a feisty woman who grew up in a suburb of Chicago and went on to graduate in 1954 from Vassar, where she played on the tennis team, and later served as national secretary for the U.S. Professional Tennis Association, which she was a member of for forty years.

"She was a big public figure back then," Virginia recalls. "She won tennis tournaments in Florida, a lot of championships. She was the writer of her own destiny, a woman who fought for other women."

Virginia recalls that her grandmother wasn't the motherly type, sending her two daughters to live with her parents so she could continue her tennis career. Shelly also had a busy social life; she was married five times before moving to Florida in 1976 with her fifth husband, Frank "Bucky" Walters.

"As a grandmother, she was crazy," Virginia recalls. "She woke up with a Bloody Mary in one hand and a cigarette in the other. She had to be fierce because she was making it in a man's world; she was a pioneer who didn't have time for bullshit."

When Virginia was eleven, her parents sent her to live with family in Salinas, California, hoping that her aunt Carol would tame her wild ways.

Virginia was in for a culture shock, coming from an all-white town of tractors and pickup trucks to a mostly black and Hispanic urban middle school that was bursting with gang violence. As a country girl, Virginia stood out. She said she was among a handful of white students and, with her long blond hair, she was often targeted by gangs.

"I did not like the school. It got to the point I refused to go because the gang members were threatening me."

She wasn't even there a year before she started planning her escape, she said, describing her ordeals in several interviews with me as well as in an unpublished book manuscript she wrote in 2011. (The memoir was filed as part of the Maxwell court case and was unsealed in 2020.)

So on Easter Sunday, with the family coming to celebrate and an elaborate party planned, Virginia packed up her meager belongings, took a shower, got dressed, and hopped out the window of her room. She hitched a ride to San Francisco, destination Haight-Ashbury—a district known in the 1960s as the heart of the nation's hippie counterculture. To Virginia, it represented a magical citadel of freedom, autonomy, and free love that she had read about in books.

"I wanted to live in a hippie town, free love and all. What I found was a nice, fancy area with uppity people. I thought, What did I get myself into? It was cold and I had no money. So I called my best friend in Florida and she told her father," she wrote.

Within twenty-four hours, her father, Sky, was on a plane to California to pick up Virginia and take her back to Florida.

For a time that summer, life seemed almost normal. The family took a cross-country camping trip with her father's side of the family. But Virginia wrote that things once again turned ugly when her father found her with a boy at one of the campgrounds they were staying in.

"My father threatened him with his life. He beat the shit out of me, threw me in the camper, and I kicked him in the groin to get him off me. He kept beating me."

Her parents then placed her in a school for troubled teens.

"It was like a jail for kids. At night, you would go to foster homes. It was easy to break away, but when I was caught, they would put me in a white room with no bed. I'd spend weeks there."

One day she escaped and hitched a ride to Boynton Beach. She bummed twenty dollars from a man who took her to the nearest train station, where she bought a one-way ticket to Miami.

She was fourteen when she arrived in Miami Beach in the summer of 1998.

She wandered to a nearby bus stop to beg for money for food, but no one offered to help. She sat on a curb and began to cry.

A long black stretch limo pulled up beside her, and a fat, bald old man opened the door. He was sitting next to a beautiful young woman in a red minidress. He asked her what she was doing, sitting alone and crying, and she told him she had run away from home, and she was hungry, hoping he would offer her some money to buy food.

He introduced himself as Ron Eppinger, owner of a modeling agency called Perfect 10, and the woman at his side as a model from the Czech Republic, who appeared to be in her teens.

He claimed that his daughter had been killed in a car accident and that he was still in grief from the loss. He stroked Virginia's hair as he told her the story, then offered to take her in, telling her, "I can be your new daddy, someone to take care of you, and you'll be my new baby forever."

He then took her to get something to eat and to buy her new clothes at Gap Kids, where he picked out tiny cutoff shorts and shirts that were too tight, even for her slight figure.

Eppinger drove her to a gleaming waterfront high-rise on Biscayne Bay, the Grand, where he owned several condos. His apartment had floor-to-ceiling windows, marble floors, and panoramic views of the water and downtown Miami. He introduced her to several other girls living there. They were nearly or completely naked, lounging around the apartment. She learned that they were escorts who were hired to accompany wealthy men with yachts and mansions who wanted female companions on their arms at parties and events.

Some of the girls were from foreign countries, and they described how their lives had changed by being introduced to well-connected men with money who bought them expensive clothes and jewelry.

Virginia's head was spinning at the enthusiasm they expressed about their work, and she began to think that this lifestyle wasn't only exciting; it was an acceptable way to earn a living.

Eppinger returned and led her to a bathroom, where he filled a cup with water, gave her two blue pills, and told her to take them. Soon he was on top of her, but in her drugged haze, she could not recall the rape. She woke up naked in bed, her head pounding, with several male voices whispering in the distance.

Eppinger was bragging about his latest conquest to his business partners. He then ordered her to come with him. That day, he took her to the hair salon to get her blond hair dyed more golden, then there was more shopping, more skimpy outfits, and, at the end of the day, she was raped again. He told her he would teach her how to please men and that she should obey or else he would throw her back on the street.

Virginia was now in training to be an escort at the age of fourteen.

MEANWHILE, EPPINGER'S MIAMI OPERATION WAS STARTING TO CRUMble. The feds had received a tip about his trafficking of young girls, but before they could act upon it, he hastily ordered Virginia and all the other girls to pack up. He moved them to a ranch in Ocala, in central Florida.

Virginia, however, had been secretly calling a childhood friend, Tony Figueroa, and telling him about what was happening to her. She would cry during those calls, but refused to call her parents, telling Tony that her parents would only send her away. She couldn't bear the thought of their abandoning her again.

One day, Eppinger burst into her bedroom, grabbed her by the throat, and threw her up against the wall, telling her how stupid she had been to call home.

"You are going far, far away from me and you better be nicer to the next man I send you to—I've heard he's not as nice as most would like. Are you fucking hearing me, bitch?" she recalled him shouting.

The girls came in to wish her farewell, some asking her why she had made those calls and risked ruining everything for them. But Virginia didn't have time to explain. She was given five minutes to pack up a small bag of what little she had, including a few hundred-dollar bills she kept hidden in the lining of a hair scrunchie.

She was promptly picked up, not knowing what horror awaited her.

chapter 18

FINDING MR. EPSTEIN

I had been monitoring Epstein's private jets for several months in the run-up to launching my series. There are internet websites that do this, but plane owners can request to be part of an aircraft-blocking program, and most commercial flight-tracking companies honor these privacy requests. It came as no surprise that Epstein's planes were part of such a program.

I found his tail numbers and registrations on his sex offender registration. I emailed one of the flight-tracking companies and gave them his numbers to see if there was a workaround.

"Isn't it that pedophile?" the man on the other end asked. His name was James Stanford, and he operated ADSBExchange, one of the last independent flight-tracking companies that didn't block planes. I told him what I was working on and he agreed to help. I tracked his plane as it crossed continents, marveling at how a child sex predator could travel in and out of the country without anyone checking who was on his plane. He could have been illegally smuggling young women from Europe and the Middle East and no one would have any idea.

By contrast, I couldn't even get past Homeland Security in the Fort Lauderdale airport without the agents seizing my moisturizer.

I tried to determine what agency would be responsible for checking people who arrive in the U.S. aboard private aircraft, and was directed to the Office of Homeland Security, which was not very helpful. I finally learned the name of the form that Epstein's pilots were required to fill out when they landed from overseas, and I placed a public records request for Epstein's. But the forms the government gave me were so heavily redacted that no one could tell who was on the plane with Epstein. They didn't redact his name, just the names of everyone else on board. It was another dead end.

I could nevertheless see where his travels were taking him, mostly to London and Paris, but also, oddly to Bratislava and Dubai. I also noticed something else: when he was coming in from Portugal, or some other far-flung country, he often flew directly into the airport at St. Thomas, bypassing the stricter customs and control that he likely would have faced if he flew into New York.

St. Thomas was notoriously corrupt, and it would have been fairly easy to get in and out of the airport without many people asking questions. It's a small airport, and the area where Epstein's jets landed was tucked away on the far side of the tarmac. His routine was to land on the runway, then hop a helicopter to his island. Rarely was he ever stopped and questioned. Air traffic controllers who worked the airport were afraid to speak publicly.

As Emily and I were preparing the documentaries to accompany my investigation, I got a call from one of my sources, telling me that Epstein was back in Palm Beach.

Emily and I collected our gear and headed immediately from Miami to the Palm Beach International Airport, a good two-hour drive, navigating the chaos of Interstate 95, hoping that the plane—and Epstein—wouldn't be gone by the time we arrived.

We got to a private aviation area of the airport, a section designated for jets owned by the millionaires of the world who make
weekend jaunts to the island. Epstein's jet was a sinister-looking, dark
blue Gulfstream IV.

The airport signs read "No Trespassing," and I wondered whether
Emily would be deterred, but she hopped out of the car, grabbed her
cameras, and walked up to a chain-link fence surrounding the tarmac. In the distance was Epstein's jet, its tail numbers clearly visible,
N212JE.

It didn't take long for a security guard to spot us, but by then
Emily had already got what she needed.

We then drove over to Epstein's mansion.

I had been by the house many times before. A few months earlier,
I accompanied one of the *Herald*'s photographers trained in taking
drone photographs, Pedro Portal, to Epstein's property. He launched
one over Epstein's mansion, taking aerial shots of the compound
from the street.

His house was no longer pink; it was now a statelier white, with
two wooden gates on either side of the house. The rear gate was open,
so Emily put a camera over her shoulder and we marched inside. I
walked up to the front door and rang the bell and shortly thereafter,
a woman came outside via a side door.

I told her I was a reporter for the *Miami Herald* and I wanted to
speak to Mr. Epstein. By now, he had to know we were working on
something because I had reached out several times to his lawyer, Jack
Goldberger.

"I am working on a story centered around the Crime Victims'
Rights lawsuit in the Jeffrey Epstein case," I had written Goldberger
in April, a month earlier. "As part of the project we are putting together a video documentary that does feature interviews with some
of Mr. Epstein's victims. Much of the information in the story is
based on court records, but we also have some new reporting connected to the case.

"To that end, I am reaching out to you for an interview. Ideally, we would like to also interview Mr. Epstein . . ."

Goldberger never responded. In hindsight, I think that had I been a reporter from the *New York Times* or the *Washington Post*, Epstein's attorneys would have paid closer attention to what I was doing. Maybe they would have even gone full throttle to quash the story.

But in the end, I think they just dismissed me as a little reporter from a local newspaper who was writing a story that no one would read.

THE WOMAN AT EPSTEIN'S DOOR TOLD US TO WAIT OUTSIDE. SEVERAL minutes went by before she returned and said that Mr. Epstein was not home.

I scrambled in my purse for a business card and cursed myself for not having one, knowing that I somehow never had one when I really needed it.

"Emily, do you have a card?"

She looked at me like I was crazy.

"Come on, give me one of your cards," I begged.

She reluctantly dug into her camera bag and pulled one out. I wrote my name and phone number on the back.

"SURE, LET HIM COME AND GET ME!" EMILY SPAT ON THE RIDE HOME, whining about how some villain would be at her house that very night stalking her family. We both laughed, but I knew her too well. She really wasn't kidding.

We would later learn that she was right to be concerned.

I guess I was bothered enough myself to call my two kids at school and tell them to be careful, to pay attention to their surroundings, and to avoid walking alone in desolate places, especially at night. Now in their late teens, they were familiar with this drill. They probably rolled their eyes, pretty much unimpressed by Mom's line of work. I had received threatening phone calls in connection with cases I had worked on before, and a couple of cop friends suggested more than once that I get a gun permit and learn to use one, especially during the years I was covering the prisons.

My boyfriend, Mr. Big, also got a little nervous. We had been together long enough that he remembered the time, years earlier, that I interviewed the former boss of the Philadelphia mob, "Skinny Joey" Merlino, who had taken up residence at a four-hundred-thousand-dollar condo in Boca Raton after serving twelve years in federal prison for racketeering. The heat from the feds was still on in Philly, where his associates were facing indictment, so Merlino traded the heat of the feds for the heat of South Florida.

THE MOBSTER NEXT DOOR, read the headline on Sunday's front page, the same day Mr. Big and I had taken a rare weekend trip.

"We are going to get killed," he said when he saw the story splashed all over the front page, complete with a graphic of a gun dripping with blood. It was an awesome front page and headline and one I wish I'd had framed.

"How'd ya find me?" Merlino asked in his thick South Philly accent. I had just knocked on his front door and I could hear a voice from above. He was standing on the balcony, wearing nothing but his underwear.

At five foot three, Joey didn't fit the description of one of the most ruthless mobsters of his time. He was an icon in Philadelphia, but no one in upscale Boca gave him a second look. Dubbed "the John Gotti of Passyunk Avenue," Merlino was a rock star back home, and I knew he had to miss the city, the cheese steaks and calamari especially, because he got VIP treatment everywhere he went in Philadelphia. I had met him once before, when I worked at the *Philadelphia Daily News* and covered his annual Christmas party for underprivileged children. In those days, mob hits happened every six weeks or so, and the media galvanized around him, waiting for him to be next. He had nearly been killed in a 1993 turf war involving mob boss John Stanfa, known as the Merlino-Stanfa war. A bunch of mobsters had pulled out their weapons in broad daylight on a South Philly street, shooting Merlino in the ass and killing his associate Michael "Mike Chang" Ciancaglini. During my time at the *Daily News* I covered my share of mob stories, including a murder trial, which was truly a scene ripped from the movie script of *Goodfellas*.

I told Merlino I was from Philly, and I think he was glad to see someone from home. I had already interviewed his neighbors, who told me he'd named his Wi-Fi connection "Pine Barrens," a reference to the heavily forested area near Atlantic City where gangsters often disposed of bodies.

IN SOME WAYS, EPSTEIN WAS LIKE MERLINO, WHO TRAVELED WITH AN entourage wherever he went, threw a lot of money around, paid people off, and threatened and intimidated prosecutors. Like any good mob boss, Epstein also made it his business to find his opponents' weaknesses, and to attack them when they were most vulnerable.

Emily and I just hoped we wouldn't end up dumped in Florida's mobster dumping ground—the alligator swamps of the Everglades.

chapter 19

MAR-A-LAGO

Virginia was driven back to South Florida and introduced to her new "owner," a man named David. In his late fifties, he was old enough to be her grandfather, but that didn't stop him from violating her the first night she arrived. She accepted this was her fate and resigned herself to a life of sexual servitude, believing that if she tried to escape, Eppinger would surely track her down and kill her.

"I thought many nights of escaping," she wrote in her memoir. "But where would I go? Would one of Ron's ever-so-connected informants find me and turn me in? I just prayed that I wouldn't be another missing person to add to the list of girls found in local ditches."

She didn't know that the FBI had been tracking her movements for weeks, having followed her from Eppinger's ranch in Ocala to the town house in Wilton Manors where she was living with David.

On June 11, 1999, at about 6:00 A.M., the FBI, along with local police, burst into David's house. They were clad in black military-style gear and helmets and armed with rifles.

Virginia was told to get dressed, and she was transported to the police station, where FBI agents questioned her for hours. She told them everything she knew about Eppinger and his sex trafficking operation. She also learned that they had found her in part through her friend Tony, who told enough people about Virginia's predicament that the FBI wiretapped their phone calls.

Before the FBI could get to him, Eppinger fled the country for the Czech Republic, where he had been traveling regularly to recruit girls for his trafficking operation. He was later extradited back to Miami and pleaded guilty in 2001 to charges of alien smuggling for prostitution, interstate travel for prostitution, and money laundering. Two Czech women were also charged as part of the enterprise, which spanned from New York to Miami.

He was sentenced to twenty-one months in prison but died while in jail.

AFTER THREE HOURS OF QUESTIONING BY THE FBI, VIRGINIA WAS LED out of the interrogation room at police headquarters to await a ride. She assumed she would be taken back to the same juvenile delinquent facility, and she prepared herself for the violent fights and strip searches, rooms with no windows, and officers armed with pepper spray. Home sweet home.

Virginia was spinning around in an office chair at the police station when she turned to see her father coming down the hall. She didn't know how to react, as deep inside, she was still full of anger over the pain that he had caused her throughout her childhood. Instead of wrapping her in his arms, he just shook his head. She knew she had to tell him what happened or the FBI would, so the story spilled out of her until he could not take it anymore, telling her to stop, his eyes wet with tears. To Virginia, however, his crying was just another sign that she had disappointed her parents again.

Her father turned to what would happen to her next, and before he could suggest another lockdown facility, she warned him that if he put her away again, she would escape to the streets and he would never see her again.

He put his head in his hands.

"Your mother doesn't want you to come home," he confessed. "She is making my life hell for even suggesting you come back."

In her memoir, Virginia recalled the last time she saw her mother.

Virginia had an eye infection and her mother put her in the car to take her to the eye doctor. To her shock, however, her mother pulled up in front of a familiar blue building and escorted her inside, where people in uniforms waited with clipboards. They walked her into a windowless room and locked the door behind her. She was left there, alone, for days, weeping at the thought that her mother had betrayed her.

Her father promised he would work something out, however, and vowed it wouldn't take more than a week or two to convince Lynn to welcome her daughter back. Virginia knew she had no choice, but warned him she wouldn't wait long. He got up and finally hugged her.

"One week, and I'm gone," she told him.

She was taken in handcuffs back to the juvenile facility that she had left more than a year earlier. She vowed to stay out of trouble, reminding herself that one way or another, she would be out in a week.

But when a week went by and her father didn't show up, she crafted her escape plan. Every so often she was taken to a lab to be tested for drugs, and one day that summer, a volunteer came to pick her up to transport her to the off-site lab facility. The car pulled into the parking lot, and Virginia took a deep breath. The driver unlocked the door and Virginia immediately bolted past him as he grabbed at her shirt. She sprinted away, as fast as she could.

She took some money from her scrunchie and bought a pair of

jeans, a shirt, and a sweater, then stopped and had a chocolate iced donut at Dunkin' Donuts. Her next stop was a pay phone to call her parents.

Her father answered the phone.

"I was just going to call you to tell you I'm coming to get you," he told her. "I found a foster home for you. It's a woman who has girls your age. Your mother was just getting ready to sign the papers."

Virginia felt anger erupt inside her at the thought of her mother still wanting nothing to do with her. She confessed to her father that she was on the run. He agreed to come pick her up so she could see her mother a final time before being shuffled off to another family.

The house didn't feel the same. Her parents had used her absence to renovate so thoroughly that she didn't even have a bedroom anymore. Her childhood space was now converted into an office, and all her belongings were gone.

"Of course, Mom didn't meet me at the gate or the front door . . . No, instead she waited for me to come find her out back smoking cigarettes and having beer," Virginia wrote. "She stood up from her seat and squinted her eyes with loathing and hatred, then she coldly slapped me hard in the face."

BOTH MOTHER AND DAUGHTER WERE BITTER AND ANGRY, VIRGINIA said. Finally, after an hour, her mother broke down and cried, agreeing to let her daughter stay—at least for the time being.

Over the next couple of weeks, there were family cookouts and bonfires, games and movie nights. She blended back into a routine, and she returned to school.

Virginia began working at fast food restaurants and later at a pet store. She had a boyfriend, James, who eventually moved in that year with her and her parents. She was just sixteen, but felt so much older than her years. The two planned to get married, and Virginia thought more about her future and what she wanted to do with her life.

In June 2000, when Virginia was sixteen, her father helped her get a summer job at Mar-a-Lago, the Palm Beach country club owned by Donald Trump.

(Virginia initially believed that she worked at Mar-a-Lago when she was fifteen, but employment records later obtained by her attorneys showed the correct time line.)

Her father had been working as a maintenance man there for many years and convinced his employers to hire Virginia that summer as a spa attendant.

She watched the masseuses at the spa and thought it seemed a serene way to earn a living.

She checked an anatomy book out of the library and began studying on quiet days in the spa locker room.

One day, as she was reading, a woman with a British accent walked up to her and inquired what she was reading.

"Do you do massage?" the woman asked.

"No, but someday I hope to study to become a masseuse," Virginia said.

"My name is Ghislaine Maxwell," the woman said.

Virginia introduced herself by her nickname, Jenna, and offered the woman, who appeared to be in her thirties, something hot or cold to drink.

She accepted a cup of tea and began to talk about how she worked for a wealthy man who was looking to hire a massage therapist. Maxwell suggested that Virginia meet him to apply for the job. Virginia was skeptical, pointing out that she didn't have the proper training.

But Maxwell assured her that she could learn on the job, noting that it looked as if Virginia was serious about her vocation—based on all the sticky notes she could see poking out of the anatomy book in her hands.

She gave Virginia her address and phone number.

"Why don't you come by after work?"

Maxwell left, with a cheery, almost motherly goodbye, and Virginia ran to tell her father about this new opportunity.

Late that afternoon, her father drove her to El Brillo Way. She remembers the house vividly—it was painted pink, surrounded by a massive wall. Her father walked her up to the large front door.

A butler in uniform answered, and immediately welcomed them inside. Maxwell floated down the long spiral stairway, kissed Virginia on her cheeks, and spoke briefly with her father before rushing him out the door, telling him that her boss was waiting to meet Virginia.

Virginia was in awe of the house, staring up at the crystal chandelier in the entry, the paneled walls and marble floors. Maxwell escorted her up the winding stairs to a dimly lit room with a king-sized bed, and just beyond the bed, there was a second, vast room with a turquoise massage table in the middle—where, to her surprise, she found a naked man.

She quietly assured herself that this good-natured, proper English woman was legitimately going to help her start a new life as a massage therapist.

Maxwell introduced the man as Jeffrey Epstein, as if Virginia would know who he was. He turned his head to the side and said, "Call me Jeffrey," and he smiled warmly, putting Virginia, for the moment at least, at ease.

This man did not look like someone to beware of, she thought.

Maxwell had prepped her, telling her to treat the session as a tryout.

"If you do well," Maxwell told her, "then maybe you could become Jeffrey's traveling masseuse, seeing the world and getting paid well for it."

In the beginning, it all seemed legitimate. Maxwell showed Virginia some techniques, starting with Epstein's feet, and then moving to his calves, instructing her to use upward strokes to push the blood up his legs. As they both continued the massage, Epstein and Maxwell began asking questions about Virginia's life.

It had only been a year since her ordeal with Ron and David, and she was still trying to reconcile the trauma she had experienced.

It didn't take long for them to coax her into talking about her childhood, and to learn that she had been a teenage runaway. They must have suspected what happened because they then began to ask blunt questions about her life on the street, which Virginia answered honestly.

They didn't seem appalled at all, but instead teased her for being such "a naughty girl."

"Not at all," Virginia replied defensively. "I'm a good girl. I just was always in the wrong places."

"It's okay," Jeffrey replied. "I like naughty girls."

With that, he flipped over, exposing his erect penis.

She looked at Maxwell for guidance, but the proper English lady was now topless. She began to undress Virginia as Epstein stroked himself. Maxwell slid off Virginia's skirt and underwear and began fondling her.

The sickness of the events brought her back to her days with Eppinger, and her body turned to stone. She mechanically went through the motions that she had been taught since childhood.

I'm not going to be worth anything at all. This is probably as good as it gets for me, she thought.

Afterward, Epstein led her into the steam room, just the two of them, and Maxwell left. He asked her to rub his feet as he chatted about the benefits of massage to help eliminate toxins in the body.

He was over-the-top pretentious, she thought, but she allowed him to enjoy the company of his own ego, imparting his supreme wisdom.

He told her he once had been a teacher, and used his intellect to earn billions of dollars as a financial adviser to wealthy billionaires.

After they had dried off, he pulled out a thick stack of hundred-dollar bills and pulled out two of them, handing them to her.

"This is probably more than you make in a whole week at Mar-a-Lago," he said, laughing.

That night, Virginia went home feeling shocked and ashamed. She wondered how she could have allowed herself to be violated again.

She got into the shower and scrubbed her body as hard as she could, trying to get the smell and feel of them off her body. She told no one what had happened, not even James, who seemed puzzled by her silence that evening.

She was supposed to return for another lesson the next day after work. She was quiet as her father drove to Mar-a-Lago that morning. Finally, he asked her whether something was wrong. She brushed him off and went to the spa, going about her day, her thoughts running from one extreme to the other—from telling herself it was wrong, to assuring herself that her new "job" might provide a path to eventual freedom, security, and prosperity.

She reasoned that if college girls could earn money by being strippers, she could certainly sacrifice her body a little bit longer to learn a vocation that would keep her off the streets. She told a friend she worked with about her new opportunity to learn massage, but inside, her stomach was full of knots.

That afternoon, her father again dropped her off at Epstein's mansion. The houseman, Juan Alessi, welcomed her in and escorted her to the kitchen, saying Maxwell would be down soon. A girl with blond curly hair was sitting behind a mound of paperwork. She introduced herself as Emmy, Maxwell's personal assistant.

"Hi, I'm Jenna," Virginia said. "I'm here on an employment tryout to become Jeffrey's personal massage therapist."

Virginia suspected from the look on her face that it wasn't the first time a girl had come for a tryout at Jeffrey's house.

The massage was the same as the day before, with both Epstein and Maxwell orchestrating the session. Virginia followed their orders like a soldier. She and Maxwell caressed each other, and the three of them began having sex.

Virginia soon realized that Epstein had an insatiable sickness that no one person, not even Maxwell, could fulfill.

"Jeffrey treated us girls like a piece of clothing he could try on for the day and get rid of the next," she would later write in her manuscript.

The routine continued for several weeks—working at Mar-a-Lago during the day and at Jeffrey's in the late afternoon into the evening. Maxwell and Epstein assured her that she was earning her masseuse stripes and that they would help her go to a proper massage therapy training program.

She began to get to know Emmy and some of the other girls, and there were times that they all chatted like friends. She said Maxwell, however, could be a tyrant, often glaring at her whenever she became distracted from her "work."

It was clear to Virginia that Maxwell was in love with Epstein. But Epstein and Maxwell rarely slept together or shared intimate moments, like holding hands or kissing. Virginia said this was because Maxwell was never able to satisfy Epstein's insatiable appetite for girls. Maxwell came to accept his obsession as long as those encounters remained purely sexual.

The two shared a kindred hedonism, Virginia said.

"It was an arrangement whereby she would bring him the girls, and he would give Ghislaine the kind of self-indulgent life that she was accustomed to growing up."

Maxwell has repeatedly denied that she ever had sexual relations with Virginia.

chapter 20

MADAM GHISLAINE

In the afternoon hours of November 5, 1991, the body of Robert Maxwell, one of the most powerful men in British publishing, was found floating naked in the Atlantic Ocean off the coast of the Canary Islands. The corpulent billionaire had last been seen in the pre-dawn hours that morning, on the deck of his 180-foot yacht, *Lady Ghislaine*—named after the youngest of his nine children.

The ship was cruising at about fourteen knots when crew members noticed their British liege on the starboard side of the yacht at about 4:25 A.M. He had a cold, and although it wasn't unusual for him to work into the early morning hours, it was quite late and the air very chilly for him to be outside. A short time later, Maxwell called the brig and asked that his air-conditioning be turned down.[1]

Earlier in the evening, the yacht's sixty-eight-year-old owner had been in a shouting match on the phone with his son Kevin over a meeting planned the following day with the deputy governor of the Bank of England. The Czech-born Jewish immigrant was notoriously stubborn, and he was procrastinating, his son would later explain. Maxwell wanted to remain at sea, putting off the meeting until the last minute. He was growing despondent over his mounting financial problems, including billions of dollars in loans for which he was in default.

By the time the ship docked at about nine thirty that morning off the Spanish Canary island of Tenerife, Maxwell, nicknamed "Captain Bob" in the British press, had disappeared.

The yacht's captain and crew were perplexed, finding it inconceivable that Maxwell could have gone overboard. For two hours, they scoured the vessel, calling his name, before resigning themselves to the possibility that something nefarious must have happened to their boss. A search-and-rescue mission was launched.[2]

Hours later, Maxwell's body was found by a fisherman, wafting faceup in the ocean, his arms outstretched, his naked body unmarked except for a small graze on his left shoulder.

A Spanish judge charged with investigating the billionaire's death declared that he had a heart attack before falling overboard, but his family were never convinced that his death was natural, accidental, or a drowning.

The questions surrounding his death, which continue to this day, mirrored the baleful air of mystery that Robert Maxwell relished in a life cloaked in money, power, and hubris.

Ghislaine was among the first family members to board the yacht the next day. At twenty-nine, Ghislaine was still the apple of her father's eye, and his most loyal confidante. Witnesses said his raven-haired daughter began frantically pulling papers from drawers and cabinets and throwing them on the floor. "I order you to immediately shred everything I have thrown on the floor," she demanded of the crew.[3]

She later denied these actions, but as the full scope of her father's financial crimes was revealed in the coming months, it appeared there was ample motive for concealing the media tycoon's corrupt business practices.

The rumor was that in the thick of his financial records Ghislaine discovered her father had been hiding money in offshore accounts, and the financier who was helping him was named Jeffrey Epstein.

The family's fortune in jeopardy, Ghislaine's brothers Kevin, thirty-two, and Ian, thirty-five, scrambled to conduct damage control for their father's crumbling empire, which included Britain's second-largest newspaper, the *Daily Mirror*, as well as the New York *Daily News* and the New York publishing company Macmillan.[4]

It turned out that, in a desperate effort to save his businesses, Maxwell had defaulted on two billion dollars in loans and then raided millions of pounds from his company's retirement fund, wiping out both shareholders and pensioners.

An investigation later revealed that Maxwell had formed a maze of shell companies and entered into illegal stock deals in a bid to keep the banks at bay and his company afloat.

The banks, however, got jittery as Maxwell's businesses lost money. They demanded more collateral, and Maxwell turned to the foreign exchange markets, gambling with funds he had looted from the pension funds of his public companies.[5]

After his death, the British tabloids relentlessly dogged the family, and photographers followed their every move.

MAXWELL'S WIFE, ELISABETH "BETTY" MEYNARD, A FRENCH PROTESTANT of Huguenot heritage, had worked for her husband's company. Meynard had studied law at the Sorbonne before meeting her future husband in Paris following the liberation of the city in 1944. The handsome British army sergeant had been born Jan Ludvik Hyman Binyamin Hoch in 1923, into a poor Orthodox Jewish family in the Carpathian Mountains of the Ruthenia region of Czechoslovakia. Most members of his family died in Auschwitz after his homeland was annexed by Hungary during World War II. In 1944, when the Germans invaded the country, he had already fled to France and joined the exiled Czechoslovak Army.[6]

An uprising within the Czech ranks led him to transfer to the British Royal Pioneer Corps, and eventually he went on to serve in other regiments across Europe, achieving the rank of captain. He was awarded a Military Cross for heroism in 1945, the same year he married Elisabeth, and he became a naturalized British citizen soon after. His children, Michael, Philip, Ann, twins Christine and Isabel, Karine (who died from leukemia at age three), Ian, Kevin, and Ghislaine, lived an affluent life of private schools, riding and tennis lessons, and extravagant birthday parties.[7]

After the war, Maxwell marshaled his military and government connections into a vast publishing business. With a background in British information services, Maxwell was among the first to understand how important technological research had been to the war effort. After the war, he collected scientific papers produced in Germany and arranged to have them published in English in the United Kingdom. In doing so, he turned academic and scientific publishing into a profitable new business model. He bought up information around the world that was often funded by public money, then translated and published the research in scientific journals that he sold by subscription. Maxwell's secret strategy was to establish such a vast number of journals that the established titles could support new ones. Circulation quite often exceeded expectations. As his enterprise grew, Maxwell rapidly began acquiring other publishing and printing companies, building an empire over the next decade.[8]

He became active in politics, and was elected to the British Parliament as part of the Labour Party in 1964, and again in 1966. He unsuccessfully tried to purchase the *News of the World*, which, at the time, was the world's bestselling English-language newspaper, a tabloid focusing on celebrity gossip and sex scandals. Australian publisher Rupert Murdoch, however, was also bidding on the paper, and Murdoch prevailed with the paper's owners, who bristled at the idea of selling it to an avowed socialist of Czech descent.[9]

Maxwell began manipulating his companies' stock portfolio by inflating sales and profits, and an audit in 1969 revealed that his financial accounts were fraudulent. He then lost control of his first and most prized publishing company, Pergamon.[10]

Condemned as a crook, Maxwell was undeterred, launching a relentless quest to buy Pergamon back, which he eventually did with borrowed funds in 1974.

Over the next decade, he bought a series of additional companies, including the British Printing Corporation and Mirror Group Newspapers, publishers of six British periodicals. He then launched a multimillion-dollar global spending spree, buying more newspapers, as well as pharmaceutical companies and TV stations, mostly bankrolled by loans.[11]

His purchase of the Mirror Group set off a legendary rivalry with Murdoch, as the two media barons spent nearly a decade slugging it out in a circulation war.

Maxwell was obsessed with beating Murdoch, and the two men later took their feud to the U.S., with Murdoch buying the *New York Post* and Maxwell, the New York *Daily News*.

As his empire grew, Maxwell was able to live an extravagant lifestyle, flying his helicopter from London to his fifty-three-room mansion, Headington Hill Hall, in Oxford, where he hosted glamorous, Gatsby-esque parties. His children were educated at the best schools, and as they grew older, he provided them highly paid jobs with his companies.

But he was an abusive egomaniac with his wife and children. He disapproved of his sons' marriages and was notoriously jealous of Ghislaine's boyfriends, believing that wives and boyfriends interfered with family duties.[12]

He beat all his children, even his favorite, Ghislaine, who, likely as a result, developed anorexia at a young age. A family friend, Eleanor Berry, described how, even as a nine-year-old, Ghislaine would order the servants around, telling them that the instructions were from her father, when that often wasn't the case.[13]

Berry, in a memoir, said Ghislaine talked about getting "hidings" from her father, and showed Berry an empty room with a table full of whipping instruments: a riding crop, a ruler, a stick, a cane, and a shoehorn.

She told Berry that her father would let her pick which instrument to use and he would then beat her with her trousers on.

In her own autobiography, Elisabeth Maxwell said the worst years of her life were 1981 until her husband's death, when he terrorized her and their children. He was known to tell them to "f— off" in front of others and treated his educated wife with particular disdain.

He had a compulsion for consuming large amounts of food, but despite his mammoth size, he exuded considerable charm and had several mistresses. He preferred to work with women around him but believed they were incapable of much more than secretarial work.

Ghislaine was doted on by her father almost from the time she was born in 1961—just days before her fifteen-year-old brother Michael was in a horrific car accident. He was in a coma for seven years until he died in 1967.[14]

During the 1980s, Ghislaine became a fixture of the London social scene, founding the Kit-Cat Club, a women's social salon that lured eligible men to meetings. But the real party was on her father's yacht, which he often brought to New York; guests sipped champagne and nibbled caviar flown in from Paris. Among the guests listed at one of the yacht parties in 1989 was Donald Trump—as well as former senators, U.S. envoys, and publishing executives. All were required to remove their shoes upon boarding.[15]

In March 1991, when Robert Maxwell signed the final agreement to take over the struggling New York *Daily News*, he vowed to rescue the city's largest tabloid following a crippling twenty-week strike. A profile of him in the *New York Times* quoted him as saying, "When I pass a belt, I cannot resist hitting below it." [16]

In London, Maxwell was ridiculed for his flamboyant ego, while in New York, he was hailed as a savior for rescuing the *Daily News*, despite his union-busting tactics. He sold Pergamon to cover his debts and then made plans to step down from his company in order to take the Mirror Newspapers Group public.

But in reality he was scrambling to keep up with his loan debt. In May 1991, he announced he would sell 49 percent of the Mirror Group to raise $228 million and reduce the company's debt load. [17]

MEANWHILE, THE WAR BETWEEN MAXWELL AND MURDOCH'S NEWS Corporation raged on as the two publishing magnates fought over coupons—one of the major revenue sources for their newspapers. The banks also wanted more collateral and $2.2 million worth of shares of Maxwell Communication stock were sold, further depressing the price of the stock. [18]

On October 31, 1991, Maxwell flew by helicopter to Luton Airport, just outside of London, and boarded his private Gulfstream jet, arriving in Gibraltar, where his yacht was docked.

From there, the yacht traveled to Funchal, on Portugal's island of Madeira. On November 4, he arrived in Tenerife, where he went ashore at about 8:00 P.M. Reports said he ate codfish cooked with clams and mushrooms, and had several beers at the Hotel Mencey, on a hillside resort in the port city. On the way back to his vessel, he asked the taxi driver to drive him around, and he stopped for coffee and brandy and then used a walkie-talkie to notify his crew that he was on his way back to the yacht.

Angus Rankin, the captain, greeted him aboard at about 10:00 P.M., news reports said.

Maxwell initially told Rankin to stay in Santa Cruz for a few days, but changed his mind and ordered him to head to the north end of Tenerife in the Canary Islands. Maxwell was restless, reports later said, and paced in and out of his stateroom most of the evening.[19]

The yacht headed toward Los Cristianos, a port on the southern coast of Tenerife. It anchored about two hundred yards from the beach near Los Cristianos at about 9:30 A.M., and shortly thereafter Maxwell's absence was noted.

The crew began searching the yacht, scouring it at least four times before calling authorities. They considered that their boss may have gone for a swim, but the distance to shore was the length of two Olympic-sized swimming pools, and it was unlikely the three-hundred-pound Maxwell would have made it.[20]

"I think we lost him overboard," came the call to marine authorities in Los Cristianos at about 11:30 A.M.

Almost immediately, theories circulated among reporters and others dispatched to help in the search. Did he fall while urinating over the rail? Did he have a heart attack? Did he decide to take his own life in the wake of financial ruin?

The original autopsy ruled he had died of natural causes, of heart and lung failure, but his family had doubts and ordered their own investigation, and further forensic tests. He was provisionally embalmed so that his body could be transported to Israel for burial, but his coffin was too large for the family's small jet and another day went by before a larger jet was chartered to carry the six-foot-seven-inch coffin to Jerusalem the following day.[21]

Maxwell's son Philip and Ghislaine stayed on board the family yacht in the days following his death.

Among those who claimed to have seen Maxwell's body was Ken Lennox, the *Mirror*'s senior photographer, who was dispatched to escort Maxwell's wife to the Canary Islands. Lennox said he agreed to identify the body to help spare Elisabeth's seeing a waterlogged cadaver.

By then, reports were being circulated that Maxwell might have been murdered, perhaps by Israeli Mossad agents.[22]

Maxwell was buried at a site in Jerusalem that he chose after visiting the Mount of Olives with Elisabeth three years earlier. It is near a memorial to the six million Jews murdered by the Nazis in World War II.

Six current and former heads of Israeli intelligence services attended Maxwell's funeral. Israeli prime minister Yitzhak Shamir eulogized him, describing Maxwell as "a person who was greatly interested in the Israeli economy, invested money in Israel, and offered to put his wide contacts on the international arena at Israel's service."[23]

Indeed, Maxwell had vast financial dealings in Israel, including a majority share in the Israeli daily newspaper *Maariv*.

He was hailed for opening factories that provided jobs and for having helped pave the way for Israel's interests around the world, by cultivating powerful people in politics and business from Moscow to London. He was personal friends with both former U.S. secretary of state Henry Kissinger and former Russian president Mikhail Gorbachev.[24]

In their 2003 book, *The Assassination of Robert Maxwell*, authors Gordon Thomas and Martin Dillon laid out evidence that for two decades Maxwell was a spy for the Mossad, who profited from disseminating Israeli intelligence-gathering computer software to Russia, the U.S., Britain, and other countries. The software was rigged with a mechanism to allow the Mossad to secretly tap into classified information gathered by the world's top intelligence agencies. The authors theorized that Maxwell was murdered because the publishing baron was so desperate to save his fortune that he blackmailed the Mossad, threatening to expose their spy activities if the agency's leaders didn't bail him out of financial ruin.[25]

JUST WEEKS BEFORE MAXWELL'S DEATH, FORMER *NEW YORK TIMES* reporter Seymour Hersh published a book about Israel's nuclear weapons program that implicated Maxwell and the *Mirror*'s foreign editor, Nicholas Davies, in a plot to help Israel capture dissident Mordechai Vanunu, a former Israeli nuclear scientist who was trying to sell Israeli nuclear intelligence to several newspapers, including the *Mirror*.[26]

Hersh contended that Davies was helping Israel broker arms sales to Iran and that Davies and Maxwell conspired to publish a disinformation campaign to discredit Vanunu as a fraud. A U.S.-born female undercover Mossad agent, posing as an American tourist, lured Vanunu to Italy, where he was captured by the Mossad and imprisoned for eighteen years for treason.

Maxwell sued Hersh, claiming the allegations were false.[27]

The exact cause of Maxwell's death remains a mystery. Three different autopsies were conducted, but the results were inconclusive. This gave rise to conspiracy theories, which his family for the most part dismissed.

After his death, his heirs were so absorbed by Maxwell's scandal that how and why he died seemed inconsequential to the goal of financial survival.

But three years after his death, his wife expressed frustration, regret, and anger that authorities had not conducted a more thorough investigation surrounding her husband's death, noting her belief that the initial autopsy by Spanish authorities was wholly inadequate and even suspect.[28]

A subsequent autopsy by the insurance company, conducted by forensic examiners in Israel, concluded that while the injuries he suffered may have suggested his death was accidental when he fell off the boat, they concluded that it was impossible to know whether it was a suicide, an accident, or murder.

His heart had been so dissected during the first autopsy that there was no way to tell whether he had had a heart attack.

"I said at the time—and will never alter my view—that Bob did not commit suicide," Elisabeth wrote in her autobiography, written in 1994.[29]

After her husband's death, their flat in London was auctioned off by Sotheby's. Then her sons Kevin and Ian, who were officers of their father's company, were forced to testify before the House of Commons with the ominous threat of criminal prosecution over their heads. The Maxwell empire was being carved up by creditors, and Elisabeth had no money and could not even secure a loan. She stated that her husband had not set aside a nest egg for her future or for the future of her children, and that she was destitute.

During this time, a financial benefactor appeared, giving her a mortgage on a home she owned in France in order to help repay some of her debts.

"Ghislaine was perhaps in the most difficult position of us all: although rumor had it she was a wealthy young woman, she was in fact left to restart her life on her own, with a bank overdraft and huge mortgage in a falling property market," Elisabeth wrote in her autobiography.[30]

Headington Hill Hall, the family's home for decades, was also auctioned, and in June 1992, her two sons were arrested. The press, having been tipped off, appeared in mobs with cameras. Bankruptcy followed.

Although she still owned a home in France, Elisabeth needed to stay in London to address the company's affairs and be closer to her children. But she was penniless, and there was no home to go to in England.

She said she approached "a friend" whom she referred to as a "white knight" who offered her a two-bedroom house. She would later describe the white knight as an American businessman whom her husband had introduced her to during his brief ownership of the New York *Daily News*. This businessman appreciated her husband's support of Israel, she said.

"He has remained unfailingly generous to me ever since," she wrote.[31]

The businessman who helped her has never been publicly identified.

But less than two weeks after her husband's death, the YIVO Institute for Jewish Research paid tribute to Robert Maxwell, an event that was planned prior to his death, to honor both him and his wife for their charitable work.

Elisabeth decided to go ahead with attending the event, held at New York's Plaza hotel on November 24.

Seated next to Elisabeth and Ghislaine at the event was a pudgy man with curly hair who was unknown at the time.

His name was Jeffrey Epstein.[32]

chapter 21

THE PRINCE AND THE PIPER

In 1992, the British media was fixated on Ian and Kevin Maxwell, who had been directors of their father's companies. Investigators alleged that the Maxwell brothers had illegally transferred ninety-one million dollars out of the public corporation's pension funds, and that their father had used that money to buy stock to prop up his failing businesses.[1]

Angry pensioners, bankers, and creditors were demanding the return of their money, as the Maxwell family empire collapsed. The New York *Daily News* filed for bankruptcy, and the family's assets were frozen. Liquidators moved in to recover whatever they could turn into cash.

Ghislaine Maxwell escaped the scandal by moving to New York and renting a one-bedroom apartment on the Upper East Side, which she furnished with flea market finds.

Despite her mother's claim that the family was broke, Ghislaine was rumored to be receiving one hundred thousand dollars a year from a million-dollar trust fund set up by her father.[2]

Detectives hired to trace her father's money were skeptical that Ghislaine had been left penniless.

"It is entirely possible, and we didn't have the resources to check, that Maxwell could have siphoned off money from some of his 400 companies in America to her. She was living on something," one investigator said.[3]

At twenty-nine, she was venturing into New York's social scene, attending fashion shows and restaurant openings. To her delight, she realized that very few people in New York cared about her family scandal. She set about reinventing herself in a way that she couldn't on the other side of the Atlantic, where victims of her father's fraud scheme were still palpably angry. On a visit to London, she wore a platinum-blond wig over her hair to disguise herself so she wouldn't be recognized by the media.[4]

Her sisters Christine and Isabel had moved to San Francisco, virtually vanishing from public life. The twins had married well and they amassed their own fortune in the 1990s Silicon Valley internet boom. One of their companies produced the internet search engine Magellan, which they sold for millions.[5]

Despite her Oxford education, Ghislaine, however, exhibited little ambition to build a business or a career. Having been born into a charmed life, she was known for entertaining, socializing, and shopping. The British tabloids took to calling her "the shopper" when she embarked on the Concorde to London for an extravagant shopping trip in November 1992. It was rumored she was living off her father's stolen money, and she showed little sympathy for the victims whom he had robbed.[6]

Upon her return to New York, she was seen accompanied by a graying, frumpy, overweight businessman who was barely noticed. Jeffrey Epstein was described as "a shadowy, almost maverick New

York property developer" who was said to be introducing Ghislaine to Manhattan's social circuit.[7]

The two had become inseparable, and within months, it was rumored that she had fallen in love with the mysterious financier. His friends attributed Epstein's rise in Manhattan society to "a remorseless attraction to well-connected, rich and beautiful women," because he had dated a former New York TV talk show hostess and several heiresses. He told people he worked for the CIA and Mossad, that he was a corporate spy and a concert pianist.

He was endlessly rich and spent lavishly on flamboyant clothes and cars. For Ghislaine, Epstein's presence in her life was familiar. Like her father, Epstein was a Svengali figure who mesmerized both men and women with his charm and intelligence. But also like her father, he had a dark, abusive, and controlling side, with little patience for those whom he considered unimportant or of inferior intelligence.

In 1999, Britain's Prince Andrew, newly divorced from his wife, Sarah Ferguson, was invited by Maxwell to visit Manhattan. Andrew had known Maxwell and her family for many years. He, too, was trying to find himself. On the heels of a messy divorce, Andrew agreed to escape to the U.S. and stay with Ghislaine at Epstein's Upper East Side mansion.[8]

Andrew was soon squiring Maxwell around Manhattan, attending social events and dinner parties. He was playing the field with a string of models whom he dated in Britain and the U.S.—and was caught on camera with a married thirty-nine-year-old woman at her bungalow in Hawaii.[9]

His flings came and went, but Maxwell remained by Andrew's side as his most loyal confidante.

In 2000, Ghislaine moved into her own lavish town house, about thirteen blocks from Epstein's mansion. Any romantic relationship she may have had with Epstein was apparently over. The New York tabloids referred to Epstein as Ghislaine's "estranged partner."

While the romance was in the past, Epstein put Ghislaine on his payroll and persuaded her to help him run his various households, plan his parties, arrange his social calendar, and hire interior designers and architects to refurbish his properties.

Soon Andrew and his ex-wife, Fergie, became regulars at Epstein's mansion whenever they came to the States. Epstein even loaned Fergie twenty thousand dollars to repay her debts. At the same time, he was using his friendship with the royals to help elevate his stature with prominent leaders in politics and government.[10]

It was rumored that Maxwell was on the verge of getting engaged to Andrew after the couple was spotted holding hands at an intimate lunch at a trendy New York restaurant. That same year, Andrew threw her a fortieth birthday party that cost twenty thousand pounds.[11]

Photographs appeared of him on a beach in Phuket, Thailand, with topless women—and he was seen socializing at Mar-a-Lago with a blond model and amateur astrologer who sold sex toys and Viagra-like impotence drugs.[12]

Epstein and Maxwell helped arrange for Andrew's entertainment, ensuring that he received VIP treatment at nightclubs in Miami and Los Angeles. Maxwell took Andrew to a "Hookers and Pimps" costume party in New York in 2000 that horrified his family.[13]

IT WAS DURING THIS TIME THAT MAXWELL WAS ALLEGED TO HAVE BEGUN recruiting young girls and women to work for Epstein, according to court records. Several women allege in lawsuits that Maxwell told them she worked for a wealthy man who wanted to hire assistants who needed help with their careers or education.

In 2001, Virginia Giuffre was still working for Epstein. She was starting to travel with him to his various homes around the country, and he was directing her to give massages and have sex with his friends. That spring, Epstein and Maxwell invited her to come and stay with them at Ghislaine's London home, a historic mews house in an exclusive section of the city, presumably purchased for her by Epstein.

"You're going to meet a prince," Maxwell told Virginia.

The two then went shopping for a new outfit.

THAT EVENING, SHE WAS INTRODUCED TO PRINCE ANDREW. MAXWELL tried to make Andrew guess how old Virginia was, and Maxwell seemed to delight in the fact that she was so young. The four of them—Epstein, Maxwell, Andrew, and Virginia—shared dinner, and then Virginia asked to take a photograph with the prince so she could send it to her family. The picture shows Andrew with his arm around Virginia's bare midriff and Maxwell smiling in the background.

They all then went to Tramp, a London nightclub. Virginia recalls dancing with a sweaty prince, who served her alcohol and put his hands all over her body.

Afterward, in the car on the way home, Virginia recalls that Maxwell told her that she should "do for Andrew what you do for Jeffrey."

Virginia was uncomfortable but obeyed. Back at the house, Virginia led the prince to an upstairs bedroom where she poured a bath and undressed. She later wrote about the encounter in her memoir, describing how the two of them got in the bathtub, and Andrew began licking her toes and caressing her body, telling her, "I love your feet. They are so irresistible."

They then had sex. "Afterward, he was not the same attentive guy I had known for the last few hours," Virginia wrote. "He quickly got dressed, said his goodbyes and slipped out of my bedroom."

She said Epstein paid her fifteen thousand dollars for her encounter with the prince. After that, she saw Andrew twice more: at Epstein's Manhattan mansion, where she had sex with the prince again, and on Epstein's island, where she claims Andrew participated in group sex with her and nine other young women.

The prince has denied all of her allegations. In a BBC interview in November 2019, Andrew said he had "no recollection" of ever meeting Virginia. Maxwell also denied that these events ever happened.[14]

ANDREW'S FRIENDS AND FAMILY HAD COME TO BELIEVE THAT HIS friendship with Maxwell and Epstein was dangerous.

"They are using him for his name and access and he is so innocent and naive that he doesn't realize they have ulterior motives," one friend told the *Mail on Sunday*.[15]

By this time, Maxwell had successfully risen to the top of Manhattan's social scene. She had become close friends with New York's elite, including the Clintons, hosting a VIP soiree to raise money for the Clinton library. In 2004, she was named by London's *Evening Standard* as one of the "Top Ten Naughty Heiresses."[16]

At parties, she regaled guests with stories about flying a Black Hawk helicopter in Colombia and firing a rocket at a terrorist camp. She joked about Prince Charles's girlfriend, Camilla Parker Bowles, and hosted parties that were so exclusive that people scrambled to obtain invitations.

Friends said she worshipped Epstein, who provided her with financial security. Maxwell, in turn, provided Epstein with connections and class. She and Epstein continued to entertain celebrities, politicians, and titans in business, science, and technology. Epstein, however, was often absent from the crowded gatherings. The center of attention was usually Ghislaine, who was colorful, outspoken, and even salacious, especially when it came to discussing sex. She once held a dinner party for socialites on the fine art of blow jobs, with dildos at each place setting.[17]

But her outrageousness on the party circuit hid a more sinister agenda that allowed her to keep up her lavish life. Working for Epstein, she took on the role of his madam, hiring young women and girls to feed his deviant sexual appetite. Some of the women and girls hired by Maxwell allege that she often took sexually explicit photographs of them and pressured them to perform sex acts with Epstein and others. Maxwell has repeatedly denied all this.

By the time Palm Beach police opened a probe into Epstein in 2005, Maxwell was dating a new man, Ted Waitt, the billionaire founder of Gateway computers.[18]

Court papers, however, claim she continued to recruit young women for Epstein. One of the women, identified as "Priscilla Doe" in a lawsuit, said Maxwell taught her how to sexually pleasure Epstein in 2006, when she was twenty.

By 2007, as the tawdry details of Epstein's crimes began to spill out, attention in the British media turned to Maxwell and Prince Andrew's connections to the disgraced money manager.

But in the U.S., Maxwell remained at the top of her game, appearing with celebrities and CEOs at one gala after another.

chapter 22

STARR POWER

On the surface, it defied logic that Jeffrey Epstein would hire an attorney made famous for authoring a steamy two-hundred-plus-page opus, known as the Starr Report, filled with graphic sexual details and moral rhetoric about one of Epstein's friends, Bill Clinton.

Kenneth Starr, the former independent counsel charged with investigating Clinton's financial dealings with the Whitewater Land Company, as well as his sexual relationship with former White House intern Monica Lewinsky, was the driving force behind Clinton's 1998 impeachment.

But the puritan compass that led Starr to climb upon a God-fearing perch and hold Clinton in contempt must have disappeared into his bank account when he agreed to help one of the most prolific and wealthiest sex predators in history.

Starr—and, indeed, all of Epstein's lawyers—has remained unapologetic for the tactics he employed in pursuit of liberty for a privileged man of perversion.

But Epstein didn't hire Starr because of his morals; he hired him for the connections he had in Washington to the Bush administration.

In the spring of 2007, Starr took center stage as part of a calculated defense strategy of trying to persuade the Justice Department that Epstein's crimes were not covered by federal law, and therefore should not be prosecuted by the Department of Justice.

Starr, along with Epstein's lawyers Jay Lefkowitz and Lily Sanchez, met with Acosta, Sloman, Villafaña, FBI agents, and Drew Oosterbaan, chief of the Justice Department's Child Exploitation and Obscenity Division. The defense argument was simple: there was no evidence that Epstein had crossed state lines to commit any crimes, thereby ruling out a federal nexus to the crimes he was accused of committing. However, the feds didn't use this mechanism for jurisdiction. They used the nexus they had successfully employed with hundreds of purveyors of child pornography via the internet, which was using "a facility or means of interstate commerce" to commit the crime. In Epstein's case, the vehicle wasn't a computer; it was the telephone, which he and his employees used to solicit girls for sex. The feds also alleged that Epstein and his co-conspirators used fraud or coercion for the purposes of soliciting someone for commercial sex. Both are federal crimes.

Still, Starr argued federal jurisdiction was weak at best, and that the crimes, if Epstein had committed any, should be left to the state to prosecute.

BY SPRING OF 2008, HOWEVER, STARR'S EFFORTS TO INFLUENCE THOSE in Washington were on full display. Emails and letters show that he and Lefkowitz were campaigning to pressure the Justice Department to drop the case.

Finally, on May 15, the Justice Department issued a decision.

Drew Oosterbaan informed Epstein's lawyers that Acosta had the right to prosecute Epstein in federal court.

"While you raise many compelling arguments, we do not see anything that says to us categorically that a federal case should not be brought," Oosterbaan wrote. "Mr. Acosta would not be abusing his prosecutorial discretion should he authorize federal prosecution of Mr. Epstein."

FOUR DAYS LATER, STARR ROLLED OUT A LAST-DITCH LETTER TO MARK Filip, a former Kirkland & Ellis colleague, who had just been confirmed as the deputy U.S. attorney general.

In the letter, Starr summoned up his most passionate legal soliloquy, using dramatic language reminiscent of the Starr report, and opening the letter with a reference to Attorney General Michael Mukasey.

"In his confirmation hearings last fall, Judge Mukasey admirably lifted up the finest traditions of the Department of Justice in assuring the United States Senate, and the American people, of his solemn intent to ensure fairness and integrity in the administration of justice," Starr wrote.

"We come to you in that spirit and respectfully ask for a review of the federal involvement in a quintessentially state matter involving our client, Jeffrey Epstein."

The eight-page letter listed all the arguments that the defense team had conjured up in the past, but added another brutal punch: allegations of prosecutorial misconduct. Specifically, Starr alleged that the tentative plea deal Epstein's lawyers struck with federal prosecutors was engineered to profit lawyers with personal relationships to the prosecutors involved in the case. Starr was obviously referring to Miami's deputy U.S. attorney, Jeffrey Sloman, whose former law partner, Jeff Hermann, was representing a number of Epstein's victims in civil lawsuits they filed against Epstein.

While it was true that Sloman had been partners with Hermann, it was only for four months in 2001, long before the Epstein case. Hermann had also built his solo practice handling sex abuse cases, having won millions in settlements for Catholic priest abuse victims.

Epstein's lawyers also went after Villafaña, alleging that she had been trying to steer a lucrative role in the restitution agreement to an attorney who was friends with her boyfriend, an allegation that she disputed.

"It was a scorched-earth defense like I had never seen before," said one prosecutor connected to the case. "Marie broke her back trying to do the right thing, but someone was always telling her to back off. We never really knew who it was, we just thought it was very odd."

The prosecutor said that it was clear that someone in Washington was calling the shots on the case. Villafaña was facing pushback, even after she warned fellow prosecutors that Epstein was likely still abusing young women and girls.

"It almost felt like they were sneaking around behind her back," the prosecutor said.

Villafaña tried to get prosecutor Andrew Lourie, who was in charge of the major crimes unit, to sign off on presenting the indictment, but he refused.

Said the prosecutor: "It was clear that she had to find a way to strike a deal because a decision had already been made not to prosecute Epstein."

In the end, prosecutors asked a judge to select the attorney who would represent Epstein's victims and help them obtain settlements. The problem, however, was that the lawyer who was ultimately selected, Robert Josefsberg, would be paid by Epstein. This created an inherent conflict of interest that remains controversial to this day. The girls who were represented by Josefsberg, for the most part, received lesser settlements than those who hired private attorneys. But in settling, Josefsberg's victims were spared some of the torture that

Epstein mounted against those girls who hired their own lawyers and fought for larger settlements.

Villafaña obviously didn't anticipate this, because the deal called for Epstein to treat victims as if he had been convicted of trafficking crimes; in other words, Epstein was required to settle the civil claims filed by the identified victims without attacking and discrediting them. But this was just another way that Epstein flouted the agreement, and prosecutors failed to hold him accountable for his civil lawyers' intimidation tactics.

ON JUNE 2, A LETTER WAS DRAFTED TO FILIP DEFENDING PROSECUTORS' ongoing probe of Epstein, and that week, additional grand jury subpoenas were prepared in hopes that Filip would allow the case to proceed. Filip was asked by defense attorneys to intervene, but there's no record whether he did or not.

Justice Department sources I spoke to, however, said that Filip, without comment, sent the case back to Acosta to handle. Acosta had the green light to prosecute Epstein.

But instead of taking the case directly to trial, federal prosecutors resumed plea deal negotiations with Epstein.

A FEW WEEKS LATER, ON JUNE 27, 2008, BRAD EDWARDS GOT A CALL from Villafaña.

"It was a Friday, and Marie called me and said that Epstein was taking a plea in state court on Monday. And I said, 'Okay, for what?' "

A plea on state charges did not necessarily mean the end of a federal investigation. Edwards asked Villafaña whether his clients, who were part of the federal case, were the victims listed in the state plea.

"No, these are not the federal sex trafficking charges," Villafaña replied, evading the question Edwards had asked.

Believing that the federal case was ongoing, and that the plea was connected to other victims investigated by the state, Edwards sent an associate to the courthouse on Monday to sit in on the hearing.

The associate called afterward.

"I'm not even sure what happened," the associate told Edwards. "They talked about prostitution charges and where he was going to jail, and neither the victims nor their attorneys were in court."

Edwards called Villafaña, who informed him that the federal case was also now settled. She wouldn't give him any details, but he sensed that she was frustrated. She told him that he could object in writing.

This gave Edwards hope that the deal wasn't final. On July 7, Edwards marched an emergency petition to the clerk's office at the federal courthouse in West Palm Beach.

"Is this a civil case or a criminal case?" the clerk asked.

Edwards, who had never filed a petition in federal court, wasn't even sure. In his petition, Edwards argued that Epstein's sentence should be suspended until prosecutors fulfilled their requirements under the Crime Victims' Rights Act. Among the law's requirements is that victims have a right to be informed about a plea deal; and victims must be given an opportunity to appear in court at their perpetrator's sentencing. Because the victims had not been told about the plea deal or the sentencing, Edwards believed that the prosecutors had broken the law.

"I want a hearing today," he told the clerk.

"This isn't even labeled an emergency," the clerk pointed out.

"Give it back to me," Edwards said. He scribbled across the top "EMERGENCY."

The petition was assigned to U.S. District Court Judge Kenneth A. Marra, a federal judge based in West Palm Beach. Marra issued an order that day, directing the U.S. Attorney's Office to file a response to Edwards's petition in two days.

Acosta assigned Assistant U.S. Attorney Dexter A. Lee to respond. Two days later, on July 9, Lee filed what would become the first of many sealed documents in the case.

Lee argued that federal prosecutors were not obliged to inform any of the victims of a state plea, only of a federal plea. They had sealed the agreement and now refused to release it.

IT WOULD TAKE TWO MORE MONTHS BEFORE EDWARDS WAS ALLOWED TO see the plea agreement—and by then it was too late. Epstein was already in jail serving his sentence.

No one, including the other victims, the media, or the public, would know for almost a year the extent of trickery that the government had used to shield Epstein, as well as his co-conspirators.

The Crime Victims' Rights case would languish for many more years, as lawyers for the victims in 2008, 2009, and 2010 filed a flurry of separate civil lawsuits against Epstein. Among the fruits of those lawsuits were the hundreds of pages of correspondence between Epstein's lawyers and federal prosecutors that Edwards managed to pry from the government during the course of the litigation.

Those emails and letters would prove to be the undoing of federal prosecutors: they illustrated in detail the extent of cooperation between the prosecutors and Epstein's lawyers.

I soon learned that just about every prosecutor or criminal investigator who touched the Epstein case saw their careers advance in the years that followed. There were a few exceptions, the most notable of which was Villafaña, who remained with the U.S. Attorney's Office in South Florida. The lead FBI agent, Kuyrkendall, eventually transferred out of her unit and retired.

WHAT MANY, ALTHOUGH NOT ALL, FEDERAL PROSECUTORS DO IS TAKE the connections that they've gained in public service straight to the bank. They go into private legal practice, or they become bankers, consultants, lobbyists, political operatives, or fixers, like Kenneth Starr, who used his political connections in the White House to get the Justice Department to review Epstein's case.

Then they can earn lots of money from wealthy people, like Epstein, who are trying to get away with bad deeds.

Of course, none of this is illegal.

chapter 23

BAIT AND SWITCH

On June 30, 2008, Jeffrey Epstein walked into the Palm Beach County courthouse with his attorney, Jack Goldberger, at his side. At the bench before them that morning, however, was not the judge who had been assigned to the case a year earlier—it was a retired senior judge who filled in.

One of the enduring mysteries of the Jeffrey Epstein case is how and why the judge assigned to Epstein's criminal case, Sandra Mc-Sorley, was absent on the very day that Epstein entered his plea and was sentenced.

The transfer of such a high-profile case from an experienced criminal judge—with a history of scrutinizing plea deals—to another judge who wasn't fully briefed on the case represented another break for Epstein that probably was no accident.

Fifteen years later, the case is still raising questions about judicial politics, procedures, and ethics.

A review of the criminal case file shows that the date of Epstein's plea hearing was set on a Friday, just three days in advance. And it was scheduled for a Monday, a day on which McSorley usually had a full docket. The signature on the document notice that was filed is illegible, and the county clerk to this day doesn't know who submitted the notice for the hearing.

Prior to the hearing, emails show Villafaña had briefed State Attorney Barry Krischer and prosecutor Lanna Belohlavek, telling them to give as little detail to the judge as possible. The actual paperwork would be sealed, so it would be Belohlavek's job to assure the judge that prosecutors—and victims—were all in agreement with Epstein's plea.

McSorley had a history of being at loggerheads with both prosecutors and defense attorneys. She was a tough judge, and her bar ratings reflected that. She was rated among the lowest in the county bar association's poll of its members.

In February 2008, McSorley was forced to step down from another case after she refused to accept the defendant's plea deal. The twenty-two-year-old defendant, Charles Tyson, was facing the death penalty if convicted of first-degree murder in the death of his nine-month-old son.

He decided to take a plea offered by, ironically, Belohlavek.

Belohlavek said that some of Tyson's family members wanted to avoid the stress of a trial and had agreed to the deal.

McSorley, however, was disturbed that the father "was not taking responsibility for his actions," adding that while the victim's family is an important factor to consider, the ultimate decision rests with the judge or a jury, calling the baby's death "egregious."[1]

A year earlier, McSorley had rejected another plea, involving a West Palm Beach man charged with vehicular homicide. The driver, who was behind the wheel of a septic tanker, ran a red light and struck a minibus carrying thirteen people from a retirement home. Two of them died.[2]

Also in 2007, McSorley only reluctantly accepted a plea involving a drunken driver who had crashed into a pregnant woman who subsequently lost her unborn child. At the plea hearing, McSorley grilled the county's veteran traffic homicide prosecutor, pointing out that the plea was too lenient, given that DUI manslaughter cases usually end with longer prison terms. The defendant's lawyer in that case was none other than Jack Goldberger, who did some legal acrobatics to make sure the deal went through.[3]

Goldberger knew from experience that McSorley might raise serious questions about Epstein's plea, and if she rejected it, her decision could be so controversial that it might lead to frenzied media attention.

"Epstein had a lot riding on this plea. There was no way that they were going to let McSorley handle it, it would have been too much of a risk," said a retired Palm Beach County judge who declined to be identified.

Jack Scarola, a former assistant state attorney who is now a veteran criminal defense lawyer representing some of Epstein's victims, said it's not beyond the realm of possibility that the judges' docket was manipulated.

"Sandra McSorley had a reputation as a tough judge. It is certainly possible for a defense attorney who is concerned about how a particular judge might react to particular circumstances to maneuver things in ways that would enable that defendant to avoid that judge on something like the entry of a plea," Scarola said.

"All it takes is for the defense lawyer and the prosecutor to inform the judge that we have a plea and we would like to present it. It's not unusual to wait for an opportunity to present that plea to an alternate judge, and with the cooperation of the prosecutor, that is possible."

McSorley, in an interview, said she couldn't recall the exact reason she didn't handle Epstein's hearing that morning.

Palm Beach police chief Reiter said he was told by the state attorney's office that McSorley called in sick. McSorley, who admitted she has a fuzzy memory of the case, said she believes she was in court that day.

"I seem to remember I was busy doing other things and someone came up to me and asked if I was available. I don't recall exactly, I may have even told them to give it to another judge," said McSorley, who is now retired.

But she insisted there was nothing unusual about a switch. Judges help each other out with caseloads all the time.

AT 8:40 A.M. THE SUBSTITUTE JUDGE, DEBORAH DALE PUCILLO, TOOK THE bench.

"Good morning, Judge. Jack Goldberger on behalf of Jeffrey Epstein."

"Good morning," Pucillo replied.

"Your Honor, we are here for a plea conference," Goldberger said. Epstein was sworn in.

For the next twenty minutes, the judge discussed the paperwork, then turned to Epstein to discuss the sentence.

"You understand once you do your twelve months following your six months in the Palm Beach County jail you will then be put on community control, which involves having an electronic monitor attached to you and—"

Goldberger interrupted, telling the judge that Epstein didn't have to wear an ankle bracelet.

Epstein was exempted from a sex offender treatment program, and he didn't have to submit to polygraph exams or serve any community service time.

One by one, the rules that applied to most sex offenders were stricken from Epstein's plea sheet.

"He has already been in treatment with a private psychiatrist," Belohlavek told the judge.

"I assume you have a law degree and do not have a Ph.D. in

psychology or M.D. in psychiatry?" Pucillo said, not hiding her sarcasm. "So it's just your judgment that his treatment with some fancy private psychiatrist or psychologist in this case is okay?"

"Yes, that's correct," Belohlavek said.

Pucillo turned to Epstein's incarceration, noting that the plea called for him to serve his eighteen-month sentence in the county jail.

"Why twelve months in the Palm Beach County jail followed by six months? Why not just send him to [state prison]?"

GOLDBERGER: "It is the agreement of the parties, your honor. We just decided that was the best way to accomplish what needed to be done here, and the parties agreed that the sentence satisfied everyone's requirements."

PUCILLO: "The taxpayers of Palm Beach County [are] going to pay eighteen months to house this guy instead of DOC [Florida Department of Corrections]?"

BELOHLAVEK: "Right."

The judge asked Epstein whether he had been given any inducements to take the plea and Goldberger responded by asking the judge for a conference at sidebar.

"The reason why I asked to come to sidebar," he whispered to Pucillo, "is there is a non-prosecution agreement with the United States Attorney's Office that triggers as a result of this plea agreement. In other words, they have signed off and said they will not prosecute Mr. Epstein in the Southern District of Florida for any offense upon his successful taking of this plea today. That is a confidential document that the parties have agreed to. Just in an abundance of caution, I wanted to tell the court."

"I would view that as a significant inducement in accepting this plea," Pucillo said.

"Are all the victims in both of these cases in agreement with the terms of this plea?" Pucillo asked in open court, near the end of the hearing.

"I have spoken to several myself, and I have spoken to counsel, through counsel as to the other victim, I believe, yes," Belohlavek said.

Pucillo: "And with regard to the victim under the age of eighteen, is that victim's parents or guardian in agreement with the plea?"

"That victim is not underage anymore. That's why we spoke to her counsel," Belohlavek said.

"And she is in agreement with the plea?"

"Yes."

CONTRARY TO WHAT BELOHLAVEK TOLD THE JUDGE, NEITHER THE GIRL at the heart of the state plea deal nor her lawyer were ever told about the deal.

All along, everyone had assumed that the victim who testified before the state grand jury—the only victim to testify, Jane Doe 1—was the girl who was the victim in the plea. Her lawyer, Spencer Kuvin, happened to hear about Epstein being in court that day and wanted to serve him with her civil lawsuit, so he appeared at the hearing.

Kuvin said he, too, assumed that at least one of the victims mentioned at the hearing was his client. In truth, Epstein's lawyers had somehow convinced state prosecutors to switch the victims. No one would learn about this until years later.

Instead of Jane Doe 1, they picked another victim, whose initials are on the plea paperwork. The agreement was sealed, however, so no one really knew for certain who the girl was.

That victim's attorney, Robert Josefsberg, insists prosecutors didn't tell him or his client that she was the victim listed in the plea deal.

So why did they switch the victims?

Because the victim named in the plea was seventeen years old, and Jane Doe 1 was fourteen, when she was molested. By picking a victim who was seventeen, it made it easier for Epstein not to have to register as a sex offender in some jurisdictions where it was legal to have sex with a girl who was seventeen, but not fourteen.

It's not clear whether Villafaña knew about the switch, but Krischer and Belohlavek had to know because they signed off on the information.

Two weeks later, McSorley—back on the case—filed another Order of Community Control in the case, reversing Pucillo's decision to allow Epstein to escape electronic ankle monitoring. McSorley signed an order mandating that Epstein be monitored twenty-four hours a day with the device, and that he serve a term of mandatory community service.

But a year later, shortly before Epstein was set to be released from jail, Epstein's lawyers filed a motion to clarify what they called a "scrivener's error" to reverse McSorley's order. They shrewdly waited to file it before another judge, Jeffrey Colbath.

chapter 24

THE GET OUT OF JAIL FREE CARD

Jeffrey Epstein stood in the doorway to his cell at the Palm Beach County jail, stark naked and angry.

"Guard! Why is my light on?" he demanded. It was late. While most inmates had to sleep with a small light on in their cells so that guards could ensure they weren't doing anything nefarious, Epstein had been allowed to sleep in the pitch-darkness of his cell, with the door open, something that was a safety concern for some of the jail deputies, especially the female officers in the unit who had no warning when he would exit his cell with his penis on display.

Corrections officer Angela Watkins looked up from her desk. The sixty-year-old sex offender ordered her to call a supervisor, telling her he had permission to sleep with the lights out. Watkins was stunned but made the call. She was told to turn the light back out.

Watkins told me she filed a complaint but later learned that it was dismissed. When I asked for records of complaints filed against Epstein while in sheriff's custody, I was told there were none.

Epstein's money and status enabled him to get many perks while in jail. His commissary account showed he had purchased two pairs of women's size 5 panties at the jail's shop, along with two thousand dollars in other items, including eight hundred cups of coffee and twenty-two tubes of toothpaste. He also asked one of his paralegals to bring him a book titled *Face Exercises That Prevent Premature Aging*. The book was confiscated as contraband.[1]

Captain Mark Chamberlain seemed sympathetic to the fact that Epstein might find a jail a bit uncomfortable.

"His financial status lends itself to his being victimized while in custody and as such, he has been placed in special management," Chamberlain wrote in an email to his subordinates. "He is poorly versed in jail routine . . . and his adjustment to incarceration will most likely be atypical. For the time being, I am authorizing that his cell door be left unlocked and he be given liberal access to the attorney room where a TV will be installed."

He was also given access to a computer. On at least one occasion, a jail deputy saw him masturbating while he was watching one of his female assistants strip naked on Skype.

THERE WAS NO PUBLIC OUTCRY WHEN THE *PALM BEACH DAILY NEWS* wrote that Epstein, within weeks, was first relocated to a special wing of the county jail and then given work release.[2]

From that point on, almost every day, Epstein's security guard and valet, Igor, picked him up at the jail each morning in a black SUV. Igor drove Epstein (with a sheriff's escort behind him) several miles to downtown West Palm Beach, where Epstein had set up an office right inside Goldberger's law suite overlooking the sparkling Intercoastal Waterway.

The sheriff's deputies, not the county corrections officers, were given the lucrative special detail assignment of checking in at Epstein's "office" from the time he arrived, at about 10:00 A.M. every day, until he left, sometimes as late as 10:00 P.M., six days a week.

I wanted to know what other benefits Epstein received and who signed off on them.

But the sheriff, Ric Bradshaw, refused to talk to me about the case, even to this day.

The Palm Beach Sheriff's Office is the largest law enforcement agency in Palm Beach County, providing police services for about a dozen municipalities and residents who live in unincorporated areas of the county. It also oversees the county jail system. However, the Town of Palm Beach, where Epstein's mansion was located, is policed by its own independent department, called the Palm Beach Police Department.

Reporters over the years have often conflated the two law enforcement agencies, wrongly leading the public to believe that it was Palm Beach *police*—and not the sheriff's office—that gave Epstein his cushy jail privileges.

Bradshaw, who has been sheriff since 2004, has long been considered one of the most powerful politicians in Palm Beach County. For years, he has mounted what I saw as a relatively successful gaslighting campaign about his role in Epstein's work release. Bradshaw maintains that, despite having a super-connected notorious sex offender in his jail, he didn't know anything about the benefits that Epstein received on his watch.

Bradshaw's spokeswoman, Teri Barbera, had given me a copy of the work release policy to clarify the agency's policies regarding sex offenders. But the document she sent me for my series clearly noted that convicted sex offenders were not eligible for work release in Palm Beach County.

When I pointed out to her that the department violated its own policy, she tried to claim that Epstein wasn't a *registered* sex offender until he was released and had to formally register. The problem with this argument is that the Palm Beach Sheriff's Office had never given any other offender charged with a sex crime work release. Only Epstein.

Villafaña learned, just days after Epstein was sentenced, that he was going on work release—and strenuously objected, writing to Bradshaw's chief deputy, Michael Gauger, that the release seemed to violate the agency's own policy, and that Epstein had clearly misrepresented details about the charity he set up for the purposes of work release.

Spending time "making telephone calls, web-surfing, and having food delivered to him is probably not in accordance with the objectives of imprisonment," Villafaña wrote on July 3, 2008.

As I dug deeper into Epstein's incarceration, I found that the first version of his "work release program" prohibited him from leaving his "office" for any reason, other than for emergency medical treatment.

But a revision of the program was made especially for him. The language was changed so that Epstein could leave his office "if authorized by [the sheriff's department's] Alternative Custody Unit."

After that, Epstein made at least sixty-nine visits in six months to doctors, sometimes for two appointments in one day. He would also travel as often as three times a week to a chiropractor in Lake Worth, records show.

He had so many appointments that the deputies assigned to monitor him struggled to keep up with his movements.

The work release was arranged by another of Epstein's longtime lawyers, Darren Indyke, who filed the initial paperwork and was also listed as vice president of the charity being run out of Epstein's office, the Florida Science Foundation, which was created just before Epstein went to jail.

"I realize that this permit is very unique," Lieutenant Steven Thibodeau wrote in an October 23, 2008, internal email discussing the changes to Epstein's work release. "However, job profiles are often modified to satisfy the client's needs or provide clarification. Considering the sensitivity of this permit, I would ask that you consider the proposed revised job profile."

I noticed how the sheriff's department was calling Epstein not an inmate but a "client."

Epstein paid the sheriff's office more than $128,000 to cover the cost of the special off-duty details. While these facts and others were reported by the *Palm Beach Daily News* over the years, I still wanted to review everything in detail, looking for something that perhaps others had missed. As a result, I did unearth new information.

Barbera, a ten-year veteran of the sheriff's office, often claimed that she didn't understand what I was asking for, or that the documents I requested didn't exist, at least not the way I was describing them. But to me, it seemed like she was being deliberately evasive. After all, her résumé said she had experience working in booking, inmate records, work release, in-house arrest, corrections administration, off-duty employment, human resources, and media relations. She was also president of a group designed "to improve communication and develop professional relationships among government agencies and the media," according to the sheriff's department website.

I piled on the public records requests until I got at least some of what I asked for. I never received everything.

I requested, for example, all the sheriff's emails that contained the name "Epstein" between 2005 and 2011. I got one email, which was completely blank except for the date at the top:

Thursday, March 31, 2005 9:04:35 A.M.

I wondered why Bradshaw would have an email about Epstein dated one week after the first victim came forward to the Palm Beach Police Department.

I subsequently learned that right around the time I was requesting public records from the sheriff's department, a meeting was held with one of its computer vendors at which the vendors were asked whether there was any way to wipe certain documents from the system. The source who told me about this meeting would not go on the record out of fear of Bradshaw, who had been accused of taking retaliatory actions against those he felt were disloyal.

However, I was unable to confirm this tip, which came from a reliable source.

The officers assigned to Epstein's work release detail were directed to dress in suits and ties, not in uniform. And because they made a lot of overtime doing these shifts, they had no reason to report him when he broke the rules. In fact, they even allowed Epstein to occasionally stop and check on his Palm Beach mansion. While he was required to wear an ankle monitor, the reports often indicated at times that the monitor "wasn't working."

After many requests, I finally received the forms that the deputies were required to fill out at the beginning and end of their shifts. There were probably at least two hundred of them. The first batch the sheriff's office delivered to me were so heavily redacted that I sent Barbera an email asking her to explain these redactions. Under Florida's public records law, the reason for redactions must be spelled out. After some back and forth, she re-sent me a new stack with fewer redactions. I took the win.

These forms were similar to time sheets. The first deputy of the day, for example, would write down his arrival time, then log visitors in and out, noting whether anything unusual happened. The next deputy would arrive to relieve the first deputy, take possession of the logbook, and continue to log in visitors.

At the end of the day, the logbook was placed back into a safe that Epstein had control of in his office.

I asked Barbera for the actual logbook and was told that it no longer existed.

I also tried without success to get some of the deputies who worked Epstein's detail to discuss their time "guarding" him. This meant also trying to figure out who they were, since their full names did not appear on the reports.

I asked for, and received, a full list of all the sheriff's department employees.

By now, many of them had retired. As law enforcement officers, their phone numbers were hidden from public databases. I contemplated how long I would be able to spend looking for sheriff's deputies who didn't want to be found, especially by reporters.

I did get a brief interview with one deputy. He told me that he had no idea what Epstein did all day because his job was simply to sit outside his office and log people in and out. He never asked questions.

"Didn't you check on him to make sure he wasn't doing anything wrong?" I asked.

"That wasn't my job," was his reply.

The logs of visitors in and out of the Palm Beach County jail were still available, and they were a who's who of high-profile names, including Alan Dershowitz, who visited Epstein on New Year's Day 2009, and Arnold Prosperi, a college friend of Bill Clinton's, who saw Epstein nearly two dozen times. But the person who visited him the most, more than one hundred times, was Story Cowles, who listed himself as a paralegal, but really just seemed to be a babysitter hired by Goldberger to keep Epstein company. Epstein's female assistants, Kellen and Marcinkova, were also frequent visitors, according to the jail logs. Kellen, who dated and later lived with Cowles, continued to work for Epstein until she married race car driver Brian Vickers in 2013.

There were so many questions raised about Epstein's incarceration that the Palm Beach Sheriff's Department posted a video explainer online in July 2019. In the clip, Deputy Chief Michael Gauger described Epstein as a model prisoner who swept floors and exhibited such good behavior that he was elevated to the job of houseman, allowed to leave his cell and collect fellow inmates' food trays.

"I'm just saddened that some people thought it was corruption, that he was given all these privileges because of his wealth," Gauger said in the video.

After Epstein's release from jail, in July 2009, Epstein's community control, a form of house arrest, was minimal at best. Records show he spent five hours a day at Home Depot and large blocks of time at Sports Authority, even though this was not permitted under the guidelines set by the Florida Department of Corrections. He received permission to travel by plane to his island off the coast of St. Thomas, and to visit his mansion in New York for business and legal reasons. His state probation officer never seemed concerned.

Once, Epstein was stopped by a Palm Beach police officer when he was walking along South Ocean Boulevard during the middle of the day. Epstein told the officer he was walking to work, but the route he was traveling was not in the direction of downtown West Palm Beach. He should have been arrested on the spot, but his probation officer intervened, saying he was allowed to have exercise.

Epstein was released from jail a month early, on July 22, 2009.

It was the same day as a rare total solar eclipse, perhaps signaling a return of the Epstein darkness.

chapter 25

SHOE-LEATHER REPORTING

During my project, I often consulted with Jay Weaver, the *Herald*'s veteran federal courts reporter. At the time, he was busy with his own work, carving out a series of stories about a complex web of drug traffickers and money launderers involved in the brutal international trade of mining gold, a project that would be nominated for a Pulitzer Prize the following year.

Jay knew the Epstein story well, especially the players in the U.S. Attorney's Office, whom he had covered during his twenty years on the beat. I wanted him to work some of his sources, and I asked him to help me with the story.

He was polite, but he didn't think anyone would talk. I don't think he really grasped the reason why I was pursuing the Epstein story again. He knew Acosta professionally, and was still close to Acosta's former deputy assistant U.S. attorney, Sloman. Jay told me that Acosta and Sloman remained loyal to each other and it was unlikely that Sloman, a Democrat, would talk because he had spear-headed a bipartisan effort to support Acosta's nomination as labor secretary.

IT WAS A PHOTOGRAPH OF ACOSTA BEING SWORN IN AS LABOR SECRETARY, with his wife and daughters at his side, that led me to dig deeper into Acosta's past. To say that his wife looked unhappy at such a proud moment was an understatement; she looked miserable. I showed Casey the photo.

"Does that look like a woman who is proud of her husband?" I said.

"Maybe she was just having a bad day," Casey said, shrugging off my observation.

I don't know what about the photo made me curious. But it was not beyond the realm of possibility that Epstein had found kompro-mat on any of the prosecutors, including Acosta.

Despite Jay's belief that no one in the U.S. Attorney's Office would cooperate with me, I did get several people who had been inside the Miami office and in the Justice Department during the Epstein case to talk to me off the record. Acosta, it turned out, wasn't well regarded by the rank and file. He was considered a career bureaucrat who didn't know much, if anything, about criminal law.

"When he came to the office from Washington, people were sur-prised," said one former assistant prosecutor in Miami. "Acosta never tried a case in his life, and didn't even understand some basic criminal legal concepts like 'burden of proof.' He was considered a light-weight who really only wanted to use the office as a stepping-stone on the way to becoming a Supreme Court justice."

The investigators and prosecutors on the case were keenly aware that Epstein might try to set them up. One of my sources close to the case told me a story about how he went on a business trip and found himself sitting on the plane next to a model-gorgeous young woman. They struck up a conversation, and she told him about how she was being threatened by an old suitor. Not thinking anything about it, the source offered to help if he could. A day later, the woman called my married source to ask for advice. But after referring her to a law enforcement agency for help, the woman kept calling him in an effort to see him. He suspected that she wasn't a victim of a bad relationship; she was trying to bait him into a honeypot trap—and that perhaps Epstein had hired her to lure him into a compromising situation. There was no way to really prove this.

I DIDN'T THINK ACOSTA WAS THE HONEYPOT TYPE, BUT AT THE VERY least, I figured I should look at his background to see whether Epstein had dug up something.

This called for some old-fashioned shoe-leather reporting.

I started with Acosta's secretaries because, let's face it, secretaries know everything.

After leaving the U.S. Attorney's Office, Acosta was hired as dean of the law school at Florida International University. FIU is a public university—which meant I could get his employment records.

It was relatively easy to find the names of his secretaries and clerical assistants in the files, because like most good secretaries, they did all his busywork.

It was one of those wet hurricane-prone summers in Miami, and every evening, a big storm would roll in, bringing traffic in Southwest Miami almost to a standstill. It was during this time that I would leave work, usually around 8:00 P.M., and drive deep into the urban sprawl of the city, looking for people who worked for or with Acosta. He had had a couple of assistants over the years. Jay told me that the one he had at the U.S. Attorney's Office was still there and would never talk to me, and I knew he was probably right.

But I heard Acosta was not liked at FIU, and I thought perhaps I could convince someone from his office to talk to me.

On this night, I was on my own, trying to look at my phone's GPS while maneuvering Miami traffic, which is not a good idea because I am a terrible driver. I went to several addresses, some of them in the kind of neighborhoods that didn't even have streetlights. I got lost a few times before I found the home of one of Acosta's former secretaries. She was a very polite Hispanic woman. She didn't speak English well, and I don't speak Spanish, so the conversation was short. She spoke well of him and didn't really want to venture deeper into a discussion over his professional or personal life, so I moved on. I made some other stops, trying to find people whom he had worked with, but after doing this for several evenings, I concluded that this path was a dead end.

Jay was kind when I told him what I had tried to do, but I'm sure he thought I was crazy.

NEXT, I LOOKED AT ACOSTA'S FINANCES. ACOSTA, UPON HIS NOMINATION as labor secretary, had put his Coral Gables home on the market. It was a luxurious, historic, four-bedroom, five-bath mansion.

I couldn't help but wonder—how does a government lawyer go from earning $140,000 a year to earning enough money to own a $1.8 million home?

Even after leaving the U.S. Attorney's Office, Acosta earned only $380,000 a year as the law school dean at FIU.

But at the same time he was at the law school, he also became chairman of Century Bank, an independent South Florida institution founded in 2003 by a group of Hispanic businessmen. Acosta was an interesting choice because the only experience he had in investment banking was a brief year working for Lehman Brothers in New York in 1990.

The bank was struggling in the aftermath of the 2009 financial crisis, and had been listed as one of the largest "undercapitalized" banks in the nation. In 2009, it received a $50 million taxpayer bailout. Acosta took the helm after the bailout, when the bank was under a federal order to stop making insider loans, as it had $134 million in losses.[1]

Insider loans—loans to directors or officers of the bank—were not unusual in the early years of a bank start-up. But Century continued to issue loans for years, many of them for speculative real estate projects. In 2011, the bank was still under federal scrutiny, and the following year, it was hit with a lawsuit by shareholders who questioned the insider loans.[2]

Under Acosta, the bank was successful in eliminating the consent order and settling its lawsuits. By 2015, it had raised $65 million and was on its way to recovery.

Upon Acosta's labor nomination, his financial forms showed that he owned less than $1 million in bank stock funds and brokerage and retirement accounts. He agreed to give up a bonus he was due from the bank, which he estimated was worth $50,000 to $150,000. Jay assured me it would be impossible to figure out where Acosta got all his money. His wife was also a lawyer and likely had her own salary, he pointed out.

After his confirmation, Acosta and his family moved into a six-thousand-square-foot, $2 million Georgian mansion in the tony Washington suburb of McLean, Virginia.

BY THE SUMMER OF 2018, I WAS ALMOST FINISHED WITH MY FIRST draft of the Epstein series. Emily and I were busy putting together the documentaries.

As we were racing to finish the project, President Trump was fuming over the decision made by his attorney general, Jeff Sessions, to recuse himself from an investigation into election-tampering and obstruction-of-justice allegations against the president.

It was rumored that Sessions had offered to resign and, as their relationship further deteriorated, Acosta was being whispered about as a replacement for the highest law enforcement job in the nation.

chapter 26

MILESTONES

The year 2018 would mark many milestones.

That January, I would pay my daughter's final undergraduate college tuition, a feat that I celebrated with buckets of tears and champagne, as her final scholarship package came through, along with my parent-plus loan—which put me into debt beyond anything I had ever imagined. I had not planned well for my kids' education, but I made it through her four years of private school and to this day, it is the biggest achievement of my life. I always tell Amelia that her education is the one thing that no one can ever take away. I promised her early on that if she got good grades in high school, I would do everything I could to help her go to college, and she wanted to return to Philadelphia, where she was born and raised until she was in middle school. Unless you grow up in Philly, it's hard to truly understand how much the city is a part of your soul. I always tell people that the best way to explain Philly is that if you are sitting in a bar anywhere in the city, and there's a Phillies game on, and there's a guy at the other end of the bar, by the end of that game you will know what neighborhood the guy grew up in, where he went to school, how he met his wife, how many grandkids he has, how he worked forty years for the transit system, where he was when the Eagles won the Super Bowl or the Flyers won the Stanley Cup.

Amelia couldn't get out of Florida fast enough.

She graduated with honors from St. Joseph's University that May and moved into her first real apartment. It was a dump, with a leaky roof and no heat, which she shared with a roommate, a dog, a cat, a hedgehog, and five pet mice. She was supporting herself by working two jobs, as a veterinary assistant during the day and a dog walker nights and weekends.

The following month, in June, my son Jake graduated from high school in Hillsborough, North Carolina, where he had spent the past few years living with his father. I was hoping he would return to Florida after high school to be closer to me and to attend college there, which he did later in 2018.

It was a busy time, trying to juggle the graduations, the celebrations, the travel, and my Epstein project all at once. There were no vacations for me that year, but those happy moments provided respite that I terribly needed. I was so incredibly full of joy that spring, seeing my children healthy, happy, and looking forward to their futures. Whatever I hoped to accomplish with my career would pale in comparison to my pride over my children.

SPRING GAVE WAY TO SUMMER, AND BY THEN, GRATEFULLY, I HAD TWO more former Justice Department sources willing to talk to me. These were people who would point me in certain directions, without really telling me exactly what I would accomplish by following their instructions. I didn't know how much they would truly help, because they wouldn't go on the record—and I had decided not to use un-named sources in the story unless it was absolutely necessary.

But the case was so voluminous that I was glad to have some conductors to help me wade through its history.

They gave me lots of angles, more than I could ever pursue in my lifetime, so I had to pick and choose which ones seemed most likely to bear fruit. I told my closest colleagues that I could have jumped down a million rabbit holes for this story, but I had to, at some point, define the parameters of the series and go to print. Besides, Casey wasn't going to wait forever.

DURING THIS TIME, A GROUP OF *MIAMI HERALD* ALUMNI WOULD occasionally meet for breakfast at a diner to discuss our latest projects and gossip a bit about the journalism troubles in our newsrooms. This group included Mike Sallah, a Pulitzer Prize–winning journalist who was then with the investigations team at *USA Today*; Audra D. S. Burch, a Pulitzer finalist now with the *New York Times*; and Sergio Bustos, who was then editor of the national desk at *USA Today*. There would be other ex-*Herald*ites who would join us from time to time, depending on their schedules. We used each other as sounding boards for our stories and for our lives, since journalism is a tough career, and few people understand that better than other journalists.

There was more than one occasion when I called upon the members of this group from secret outposts in back closets of the *Herald* newsroom, mostly crying about my latest struggle with Casey, fueled by pressure and exhaustion. It was good I had four of them, because I took turns so as to not wear any one of them out.

Emily, too, was going through her own struggles with putting together the documentaries. I was completely wrapped up with the research and writing. I thought that what she was doing looked amazing, so in hindsight, I really wasn't as supportive as I probably should have been. When you have over twenty-five hours of video, it's a real challenge to whittle it down to a seven-minute documentary. We also had to make sure that the video was as legally sound as the stories. This was especially difficult because of all the influential people Epstein associated with who had the potential to sue us if we messed anything up.

Emily and I carefully wrote the scripts together, then Emily added the narration.

Emily is so incredibly gifted as a visual journalist that she would find significant things in interviews that I didn't even remember. I would watch her work, and then tell her to send me the snippet she had pulled from the interview so that I could put it into the story.

As the project moved along, and we obtained more interviews and records, it became a challenge to keep track of everything. I prepared myself for the drill that, in journalism jargon, we call having your story "lawyered." I expected to hear things like "Where did you get that?" and "How do you know that?" and "Where's the document that says that?"

I attached all the documents to back up the story on clipboards.

As the publishing date got closer, I began to work more closely with Emily, listening to sound and watching video, over and over. Altogether, we had a one-minute video trailer that summarized the series; a twelve-minute mini-documentary featuring the victims, the lawyers, and Reiter; a seven-minute video featuring Virginia; and a five-minute recap of the various people involved in Epstein's case.

It was a humbling experience, hearing the women's voices, watching them cry, get angry, and cry again. It made me want to stand up and scream sometimes.

That summer and fall were hard on us both. McClatchy was tightening its belt (again) and offering buyouts to senior staff writers; a whole slew of our colleagues left the paper. The younger reporters felt cast adrift, as many of them had come to the *Herald* to be mentored by more seasoned journalists, and now most of the veterans were leaving. I didn't get a retirement package, even though I was in the target age group that they wanted to downsize. As is typical of the chaos of my life, I wasn't sure whether or not I even had a *Herald* pension. I asked about it a few times, but no one could find me an answer, and I was too overwhelmed by my work to pursue it.

Casey was now the investigations editor for the whole world, or so it seemed, because he was charged with supervising projects for other McClatchy papers in the country, as well as the *Herald*. I honestly couldn't keep track of all the work that was on his shoulders, and being the selfish journalist that I am, I was more than a bit relieved that he was too busy to monitor my progress very closely.

I was getting near the finish line. To that end, I reached out to every person named in the series, from Epstein himself to Sarah Kellen, Ghislaine Maxwell, Acosta, Villafaña—just about everyone. I not only emailed and called, but I sent out about twenty-five to thirty certified letters requiring their signatures on return receipts. Almost all of the receipts came back signed.

Acosta's spokesman in the Labor Department referred me to the U.S. Attorney's Office in Miami, which made no sense because Acosta no longer worked in the USAO's office. I patiently tried to explain this to him, but it was like talking to my hand.

Almost no one would comment for the story.

Even the legal experts I reached out to didn't want to comment on a case that was so controversial and complicated.

Epstein also didn't respond to any of my queries.

He had returned to his jet-setting life, convinced that he had beaten the system.

But 2018 would become a milestone in his life, too.

He just didn't know it yet.

chapter 27

MORNING SICKNESS

Journalists often compare going through the rigors of an investigative project to having a baby. Birthing a project, and the months leading up to it, are full of morning, afternoon, and evening sickness, the joys that come with new discoveries, exhaustion, depression, anxiety, and just being pissed off at everything. Having done almost every aspect of journalism short of being at the top of the food chain, I can say that investigative journalism is probably the most difficult path to choose in this line of work. It can also be the most rewarding.

In the run-up to the series, the time when I was putting the pieces together and writing, I was also still juggling prison stories. There was a murder at Columbia Correctional Institution and a riot at Hamilton Correctional, both brutal facilities in North-Central Florida. I was getting emails and letters from inmates and their families all over the state, begging me, almost on a daily basis, to help deliver them from the abuses they were suffering. I knew I couldn't help them all, but I diligently responded to almost every email I received, giving them a list of resources and phone numbers for inmate advocates like the ACLU, Disability Florida, and the Southern Poverty Law Center. I would advise them to document their issues in writing, and to make sure there was a notice in their prison file giving a family member or friend permission to obtain information about them in case they were incapacitated or placed in solitary confinement. If an inmate doesn't do this, they can disappear into the system and their family will never be able to find out what happened to them unless they turn up dead.

After each story interrupted my project's rhythms, I would return to writing, mostly from home. But there came that time that all *Miami Herald* writers dread—the day you have to put your stories into Cue, the *Herald*'s computer publishing program. Casey usually did this for me because it is so laborious that I didn't have the patience. I also tended to lose the stories into the ether.

I called our company's central help desk so many times that I'm sure they called me the crazy lady from Miami. Once all the stories were in the system, then the real nightmare called "editing" begins.

One of the best things about working with an editor like Casey for so long is that you can almost predict what your editor is thinking. And one of the worst things about working with an editor for so long is . . . you can almost predict what he's thinking.

I had worked with Casey almost the entire fifteen years I had been at the *Herald*. He wasn't always my direct boss, but we had an analogous sense of what made a kick-ass story. He used to be the *Herald*'s front-page editor, so I would always pick his brain to ensure that I was headed in the right direction because, like most reporters, I always wanted my stories on the front page.

He then became the Sunday editor. Now, the only thing better for a reporter than being on the front page is being on the *Sunday* front page. This was back in the days when big stories appeared in print first, not on the internet.

Casey is, for the most part, very calm, soft spoken, and mild mannered. Even when he is excited or mad, his emotions brew just beneath the stratovolcano surface, contained—but evident in the slightly seismic movements of his hands, legs, and eyes. His words eventually spill out like molten lava, opening fresh craters of self-doubt in the fragile confidence I always have in my work.

This happened frequently in the days before the launch of the Epstein project, and our headstrong natures became quite challenging for us both. As my former colleague Mike Sallah says, "There is a lot of blood spilled when you are launching a project."

There are few editors on Casey's level willing to bury themselves in the denseness of an investigative project, right down to poring through the most boring pile of documents imaginable just so he can truly understand all the minutiae that, when put together, often give the story its impact.

But as in any relationship, it takes a lot of patience and hard work to make the partnership succeed. And the process wasn't always pretty, largely because I'm not an easy reporter to work with. For most of my career I was so obsessed, competitive, and worried that I would be laid off that I was truly oblivious to how unforgiving I was to those who, in my mind, were not as relentless and obsessed as I.

Often, Casey's comments hinted that I wasn't working hard enough or, particularly if I was home or on the road on assignment, that I wasn't working at all. I would feel guilty for every moment I took to breathe or take care of myself. I know this wasn't his intent. There were a lot of demands on him, and I could sense those pressures being passed on to me in not-so-subtle ways.

One time, when I spent my long, horrible commute to work on the phone with Jay Weaver, talking about the Epstein case the entire time, I got in trouble because Casey had been trying to call me the entire forty-five minutes. I was so pissed at him for scolding me that for weeks after that, I sent him an itinerary every day that listed what

I was doing every minute, including, I think, when I went to the bathroom.

Here's the thing: even when I wasn't physically writing or reporting the story, I was still working on it in my head. I thought about the story from the time I got up until the time I went to sleep—if I slept. On my morning runs, I would try to clear my head, but my thoughts were always on who I was going to call and interview, how I was going to get more information from them, and what I needed to do after that.

After my run, I was immediately on the phone—even if I was sitting having coffee at Food King, my favorite deli on the beach. A lot of people also don't know this about sources: sometimes you have to talk to them for hours—or call them dozens of times—to get them to trust you and open up enough so that you finally get what you *really* need from them.

How do you explain to your editor that you spent an hour listening to a source talk endlessly about his or her marital problems?

I finally assigned Casey's cell phone number a special ringtone so I knew when he was calling and I could drop whatever I was doing and answer. Even to this day, that damn ringtone "I don't want to work, I want to bang on the drum all day," by Todd Rundgren, startles me every time it goes off.

With the Epstein project, Casey and I went back and forth a lot, arguing loudly at times. He would change something, and I would change it back, then he would change it again. Around and around we would go with the first drafts.

The editing process is probably the most painful part of any journalism project. Writers often get wedded to a certain angle on a story, and even to certain words or phrases in the piece. Editors then can throw a wrench in the whole approach to the story and slash sentences that writers may have spent days or even weeks carefully crafting.

I write with my ear, which means that at any given time, if you walk over to me when I'm writing, you will see my lips moving, and I will be whispering the words to myself as I'm typing. So the narrative has a cadence to it, at least in my head. Casey can easily mess up that flow by moving words and sentences around, and I hate that.

Coming up with a title or a headline is often key to the whole package. It has to be catchy without being too cute, hard-hitting without being too obvious. I didn't always like the titles the editors came up with, and sometimes I had to come up with my own. Sometimes, it took weeks to come up with a title.

But this time, early on, when I asked Casey what he thought we should call the series, he quickly came back with "Perversion of Justice."

I thought it was perfect. At least we agreed on something.

THE EDITING ROUTINE CONTINUED. CASEY WOULD MAKE SOME CHANGES that I accepted. Others I stood firm on. I refused, for example, to call the women "alleged victims." I reasoned that we don't call people who are burglarized "alleged burglary victims." I also pointed out that in this case, the victims were all listed as *victims* by the U.S. Attorney's Office as part of the final plea agreement that Epstein signed.

But our loudest argument was over a single phrase that I refused to take out of the story:

"The women—now in their late 20s and early 30s—are still fighting for an elusive justice that even the passage of time has not made right."

"I don't even know what that means," Casey said, in striking the sentence out.

"What do you mean? Casey, we all know that sometimes, the way we look at things can change over time," I argued.

I could see he was digging in his heels, and it was making me mad.

I pointed out that the Bill Cosby case was one where victims finally got their day in court as a result of years of pressure. In that case, I reminded him, a new prosecutor was elected who finally brought charges against the disgraced comedian—and those charges led to his conviction.

Our voices grew louder in the newsroom, drawing attention. We finally took the debate into a conference room, where we screamed and yelled over things that really had nothing to do with the sentence. Whatever it was that was really bothering us, we got it out of our system. I retired to the back-issues room, swallowing my tears, and called Emily.

In the fall of 2018, we were still struggling to find a weekend slot to launch the story, and Emily and I were working nearly every day to finalize the documentary. Every now and then, someone in the photo/video department would pop into the project and ask how we were doing, but then disappear, having their own workload to navigate. Once, deep into our video work, we were informed that one of the video producers with no knowledge of our project had been assigned to take the reins. Emily was annoyed, but I gently reminded her to keep going, and of course, we were soon back to working on our own. The videos were and remain to this day the most powerful part of the project.

The last days of the video edit were over Thanksgiving weekend. Emily took a break from making pies with her aunt and sister to do a conference call with me, Casey, and our lawyers, who had reviewed the documentary. A decision was made to pull some photographs from a portion of the video because of legal concerns. This meant that Emily had to rework the whole documentary—and rerecord the narration on Thanksgiving.

"I remember shutting down the computer on Thanksgiving and trying to set it all aside, sitting at the table with my family. I said a silent, thankful prayer for the brave young women who had trusted us with their stories," Emily later told me.

To this day, no other media outlet, producer, or journalist will ever be able to capture the same raw emotion that those four women shared with us for the first time.

I WENT THROUGH DAYS WHEN I THOUGHT WHAT WE HAD ACCOMPLISHED was something to be proud of, and other days when I thought that I had completely failed at what I had set out to do.

On November 27, the day before the series was set to run, we were going through the last edits with our attorney, Steve Burns. Casey was sitting at the table, his leg nervously twitching. It was making me apprehensive. Steve was calm, however, and actually made me feel like I had done a good job; the stories, he said, were legally sound.

The last few hours were dedicated to reviewing the documentaries. Emily had set up a conference room, and invited Casey, along with some of the younger reporters in the newsroom and our social media producers, who were writing up feeds to share on Twitter, Instagram, and Facebook.

The room was dark as the women came on-screen. I was using all the energy I had left to keep going and not break down. Casey asked us to tweak a couple of things, then abruptly left. Emily and I felt the wind go out of our sails.

I turned to the young reporters in the room and asked them what they thought. I could see in their faces and body language that they were moved by the survivors' voices.

That afternoon, I convinced myself that the stories were way too long, and that a three-part series with hundreds of inches of copy would never hold readers' attention. I began deleting huge chunks of words from the story. Finally, Mary Behne, the paper's best copy editor, said something to Casey. He marched over to my tiny cubicle in the center of the newsroom. It was good he was tall, because I'm only five foot two and anyone else wouldn't have been able to see me behind the tall stacks of records and file boxes I had finally brought from home and piled on my desk.

"What are you doing?" Casey asked me.

"No one is going to read all this," I told him as I kept hitting the delete key.

"Leave it alone. Put it all back," he said.

THE LAUNCH TIME FOR THE ONLINE VERSION OF THE STORY KEPT changing, but we finally landed on November 28, at 7:00 A.M.

I went home that night and tossed in bed, unable to sleep. I finally gave up and got up about 4:00 A.M. I headed to the gym at 5:00 and climbed on the elliptical trainer. I remember praying the entire time I was on the machine that my story would at least last one day online before being forgotten.

I went home, showered, threw on jeans and a T-shirt, and drove to the Doral newsroom just after dawn. I stopped and bought sixty dollars' worth of bagels and coffee for the crew that morning, hoping I had enough money in my bank account to cover the expense.

When I walked into the newsroom, I looked at the large digital screen in the center of the room that lists the *Herald*'s most-read stories that morning.

At the top of the list was a story about a woman who had farted in a dollar store.

WOMAN PASSES GAS IN STORE, THEN PULLS KNIFE was the headline.

It was getting thousands of hits.

I almost never paid attention to the stories at the top of the board. They were often "clickbait" that we and other newspapers use to lure our readers to the other, more "serious" journalism on our website.

At about 8:00 A.M., the three parts of the series, along with a massive graphic, all the videos, a time line, and a piece called "How We Got the Story," were launched under the headline HOW A FUTURE TRUMP CABINET MEMBER GAVE A SERIAL SEX ABUSER THE DEAL OF A LIFETIME.

I began tweeting out the stories. I hardly had any followers on Twitter, so it was a short task.

Our two social media talents, Noel Gonzalez and Adrian Ruhi, were busy blitzing the stories across the internet universe.

I had a bagel and watched the board, with my stories at the very bottom of the list, then began packing up with the intention of going home to sleep. I was relieved my work was done.

The newsroom was starting to get busy as more staff arrived for work. Suddenly, reporter Rene Rodriguez shouted over: "Have you seen the board?"

I walked over, and my stories, all three of them, were climbing fast. The first one had thousands of hits.

"Well, it's never going to top that fart story," I said, walking back to my desk.

Before turning off my computer, I looked at my Twitter account. I suddenly had thousands of followers.

Then the unbelievable happened.

It beat the fart story.

The room erupted in applause.

My phone started ringing, and my computer mailbox was filling up with congratulations.

The first call I took was from Mike Reiter. He was more than elated. Finally, he said, someone had put together the Epstein story in a way that would make people understand the scope of his crimes and worse—how prosecutors helped Epstein get away with them. Reiter's words meant the world to me.

I tried without success to reach Michelle, and then Courtney, who had been released from prison just two months earlier. It was the middle of the night in Australia, so I couldn't call Virginia. I did speak to Jena-Lisa, who had been very worried about how her grandparents would react to her story.

She was in tears.

"My grandma told me she was never more proud of me," she said.

In Palm Beach, Jennifer Recarey was home with her two boys that morning. Reiter called her to tell her the story was up on the

Herald's website. When she read the story, she instinctively reached for her phone, intending, for a second, to call Joe.

"It was the first time in a long time that I did something like that. It was instinctive. Joe would have been so happy to see what happened," she later told me.

TODAY, MOST NEWSPAPER STORIES ARE PUT ON THE INTERNET BEFORE they are published in print. So two days after the story went online, I returned to the newsroom. It was about 8:00 P.M. and the delivery trucks were already parked outside ready to be loaded with the next day's papers. The pressmen were preparing the machines, and I bathed in the smell of fresh newsprint, recalling my early years in the business and how exciting it still was, forty years later, to see the delivery trucks idling outside and watching the presses roll. A camera team from a production company working on an Epstein documentary had asked the *Herald* for permission to film the run. I agreed to accompany them, although I was much too nervous and tired to talk about my story on camera. I hardly ever watched the presses anymore, so when the lumbering equipment began booming, with my story furiously spinning down the racks, I was overjoyed I was there to see it.

I thought I would finally be able to get some rest. After a big story, you always hope to get a break, but if the story is successful that rest doesn't come.

I had no idea what was awaiting Emily and me around the corner.

That day, a van pulled up outside Emily's house and parked. It was there all day, and the next. Finally, her husband, Walt, called the police.

chapter 28

AFTERSHOCKS

I hate doing television interviews. I have done many of them during my career, and the exposure of your story on television can go a long way toward forcing people to make important change, hold leaders accountable, solve crimes, and help people you are writing about who need it.

I was exhausted, however, and felt TV could wait. But before I had a chance to make my escape, I was sitting in the middle of the newsroom wearing a borrowed black blazer and a black T-shirt I bought at the Doral Walmart, and had a makeup artist and a camera in my face. By that evening, the story was all over the national news.

I received kind words from fellow journalists, sexual abuse victims, lawyers, judges, and victim advocates. I heard from people whom I had worked with early in my career, and old friends I had lost touch with decades ago.

I returned to my apartment late that night, oblivious to everything except the salty sea wind that always hits me in the face as I step out of my car after a long day. It felt good to be home. My apartment was in a small boutique building with a 1980s brownstone façade that had seen better days. The elevator was constantly out of service, the hallways flooded with water, and my car was often broken into. But I had a view of the Intercoastal Waterway, and I was only one block from the beach.

That night, I began receiving incessant FaceTime calls from numbers I didn't recognize. I was also getting deluged with nonsensical emails to my work email address. I turned off my phone and went to sleep.

Meanwhile, the van parked directly in front of Emily's house had not moved. The local police arrived and surrounded the vehicle. The man behind the wheel claimed he was a private investigator working a case in the area.

The suspicious activity in my life continued. People I didn't recognize through the peephole knocked on my door. Emily warned me not to answer the door for strangers, but I rarely ever had strange people knock on my door, except for now. One of the men claimed he had a pizza delivery for me.

"I didn't order pizza," I told him through the door.

"Well, it's for this address," he claimed.

"Well, all I can tell you is I didn't order a pizza."

He left and I waited a few hours before leaving my condo. Soon after, I installed a video camera outside my door. Over the next several months, there were other strangers at my door. One of them appeared several times and took selfies of himself in a mirror in the hallway outside my apartment. I still don't know what that was all about. Did they need to show someone proof that they had found me?

I felt like I was being watched. I kept seeing familiar vehicles in my rearview window. I told myself I was being paranoid. But I knew Epstein's people were probably looking into my background, trying to unearth something in my past, just as he had done to his victims. I searched my memory to recall whether I had ever done anything that could cause me embarrassment. There were times I had a couple too many beers at Nick's, the local watering hole, and had left my shoes behind because heels don't work walking home on the beach. I knew I had more than a few parking tickets and a lot of unpaid bills. I was glad my children were away at school. My boyfriend, Mr. Big, was oblivious to the success of the story and how much it was shaking up the quiet life that I had constructed around him and my work. We were not seeing each other as often because of the time I needed to put into finishing the project. He was jealous that perhaps I was seeing someone else, which didn't make sense because our relationship was never exclusive, especially on his part. Suddenly, he seemed needy. He didn't like the attention I was getting.

Yet he knew, perhaps more than anyone else in my life, the sacrifices I had made, how hard I had worked, and the pennies I had scraped together to take care of my children. In the midst of the biggest success of my career, he couldn't even bring himself to be happy for me. For the first time during all our years together, I didn't have the time or even the yearning to cry over him.

WHAT I DIDN'T KNOW AT THE TIME WAS THAT MY SERIES HAD SET OFF a bombshell of events not only in my life but also within the U.S. Department of Justice. Almost immediately, members of the public corruption unit at the U.S. Attorney's Office in the Southern District of New York took my story to their boss, Geoffrey Berman, who had been tapped earlier that year to replace Preet Bharara, a longtime SDNY federal prosecutor who had been fired by Trump.

The Manhattan U.S. Attorney's Office is arguably the most influential, independent, and prestigious in the country. Its prosecutors usually go on to lucrative jobs at corporate law firms or are appointed to high-profile government posts.

Bharara had a reputation as a tough, independent prosecutor who took on a long list of public corruption and Wall Street cases. While he was considered an outspoken "crusader" who successfully prosecuted insider trading and securities fraud cases, he had been criticized for an unwillingness to go after some powerful and politically connected figures.[1]

Bharara, who was now a TV commentator, had been in charge of SDNY when Virginia Giuffre went public with allegations that she was abused by Epstein, Dershowitz, Prince Andrew, and a number of other prominent men at Epstein's New York mansion. Lawyers representing Epstein's victims had met several times over the years with New York federal prosecutors in hopes of convincing them to prosecute Epstein on charges in New York.

Bharara, a former chief counsel to Democratic senator Chuck Schumer, never took up the Epstein case, even when new evidence and witnesses surfaced. He has never explained why his office didn't act. Nor has he answered any of my email or phone queries about the case.

Berman, however, wasn't going to let Epstein slide this time. He gave his team the green light to investigate.

MY SERIES ALSO DID NOT GO UNNOTICED BY EPSTEIN. TWO DAYS AFTER it ran, he wired $100,000 to one of his co-conspirators and three days later, wired $250,000 to another. One of those who received money, sources later told me, was Sarah Kellen, and the other was Lesley Groff, who was in charge of Epstein's Manhattan office. The story also alarmed Epstein's financial institution, Deutsche Bank, where some employees had already been raising flags about Epstein's accounts.

Over the years, Epstein had opened forty different accounts with the bank, and had made millions of dollars in transfers and other suspicious transactions that should have raised scrutiny with bank officials because of his criminal past.

The money he moved included payments to lawyers, victims, Russian models, and tuition payments and checks written directly to women "with Eastern European surnames," federal authorities would later discover.

Then there were at least seventeen out-of-court settlements to Epstein's victims, totaling more than seven million dollars.

The same day that Epstein made the payments to Kellen and Groff, Nebraska senator Ben Sasse, a Republican member of the Senate Judiciary Committee, wrote a letter to the Justice Department, demanding an investigation into Acosta's handling of the Epstein case. Citing my series, he wanted a review of the entire prosecution, and by the end of the month, he was joined by a chorus of lawmakers, both Democrat and Republican.

THE PROJECT WASN'T PRAISED IN ALL QUARTERS. THOSE WHO criticized my work fell into several categories: journalists who knew about the case, had written about it years earlier, and thought my project was nothing but a redo; Epstein prosecutors who were not happy at the way they were portrayed; and Epstein's co-conspirators, enablers, and lawyers.

But it was a former writer for the *Daily Beast* who took criticism of the series to a completely different level.

At first, Conchita Sarnoff congratulated me on the project in a breezy, cheerful email. Then, as the story received more attention, she grew angrier and angrier, demanding that I call her because she said, "I broke the Epstein story in 2010."

She then reached out to one of our columnists whom she knew personally, and he forwarded her concerns to Mindy Marqués, who by then had been promoted and was now the *Herald*'s publisher.

Up until then, I had only read one story Sarnoff wrote about Epstein—and the only reason I read that one was because there was a copy of it in the FBI files. A socialite turned journalist turned human trafficking activist, Sarnoff was divorced from Daniel Sarnoff, whose grandfather, David Sarnoff, founded RCA and NBC. After reading the story in the FBI file, I saw that she had in fact self-published a book about the Epstein case years earlier. By January 2018, however, Sarnoff was running a nonprofit organization for victims of human trafficking.

Since she was now an activist on the topic of trafficking, I thought I might interview her for my story.

I don't remember all the details of our conversation, except that I found it difficult to get a word in. It also seemed that she felt she was the only person who knew the Epstein story. I quickly realized that it would be better not to tell her I had interviewed several victims. All I remember thinking after hanging up the phone was "I am never going to read that woman's book." To this day, I never have.

After the series was published, she wrote letters to my editors, my publisher, and the Pulitzer Prize board. At first, she indicated she was upset that she didn't get credit for being the person who broke the story. We checked the clips. The problem was, she didn't "break" the story. The *Palm Beach Post* was the first paper to write about Epstein, in 2005.

Then she claimed that I had "repackaged" her work. As evidence of her "great expertise" on the story, she listed all the pertinent people whom she had interviewed over the years, including Acosta. However, we couldn't find any of those interviews in her stories. The last story I could find that she wrote about Epstein was in 2011, seven years before.

After speaking to some of the people she claimed she had "interviewed," I was told that she used her society connections to interview them at cocktail parties and charitable events. Anything they might have told her, which wasn't much, was off the record, according to several people who said she cornered them at these functions.

Mindy wrote Sarnoff a lengthy letter, addressing every allegation she had made, disputing each one of them.

Sarnoff then called former Palm Beach police chief Mike Reiter to ask him whether he had actually spoken to me. Reiter was as baffled as I was, because after all, we had him on camera.

When that approach didn't work, she moved on to accusations of plagiarism. Casey had to buy her book and read it.

The *Herald* put my entire series through a program that detects plagiarized material and found nothing.

Next, she began to show up at events where I spoke or appeared. Once she actually stood up at a *Miami Herald*–sponsored town hall in Coral Gables, displaying her book and speaking about the case until the moderator cut her off. The *Herald* considered seeking a cease-and-desist order, but I think they believed that would only call more attention to her.

Sarnoff continued to make allegations, some of them in writing to prominent people, who showed these communications to me. I finally hired a lawyer myself to send her a cease-and-desist letter.

Meanwhile, the *Washington Post* began quoting Sarnoff as an expert in their Epstein stories. The pieces, written by journalist Marc Fisher, were gymnastically written—as if he purposefully avoided mentioning the *Miami Herald*'s series. I wasn't the only person who noticed this.

It wasn't as if the *Washington Post* didn't know I had been up to something. During the reporting phase of my project, a member of the *Post*'s investigations team called lawyer Brad Edwards to ask him what I was working on.

"She asked me whether your story had anything to do with Trump. I told her no, and she basically hung up. That was it," Edwards told me.

JOURNALISM, BY ITS VERY NATURE, IS COMPETITIVE, EVEN AMONG those whom you work with. I was warned from the day I started in this business that I needed to watch my back because reporters and editors can be fierce. I was forced to develop a thick skin at the *Herald* after I was stepped on a few times.

Still, the competitive tension in a newsroom usually fades with the success of a big story. The staff almost universally recognizes something that spotlights our work as a publication, leads to positive change, rights wrongs, or saves lives. This is good for the newspaper and good for journalism.

There were noticeable exceptions to this with the Epstein story. One of them was reporter Jay Weaver, who posted on Facebook old stories he had written about the case to emphasize that he had covered it years earlier. Another was Curt Anderson, the legal affairs reporter of the Associated Press in South Florida, who took to Twitter to also dismiss my series.

It was as if all the work I did tracking down the survivors, getting them and the lead detective and the police chief to trust me, didn't count at all. Somehow, it seemed insignificant to these critics that I had taken apart the case and put it back together in a way that made people angry enough to want to do something about it. Isn't that what journalists are supposed to do?

It was a slap in the face that everyone in the newsroom noticed. I tried to brush the criticism off, but Jay's comments really hurt because I admired his work. He would later apologize to me.

REPORTERS ARE NATURALLY PROTECTIVE OF THEIR BEATS AND SOURCES. One of Jay's longtime sources, Jeff Sloman, also wasn't happy about the series. Although Sloman was now in private practice, the former deputy U.S. attorney under Acosta first took his gripes to Jay, and then to the editors of our opinion page. He wrote (and the *Herald* published) a scathing column to discredit my series. I'm not sure that giving a bundle of excuses for letting a pedophile off the hook is ever a good idea. To me, there was no excuse for keeping the deal a secret from Epstein's victims—and that was probably the most egregious part of the story. Sloman didn't mention that detail in his column.

Sloman called Acosta "an outstanding public servant . . . at risk of becoming collateral damage in Washington's latest polarized conflagration." He also insisted that Epstein's lawyers' aggressive tactics had no bearing on the case, adding that it was "at heart a local sex case." Attorney Jack Scarola, who represented several victims, called Sloman's assessment of the case a "gross mischaracterization," pointing out that it was not a minor local sex case; it was a federal sex trafficking crime involving minor girls.

WE HAD TIMED MY SERIES TO COINCIDE WITH THE UPCOMING LEGAL showdown between Epstein and Brad Edwards. A hearing on the civil lawsuit involving jailed lawyer Scott Rothstein's effort to sell Epstein's legal settlements in a Ponzi scheme was scheduled to begin the week after my series launched.

Edwards and his lawyer, Scarola—a former Palm Beach prosecutor—had already proven that Edwards wasn't involved in Rothstein's fraud, but the legal battle raged on as Edwards sought to prove in civil court what federal prosecutors had failed to do in criminal court: that Epstein had sexually abused, raped, and trafficked countless girls.

Emily and I had inquired about whether cameras were going to be permitted in the courtroom, and were told that the *Palm Beach Post* had what they called the "pool" camera—which meant that one videographer would be in the courtroom and share video with all the other news outlets. But when the proceedings began, no one from the *Post* was at the courthouse.

Luckily, that morning there was a film crew there from the Netflix documentary production company working on their Epstein project, and they agreed to be the pool video camera.

By then, we had already heard that Epstein wasn't going to appear in court. But his victims perhaps would, as Scarola intended to call some of them as witnesses during the trial. This would be the first time that victims would testify about Epstein's crimes, so there was a palpable tension in the courtroom, which was packed with media.

After the judge entered the courtroom and everyone sat down, Scarola stood up to make an announcement. Instead of speaking to the judge, he turned to face the audience. There had been a settlement in the case, he announced, and as part of the deal, Epstein's lawyers were required to read an apology from Epstein.

It was short.

"While Mr. Edwards was representing clients against me, I filed a lawsuit against him in which I made allegations about him that the evidence conclusively proves were absolutely false," Epstein said in the statement. "The lawsuit I filed was my unreasonable attempt to damage his business reputation and cause Mr. Edwards to stop pursuing cases against me."

There was a stunned silence in the courtroom, as people began congratulating Edwards. I looked for victims in the room. There didn't appear to be any.

The problem, to me, was that, while it was important that Edwards was vindicated, what about Epstein's survivors?

"I'm still waiting for our apology for ruining our lives and taking away the innocence from every one of us," Michelle Licata told me by phone afterward.

Outside the courthouse, Edwards and Scarola had set up a press conference in front of a wall of case files with the name "Epstein" written on each one.

With all the cameras clamoring for a spot, I sat on the pavement to not block their lenses. I was still running through my mind what had happened, and taking notes, when Edwards suddenly mentioned my name. He said something about me being the only reporter, among many, who had reached out to him. He explained that I had finally written the story that other reporters had failed to do.

Later that afternoon, I asked Scarola what Edwards meant.

"Over the years, there were a lot of reporters who tried to do this story," Scarola said. "We told them all the same thing: Here's the court file, call us when you read it. You were the only one who called us back who had actually read it."

chapter 29

DERSHOWITZ V. BROWN

Alan Dershowitz, Harvard professor emeritus, constitutional law expert, and TV pundit, somehow thought that my story about Epstein was all about him.

I actually went to great lengths in my work to stick to what was already in the court record about Dershowitz; I didn't embellish it with additional material or reporting. In fact, after speaking to him, I added several paragraphs from him disputing Virginia Giuffre's sex-abuse claims.

We pretty much tiptoed our way over Dershowitz's part of the story because we wanted to focus on the failure of prosecutors. In hindsight, I wish I had included more about Dershowitz.

For example, I could have put in some of the inconsistencies contained in his depositions or all the times that Dershowitz was on Epstein's plane. I could have written about how Dershowitz spent time at Epstein's home, or how he was so close to Epstein that he would ask him to review his book manuscripts.

I could have added that there was at least one other woman, besides Virginia, who had claimed that she was also ordered by Epstein to have sex with Dershowitz. I could have pointed out that Dershowitz once wrote an opinion column that called statutory rape an irrelevant concept.

Perhaps I should have mentioned that Dershowitz had had a massage at Epstein's house—with a large Russian woman—and kept his underwear on.

Instead, I stuck with what everybody basically already knew about Dershowitz and Epstein.

But after the story ran, the eighty-one-year-old legal eagle launched an all-out attack against me and the *Herald*. His hysterics were so over the top that I began to wonder whether Dershowitz was doing this as a distraction on behalf of Epstein.

Even some of his own legal colleagues began reaching out to me via Twitter, saying "WTF is Alan doing?"

I FELT THAT DERSHOWITZ NEEDED A FULL HEARING OF THE EVIDENCE that he claimed he had to disprove Giuffre's allegations and those of his other accuser, Sarah Ransome. Ransome, in a sworn affidavit, said she was twenty-two when she met Epstein in the summer of 2006, a time during which Dershowitz was defending Epstein from underage sex allegations in Florida.

Ransome said she was flown to Epstein's island, where her passport was seized and she was forced to have sex with Epstein and his associates. On one occasion, at Epstein's New York mansion, she was in bed with Epstein and one of his girlfriends, Nadia Marcinkova, when Dershowitz walked in.

"Dershowitz entered the room, after which Jeffrey left the room and Nadia and I had sex with Dershowitz. I recall specific, key details of this person and the sex acts and can describe them in the event it becomes necessary to do so," Ransome said in the affidavit, filed in 2019 as part of Virginia Giuffre's defamation suit against Dershowitz.

Dershowitz aggressively denies he had sex with either woman, and he says he can prove it. The problem, I soon learned, is that Dershowitz wouldn't produce that evidence. I'm not saying that this is because the evidence doesn't exist; it's just that he has thus far refused to turn over the evidence or make it public.

He claimed, for example, that an investigation that he commissioned by former FBI director Louis Freeh concluded that Dershowitz could not have had sex with Virginia. But neither Dershowitz nor Freeh has released anything about the investigation except for a single-page "To Whom It May Concern" letter. We asked for the full report, and Dershowitz said he didn't have a copy of it.

What followed was a dance, not one that would help enlighten anyone to what happened or didn't happen; Dershowitz would just constantly send me threats. He even hired a libel lawyer to send the *Herald* a clear message that he was prepared to take us to court if we stepped out of line.

I started forwarding Dershowitz's emails to our *Herald* attorney, Sandy Bohrer, and not even responding to the threats.

Finally, Sandy, a gentlemanly seventysomething lawyer whom I had never seen lose his cool, sent Dershowitz an email like no one at the *Herald* probably had ever seen from Sandy. Sandy doesn't ever get angry; in fact, it's almost strange how he never gets flustered. So when I saw what he sent to Dershowitz, my jaw dropped. I won't go into specifics, but Sandy spoke to Dershowitz lawyer to lawyer, taking him to task for some of his outlandish unprofessional behavior. I remember walking into the newsroom that morning, after reading Sandy's email to Dershowitz. I walked right into Mindy's office, where she was sitting with Casey and Rick Hirsch, the *Herald*'s managing editor. They, too, had just read the email.

"What just happened?" I said.

They all looked just as shocked as I was.

THE PROFESSOR'S ANTICS CONTINUED. I CAME TO CALL HIM ALAN, AS if he were a child who needed special attention, saying things like, "Okay, Alan," or "I'm sorry, I can't do that, Alan."

He kept referring to information that was contained in sealed documents. He accused the newspaper of not reporting "facts" that he said were in those sealed documents. The truth is, I tried to explain, newspapers just can't write about things because Alan Dershowitz says they exist. We need to see them. We need to verify them. Then, because I said "show me the material," he publicly accused me of committing a criminal act by asking him to produce documents that were under court seal.

This is the way that Dershowitz operates.

What disturbs me the most about Dershowitz is the way that the media, with few exceptions, fails to critically challenge him. Journalists fact-checked Donald Trump and others in his administration almost every day, yet, for the most part, the media seems to give Dershowitz a pass on the Epstein story.

In 2015, when Giuffre's allegations first became public, Dershowitz went on every television program imaginable swearing, among other things, that Epstein's plane logs would exonerate him. "How do you know that?" he was asked.

He replied that he was never on Epstein's plane during the time that Virginia was involved with Epstein.

But if the media had checked, they could have learned that he was indeed a passenger on the plane during that time period, according to the logs.

Then he testified, in a sworn deposition, that he never went on any plane trips without his wife. But he was listed on those passenger manifests as traveling multiple times without his wife. During at least one trip, he was on the plane with a model named Tatiana. It might not prove that he had had sex with anyone other than his wife, but it certainly raises questions about his recall.

DERSHOWITZ WAS SO AGGRESSIVE IN HIS ATTACKS AGAINST GIUFFRE and Ransome that at least three women reached out to me with new information because they couldn't stomach his behavior on television. From one of them I received unsolicited material, including copies of court papers involving Dershowitz's contentious 1976 divorce from his first wife, Sue Barlach, whom he had been married to for fourteen years. In the court's findings of fact, the judge concluded that Dershowitz subjected Barlach to so much abuse that she required mental treatment. Barlach, in a report she submitted to the court, said she was so abused by Dershowitz that she had an abortion rather than give birth to their third child.

While she was initially given custody of their two children, a subsequent battle over child support and alimony led to Dershowitz's being awarded full custody based in part on phone calls with his distraught wife that he had secretly recorded. The recordings, submitted to the court, showed that she was unraveling. The judge noted that she referred to Dershowitz in disparaging terms and was interfering with his visits with his children. Years later, Barlach committed suicide, but it's unclear exactly how. Dershowitz insists that rumors perpetuated over the internet erroneously say that she jumped off the Brooklyn Bridge on New Year's Eve 1983. He maintains that she "drowned in the East River in an apparent suicide."

Autopsy reports are not public in New York, and the New York medical examiner has declined requests to release Barlach's.

I find it telling that there is virtually nothing to be found on Barlach, not even a grave marker. There is a legacy.com entry, grave marker, and obituary for Barlach's sister, Marilyn, who married Dershowitz's brother, Nathan. Marilyn Barlach was killed in 2011 after being struck by a postal truck while bicycling in Manhattan with her husband.

CASEY AND I MET WITH DERSHOWITZ FOR FIVE HOURS AT HIS HOME IN Miami Beach, fittingly, on April Fool's Day 2019. We wanted to give Dershowitz an opportunity to show us the evidence he claimed he had that exonerated him. In his beachfront condo, he had reams of paper stacked in piles on a table. He explained that the pages were copies of his calendars and appointment books during the time that Virginia says she was abused by him. After the interview, he said, "Okay, you can now sit here and go through all my records, take as long as you want."

It was the first time in my career that I had ever asked an editor to accompany me to an interview. I was happy that Casey did most of the talking. He explained, very professionally to the professor, that we needed copies of his calendars and documents in order to verify them.

"No, you don't, you can just sit here and copy them all down by hand. Take your time," he said.

My eyes drifted over to the piles of papers on the table, about five of them, each at least two feet high. We would have been there for days.

He claimed he couldn't give us copies because some of the calendars contained privileged legal information. Casey suggested that Dershowitz redact the privileged material and then let us examine the copies.

Dershowitz changed the subject.

He played us a tape he had recorded of a 2015 phone conversation with the lawyer David Boies, claiming that Boies, who represented Virginia Giuffre, admitted on the tape that Virginia was lying about having sex with the Harvard professor.

But the recording was full of static and cut out at several points, making it difficult to discern anything Boies said. Dershowitz had conveniently typed up a script for us to follow, but there was no way to confirm the script was an accurate transcription of the audio because portions of the audio were so muffled.

Later, I spoke to Boies about the taped conversation he had had with Dershowitz. Boies said the conversation was taped without his knowledge, may have violated legal canons of ethics, and was perhaps even illegal because Boies said that the conversation happened when he was in California, not in New York, where only one party needs to give consent for recording. California, like Florida, requires two-party consent. Dershowitz maintains it was legal because Dershowitz recorded it while he was in New York.

Boies acknowledges that he told Dershowitz that *if* he found that Virginia was lying, or that she had been mistaken, then he would direct her to correct her statements about Dershowitz. But the two lawyers were discussing a hypothetical situation, Boies said.

Later, Boies did his own investigation into Virginia's claims and found her to be truthful. She also passed a lie detector test. Both Boies and Giuffre have since filed civil defamation claims against Dershowitz, who countersued. Those cases remain pending.

TWO DAYS AFTER MEETING WITH DERSHOWITZ—AND TWELVE DAYS BEFORE the Pulitzer Prizes would be announced—Dershowitz wrote an open letter to the Pulitzer board titled "Don't Reward Fake News," labeling my stories as "shoddy journalism" and urging the Pulitzer committee to eliminate my series from consideration.

Dershowitz contended that "Brown refused to investigate and/or publish highly credible information that undercut the simplistic and largely false narrative fed her by her biased sources."

He added: "I have been providing her with much of the documents and information she chose to bury rather than report."

Let's be clear: Mr. Dershowitz has never, to this day, provided me with a single document, other than his transcripts of static-filled audiotaped conversations and the one-page Freeh report, which had already been made public.

I TRIED TO REMAIN PROFESSIONAL, BUT IT WAS GETTING DIFFICULT TO not stand up to him. My instinct is always to fight back.

Then my kids reminded me of something that I always tell them when confronting bullies.

Take the high road.

This was one of those times that my kids told *me* to take the high road.

And so I did and moved on.

chapter 30

THE FEDS

By January 2019, there was intense pressure for Acosta to resign his post as Trump's labor secretary.

I had also heard, but could not confirm, that the FBI and federal prosecutors in New York had opened up a criminal probe on Epstein.

Brad Edwards had been trying, without success, to get the attention of prosecutors in New York for years. Up until my series ran, however, Edwards had been unable to convince law enforcement authorities to take up the case.

I couldn't confirm the probe, but suspected it was happening, largely because Edwards inexplicably began ignoring my phone calls, emails, and texts.

Or, there could be another explanation—that he was now a very popular attorney at the center of one of the biggest stories in the world, and he was simply busy with new clients.

As I worked to confirm whether there was a new probe, I began combing through the pile of tips I had received since publication of the series.

One of them was from a friend of an air traffic controller (ATC) at the airport in St. Thomas who told me the ATC had mentioned that Epstein frequently landed his private plane there and disembarked with young girls. I contacted the tipster and asked him to reach out to his friend to see if he or she would talk to me.

In the meantime, I had already been digging into Epstein's exploits in St. Thomas. I had obtained, from a source, documents that showed Epstein had illegally qualified for a lucrative program that saved him millions of dollars in taxes. The source suggested that Epstein paid off local government officials in order to obtain the tax break, which allowed him to write off 80 percent of his income.

But I needed to go to St. Thomas to do the story, and couldn't get there right away. I had been tasked by Casey with other work. I was back in the reporting mix.

PRESIDENT TRUMP THAT MONTH NOMINATED WILLIAM BARR TO BECOME the new attorney general. Barr, a former attorney general under George H. W. Bush, also was an alum of Acosta's former law firm, Kirkland & Ellis—which was the same firm that Epstein's lawyers Kenneth Starr and Jay Lefkowitz worked for.

At Barr's confirmation hearing, Senator Ben Sasse asked Barr whether he was committed to a "full and thorough" investigation into the way the Justice Department handled Epstein's case.

"Senator," Barr replied, "I have to recuse myself from Kirkland & Ellis matters, I am told, and I think Kirkland & Ellis was maybe involved in the case. So I need to sort out what—what my role can be, but, you know, I will say that if—if I'm confirmed, I'll make sure your questions are answered in this case."

Sasse was concerned that the DOJ might let the case slip through the cracks again.

"More broadly than the miscarriage of justice in this particular Florida case," Sasse said, "would you not agree that justice has nothing to do with the size of your bank account or the number of attorneys you can hire?"

But what Sasse and other lawmakers failed to ask—and should have—is whether William Barr knew Epstein.

It was certainly possible they knew each other, since Barr's father had hired Epstein at Dalton and the attorney general and Epstein would have been about the same age at the time.

IN EARLY FEBRUARY, THE DEPARTMENT OF JUSTICE OFFICIALLY OPENED a federal probe into whether Acosta and other prosecutors assigned to the 2007–08 Epstein case had committed any wrongdoing. The inquiry was assigned to DOJ's Office of Professional Responsibility, which is akin to an internal affairs unit, except that OPR often keeps its findings secret and rarely finds fault with federal prosecutors accused of misconduct.

Sasse wanted DOJ's inspector general, Michael Horowitz, to handle the case, but Horowitz, whose office is considered more independent than OPR, didn't have the legal authority. Unlike other federal agencies, DOJ insulates its lawyers from congressional and public scrutiny.

In a letter to Congress about the matter, Horowitz faulted DOJ's investigative process, saying it "shields prosecutorial misconduct from review by a statutorily independent Office of Inspector General."

But Congress failed to change the Justice Department's review process, and OPR remained in charge of the Acosta probe.

AS IF ACOSTA'S PROBLEMS COULDN'T GET ANY WORSE, ONE WEEK later, the federal judge in Palm Beach presiding over the Crime Victims' Rights Act (CVRA) lawsuit finally issued a ruling.

In a thirty-three-page order, U.S. District Judge Kenneth A. Marra put an official stamp on what lawyers Brad Edwards and Paul Cassell had been claiming for years—that federal prosecutors broke the law when they gave Epstein a non-prosecution agreement without notifying his victims.

Cassell called me that afternoon as soon as he got word. The normally composed former judge could not hide his happiness. He and Edwards had been fighting the case for almost eleven years, at great personal and financial sacrifice.

Not only did the judge say that the deal was illegal, but in a sharply worded rebuke, Marra noted how prosecutors deliberately misled Epstein's victims by seeking "to conceal the existence" of the agreement.

"When the Government gives information to victims, it cannot be misleading. While the Government spent untold hours negotiating the terms and implications of the [agreement] with Epstein's attorneys, scant information was shared with victims," Marra wrote.

The judge had reviewed depositions and other evidence that had not been made public, so it was also telling that Marra affirmed that Epstein was running an international sex trafficking operation.

"Epstein worked in concert with others to obtain minors, not only for his own sexual gratification but also for the sexual gratification of others," the judge wrote.

But he stopped short of issuing any kind of punishment, or doing what Courtney and the other victims really wanted—which was to void the deal and lock Epstein up in prison.

To me, however, the victory was not a hollow one.

I knew what it meant for the survivors.

It meant that they were finally being treated as real victims instead of prostitutes.

THE FOLLOWING MONTH, A HEARING WAS SCHEDULED ON A MOTION that the *Miami Herald* had quietly filed almost a year earlier in federal court in New York. We were seeking to unseal documents in the defamation case brought in 2016 by Virginia Giuffre against Ghislaine Maxwell.

During the 2016 litigation, the judge allowed the blanket sealing of a vast trove of documents, including the testimony of witnesses and other sensitive evidence that was gathered during discovery in the case. The testimony, in particular, was said to reveal new details about Epstein's sex trafficking operation, including the names of other prominent men who were involved.

Dershowitz tried unsuccessfully to get a select number of documents unsealed in 2016 when the case was still being litigated. He maintained that there were emails between Giuffre and *Daily Mail* reporter Sharon Churcher that proved that Giuffre was being pressured to lie about him. Dershowitz wanted those emails to be made public.

Conservative blogger Michael Cernovich, an aggressive critic of the Clintons, also filed a similar motion, hoping to get information against them. The judge, Robert W. Sweet, denied the motions, saying their release could taint a potential jury pool.

But with the case between Giuffre and Maxwell now settled, the *Herald* in April 2018 filed a more extensive motion arguing that since the case was closed, all the documents should be made public. Sweet rejected our motion in October 2018, just before the series was published.

But we appealed the decision to the U.S. Court of Appeals for the Second Circuit in New York.

The *Herald* argued that the importance of the public's right to access information about such a serious crime outweighed any privacy concerns that may have led to the sealing of the documents.

"In connection with its ongoing investigation, the *Miami Herald* has sought to access public court filings that will shed light on the Epstein scandal and address questions of serious public concern," our motion read. "These include how the Epstein case was disposed of by the criminal justice system, whether victims were treated properly, whether Epstein's victims were unfairly kept in the dark, whether Epstein was given favorable treatment because of his wealth and status, in short, whether the public interest was served."

The First Amendment imposes a heavy burden on those who seek to limit public access, and we were arguing that that burden had not been met in the Maxwell case.

Subsequently, the Reporters Committee for Freedom of the Press and thirty-two other media companies, including the *New York Times*, the *Washington Post*, Fox News, Gannett, *Politico*, and the Tribune Publishing Co., filed briefs in support of our motion.

On March 6, a public hearing was held in New York, with Sandy Bohrer, our attorney, arguing before the three-judge appeals court.

Paul Cassell, representing Virginia Giuffre, told the court that the testimony of other witnesses in the case would implicate some prominent men involved in Epstein's operation. "When all the records come out, it will show that Epstein and Maxwell were trafficking girls to the benefit of his friends, including Dershowitz," Cassell said at the hearing.

Lawyers for both Dershowitz and Cernovich renewed their motion to release portions of the case. Meanwhile, Maxwell's attorneys argued that unsealing the case would constitute an invasion of privacy.

Later, outside the courtroom, Dershowitz proffered an elaborate conspiracy theory he insisted was behind Virginia's allegations: that Giuffre, together with her lawyer, David Boies, had concocted the false claims of sexual abuse against Dershowitz as a means to extort Les Wexner, the eighty-three-year-old billionaire CEO of Victoria's Secret and the Limited stores.

Dershowitz claimed that Boies forced Giuffre to publicly name Dershowitz to send a message to Wexner, whom Virginia had only privately named as an abuser. Dershowitz contended that by naming Dershowitz, it would rattle Wexner enough to pay a secret settlement to Giuffre to keep his name from becoming public in the same way Dershowitz's had.

There are at least two problems with this story. First, Boies wasn't

Virginia's lawyer when she outed Dershowitz; Brad Edwards was. Second, Wexner's lawyer would later testify under oath that no financial claim was ever made by Giuffre or her lawyers against the billionaire retailer.

The damage, however, to Wexner's reputation by Dershowitz's statements had been done. Wexner was now facing scrutiny from his stockholders, and the adverse publicity over his connections to Epstein was affecting his corporate bottom line. He issued a statement apologizing for ever associating with Epstein, insists he has never met Giuffre, and continues to deny that he did anything improper or illegal. Wexner would eventually step down as chairman and retire from the board of his company.

THE NEW YORK APPEALS COURT ISSUED AN ORDER TO UNSEAL PORTIONS of the Maxwell case about a week later. While we would not get those documents for months, it was a significant victory. The release was delayed, however, to give all parties a window of time to file objections. Sure enough, two mystery parties, labeling themselves as J. and John Doe, filed legal briefs to block the documents from becoming public. "J. Doe" appeared to be a victim who didn't want to be identified; and the identity of "John Doe," who claimed he was not party to the Maxwell suit, is still a mystery.

ON MARCH 4, EPSTEIN'S LAWYERS, RESPONDING TO A BLISTERING editorial in the *New York Times*, took the bold step of writing a letter published in the paper, defending Epstein's plea deal. Among other things, they claimed that the case wasn't prosecuted because there was no "credible and compelling proof" that Epstein committed any federal crimes.

"That the guilty plea was required in a state, not federal, court reflected the absence of evidence that Mr. Epstein used the internet, traveled to a location away from his home for the purpose of having illegal sex, commercially trafficked women to others, engaged in force, fraud or coercion, used drugs or alcohol to entice young women who came to his house to exchange sexual massages for money, possessed child pornography or in other ways violated federal law."

The letter was signed by Kenneth Starr, Martin Weinberg, Jack Goldberger, and Lilly Ann Sanchez.

THAT SPRING, THE COUNTRY WAS CONSUMED BY THE REPORT ISSUED by Special Counsel Robert Mueller.

Mueller had been appointed to investigate Russian interference in the 2016 presidential election. He submitted his five-hundred-plus-page report to Attorney General William Barr. The much-anticipated tome confirmed that the Russians had interfered with the election. It stopped short, however, of directly tying President Trump to illegal activities, even though it suggested that he obstructed justice by interfering with the probe.

Meanwhile, the call for Acosta to step down was growing louder each day. Trump's press secretary, Sarah Huckabee Sanders, was asked about the Epstein case at a White House press briefing but would only say that "we're certainly looking into it."

It was telling that the president's spokeswoman failed to issue a statement in support of Acosta, as Trump had often done for other members of his administration who were under fire.

Over the next several months, the news cycle was dominated by stories about Mueller as Democratic members of Congress mobilized their own investigation into foreign interference in the election.

It seemed that Epstein was once again a footnote in Washington.

I CONTINUED TO ANALYZE EPSTEIN'S TRAVELS, WONDERING HOW HE managed to fly in and out of the country, untouched. Finally, after countless calls to federal agencies, my queries to the Department of Homeland Security were noticed by the Office of Customs and Border Protection (CBP). In June, an agent with the U.S. Marshals Service emailed me about one of my queries in which I mentioned that I had a source who told me that air traffic controllers had seen Epstein deplane with young girls at the St. Thomas airport. The marshal, Brad Bolen, wanted to know more—and I wanted to know what the Marshals Service was up to, so I agreed to meet him.

We met at the Moonlite, a throwback 1950s diner in Hollywood, Florida, filled with old movie posters, chrome counters, and red vinyl booths. It was the same place I often met my journalist breakfast buddies, because it was centrally located in Broward County, just south of Fort Lauderdale and right off Interstate 95.

Bolen arrived with another agent, and they presented their badges. They informed me that CBP had opened an investigation into whether Epstein was trafficking minors using his private plane. They were fishing for information from me, assuming that I knew an air traffic controller at the airport who had seen Epstein—which was not the case. However, I didn't correct him.

Bolen wanted to speak to the air traffic controller and anyone else I knew who had information about Epstein's movements in and out of St. Thomas or New York.

I told him I needed to talk to my source and couldn't promise anything. After all, I didn't know who the air traffic controller was. I was still hoping the ATC's friend would persuade him or her to talk to me.

I began planning a trip to St. Thomas and Epstein's Pedophile Island.

chapter 31

THE JOURNALISM RESISTANCE

I was beginning to think that the only way to get justice for Epstein's survivors was to keep writing hard-hitting stories, hoping that the national attention would ensure that his victims would not be forgotten with the next news cycle.

But the TV appearances and publicity, it turned out, had far-reaching effects that I could never have predicted. One of them was that I began hearing from sexual assault victims all over the world. Journalists rarely get supportive letters, so I was incredibly moved by all the cards, letters, and emails from people, both men and women, sharing their stories of sexual assault and abuse.

I would return from trips to New York to find my desk covered with mail. Beautiful letters, sometimes even gift cards, flowers, and hand-drawn thank-you notes. One woman sent me an envelope with five blank cards inside, along with a stamped, self-addressed envelope. She asked me to sign my name on each and mail them back to her so she could give the autographs to some of her grandchildren.

The letters made me cry. I did not have time to respond to them all, but I read every one. I still have them.

AT A TIME WHEN OUR PRESIDENT WAS CALLING REPORTERS "THE ENEMY of the People," I discovered that my work was suddenly being used as a positive example of the importance of local journalism. Over the next year, the *Miami Herald*'s digital subscription base began to grow. Readers from Hawaii to Maine purchased subscriptions to support our work or even offered outright donations. This was not the first time the *Herald* had garnered this kind of attention for a story, but the offers of contributions to our paper grew so voluminous that the *Herald* and our parent company, McClatchy, set up a nonprofit arm to help fund investigative journalism.

The series also inspired countless young journalists who reached out to me seeking advice on their careers. I remembered how lost I felt during college, with no mentor to guide me through the maze of decisions that I faced. So I accepted just about every request I received to talk to student journalists during this crazy time in my life. I think besides helping them, the conversations also helped me remember how I got to where I am.

I was exhausted, however, and tiring of the television appearances. I wanted to get back to working on the story, and I needed to spend some time with my children.

One early evening, when Emily and I were in New York on assignment, I got a call from my daughter, Amelia. She was having a panic attack over the deadline for her applications to vet school. She couldn't bring herself to finish them. She was convinced she wasn't going to get accepted anywhere, and had managed to work herself into a frenzy of anxiety.

I was in a bind because I had promised to do a segment on ABC the following day, and they had paid for our hotel that night in New York.

The next morning, I called ABC and told them I had to cancel. I hopped a train to Philadelphia. That weekend, I made Amelia tell me everything she knew about being a veterinarian and why she wanted to become one.

Then I told her to put the words she told me on paper. The applications took all weekend, but we got them done.

My son, Jake, meanwhile, was applying to college, with hopes of going to Florida State. I was juggling his applications, too, and once again trying to figure out how to pay tuition.

It was right around this time that Emily and I received a cryptic message that our publisher wanted to see us separately in her office as soon as possible. We had to make appointments with her secretary.

It's rare that reporters are called into the publisher's office, unless it's for a very bad reason.

I of course assumed the worst. I told Emily we were probably getting fired, or laid off, or maybe it was just another unpaid furlough. The best-case scenario in my mind was we'd get a scolding about our expenses.

I made Emily go first.

It turned out that McClatchy's CEO, Craig Forman, was giving us a bonus.

It was beyond belief—and relief—as I was still taking biweekly payday loans to make ends meet. I was going to the Check Cashing Store so often that the woman who worked there knew me by my first name.

"How is your daughter? Did she get into vet school?" she would ask. We would chat briefly about her own daughter, who seemed smart and was doing well in school.

Not long ago, I went by the Check Cashing Store and it was closed for good. I hope that the nice woman who worked there was able to land on her feet, as I finally was able to do.

THE PULITZER PRIZES ARE SUPPOSED TO BE A SECRET, SOLEMN PINKY-
swear selection process. But it's asking the impossible to keep the
nominations under wraps from a group of people who make a living
out of getting information they aren't supposed to have.

"Perversion of Justice" was entered in two categories: investigative
journalism and local reporting. Investigative journalism is arguably
the toughest category to win, and I was up against some exhaustively
researched projects from 2018, including one by the *New York Times*,
a blockbuster about Trump's businesses. I knew it would be impossible to beat that series, but I was hopeful that my project would at
least be nominated and make the finals.

But in March, I learned I hadn't made the cut.

"Dirty Gold," the *Herald* series by Jay Weaver and reporters Kyra
Gurney, Jim Wyss, and Nicholas Nehamas, was a finalist in the explanatory journalism category.

As it turned out, the *New York Times*' Trump series was also
moved to that category, explanatory, and won. The same *Times* series
was also a finalist in the investigative journalism category, which was
won by the *Los Angeles Times*, for a project about a former gynecolo-
gist at the University of Southern California who was accused of sexually abusing hundreds of students during three decades working at
a campus clinic. The series triggered local, state, and federal probes,
as well as the resignation of the university's president.

I WOULD NEVER KNOW WHETHER THE EFFORTS BY SOME IN THE
journalism industry to undermine my series impacted the decision-
making that went into that year's Pulitzer Prizes. But it truly didn't
matter to me all that much. I was aiming for something greater than
a Pulitzer: justice.

chapter 32

KATIE JOHNSON

That summer I was assigned, along with *Miami Herald* reporter Doug Hanks, to investigate a story about Jerry Falwell Jr., the president of Liberty University. Falwell, one of the leaders of the Christian right, was in a mysterious business relationship with a male pool attendant whom he and his wife, Becky, had met at the iconic Fontainebleau hotel in Miami Beach.

Doug had learned that naked photographs of Falwell's wife—and a few others of her fully clothed sitting on the pool boy's lap—had landed in the hands of someone who wasn't supposed to have them.

It was another one of those only-in-Miami stories that you just can't make up. Where else can one of the world's most prominent evangelical leaders frolic with his wife and a pool boy?

If that wasn't wild enough, comedian Tom Arnold also had a cameo in this story, along with Trump's fixer, lawyer Michael Cohen. Arnold had recorded Cohen saying he had seen the naked photographs. Doug's source told him that a man with a thick New York accent had called and threatened to harm him if he didn't keep quiet about the naughty pictures. Falwell, a loyal Trump supporter, denied that anything illegal or immoral had happened.

In order to confirm that some of these photographs were authentic, we had to see them and then confirm where they were taken and when. We knew from Falwell's Instagram account that the couple had spent a lot of time at the Fontainebleau—and at a resort in Islamorada. One of the photographs we were shown was of Becky Falwell naked in a shower. We were told that shower was at a fancy resort in the Florida Keys.

I managed to talk Casey into letting me take a trip to the hotel, Cheeca Lodge, an exclusive retreat for the rich and famous, about a two-hour drive from Miami.

"I have to stay at the hotel in order to look at the rooms, as well as the property, you know, in order to match the location with the actual photographs," I told Casey. "It's such a private resort that they don't just let reporters in there to walk around."

My tactic worked.

So in early June, I was on another investigation. But at least I was getting a trip to the Keys out of it.

I took one of my friends with me as a bodyguard. Lois is eighty-one years old, but she has been a physical education teacher for sixty years, and at the time she was still teaching high school students aerobics and sex education. She is in better shape than most people half her age, and I have a hard time keeping up with her.

We packed overnight bags. I threw on a pair of jeans and a tank top; Lois donned her big floppy hat and Ray-Ban sunglasses—and we hopped in her white Volkswagen Beetle convertible, which always attracted attention because she had giant eyelashes attached to the car's headlights.

The object of my trip, however, was not to sit on the beach and sip champagne; although at this resort, that's the first thing they give

KATIE JOHNSON | *313*

you upon check-in. This was definitely a step up for me. My get-away weekends to the Keys were usually spent at what I called cheap BYOBs—"Bring your own bedding" motels.

We walked around to get a look at the lavishly landscaped property, which included two large tiki bars, two swimming pools, and a beach, which, that weekend, happened to be covered with so much smelly seaweed that it was impossible to go in the water even if we wanted to. I thought about all the people who were spending six hundred dollars or more a night to stay there and was glad that the *Herald* was picking up my tab.

It didn't take more than a day to identify the pier in the background of the Falwell photo and the unusual palm tree at the water's rocky edge, or to confirm that several of the naked photos of Mrs. Falwell were taken in a shower in one of the rooms of the resort. The bath/shower area had unique tiling and fixtures that matched the photographs exactly.

Before leaving the following day, Lois and I decided to take a swim in the adults-only pool. Our conversation turned to the Epstein case. Shortly thereafter, a woman who was swimming nearby approached me and, after a brief, probing conversation in which she asked where we were from, the woman identified herself as a private investigator employed by Jack Goldberger, Epstein's Palm Beach attorney.

I don't really believe in coincidences. I wondered if Goldberger had hired her to follow me. I told her to tell Jack I said hello and to remind him that I had been trying to talk to him for almost a year.

She gave me her business card and we parted ways, as it was time for us to head home.

As for the Falwell story, Doug and I worked on it for another week and it ran on the front page of the paper. A year later, Falwell would step down as president of the university after another naughty photograph was made public of him with his pants unzipped and his arms around another woman whose pants were also unzipped. The pool boy then went public, claiming that Falwell directed him to have sex with Falwell's wife, Becky, so that Falwell could watch. Falwell denied this part of the story.

TOM ARNOLD, WHO WAS ACTIVELY PURSUING THE FALWELL STORY ON Twitter, not only seemed to know a lot about Falwell's pool boy; he also claimed to know some of the people around Ghislaine Maxwell, who had for many years dated and been engaged to a friend of Arnold's from Iowa, Ted Waitt. I reached out to Arnold to see what he knew.

He said that Maxwell and Waitt had been together almost eleven years, and that Waitt probably knew her better than anyone. During the couple's time together, Maxwell founded the TerraMar Project, a research and environmental organization dedicated to protecting the world's oceans. She spoke at the United Nations and also gave a TED Talk about the organization's efforts in 2014. That same year, she spoke at the Council on Foreign Relations in Washington, D.C.

According to tax records, TerraMar never gave out grants, but the *New York Times* reported that the nonprofit did have a partnership with a luxury bedding company to produce "water inspired" sheets.[1]

I suspected that Maxwell was spending more ocean time lounging on luxury yachts than actually saving the seas from pollution.

Many wondered whether the charity was really a mechanism for Maxwell to cleanse her reputation after her rumored involvement with Epstein's sex trafficking ring.

Arnold would continue to call or text me from time to time, hinting that he had some tidbit about Maxwell that I should look into. But none of the people associated with Maxwell would talk to me when I tried to contact them.

Arnold was also talking to Michael Cohen, who had helped Trump cover up one, and possibly several, affairs. On Twitter, Arnold was urging Cohen to go public with Trump's sexual escapades.

One of Trump's alleged mistresses was porn star Stormy Daniels. The *Wall Street Journal* reported that Cohen had paid Daniels $130,000 in October 2016—a month before the election—in order to silence her about an affair that she had had with Trump in 2006.[2] The story snowballed, leading to a federal investigation, and in August 2018, Cohen pleaded guilty to eight criminal counts, including tax evasion, lying to a financial institution, and federal campaign violations. He eventually admitted that he had paid Daniels at Trump's direction to silence her in advance of the election.[3]

Cohen's role in squashing such Trump scandals made me wonder whether a similar or parallel playbook was used to silence another woman who made claims against both Trump and Epstein during the 2016 campaign.

IN EARLY 2016, AN ANONYMOUS WOMAN FILED A CIVIL COMPLAINT IN federal court in California, under the pseudonym "Katie Johnson." She alleged that she was sexually abused and raped by Trump and Epstein when she was thirteen, over a four-month period from June to September 1994.

Johnson said that Epstein invited her to a series of "underage sex parties" at his New York mansion where she met Trump. Enticed by promises of money and modeling opportunities, Johnson said she was forced to have sex with Trump several times, including once with another girl, twelve years old, whom she labeled "Marie Doe."

Trump demanded oral sex, the lawsuit said, and afterward he "pushed both minors away while angrily berating them for the 'poor' quality of their sexual performance," according to the lawsuit, filed April 26 in U.S. District Court in Central California.

Afterward, when Epstein learned that Trump had taken Johnson's virginity, Epstein allegedly "attempted to strike her about the head with his closed fists," angry that he had not been the one to take her virginity. Johnson claimed that both men threatened to harm her and her family if she ever revealed what had happened.

Johnson filed the suit on her own behalf, just as Trump emerged as a front-runner for the 2016 election. She was seeking one hundred million dollars in damages.

Very few American newspapers covered the lawsuit when it was initially filed. At the time, Trump's attorney Alan Garten told the *Miami Herald* that it was "unequivocally false."

The lawsuit was subsequently dismissed because Johnson had failed to file it under the correct statute, and there was no evidence that she lived at the address she noted in her paperwork. Then, in June 2016, she refiled the lawsuit in the Southern District of New York. It was amended in late September, little more than a month before the presidential election.

This time, using the pseudonym Jane Doe, Johnson sued Trump and Epstein for sex crimes, assault and battery, false imprisonment, and defamation. She sought a protective order because she feared retribution from Trump and Epstein. She also provided more detail about the alleged incidents, saying that she traveled by bus to New York City in 1994 to start a modeling career. After being told by several modeling agencies that she needed a portfolio, she decided to return home. She went to the Port Authority to buy a bus ticket. There, she said, she met a woman named Tiffany who told her about a number of parties where she could meet prominent people who could help get her into modeling. She was told she would be paid to attend the parties, which she later learned were held at a mansion being used by Epstein.

Johnson said she attended at least four different parties that summer at the mansion. There were a number of young girls at the parties, as well as older guests, including Trump. Her affidavit provided the same details as her earlier lawsuit, including descriptions of the brutal rape and physical abuse she said she endured from both Trump and Epstein.

"I loudly pleaded with Trump to stop," she said in the lawsuit, describing Trump raping her. "Trump responded to my pleas by violently striking me in the face with his open hand and screaming that he could do whatever he wanted."

In a YouTube video posted before the November 2016 election, a woman who purported to be Johnson (her face blurred) talks about the sex parties that Epstein hosted and her interactions with both men.

The videos appeared to be politically motivated, as Johnson returns time and again to Trump and how she feared his being elected president.

Wearing a blond wig and sitting in front of a curtain beside a table with a lamp, she describes meeting "Tiffany," who worked for Epstein in 1994.

A woman named "Tiffany Doe" filed an affidavit with the lawsuit in which she said that when she was twenty-two years old, she was hired by Epstein as a party planner. She said she was instructed to hire adolescent girls to attend parties, most of which were held at 9 East Seventy-first Street, which was Epstein's massive town house, then owned by billionaire Leslie Wexner. (Wexner later transferred ownership of the property to Epstein.)

Among the places Tiffany looked for girls was the Port Authority Bus Terminal. She recalled recruiting Johnson ("Jane Doe") and luring her to attend several parties, where she said she personally witnessed Johnson being forced to perform sex acts with Trump and Epstein.

She went on to claim that she witnessed both Trump and Epstein rape Johnson and alleged that Epstein sexually and physically abused other minor girls at the mansion.

"After leaving the employment of Mr. Epstein in 2000, I was personally threatened by Mr. Epstein that I would be killed and my family killed as well if I ever disclosed any of the physical and sexual abuse of minor females that I had personally witnessed by Mr. Epstein or any of his guests," she said in the affidavit.

In her lawsuit, Johnson also refers to twelve-year-old Maria, who she said was involved with her in one of the sex incidents involving Trump.

A THIRD WOMAN, IDENTIFIED AS "JOAN DOE," FILED A DECLARATION
saying that in the "1994–95 school year," Jane Doe (aka Katie Johnson) had told her about the abuse with Trump and Epstein.

In the video, Johnson adds more detail about her encounters with
Trump, saying that Epstein hired her and other girls to entertain and
perform for the wealthy men at the parties he hosted at his mansion.

It appears that Epstein and Trump met about 1987, often attending the same parties and social events in New York and Palm Beach.
NBC News, in July 2019, unearthed some film footage of Epstein
partying with Trump at Mar-a-Lago in 1992. The video showed
Trump greeting Epstein during a party with cheerleaders from the
Buffalo Bills and Miami Dolphins. Divorced at the time the video
was shot, Trump can be seen whispering to Epstein and pointing to
one of the women, as Epstein doubles over and laughs.[4]

Brad Edwards, who spoke to Trump during his investigation into
Epstein, claimed that, according to Trump, the problems between
the two started when Epstein hit on the daughter of a Mar-a-Lago
club member. Trump got angry and banned him from the resort.

But Epstein's brother Mark had a different view of Epstein's relationship with Trump. In a civil deposition, Mark Epstein stated that
Trump had flown several times on Epstein's plane and that the two
were good friends.

"I know Trump is trying to distance himself, but they were," he
said, adding that Trump used to comp Epstein's mother and aunt at
one of Trump's casinos in Atlantic City.[5]

Epstein had twenty different numbers for Trump in his so-called
Black Book, or phone book, including numbers for Trump's car, his
houseman, his security detail, and one labeled "Norma—emergency
contact." Norma Infante Foerderer was Trump's longtime executive
assistant who died in 2013.

Of course, portions of the book were compiled by Maxwell, who
was also a friend of Trump's and had reportedly introduced Trump
to his future wife and First Lady, Melania.

THE REAL BAD BLOOD DEVELOPED BETWEEN THE TWO OF THEM OVER A 2004 real estate deal. Trump learned that Epstein was eyeing one of the largest mansions in Palm Beach, a seven-bedroom oceanfront estate along the iconic Raider's Row, nicknamed for the large number of Wall Street investors who live there. Ironically, the property had once been owned by Les Wexner, Epstein's top client. Wexner sold it in 1988 to nursing home developer Abe Gosman for $12.1 million.[6]

Gosman lost the property when he filed for bankruptcy in 2001.

When it came time for auction, Epstein tried without success to get Trump disqualified from the bidding. After the last bidder bowed out, Epstein was unable to top Trump's offer, and the property went to Trump for $41.1 million.[7]

Trump refurbished it and put it on the market for $125 million. He eventually sold it in 2008 to a Russian businessman for $95 million.[8]

MORE DETAILS OF EPSTEIN'S FORAY INTO THE MODELING BUSINESS were revealed when one of Epstein's bookkeepers testified during a 2010 sworn civil deposition that Epstein invested a million dollars in a Miami-based modeling agency, Mc2, a partnership with French modeling scout Jean-Luc Brunel, who had launched the careers of many famous models.

The deposition had never been made public, so when it was leaked to me, I reported on it for the first time in my series.

Brunel's bookkeeper, Maria Vasquez, said that she arranged the paperwork for the deal. Epstein was explicit: he wanted his company set up just like Trump's modeling agency, Trump Model Management, she testified in the deposition, which was taken by Brad Edwards. At first, Epstein didn't want to be identified with the agency, but Vasquez said the bank insisted that Epstein sign the paperwork since he was putting up the money.

Brunel, who called himself a "scouting tsunami," had a dark

past. Like Epstein, he had been accused numerous times of sexual assault, often with minors. During the 2005–06 police investigation, police found phone messages from Brunel, one of them in which Brunel hinted that he had twelve-year-old twins to send him.

Vasquez had been working for Brunel since 1998. She said Epstein asked her to arrange for women and girls to come to the U.S. on tourist visas.

"Many girls coming here first, without a visa, without a working visa," Vasquez said. "Most of the girls, they were coming in to the States as tourists."

She said Brunel was collecting 30 percent from their income and didn't pay their taxes or Social Security.

Later, Epstein became concerned that they were going to get caught, so they hired lawyers to obtain work visas for the women.

Vasquez said the agency was providing models for legitimate assignments, but the agency was also used as a party pipeline. She said some of the lower-tier models, especially those who were very young, were sent to parties at Epstein's various homes in New York and Florida and on his island, as well as to other assignments where they were expected to provide sexual favors for those who hired them. If they didn't acquiesce to sex, Vasquez said they often weren't paid.

Trump also held his own model parties in New York, according to Michael Gross, who wrote an exposé in the *Daily Beast* in 2016 about Trump's party exploits where underage models were among the attendees.[9]

A photographer Gross interviewed for the story said that some of the girls were as young as fifteen.

"Trump would go 'room to room,' said the photographer. . . . 'It was guys with younger girls, sex, a lot of sex, a lot of cocaine, top-shelf liquor' but no smoking. Trump didn't approve of cigarettes." Trump, the photographer said, would "wander off with a couple of girls. I saw him. He was getting laid like crazy."

Trump has denied that he was ever involved with underage girls, and his spokespeople have repeatedly attacked Katie Johnson's story.

Johnson, in her lawsuit and video, said that Epstein's parties were similarly bizarre.

At the end of each event, the models would meet with Epstein, she said, and he would ask them about the men that they had been with, including what they liked and didn't like, and then each of them would be paid.

Trump, she said in the video, didn't participate in the orgies that often happened at the parties. But he liked to watch them. At one of them, she said he called her over and asked her to give him a hand job as he watched others having sex. Trump, a known germophobe, also insisted during another encounter that she give him oral sex while he was wearing a condom.

In 2018, I contacted one of Johnson's attorneys, Thomas F. Meagher, who cited attorney-client privilege for not giving me an interview. He did, however, assure me that he was confident in his case, and felt his client was credible and truthful.

While there were obvious political motives for Johnson to go public, that nevertheless doesn't mean that she was lying; perhaps it meant that she had fallen prey to people who wanted to use her story for political gain.

As the lawsuit advanced in New York, and a pretrial conference was set, Meagher reached out to Lisa Bloom, a Los Angeles attorney who represents victims of sexual abuse and harassment, particularly those who make allegations against prominent men.

I was unsuccessful in my attempts to talk to Bloom prior to the series. But in a recent interview, Bloom said she thoroughly vetted Johnson and believed she was truthful.

"Tom Meagher reached out and begged me to work alongside him. She [Johnson] was about to do a CNN interview, and he was afraid it was like throwing her to the wolves. She was a frightened young woman doing her first interview with CNN. He wanted her to be prepared and I felt I had an obligation to do what I could," said Bloom, who had represented other women who have accused Trump of sexual harassment and assault.

"You can never know for sure, but I make my own determination if someone is credible, and I thought she was and that the media should be reporting on it. It was also part of a larger concern that women who were making allegations against Trump were not getting covered," Bloom said.

In June 2016, Bloom wrote a piece for the *Huffington Post* accusing the mainstream media of ignoring Johnson's lawsuit.[10]

Bloom, the daughter of the civil rights lawyer Gloria Allred, raised questions about why journalists had been ignoring the Trump rape allegations, pointing out that the media had failed to adequately cover allegations of rape against another powerful man, comedian Bill Cosby.

"If the Bill Cosby case has taught us anything, it is to not disregard rape cases against famous men . . . now history is repeating itself," Bloom wrote, laying out a clear argument for why the media should be taking the rape allegations against Trump more seriously.

Bloom suggested that the allegations were too credible to ignore, especially against a man running for president.

Bloom accompanied Johnson to her interview with CNN. The story has never aired.

"They [CNN] never firmly said they weren't running it, and I always got the impression they were still working on it. I don't remember them giving us a hard no."

But as the election drew closer, Bloom decided to get Johnson's story out to the American public in another way: she scheduled a press conference for November 2, six days before Election Day.

"I met with her near her home a couple of hours away from me, and she came up and I met with her and several members of her team," Bloom recalled. "The day of the press conference we hired a hair and makeup person, and we sat in my office with her for an hour or two, fixing her hair."

By then, the media was interested. The *Washington Post* had just published a story, along with a video, about an interview that Trump did in 2005 for *Access Hollywood*. In the video, Trump tells the host, Billy Bush, how he often seduced married women.[11]

Dozens of media crammed into a conference room at Bloom's Los Angeles office for the 3:00 P.M. press conference at which Johnson was going to "break her silence" about Trump and Epstein, Bloom announced in her press release.

But when the time came, Bloom suddenly canceled.

"I have bad news. Jane Doe has received numerous threats today as have all Trump accusers I have represented. She is living in fear," Bloom said, adding that "we are going to have to reschedule."

Bloom said Johnson was at her office most of the day preparing.

"I was trying to go in the direction of airing her story publicly, and it was frankly embarrassing for me to cancel it. I took her out the back stairway and she instructed me to drop the case. I told her she should sleep on it. The next day she confirmed she dropped the case and she did not want us to ever talk about it again."

Since then, Johnson seems to have disappeared.

"I don't know where she is and haven't spoken to her since 2016," Bloom said.

Speculation soon circulated that the suit was dropped after a payoff by Trump or someone on his behalf, but Bloom brushed aside those rumors.

"Trump's people never reached out," Bloom said. "There was absolutely no communication with anyone in the Trump team."

After my series ran, I was contacted by dozens of readers, most of them just regular folks who demanded to know why I didn't write anything about the Katie Johnson lawsuit and the allegations she had made against Trump. In my mind, and I think in my editor's mind at the time, we felt that part of the problem with the coverage of the

Epstein story was that journalists had spent so much time trying to tie the story to politicians and celebrities that they missed the larger narrative about the negligence and possible corruption of the criminal justice system. In hindsight, I wish I had included the Johnson lawsuit.

Trump and Clinton were both friends with Epstein at a time when Epstein was clearly involved with girls. While that certainly calls their judgment into question, there has never been any evidence that either one of them had inappropriate sexual relations with minors.

Until victims come forward saying otherwise, engaging in innuendo does a disservice to those sexual assault victims who have been brave enough to tell their stories.

chapter 33

FIREWORKS

On July 6, 2019, Jeffrey Epstein was aboard his Gulfstream jet headed to New Jersey's Teterboro Airport after what had become an annual ritual: a summer holiday at his luxurious apartment on the exclusive Avenue Foch, near the Arc de Triomphe, in Paris.

He had some special playlists made for these Parisian holidays, music that ranged from rock songs like "Running with the Devil" by Van Halen and "Fun, Fun, Fun" by the Beach Boys to jazz favorites by Charlie Parker. Epstein was obsessed with playlists and had compiled these Paris playlists on Spotify.[1]

Teterboro, about twelve miles from downtown Manhattan, is the oldest operating airport in the New York City area. Its landing strips, surrounded by wetlands, have served as a gateway for some of aviation's most iconic figures, such as Charles Lindbergh and Amelia Earhart; and its tarmac has been graced by a litany of the world's rich and famous who can slip in and out of their private planes into waiting limos without being bothered by paparazzi and overzealous fans.

On that afternoon, however, the FBI had been monitoring Epstein's flight path, and by the time Epstein was flying over the Atlantic Ocean, the feds had mobilized an FBI welcome at Teterboro.

I HAD SPENT THAT JULY FOURTH WEEKEND AT HOME, WORKING ON A story about the feud between Alan Dershowitz and David Boies. For some reason, I hate being alone on the Fourth of July, especially in Florida. But since Jake was with me, it brought me solace, especially after dealing with a Dershowitz headache all weekend.

I spent most of the holiday fielding emails from him and forwarding them to our lawyer, Sandy Bohrer. Dershowitz was demanding, among other things, that I send him copies of lawyers' affidavits that were part of the public court file in his own defamation case.

"Name the other lawyers," he demanded in one email. "I don't have access to their affidavits."

Sandy was skeptical, saying that he certainly had access, but he was using this as a delaying tactic.

Casey was over it.

"Heading out to mow the lawn. Will be incommunicado for a while," he said in an email.

I spent the day going back and forth with Dershowitz, who threatened me repeatedly with legal action.

"Stop threatening me. I am not intimidated by you. Try keeping things professional," I wrote. "I respect the fact that you are dealing with a difficult situation, and I am trying my best to give you the benefit of the doubt even in the face of your attacks," I repeated.

I finally filed the story, then spent the evening watching fireworks over the ocean with Jake.

The following afternoon, Dawn Schneider, Boies's spokeswoman, sent me an email with the final arrangements for a trip Emily and I planned to take on Monday to Arkansas.

I had tried for almost two years to interview Annie and Maria Farmer, sisters who had long ago tried to tell their story about how they had been abused by Epstein and Maxwell. I was unsuccessful in getting them to talk, largely because Maria had been quite ill with cancer, and her sister was uncertain about being involved in my project. But I kept reaching out to their lawyers, hoping that the women would eventually agree to be interviewed.

Maria had had surgery in May 2019 and was still recovering. As we waited for the release of the sealed documents that the *Herald* had secured in its case against Maxwell, I had continued discussions into June with both Boies and Schneider to interview Maria and Annie, together.

Maria now lived in Paducah, Kentucky, and Annie lived in Austin, Texas. It wasn't an easy interview to coordinate.

We wanted photographs of both sisters, and also of Maria's art, which I suspected would show the trauma she had gone through all these years.

"We can agree to one photo of the two sisters if that's all she will agree to," I told Dawn after she said Maria was reluctant to have photographs taken.

"Best I can say is we'll try . . . if I push too hard around this mine field, I may lose them," Dawn said.

We arranged to do the interview on July 8 outside of Little Rock, Arkansas. Boies's law partner, Sigrid McCawley, was to fly in from Fort Lauderdale, Dawn was to fly in from New York, and Emily and I were flying in from Fort Lauderdale. The *Herald* agreed to pay for Annie's flight, and we brought her in a couple of days early, allowing her to spend the July Fourth weekend with her sister.

I braced myself for some pushback from the *Herald* at the cost of the trip. There is no easy way to get to Arkansas, and it was a holiday weekend, so Emily and I had to fly through Atlanta. The airfare for both of us, combined with the cost to fly Annie to Arkansas, was thousands of dollars.

Still, the trip was approved.

"Let's plan on starting at ten A.M. on Monday. I sent you the address . . . I hear the humidity level in Hot Springs is off the charts high. Going to be a bad hair day for me!" Dawn Schneider wrote.

"Ok, not even had a chance to look, been working around the clock, all day yesterday and today on this story. Have not even taken a shower today," I wrote.

Dawn asked about the story I was working on.

It was a semi-profile of Boies and Dershowitz, mostly about the ugly war between them that had been simmering for years.

Dawn got concerned.

"Does David know you are doing this?"

I told her I had spoken to David for the story.

That evening, the story went online and I sent a link to Dawn.

The headline: DERSHOWITZ V. BOIES: JEFFREY EPSTEIN CASE UN-LEASHES WAR BETWEEN TWO LEGAL GOLIATHS.

The story detailed the bitterness between two of the country's most powerful lawyers, involving accusations of extortion, surreptitious recordings, unethical conduct, and in Dershowitz's case, underage sex.

Dershowitz, then eighty, had filed bar complaints against Boies and McCawley in three states, while Boies, seventy-eight, represented victims who had alleged that Epstein had trafficked them to Dershowitz.

It was a story that I knew neither one of them would like. Boies does not like to be compared in any way to Dershowitz. Dawn immediately informed me that he was not pleased.

I spoke to Boies the following morning. Unlike Dershowitz, Boies has a way of letting you know he doesn't like something without throwing you headfirst into a plate-glass window.

Afterward, I started packing for the next day's flight to Arkansas.

AT 7:53 P.M. THAT NIGHT, A SATURDAY, I GOT AN EMAIL FROM SOMEONE on the *Herald*'s night desk, with the *Daily Beast* headline: JEFFREY EPSTEIN ARRESTED FOR SEX TRAFFICKING OF MINORS.[2]

I thought perhaps it was a mistake, but then my phone began ringing and didn't stop.

I called Emily, or she called me, I can't remember. We were in shock.

I called some sources who confirmed Epstein's arrest that evening at Teterboro Airport.

I honestly believed that he would never be held accountable. After eleven years, had the law finally caught up with Epstein?

At 5:30 P.M., about the same time as his arrest, about a dozen federal agents broke down the door to his Manhattan town house to execute search warrants.

Such commotion on the Upper East Side isn't common, and neighbors described for me the scene: "We heard the loud banging and we walked over and saw all these FBI agents just pounding down the door."

This meant a change of plans, as there was an indictment to be unsealed on Monday in federal court in New York.

I called Dawn to tell her I had to cancel the interview. She understood. I made it clear that I wanted to reschedule the interview with the Farmers as soon as we could.

Besides Epstein finally being behind bars, another thought brought me joy.

I knew Maria and Annie Farmer were together in Arkansas when they heard the news of his arrest.

EMILY AND I FLEW INTO NEW YORK THE FOLLOWING NIGHT, ARRIVING at our hotel late. We asked McClatchy corporate to book us a hotel as close to the courthouse on Pearl Street in downtown Manhattan as we could, since Emily had a lot of gear to carry and the arraignment was early.

I don't know whether it was because there weren't many rooms left, or whether McClatchy was just being generous, but the hotel was nicer than we had ever stayed in before.

It felt like we had barely put our heads to the pillow before it was time to wake up. It was before dawn, but Emily wanted to be at the federal courthouse to secure her spot. She knew it would be, in journalism lingo, a clusterfuck. We walked the half mile or so to the courthouse, gear in tow. There were already camera crews there; some of them had probably been there all night. I left her to set up and I set out to find coffee, which wasn't as easy as one might think in New York City that early in the morning.

I returned with our much-needed caffeine and waited several hours with Emily as the media descended upon the courthouse. I tried without success to reach Brad Edwards. I learned that he had possibly flown to New York with Courtney, and that other victims might also be arriving.

Cameras aren't permitted in the federal courthouse, so when the hearing was set to begin, I went inside to find a seat while Emily remained on the courthouse steps.

Sixty-six-year-old Jeffrey Epstein appeared in a blue prison jumpsuit and orange sneakers. He was unshaven, and his hair was disheveled after spending two nights at the Metropolitan Correctional Center, a hellhole of a federal prison notoriously understaffed and filled with vermin. Two of Epstein's victims whom we had interviewed, Courtney and Michelle, were in the courtroom. It was the first time they had seen him in a decade.

I was sitting only a few feet behind Epstein.

I remembered thinking that for a man who loomed so large, Epstein seemed quite small that day.

The magistrate read the charges: one count of sex trafficking of minors and one count of conspiracy to engage in sex trafficking of minors.

Epstein was asked how he intended to plea.

"Not guilty, Your Honor," he replied.

The indictment involved two unnamed victims who were underage at the time of the abuse, and another victim who had helped Epstein recruit. But prosecutors made it clear that they intended to expand their case to include additional victims.

At the press conference that followed, U.S. Attorney Geoffrey S. Berman of the Southern District of New York issued a public appeal to Epstein's victims, announcing that he had set up a special phone hotline for them to call.

Berman said Epstein's conduct "shocked the conscience" of America, and he issued a veiled rebuke to Florida authorities who had failed to prosecute him a decade before, saying, "My office is proud to stand up for these victims by bringing this indictment."

He was asked at the press conference why he had taken up this case after so much time had gone by.

"We were assisted by some excellent investigative journalism," Berman said, glancing briefly at me, sitting in the front row.

Afterward, I left the courtroom and faced a regiment of camera lenses in my face.

"No, sorry, guys, I really can't talk right now," I said, still trying to wrap my head around what had just happened. Besides, I was on deadline and had a story to write.

Emily stayed at the courthouse to get footage of the victims who attended the hearing, while I dashed back to the hotel to write one of the biggest stories of my career.

ATTENTION SWIFTLY TURNED TO EPSTEIN'S BAIL HEARING AND TO Acosta, with renewed calls for his resignation as labor secretary. House Speaker Nancy Pelosi called Acosta's deal with Epstein "unconscionable," and demanded he resign. Acosta's office wouldn't comment.

Neither would the White House or the Justice Department.

There was concern behind the scenes that Epstein's arrest, which was being handled by the SDNY's public corruption unit, was going to cause difficulty for Trump, who immediately tried to distance himself from Epstein by claiming that he hadn't spoken to him in years.

Bill Clinton also felt compelled to finally make a statement about his relationship with Epstein, claiming that he "knew nothing" about the crimes that Epstein was accused of. In a statement from his spokesman, Clinton acknowledged he took four trips on Epstein's airplane in 2002 and 2003, had one meeting with him in Clinton's Harlem office in 2002, and made a brief visit to Epstein's New York apartment with his security detail around the same time.

"He has not spoken to Epstein in well over a decade and has never been to Little St. James Island, Epstein's ranch in New Mexico or his residence in Florida," the statement said.

Epstein's criminal lawyer Reid Weingarten called the new charges a "do-over" of the Florida case.

"This is old stuff, this is ancient stuff," he said.

William Barr, the attorney general, recused himself from the case because of his ties to the Kirkland firm.

In another crazy twist, part of the public corruption team prosecuting Epstein was Assistant U.S. Attorney Maurene Comey, the daughter of former FBI director James Comey, who had been fired by Trump in 2017. Comey, along with the other prosecutors on the case, Alex Rossmiller and Alison Moe, requested that Epstein be held without bail until trial. A hearing was scheduled for July 15, the following Monday.

ALL OF A SUDDEN, EVERY MEDIA OUTLET IN THE WORLD WAS REPORTING on Epstein. Casey, feeling the pressure, wanted me to write a story about Epstein's early days teaching at Dalton, something I felt I couldn't do immediately. There were still too many missing pieces to the story of his arrest, and that was a trail I felt I needed to follow.

While I was in New York, I met with David Boies at his sprawling new office overlooking the Hudson River at Hudson Yards. The smells of sawdust and fresh paint were still in the air as we discussed, among other things, rescheduling my interview with Maria and Annie. With the media frenzy following the arrest, he said he didn't think it was a good time to do so. I told him to let me know when the timing was better, and I assured him that I was still eager to tell their story.

Instead, however, a few weeks later, he gave the story to the *New York Times*. I was disappointed and more than a bit angry, and I let both David and Dawn Schneider know that I was upset.

I suspected that the reason the *Times* got the story was that David was livid about the article I had written on him and Dershowitz. Perhaps it was also a way for him (or perhaps for Dawn) to try to repair their relationship with the *Times*, which had fractured after the Harvey Weinstein scandal.

THE DAY OF EPSTEIN'S ARREST, A REPORTER FROM THE *NEW YORK Times* called Monika Leal, the *Herald*'s librarian, wanting to get in touch with me.

No reporter wants to be part of their own story. I wanted nothing more than to be invisible again.

"They promised they will come to you and it will only be no more than an hour," said Melanie Jensen, my "fixer" in McClatchy corporate who handled media calls.

I told her I would not do the interview without Emily.

So that is how a profile of Emily and me ended up in the business section of the *New York Times*.

Emily and I met with the reporter, Tiffany Hsu, in the restaurant of our hotel the next morning. It was truly funny to us that we were having breakfast at a white-tableclothed restaurant with a reporter from the *New York Times*.

The *Times* story ended up capturing, pretty well, the struggles that Emily and I had faced working in the news business at a time when journalists were considered the "Enemy of the People," and local papers like the *Herald* were cutting their staffs or disappearing altogether.

We talked about, among other things, how Emily was now the only female photographer on staff, and how we often elected not to put in all our expenses out of anxiety that the cost would prevent us from being able to do other challenging assignments that required travel.

We were informed the next day that corporate wasn't pleased about our honesty.

I reminded Casey how earlier that very same year, after the George Polk Awards, I went out to dinner with a few fellow journalists and, upon seeing the bill on my company credit card, I freaked out at the cost, marked it as a "personal expense," and paid for it out of my own pocket.

That wouldn't be the end of my conversations with the *New York Times* that week.

On Wednesday, the day after the *Times* piece ran, I got a message via Twitter from Marc Lacey, the *Times'* national editor, who asked me to stop by the newsroom to chat.

I had only been to the *Times* building once before, for a job interview that obviously never led to a job.

The best way to describe the awe for any journalist walking into the *New York Times* is to think of it the way a priest would feel the first time he walks into the Vatican. The *Times* tower, between Fortieth and Forty-first Streets, has a cavernous bright orange lobby with vast ceilings and a magnificent 360-degree view of a woodland courtyard with fifty-foot birch trees towering over a carpet of ferns.

I don't really get nervous at job interviews, so I was pretty calm and confident until Marc Lacey greeted me and took me straight to the pope.

That's Dean Baquet, the executive editor of the *New York Times*.

Honestly, I don't remember what Mr. Baquet said or what I said. It happened so fast, I was stunned.

From there, Marc led me down a corridor past a conference room filled with what appeared to be college or older high school students. He brought me into the room and introduced me as the journalist who wrote the Epstein series. The group burst into applause, and I grew more uncomfortable.

From there, he walked me through the newsroom. Or, I think it was the newsroom. I could see people coming out of their offices walking toward me, as Marc ushered me into a large room with a sofa and conference table, which he called "the Dignitary Room," where editors and reporters interview important people, like presidents and foreign dignitaries. Among those who followed us into the room whom I recognized were Carolyn Ryan, one of the paper's managing editors, and reporter Jodi Kantor, who, along with Megan Twohey, had won a Pulitzer Prize the year before for their coverage of the Weinstein case.

There were other editors there whose names I can't recall. They all began asking me questions about the series, pumping me about whether there were angles to the story that I hadn't yet explored.

I was so caught off guard that I blabbed something about Epstein belonging to a secret Billionaire Boys Club, along with some of the wealthiest people in the world, like Bill Gates and Jeff Bezos. It was after I opened my fat mouth that I suddenly realized what they were doing. Damn, I had just been punked by the *New York Times*.

I smiled sweetly and told them that I'd figured out what they were trying to do. Sorry, I wasn't going to give them anything from my Epstein story list.

Carolyn Ryan offered to introduce me to some college students who would be willing to help me with my work. I was appreciative but still a bit pissed at myself when I left the newsroom and returned to the lobby. I should probably have been angry at them for treating me like a poor stepchild from a little local paper, but I wasn't.

I sat on a step overlooking the *Times'* million-dollar garden, thinking about the view we had from the *Herald* newsroom overlooking grubby warehouses in Doral. It was a million miles away from the beautiful bayfront building the *Miami Herald* used to occupy, before the company sold our signature headquarters in downtown Miami, demolished our storied newsroom, and banished us to a two-story office compound out by the Miami airport.

I didn't have time to feel sorry for myself. Alex Acosta had finally decided to break his silence. He had scheduled a press conference that afternoon.

I called Casey, who I figured had been wondering where I was because I had not checked in for a few hours.

"Hi, thought I would check in," I said, sounding pretty somber.

"Oh. Okay. How was the Dignitary Room?" he asked.

"What?"

"The Dignitary Room at the *New York Times.*"

"How did you know?" I asked.

"Let's just say someone sent me a message."

chapter 34

NO APOLOGIES, NO REGRETS

Alex Acosta took to the podium with the confidence of a secretary of labor about to do a victory lap over his latest jobs report.

About two dozen staffers attended the press conference in the dated, wood-paneled press briefing room at the Department of Labor in Washington. Alex Daugherty, a reporter from McClatchy's Washington bureau, called it "an unusually high-profile affair for what is otherwise a low-key office."

It was July 10, four days after Epstein's arrest.

Acosta, dressed in a charcoal-gray suit, crisp white shirt, and red tie, came prepared with a satchel of documents and a story. He was hoping to impress the president and save his job.

"Let me start by reiterating that I am pleased that the New York prosecution is going forward," he began, sounding upbeat and almost smiling. "They brought these charges based on new evidence against Jeffrey Epstein, who is now a registered sex offender, and this is a very, very good thing. His acts are despicable, and the New York prosecution offers an important opportunity to more fully bring Epstein to justice."

What followed was a painfully long and distorted retelling of the steps that he and other federal prosecutors took when Acosta had supervised the case a decade earlier in the Southern District of Florida.

For nearly an hour, Acosta asserted that he had done the best that he could do, given the cards that he was dealt by a state prosecutor who had been prepared to let Epstein walk without any charges at all.

"Simply put, the Palm Beach state attorney's office was ready to let Epstein walk free, no jail time, nothing," Acosta said, referring to Barry Krischer.

Describing going to trial as "a roll of the dice," Acosta cited two key people involved in the case as having serious doubts whether they would be successful—the lead prosecutor, Marie Villafaña, and the FBI case agent, Nesbitt Kuyrkendall.

Villafaña, he said, talked about victims who were scared or refused to testify, how some victims exonerated Epstein, and how many of them fretted about their names coming out and their families finding out what they had done.

"After the fact, people alleged that Epstein would have been easily convicted," said Acosta, reading directly from Villafaña's affidavit, which she filed in 2017 as part of the Crime Victims' Rights civil case. "As the prosecutor who handled the investigation . . . these contentions overlook the facts that existed at the time."

But like any lawyer, Acosta didn't put the affidavit in its full context, nor did he point to other parts of the document in which Villafaña questioned the decision not to prosecute Epstein.

Acosta also misrepresented Kuyrkendall's affidavit, filed in 2017. Most of that document concerned a single victim, identified as Jane

Doe 2, who refused to cooperate with the investigation. While Kuyrkendall conceded that other victims were interviewed, and many of them also expressed reluctance to testify, her final conclusion was far from how Acosta characterized it.

"No victims expressed a strong opinion that Epstein be prosecuted," Kuyrkendall wrote.

Victims are often reluctant to testify; good investigators and prosecutors know how to prepare witnesses for trial.

Acosta also seemed to forget the obvious: prosecutors didn't need *all* the victims to cooperate. All they needed was one or two. They had thirty-four.

Acosta also alleged that because this happened so long ago, the norms and perceptions in 2007 would have somehow adversely affected how the case was looked upon by jurors. The victims would have been subjected to "victim-shaming," for example, he said. That argument, however, fell flat for just about every prosecutor who analyzed it later.

"It was 2007, not 1958," wrote former prosecutors Mimi Rocah, Jennifer Rodgers, and Berit Berger in the *Daily Beast*.[1] "Child exploitation and child pornography were believed to be just as abhorrent then as they are now. In all relevant ways, the case would have been charged, tried, and decided exactly the same way in 2007 as it would be today."

Acosta also misled the public about the status of negotiations when he had that breakfast meeting with Epstein lawyer Jay Lefkowitz in October 2007. He claimed the meeting was arranged well after the agreement was signed, which was true—but then he contradicted himself by admitting that Epstein and his lawyers continued to argue with prosecutors about elements of the plea for eight months—all the way up until Epstein pleaded guilty in June 2008. Emails between Acosta and Lefkowitz after that breakfast also support the fact that there were ongoing negotiations about various portions of the agreement before, during, and well after Acosta and Lefkowitz had pancakes that morning.

A letter written by Lefkowitz indicates that, at that breakfast meeting, Acosta promised to not inform Epstein's victims about the deal, which was of critical importance to Epstein and his attorneys.

But perhaps the most disturbing part of Acosta's press conference was his refusal to apologize or express any regret for how Epstein's victims were treated, even knowing just how betrayed they felt by his actions.

Again, Acosta seemed to place blame on Villafaña's shoulders, saying it was she who raised concerns about telling the victims about the plea deal.

Afterward, even Republican lawmakers were frosty.

Senate Majority Leader Mitch McConnell deferred to the president for comment.

"Epstein is clearly a sick pig," said Republican Florida senator Marco Rubio, who had introduced Acosta—a fellow Cuban American—at his confirmation hearing with much praise and fanfare.

"Was it a difficult prosecutorial decision that was made at the time given the evidence, the number of witnesses at the time?" Rubio asked. "Or was it a decision that was made on the basis of political influence? And that's what we're hoping the Department of Justice's review of it will show."

Even former Palm Beach state attorney Barry Krischer, who had been silent since the case ended, was moved to write a public response to Acosta's statement.

"I can emphatically say that Mr. Acosta's recollection of this matter is completely wrong," Krischer said in an email to me and other reporters. "No matter how my office resolved the state charges, the U.S. Attorney's Office always had the ability to file its own federal charges," Krischer said. "If Mr. Acosta was truly concerned with the State's case and felt he had to rescue the matter, he would have moved forward with the 53-page indictment that his own office drafted. Instead, Mr. Acosta brokered a secret plea deal that resulted in a non-prosecution agreement in violation of the Crime Victims' Rights Act. Mr. Acosta should not be allowed to rewrite history."

I FLEW HOME ALONE THE FOLLOWING DAY. EMILY STAYED A BIT LONGER in New York to get photographs of Epstein's town house, Dalton, and other locations germane to his life. During the trip home, I thought mostly about Villafaña and Kuyrkendall, and how Acosta had used their own words to manipulate the facts in an attempt to save his career.

Villafaña and Kuyrkendall, the two women at the center of the federal case, had also been silenced by their bosses and said nothing. This allowed the powerful men involved in the case to spin history in Epstein's favor for more than a decade.

THE NEXT MORNING, I DESPERATELY NEEDED A RUN. I LACED UP MY sneakers and pulled my running playlist up on my iPhone. Pink's "Hustle" came on first, a fitting song for how I felt.

I had gone about three miles along the beach when my phone started ringing. It was a New York City area code, and I figured that it was another TV producer wanting me to go on a program, so I ignored it. Then the call came through again. And again.

I reached George's Market, at the other end of the beach from my apartment, and poured a cup of coffee. Acosta's press conference from two days earlier was playing on TV.

My phone rang again.

It was a TV producer, as I suspected.

"Acosta just resigned," she said.

I walked over closer to the television so I could listen.

"Hey, Joanne, can you turn it up?" I asked the clerk behind the counter, a friend with whom I kvetched with most mornings.

Acosta was standing on the south lawn of the White House, next to President Trump.

"I called the president this morning. I told him that I thought the right thing was to step aside. Cabinet positions are temporary trusts. It would be selfish for me to stay in this position and continue talking about a case that's twelve years old rather than about the amazing economy we have right now.

"So, I submitted my resignation to the president, effective seven days from today."[2]

It was the equivalent of a Friday Night news dump, a resignation on a Friday morning the weekend before Epstein's bail hearing in New York.

I called Casey, then Emily. Chief Reiter had already texted me.

Then I put my headphones back on and ran.

chapter 35

INMATE 76318-054

I started experiencing stomach cramps and nightmares. It didn't help that Emily, usually the voice of reason, started piling furniture in front of her hotel room door at night out of fear that someone would break in.

I was plagued by a recurring dream that someone, usually Epstein, but sometimes Maxwell, was pushing me off a cliff. I was mindful of being in the spotlight now, and both Emily and I were paying close attention to our surroundings. We were so busy with work, we didn't have time to think about adopting stricter security protocols, but we did start to monitor each other's location through an app on our iPhones.

I was asked at several functions that I attended whether I was ever worried about my safety covering this story.

My answer was always "only when someone asks me that question."

On Monday, at the federal courthouse in Lower Manhattan, Epstein, appearing a bit more scrubbed and coiffed than last time, sat stone-faced as his lawyers argued in favor of releasing him on bail to await trial. They told judge Richard Berman that Epstein was now reformed. He was complying with his sex offender registration requirements and had been living a clean life since his arrest in Florida a decade ago.

As proof of that, they claimed that there had been no complaints filed in recent years alleging that he had abused minors. Defense lawyer Martin Weinberg argued that because of Epstein's high profile, it would be almost impossible for him to get away with any kind of abuse without it being reported.

Weinberg repeatedly told the judge to put aside the issue of consent.

"It's not like he's an out-of-control rapist," Weinberg said. (As if having sexual contact with girls three or four times a day wasn't "out of control.")

Berman, arguably best known as the judge who overturned New England Patriots quarterback Tom Brady's four-game suspension in the 2015 "Deflategate" scandal, wasn't buying Epstein's story of being a changed man.

Berman, in addition to sitting on the bench for two decades, was a licensed social worker and had a master's degree in the field. He had authored a number of articles in the *New York Law Review* about child abuse, including "Seven Steps to Protect Children." He was also a member of the New York State Permanent Judicial Commission on Justice for Children.[1]

Berman said the evidence wasn't clear-cut on whether pedophiles can reform themselves.

"There is other discussion in some of these studies that sex crimes are the most difficult to evaluate in relation to recidivism and a lot of other concepts because in sex crimes, victims very often don't come forward," Berman noted.

He added that he was also disturbed by a *New York Post* story that had run a few days earlier, reporting that Epstein never checked in with New York City police in the eight-plus years since he was ordered by a judge to do so as part of his sex offender requirements.[2]

Apparently, NYPD never enforced the judge's order.

To that end, Berman said he had reviewed the judge's decision and the transcript of Epstein's 2011 hearing where New York Supreme Court Justice Ruth Pickholz sternly rejected Epstein's effort to downgrade his sex offender status.

What is noteworthy, besides Epstein's unrelenting endeavor to game the system, was that he managed to enlist New York District Attorney Cy Vance's office to help him. Pickholz noted that in all her years on the bench she had never seen a prosecutor try to ease the registration burden for a convicted sex offender.

Berman agreed.

"The prosecutor, the DA's office, and the defense joining together in making such an application is very unusual, I think is what she said," Berman noted.

The New York City officer who was assigned to monitor Epstein repeatedly complained to Vance's sex crimes unit that Epstein wasn't in compliance.[3]

Vance flat out denied that his office was ever told Epstein was violating his registration, saying that NYPD informed his office just the opposite—that Epstein was in full compliance.

Epstein's stubborn persistence to do whatever he wanted, however, was finally coming back to haunt him.

The bail package that Epstein's lawyers proposed was fit for a king. Instead of sitting in the Metropolitan Correctional Center with other people accused of sex crimes, Epstein wanted to be confined to his seventy-seven-million-dollar Manhattan mansion until trial. He offered to post a substantial bond as insurance. He would wear a GPS monitor, ground his private planes, hire twenty-four-hour armed guards, and install surveillance cameras at his mansion that could be monitored by federal authorities.

He was also prepared to put his mansion and his private jet up to secure his bail. Prosecutors, however, said that they intended to seize those assets under federal forfeiture laws, which would mean they couldn't be used for security.

Then Assistant U.S. Attorney Alex Rossmiller dropped a bomb.

"Any doubt that the defendant is unrepentent and unreformed was eliminated when law enforcement agents discovered hundreds of thousands of seminude photographs of young females in his Manhattan mansion on the night of his arrest, more than a decade after he was convicted of a sex crime involving a juvenile," he wrote.

Rossmiller also revealed that a phony Austrian passport and millions of dollars in diamonds, some as large as 2.38 carats, together with a pile of cash were found in Epstein's safe. Epstein had used the now expired passport with a fake name to enter countries in the 1980s, including France, Saudi Arabia, and Spain, prosecutors said.

Rossmiller also raised the specter of witness tampering, pointing out that Epstein had recently sent payments to two of his 2008 co-conspirators. Rossmiller said it was clear that Epstein was trying to send a message to the two women that they should keep their mouths shut.

But Epstein's lawyers scoffed at the idea that the transactions were hush money.

"The payment of an employee and the payment of a friend is not witness tampering because the *Miami Herald* exposé was first published last November," his lawyers said in their written response to prosecutors.

Berman, however, bypassed the bail issue for the moment.

He was curious about the "sweetheart deal" that Epstein had received from federal prosecutors in 2008.

"You mentioned in your submissions . . . that high-level Department of Justice officials approved the non-prosecution agreement," Berman said.

"Yes, Your Honor," said Weinberg.

"Who are they?"

I leaned over and almost fell out of my chair. It seemed as if we might finally learn who in the halls of Washington had given Epstein a pass.

Weinberg revealed, perhaps for the first time, the trajectory of Epstein's plea deal—at least from his perspective.

He explained that in late 2007, Alice Fisher, head of DOJ's Criminal Division, assigned the review of the Epstein case to Deputy Assistant Attorney General Sigal Mandelker.

Epstein's defense team met in Washington with members of the Justice Department in the spring of 2008, hoping to persuade them to drop the case.

Weinberg explained that while Justice Department officials recognized that aspects of the case were "novel" and "unusual," they ultimately ruled that Acosta had the discretion to prosecute Epstein on federal sex trafficking charges, if he chose to do so.

Weinberg said the defense team then appealed that decision to the Office of the U.S. Deputy Attorney General at the time, Mark Filip.

Filip assigned John Roth, a former federal prosecutor in Florida, to handle the appeal, Weinberg explained. Roth reaffirmed that the decision whether or not to prosecute Epstein was Acosta's.

"Is Mr. Filip the highest-level official in the Department of Justice?" Berman asked.

"Yes, he was one step below the attorney general," Weinberg replied.

Weinberg explained that it was Acosta who decided to give Epstein immunity and send the case back to the state. The DOJ required Krischer add a charge of solicitation of minors, which forced Epstein to register as a sex offender.

It was probably the most detailed accounting yet of who was involved in the decision.

Of course, that was the story from Epstein's camp.

THE MOST POWERFUL FORCE AT EPSTEIN'S BAIL HEARING WAS NOT THE prosecutors, the judge, the high-priced defense attorneys, nor even Epstein himself. It was two women who braved their demons to stand up and tell the judge that it was time to send a message to Epstein's victims.

"I was sixteen years old when I had the misfortune of meeting Jeffrey Epstein here in New York," Annie Farmer told Berman in open court.

"He later flew me to New Mexico to spend time with him there. I wanted to voice my support for the government's request that his bail not be set," Farmer said.

Epstein, sitting only a few feet away, turned his head and set his gaze directly on the women.

"Hi, Your Honor. My name is Courtney Wild. I was sexually abused by Jeffrey Epstein starting at the age of fourteen. And I would just like to ask the court to not grant him bond, to keep him in detention just for the safety of any other girls out there that are going through what I'm going through. It's a public case—and it's just—he is a scary person, he should not be walking the streets."

She and Farmer both told Berman that if Epstein were released on bail, it would pose a threat to them and other women who were abused and threatened by him.

After the bail hearing, Brad Edwards, with Courtney and Annie at his side, held a press conference and dropped another piece of new information.

Turns out that Epstein wasn't just pushing pencils when he was on work release in his cozy West Palm Beach office. He had company, and plenty of it.

Edwards announced that he had a new client who had visited Epstein at his "office" while he was on work release. She alleged that she was coerced by Epstein into having sex several times with him in his office, while sheriff's deputies were stationed outside his office door.

"It was not for some business arrangement, and it was for . . . improper sexual contact," Edwards said.

Later, in a lawsuit filed by the unidentified woman, she said that Epstein met her when she was seventeen, just before his 2008 arrest. He offered to help pay for an expensive surgery she needed. When he was serving his sentence at the Palm Beach County jail, he wrote to her and asked her to come work for him at his office.

"Specifically, while in Jeffrey Epstein's 'office' . . . plaintiff was made to engage in sexual encounters with Jeffrey Epstein, both alone and with Epstein during which she engaged in sexual intercourse, and also on one occasion with another young female and Epstein," the lawsuit said.

I always suspected, but could never prove, that Epstein—who was able to use his money to get whatever he wanted—made sure that he could continue his obsession while he was incarcerated.

Palm Beach Sheriff Ric Bradshaw, the elected official who should have been overseeing Epstein's work release, refused to comment.

It's hard to fathom how young women were able to come and go from Epstein's "office" without a single deputy raising a concern—unless they were instructed to look the other way.

Within days of Epstein's New York bail hearing, Bradshaw, hoping to head off more criticism, ordered an internal investigation into whether any of those deputies committed wrongdoing while supervising Epstein.

This was also a mechanism for him to be able to refuse to turn over public records, since one of the exemptions in Florida to releasing public documents is if the matter is part of an ongoing criminal investigation.

Bradshaw, in a subsequent interview with Miami's WLRN Sundial program, said: "All we did was house him. . . . He met the criteria for work release. He was not adjudicated as a 'violent' sex offender—he wasn't even adjudicated as a sex offender."

But Epstein's sentencing paperwork clearly stated he was a sex offender. In fact, Epstein had to sign numerous documents checking off all the restrictions he had to comply with as a registered sex offender in Florida.

Unfortunately, like most of the federal laws that are supposed to monitor sex traffickers who have private planes, the requirements for sex offender registration in Florida were so confusing that nobody seemed to know what Epstein was required to do and who was responsible for ensuring that he complied.

The sheriff's department claimed it was the state's job to monitor him after his release, and the state claimed that it was the sheriff's job. Epstein did check in at various times of the year, but it's not clear whether he ever appeared in person. Emails suggested that he was on a first-name, chummy basis with several of PBSO's commanders.

When I was working on the series and began asking questions to the sheriff's department about Epstein's registration, Epstein suddenly left New York and flew to Florida and registered, even though he had already registered earlier in the year.

It was clear that someone at the sheriff's office was watching his back.

Authorities in both New York and Florida had to be wondering how far the corruption went. Who was involved, and at what level?

AFTER THE BAIL HEARING, BRAD BOLEN, THE U.S. MARSHAL, CALLED again. He wanted to know whether I had contacted the air traffic controller.

I had finally gotten her name, but she wouldn't talk to me on the record. I didn't tell her that the marshals wanted to speak to her because I was still working on getting her to talk, and I knew once the marshals stepped in, I'd lose my chance. I called her again that afternoon following the bail hearing. I thought that, with Epstein now in jail, she might be more willing to go public, but she wasn't. I kept my word with Bolen and asked her whether she would talk to the marshals about what she had seen at the airport in St. Thomas.

She agreed to let me give Bolen her phone number, which I did.

A few weeks later, a report filed by Bolen was released as part of a massive FOIA (Freedom of Information Act) records dump obtained by the website Muckrack.com.

I was physically sick to my stomach when I read his report. He claimed that at our very first meeting at the diner, I walked in, sat down, and in no short order, gave him the name and phone number of the air traffic controller. In other words, I had given up my source to a federal marshal whom I didn't know and had never met before.

I immediately called Bolen.

"What the hell? Brad, you know I didn't give you her name or her number until I cleared it with her weeks later. Why would you write something like that?"

He had no good answer. He offered to ask his superiors to correct the report, but I knew that wasn't ever going to happen.

The Office of Homeland Security, in less than six months, closed their investigation into whether Epstein was trafficking women and girls from overseas using his planes. To this day, the names of the passengers on those Homeland Security forms that Epstein's pilots were required to complete for flights in and out of the United States have never been made public.

chapter 36

PEDOPHILE ISLAND

It was past 8:00 P.M. when Emily and I set out in a rented blue Jeep to find the bungalow I had rented on the island of St. Thomas. We had an address, but the deeper we drove into the mountains, and the steeper the slope of the roads, the more my nails dug into my knees. Our phones' GPS became useless. It also didn't help that we had to drive on the left side of the rugged roads. This would have been impossible for me because I can't even drive well on the right side of the road.

But at night, even Emily was nervous about where we were going and how the hell we were going to get there.

I had this brilliant idea, or at least I thought so at the time. Instead of staying at a crappy hotel, I would treat Emily to a lovely Airbnb bungalow, high on a cliff with large windows and a deck with a 180-degree view of the Caribbean. The description sounded perfect, the photographs were breathtaking, the price was reasonable. What could go wrong?

I called the owner a few times, but her directions went something like this: "Go to the end of the street with the blue house, make a right at the mailbox, make another right at the cows, look for the white wall, and then the driveway is right there."

Blindly navigating the narrow roads winding around the mountains of St. Thomas reminded me of the classic car-chase scene in the Alfred Hitchcock movie *To Catch a Thief*, with Grace Kelly behind the wheel of a powder-blue roadster convertible driving full throttle along the French Riviera. A wrong turn would have sent us flying right off the side of the mountain. I had to close my eyes and hold my breath at the top of every steep slope. On the way down, I would wail in fright, grasping the dash as if we were going to tumble into the Caribbean.

We probably would have never found the house, or even a way back to town, had we not had an escort. I had been talking to several sources on the island for months, and one of them, whom I will call "Island Mike," must have predicted that we didn't know what we were in for trying to find a house up in the cliffs.

When we finally got to the driveway, we had to drive straight up an almost ninety-degree incline to get to the house. Island Mike, who was driving an SUV and accustomed to the terrain, coached us up the hill.

The cottage was bathed in a deep red glow, and inside, it looked nothing like its photos on Airbnb. There was no air-conditioning, and the windows were covered in sheets. Emily took pictures to show that the house was not exactly the romantic island getaway that was advertised. It was late, so I suggested we make do, then set out in the morning for a new place to stay.

Emily would have none of it.

"Are you kidding me? We're not staying here. This is the perfect place to get killed! No one would ever be able to find us," she groaned.

Island Mike agreed that it wasn't the kind of place where two women should be staying alone. It was so remote that our phones didn't work. He offered to help us find a hotel, which wasn't easy because the island was still recovering from Hurricane Irma, which devastated St. Thomas in September 2017. Many of the hotels were still being repaired or had shut down altogether. I didn't have time to argue, as I was meeting another source later that evening at a bar downtown.

Island Mike led us back down the mountain, as I prayed a car wouldn't come barreling in the other direction. I kept wishing my cell phone would work so I could play Bruce Springsteen, since he always calms my nerves.

Emily still has those photographs of our idyllic island retreat.

She calls it "the Murder House."

I HAD BEEN TRYING FOR MONTHS TO CARVE OUT SOME TIME TO VISIT St. Thomas and take a trip out to Epstein's "Pedophile Island," which was also sometimes called "Orgy Island." Sources on St. Thomas were sending me information about Epstein's exploits on his island, Little St. James, as well as documents about his purchase of the larger island nearby, Great St. James.

A lot of people suspected that Epstein's island was being used for sex trafficking, its remote location, accessible only by boat or helicopter, providing a perfect cover for the sexual abuse that Virginia and other women were alleging happened there.

I was also planning to meet with a source who called himself Chef James. His emails suggested that he knew a lot about Epstein. He told me, for example, that while Epstein was on work release he spent over one hundred thousand dollars in catering bills for food that he brought into his "office." A lot of that food went to deputies who were making upward of forty-two dollars an hour monitoring him.

I thought Chef James may have worked for Epstein, but given the avalanche of tips I had to wade through, I honestly didn't have time to find out who he was.

Both Chef James and Island Mike claimed, without proof, that Epstein had the fix in with the former governor of the U.S. Virgin Islands, John de Jongh Jr., and Epstein had even hired the governor's wife, Cecile, to work for him at his St. Thomas–based company, Southern Trust, which was purportedly a data-mining venture.

St. Thomas is a poor island, and it wouldn't take a lot to get the local politicians to look the other way when it came to doing what Epstein wanted.

In fact, St. Thomas was probably the perfect place for Epstein.

The U.S. Virgin Islands are a territory of the United States. Besides St. Thomas, the USVI includes St. Croix, St. John, and many other smaller islands, such as Epstein's Little St. James. They are geographically in the Virgin Islands archipelago, to the east of Puerto Rico and west of the British Virgin Islands, or BVI, a territory of Britain.

The capital of the territory, Charlotte Amalie, is on St. Thomas, which, as of the 2010 census, had a population of 51,634.

By the time Emily and I arrived on St. Thomas, the feds had already raided Epstein's island. I was talking to a woman who worked on the compound briefly, and whose boyfriend was still employed by Epstein at the time of his arrest.

The couple told me that, immediately upon Epstein's July 6 arrest, one of his employees, Lesley Groff, arrived from New York and began dismantling the camera system on Epstein's island. His computers were moved, as well as boxes of unknown items. They also said a giant steel safe in his office was carted away. (Groff's spokeswoman said Groff was not on the island after Epstein's arrest, and Groff was not aware of any cameras on the island.)

The couple was afraid, however, and wouldn't talk on the record. They claimed they had been required to sign nondisclosure agreements with a one-million-dollar penalty.

The male employee said when the FBI agents arrived, all the employees were asked to leave.

"By then, all the cameras were already gone," the employee said. "We were surprised that they waited so long to raid the island."

The other new arrivals in St. Thomas were caravans of media crews. Before I could even get my bearings, *Vanity Fair* churned out a strong piece about Epstein's exploits on the island, with locals alleging that the sex trafficker had been bringing in girls as recently as 2018.

He had often been seen boarding his private plane at the St. Thomas airport with what appeared to be minor girls.

"There were girls that look like they could be in high school," one employee of the airstrip told the magazine. "They looked very young. They were always wearing college sweatshirts and they were always carrying shopping bags."[1]

The island's police chief, William Harvey, claimed he didn't even know who Epstein was.

After purchasing Little St. James in 1998, Epstein invested millions to clear his seventy-acre piece of paradise on Little St. James, bulldozing most of its lush forests to make way for roads and buildings. Besides the main compound, the island has a movie theater, a library, a gym, a music studio, and a Japanese bathhouse. Records show that complaints were repeatedly filed with environmental agencies that fought unsuccessfully to limit the island's development in order to save wildlife and prevent the invasion of non-native plant species. Each time, Epstein paid the fines or donated to charity in lieu of fines in order to get around the environmental regulations.

Steve Scully, a data and communications specialist who was hired by Epstein in 1999, said Epstein poured a crazy amount of money into wiring the island with fiber optic cable so he could have dedicated power and data service to keep constant tabs on financial markets around the world.[2]

Epstein, like other employers on the island, paid for private school for the children of his employees, including the children of the former governor, de Jongh.

But one island wasn't enough. In 2015, Epstein set his sights on a body of land across the channel from his, Great St. James, which sprawled 165 acres, more than double the size of Little St. James.

A Danish family had owned the island since the 1970s, although there was a brief battle over a sale to Miami Dolphins player Jason Taylor that was settled in 2013. The island remained in the hands of the Danish family, who put it up for sale a year later.

The family's heirs, however, did not want to sell the island to Epstein because of his sex trafficking history.

So Epstein did what he always did: he found a way to get what he wanted using his money and resources.

He set up a shell company to make it appear that the true buyer was Sultan Ahmed bin Sulayem, a wealthy Dubai businessman with connections to Dubai's royal family.

After the $22.5 million deal was signed, and the buyer began bulldozing the island, it was discovered through work permits that Epstein was actually the real owner.

Sulayem confirmed to the *Herald* through an aide that Epstein had asked to use his name in a business venture but that Sulayem had refused.

I could never get an answer from USVI authorities as to whether Epstein was complying with the territory's sex offender registration requirements.

In March 2019, I reached out to Stacey Plaskett, who represented USVI as a delegate to Congress, asking her staff to help me determine who was monitoring Epstein, and whether he was adhering to sex offender laws. I pointed out, for example, that I had reports that young women were seen disembarking from his plane at the airport in St. Thomas.

Born in Brooklyn, Plaskett, fifty-four, attended Choate Rosemary Hall boarding school, and Georgetown and American universities before starting her career as an assistant district attorney in the Bronx. She later served as a Republican-appointed lawyer in the Justice Department under President George W. Bush but switched to the Democratic Party in 2008.

After moving to her parents' native St. Croix, she unsuccessfully ran as a USVI delegate to Congress in 2012. In 2014, she was elected to her first term in Congress. As a delegate, she represents the territory, but she has no voting power on the floor of the House of Representatives.

Federal election records showed that Epstein had given at least eight thousand dollars to Plaskett's political campaigns, starting in 2016. But lawyers representing Epstein also donated over ten thousand dollars to Plaskett's campaigns from 2013 to 2018, records show.

In 2006, after Epstein's arrest in Palm Beach, former New Mexico governor Bill Richardson, who received fifty thousand dollars from Epstein, along with a number of candidates for public office, announced that they would donate Epstein's political contributions to charity.

In March 2019, Plaskett's spokesman, Mike McQuerry, told me that Plaskett accepted Epstein's money, despite his sex-offender history, because Epstein passed a litmus test she had for her donations that went something like this: if one's wealth and money was obtained legally and there were no strings attached, then the donation was accepted.

McQuerry said Epstein had never asked Plaskett to do him any favors, and Plaskett had no intention of returning his donations.

Four months later, when Epstein was re-arrested in New York, Plaskett stuck to her convictions, saying she would keep Epstein's money. But after a barrage of criticism, she quickly reversed course and donated the money to USVI charitable organizations that work with women and children.

Plaskett had other connections to Epstein, having served as general counsel for the Virgin Islands Economic Development Agency from 2007 to 2012, when Epstein received a 90 percent tax break.

John de Jongh was the USVI's governor, and Albert Bryan, the current governor, was chairman of the EDA at the time that Epstein was granted his tax windfall in 2012. Records show that the EDA board re-upped Epstein's tax exemptions, even though they knew he was a convicted felon and a registered sex offender. As a resident of St. Thomas, Epstein received more than $144 million in government tax exemptions over twenty years through various companies, even though there was evidence that he wasn't qualified for the tax program because many of his company's employees didn't reside in the USVI, which was one of the requirements.[3]

In January 2020, USVI Attorney General Denise George filed a civil racketeering lawsuit against Epstein's estate, alleging that Epstein trafficked hundreds of young women and girls on his island, using the territory as a nexus for his sex trafficking operation. George claimed that Epstein used the tax benefits he received in the islands to help fund his criminal enterprises, and used a revolving number of local helpers to move women and girls in and out of the island, often holding the victims hostage by withholding their passports.

Epstein's longtime lawyer, Darren Indyke and his accountant, Richard Kahn, were also named in the complaint.

Even though the island's former First Lady, Cecile de Jongh, worked for Epstein for two decades, George said Epstein was able to obtain his tax breaks by providing false information to USVI government officials.

Did Epstein accomplish all this with the knowledge of the islands' political and financial leaders, using the same guile that enabled him to win immunity in 2008?

George said she has thus far uncovered no evidence that political leaders in the USVI committed any wrongdoing.

ON OUR FIRST NIGHT IN ST. THOMAS, EMILY AND I FINALLY SECURED two rooms with the help of Island Mike and then set out to meet Chef James at a little restaurant in town.

Mike must have been a little worried about us, because he offered to come along and just sit at the other end of the bar to keep watch. I wasn't worried, but Emily, as usual, kept asking questions.

"Who is this guy again?"

"How do you know him?"

"So, let me get this straight, you don't have any idea who he is?"

In hindsight, I should have done more homework.

That evening, as I was waiting for the Chef, I was exchanging texts with Lauren Book, a Florida state senator and child abuse survivor who had become involved in pushing for an investigation into whether there was any wrongdoing on the part of the Palm Beach sheriff in connection with Epstein's work release scam.

Chef James was supposed to join us about 10:00 P.M., after he got off work, presumably from his job at a restaurant on the island.

As we waited, Emily became more nervous. I kept texting Lauren about the investigation, wondering whether I should return to the hotel and write a story that night. It had already been a long day, and I couldn't even recall whether Emily and I had eaten anything.

Then Lauren mentioned that she had received a number of threats from people who were warning her against pursuing anything connected to Palm Beach Sheriff Ric Bradshaw. This got my attention. This was a gutsy move because Lauren's father, Ron Book, is one of the most powerful lobbyists in Florida.

I then called Ron Book to find out more. I knew he was using all his political clout to determine where the threats were coming from.

"Well, a while back there was this guy who kept sending Lauren these terrible emails; she was afraid for her life," Ron said. "We had to hire security and try to find the guy. He only went by the name Chef James."

"Chef James? Are you sure?" I said, leaving the restaurant and walking outside so that no one could hear the alarm in my voice.

I told Ron that a guy using that very name was about to come to the restaurant to meet with Emily and me.

"Get out of there fast," Ron said.

I returned to the bar and searched my email for Chef James's email address. I couldn't believe it. This guy had sent me more than fifty emails since 2016, well before I even wrote about Epstein. He had first written me about my prison series. Turns out he claimed to be a former inmate at Suwannee Correctional Institution in Florida who had served twenty-five months for a sex crime he claimed he had never committed.

It was well past ten and no one had showed up looking for us, so that was a good sign. But as we were paying our bill, two men appeared and sat at the bar, staring at Emily and me. I asked them where they were from, and they told me the Middle East.

Island Mike, who knows everyone on St. Thomas, didn't recognize them and motioned for us to leave. Seeing that we were getting up to go, they sneaked away first. Mike escorted us outside, where the men were standing smoking cigarettes. Mike asked for a smoke, and they began chatting.

Mike was still talking to them when we pulled away and headed to the hotel. We were both a bit shaken.

We got to our rooms and I could hear Emily in the room next door, piling the chairs and a nightstand in front of her door.

I put my night clothes on, fell into bed, and slept so soundly that I didn't hear my phone or Emily knocking at my door around midnight.

NBC had just published a story about Epstein being found unconscious in his New York jail cell.

When I awoke and checked my phone the next morning, and saw all the messages, I immediately knew that I wasn't going to be able to make the boat trip to Pedophile Island with Emily and Island Mike that morning.

Reports were sketchy, but it appeared that on Tuesday, Epstein had been found unconscious, with injuries to his neck, on the floor of his cell. It was not clear whether he had tried to commit suicide or whether he had been attacked. Initial reports were that Epstein had been moved into a more secure protective custody unit because he had received threats from other inmates.[4]

Depending on which account you read, his cellmate, a corrupt former cop named Nicholas Tartaglione, had either tried to kill Epstein or he had prevented Epstein from hanging himself.

Tartaglione, fifty-one, wasn't talking. His attorney said his client claimed he was friendly with Epstein and had nothing to do with what happened. He theorized that Tartaglione was being set up because the ex-cop had filed complaints on the prison's inhumane conditions.

The incident happened in a secure cellblock. The two were housed in a windowless room, infested with insects and rats, with standing water on the floor.

For reasons that remain unexplained to this day, the Metropolitan Correctional Center had bunked a hulking accused quadruple murderer with a sixty-six-year-old nerd with an egg-shaped penis who happened to be the nation's most famous child molester.

A SERIES OF SUSPICIOUS EVENTS FOLLOWED. FIRST, THE SURVEILLANCE video of the incident disappeared. Prison officials said it was inadvertently destroyed. Tartaglione had an illegal cell phone, but the government wasn't releasing its contents. To this day, authorities have never released a report on their investigation into the event.

Epstein's injuries were not serious, and he was placed on a suicide watch.

Meanwhile, the Capitol Police in Tallahassee, Florida, were investigating threats made against Florida state senator Lauren Book, who had made an appeal to Florida governor Ron DeSantis to investigate Sheriff Bradshaw's handling of the Epstein case. Two days after calling for the Bradshaw probe, she got several calls from the sheriff's supporters warning her to stop.

"Little girl, you don't know what you're getting into," one of the callers reportedly said.

I was racing to get my story filed from the hotel room that morning when there was a knock on my door. It was only 11:20 A.M. and we had arranged for late checkout. I called the desk to remind them and was told there was no late checkout, and I had to be out—now. I felt it was strange that they seemed so insistent, considering the hotel wasn't full.

I pleaded with them, as I was still in my pajamas and had not showered. They gave me until noon. I was still furiously writing when there was another knock, this one more forceful. It was not yet noon. I opened the door to find a maid and a manager standing there.

"If you don't leave right now, we are calling the police," the manager said gruffly. Damn, they don't play games here, I thought.

I slammed the door shut, and took the fastest shower I had ever taken. I couldn't wait to get out of that hotel.

We found a room in a little hotel in a sketchy part of town. There was no elevator, so we had to lug our suitcases up a set of steep stairs. The windows of the room were still boarded up with old plywood from the hurricane. Emily surveyed the room and proclaimed that any self-respecting murderer could easily hatchet his way into the room at night. She called Walt, her husband, and told him to keep track of her whereabouts using the GPS on her cell phone. But the GPS on our phones didn't work in St. Thomas.

I TRIED WITHOUT SUCCESS TO SPEAK TO THE GOVERNOR, ALBERT Bryan, but he wasn't available. Neither was the former governor, de Jongh, or his wife. No one was in the offices of Epstein's Southern Trust company in the town of Red Hook, and when we went to the local bar and mentioned Epstein's name, I swear the whole place went silent.

We spent the next couple of days trying to track down people who had worked on Little St. James. We met two, who would not go on the record, and basically confirmed the information we already had. Except for the beautiful drone footage that Emily had filmed of the island from the boat that morning, the trip was proving to be a bust.

I told Mike I was a bit frustrated, and he suggested that I go on the local radio talk show and try to drum up people to interview. He had a contact there, and so the following morning, I met with Lesley Commissiong, who has a morning drive time talk program on St. Thomas. She ran the show live on Facebook as well as on the radio. We had a lively discussion about Epstein and how he could have operated in secret in the USVI for so long. A few of the callers criticized local politicians for not monitoring him after his 2008 arrest. But for the most part, residents of the island were unfazed by the scandal. They had bigger worries, with 22 percent of the island living below poverty level, half of them single mothers.

The price of living in paradise for the people of St. Thomas was crushing. USVI has one of the highest infant mortality rates in the world, and its education system had been in decline for decades. More than 60 percent of public school children in the eleventh grade do not read at that level. This means that even children who graduate struggle to obtain employment to sustain their families.[5]

Island Mike and others we interviewed on the island had resigned themselves to the corruption that had become part of the territory's fabric.

"We make Chicago politicians look like amateurs," Mike said.

MIKE GOT ACCESS TO ANOTHER BOAT THE NEXT DAY, AND EMILY AND I headed out with him toward Epstein's orgy island. Emily wanted to get more drone footage and photographs, and I wanted to see it for myself. It's incongruent to imagine such an evil place in the midst of such immense beauty. Epstein's giant American flag was still flying on the island's tallest perch.

He might be in jail now, but the crews boarding the ferries each day to work on his island never stopped. We could see the men on the beach, working, as we got as close as we could to try to see what they were doing.

There was construction happening on the big island as well. The rumor was that Epstein intended to subdivide it and sell some of the properties. For now, they were mostly clearing the land. It was a clear and sunny day, far better than when Emily had first flown her drone under gray skies.

Epstein's main compound was on one side of Little St. James, with several blue-roofed buildings surrounding a vast infinity pool. There was a helicopter pad, and an area with metal buildings and, curiously, an ambulance, parked high above the compound. Closer to the beach were benches overlooking a Zenlike garden. On the hill above was a tall, striped, Egyptian-looking building that once had a gold dome that was ripped off during a bad storm. Conspiracy theorists had long speculated that the building contained all the bodies of people Epstein had killed. In reality, his employees confirmed that the building was a concert hall where Epstein would often play the piano. At the foot of the compound by the beach was a pier.

The other side of the island had a rougher surf, and its terrain was lined with rocks and cliffs. There was a dark, dungeon-like shelter built out of the rocks and steps that wound down to the ocean's edge. It was so treacherous and remote on this side of the island that it would have been impossible for anyone to escape.

THE NEXT DAY, WE RETURNED TO RED HOOK TO TRY TO FIND MORE LOCALS to interview. We had lunch at a little Chinese restaurant. As we were paying our bill, the waitress came over to me and asked me if I was Julie Brown. There was a phone call for me.

I figured it was probably the bank telling me my credit card was declined, but it turned out to be a local television reporter who had heard I was on the island. It was very odd that she knew where I was having lunch. I wondered if the walls had ears.

Emily was terribly creeped out.

After two more days of dead ends, we finally decided to book a flight home.

Still not ready to give up, I told Emily to head to the airport a few hours early so that we could scope out the landing strip that Epstein used and possibly track down airport workers or air traffic controllers. We even tried the local fire station. But no luck.

The airport was small and hot and stuffy. It was impossible to buy even a bottle of water. I couldn't wait to get home.

chapter 37

HARVARD, MIT, AND THE BILLIONAIRES CLUB

In December 2011, Jeffrey Epstein brought together some of the most brilliant scientific minds in the nation on his remote island, better known to his friends as "Little St. Jeff's." The purpose of this event belied the lavish, pristine surroundings and the extravagant food laid out in front of the guests who flew in from around the country. In the aftermath of the earthquake and tsunami in Tohoku, Japan, the meeting was called "Coping with Future Catastrophes."

It was, essentially, a Global Doomsday conference.

The attendees were instructed to identify some of the greatest threats to the earth, contemplating such phenomena as bioterrorism, nuclear warfare, nuclear catastrophes, overpopulation, asteroid and meteor collisions, supervolcanoes, earthquakes, rogue machines and computers—and what a press release called "high-energy chain-reactions that could disrupt the fabric of space itself."

The meeting was organized by Marvin Minsky, a professor of electrical engineering and computer science at the Massachusetts Institute of Technology (MIT) and cofounder of MIT's Artificial Intelligence Lab.

A rich array of renowned scientists, authors, and entrepreneurs attended the conference, with the goal of prioritizing a list of threats and forming panels of experts in various fields to review this list and then work on solutions for each item.

Among those at the conference was Martin Nowak, a biology and mathematics professor at Harvard University, whom Epstein had supported with millions of dollars for research in the field of evolutionary dynamics.

TWO YEARS AFTER BEING RELEASED FROM JAIL, EPSTEIN HAD REMADE himself as a maverick science philanthropist who was flying some of the world's most famous geniuses around the world in his private planes for conferences, meetings, and TED Talks, branding himself as someone who was dedicated to the protection of the planet. Celebrated physicist Stephen Hawking was another scientist with whom Epstein cultivated a relationship. In 2006, Hawking was photographed at Epstein's island after the financier reportedly paid to have a submarine specially equipped for Hawking, who had never been underwater before.[1]

Epstein was burnishing his image by giving grants to scientists and dangling connections to wealthy donors who could bankroll their work. For Epstein, the conferences were not just a vehicle to rub elbows with academics and philanthropists; they were also a way to scrub his soiled reputation—and make money through these potential investors—amid a loss of tens of millions of dollars in legal fees and a barrage of civil lawsuits he had settled with underage victims.

During the research for my series, I saw all the press releases that Epstein and his new charitable foundation, the Jeffrey Epstein VI Foundation, had put out on PR Newswire, starting in 2012. It was quite remarkable, really. I showed some of them to Casey, and while the foundation was only mentioned briefly in the series, I planned to focus more on that aspect of the story. I knew it would require a lot of digging to determine whether Epstein had ever followed through on all the promises he made and the money he pledged in all his hyperbolic press releases.

Among other things, Epstein established a fellowship at the International Peace Institute, an international nonprofit that promotes peace around the world; pledged to build the largest school in earthquake-ravaged Haiti; announced funding for charter schools in inner-city neighborhoods; supported music therapy research for premature babies; helped develop computer coding for toddlers; and launched an online learning program about brain science called *NeuroTV.*

There were press releases about Epstein's endeavors nearly every day, announcing gifts from "Science philanthropist Jeffrey Epstein," "Education activist Jeffrey Epstein," "Evolutionist Jeffrey Epstein," "Science patron Jeffrey Epstein" and "Maverick hedge funder Jeffrey Epstein."

There were gifts to fund research at universities, research institutions, and nonprofits in the search for cures for melanoma, ovarian cancer, multiple sclerosis, Alzheimer's disease, Crohn's disease and colitis, Parkinson's disease, diabetes, breast cancer, and AIDS.

In the Virgin Islands, he launched a youth football training camp, a youth orchestra, the territory's first humane society, its first Head Start program, and its first student radio station.

His more ambitious quests included funding for artificial intelligence, developing free-thinking robots, creating software that mimics human thinking, the first "humanoids" in Berlin, and a ban on shark fin consumption in China.

He promoted himself as a former board member of Rockefeller University, the New York Academy of Sciences, and the Mind Brain Behavior initiative at Harvard University. He was also a former member of two think tanks promoting global political and economic cooperation, the Council on Foreign Relations, and the Trilateral Commission—forums whose members include leaders in banking, business, government, academia, and science.

I RETURNED FROM THE VIRGIN ISLANDS WITH PLANS TO DIG INTO ALL Epstein's alleged charitable endeavors, as well as the little information I had gleaned about a Billionaires Dinner run by the Edge Foundation, a mysterious salonlike gathering of guests representing a who's who of scientists, intellectuals, and rich elites, including Epstein. The group met annually to answer a single question, which was different each year, and tailored to provoke debate on various esoteric subjects.[2]

The Billionaires Dinners were hosted by John Brockman, a literary agent behind the foundation. Renowned entrepreneurs who attended these high-brow affairs included Amazon's Jeff Bezos, Tesla's Elon Musk, and YouTube's Salar Kamangar, as well as countless authors, musicians, and writers, members of the media, and academics from all over the country. Epstein was able to get invited by bankrolling a portion of the Edge Foundation's events.

ON JULY 31, 2019, THE *NEW YORK TIMES* BEAT ME TO THE PUNCH. THEY ran a story about how Epstein had a dream of seeding the human race with his own DNA by creating a baby ranch at his New Mexico compound. The *Times* reporters had interviewed a number of Epstein's scientific and academic acquaintances, some of whom attended various dinner parties he hosted at his home or conferences where he held court at Harvard.[3]

The fact that this *New York Times* story likely derived from my stupid slip about the Billionaire Boys Club at that meet and greet with the *Times* was too painful for me to think about. I should have, immediately after mentioning it to the *Times*, started working on my own story about the Brockman salons. But the thicket of stories to be done about Epstein was so dense that neither I nor the *Herald* could possibly cover them all.

Part of me was glad that someone had written it, because it was an important story, revealing so much not only about Epstein but about the ethics of those scientists, wealthy individuals, publicists, and institutions, like Harvard and MIT, that took Epstein's money.

The *Times* article about Epstein's desire to perfect the human genome through his own DNA revealed that, while some scientists were revolted by his plans, his ideas weren't entirely rejected, either. Many found him charming, a bit full of himself—but nevertheless an emperor worthy of entertaining because there was cash in those new clothes.

Epstein was also obsessed with cryonics, the transhumanist philosophy whose followers believe that people can be replicated or brought back to life after they are frozen. Epstein apparently told some of the members of his scientific circle that he wanted to inseminate women with his sperm for them to give birth to his babies, and that he wanted his head and his penis frozen.[4]

IN LATE 2019, HARVARD UNIVERSITY, FACING PUBLIC PRESSURE, BEGAN an investigation into its relationship with Jeffrey Epstein. The release of the findings, in the midst of a growing pandemic in May 2020, received little attention in the Trump-dominated media ecosystem.

Based on interviews with more than forty individuals, including senior members of the administration, faculty and staff, and a review of 250,000 pages of documents, the Harvard investigation detailed the story of Epstein's tawdry relationships with Harvard professors, some of whom visited him in jail, and how Epstein enlisted the institution's academics to help boost his image by posting information about his philanthropy on the university's website—including false claims about the money he gave Harvard.

Epstein not only had a key card and pass code to the building hosting Harvard's Program for Evolutionary Dynamics, but he also had an office that was called "Jeffrey's Office," which he visited more than forty times between 2010 and October 2018.[5]

While Epstein attended undergraduate math classes, and was often accompanied by young women, the university investigation found no evidence that he engaged with Harvard students.

As a footnote—yes, a footnote—it revealed that an untold number of Harvard faculty members interviewed for the report admitted that they had visited Epstein at his homes in New York, Florida, New Mexico, and the Virgin Islands. They flew on his planes and dined on his food.

There was little mention in the report about Epstein's friendships with former university president Larry Summers, or with professor emeritus Alan Dershowitz, who helped Epstein secure his federal plea deal.

The university agreed to donate $200,937 in remaining unspent Epstein gifts to organizations that work to end sex trafficking.

Epstein's relationship with Harvard began in the late 1990s, when he announced that he would give thirty million dollars to launch the Program in Evolutionary Dynamics; researchers in this field apply mathematical formulas to genetics in order to find cures for cancer and other diseases. The program's director, Martin Nowak, was introduced to Epstein through Stephen M. Kosslyn, then chair of the university's psychology department.[6]

Kosslyn, who has since left the university, also designated Epstein as a visiting fellow in the Department of Psychology in 2005. The title is normally awarded only to an independent researcher registered with the Graduate School of Arts and Sciences. The university later found that Epstein was not qualified, either academically or by university policy, to be in the program.[7]

Altogether, the university received $9.1 million from Epstein between 1998 and 2008, prior to his conviction on underage sex charges. But Epstein was still welcomed at the university following his 2006 arrest, which was prominently reported by its own student newspaper, the *Crimson*, in July of that same year. Still, Harvard continued to bend its policies to suit Epstein—and his money.

Even after Epstein's release from jail, the university accepted millions of dollars from donors who were friends of Epstein's, mainly the billionaire financier Leon Black, chairman of Apollo Global Management, and his wife, Debra, through their Black Family Foundation, which gave Nowak and his evolutionary dynamics program seven million dollars from 2011 to 2015, Harvard records show.[8]

Nowak acknowledged he had no preexisting relationship with the Blacks, but he argued that Leon Black, a Harvard alumnus, had made other donations to Harvard. The Harvard investigation found that development offices for the medical school and faculty in the arts and sciences asked Nowak to reach out to the Blacks and Epstein for more support after Epstein got out of jail.

On a parallel front, Nowak and others were trying to pressure Harvard's administration to reconsider its decision not to accept money directly from Epstein, a policy that had been in place since Epstein's 2008 conviction.

The New Yorker's Ronan Farrow would later write an exposé on Epstein's fundraising relationship with MIT's Media Lab, and how the lab tried to keep those donations secret, knowing that Epstein, after his conviction, had been disqualified from MIT's donor database. The lab, and its director, Joi Ito, however, continued to accept gifts from Epstein and donors he directed to them, including millions from Microsoft cofounder Bill Gates and Black.[9]

"The effort to conceal the lab's contract with Epstein was so widely known that some staff in the office of the lab's director, Joi Ito,

referred to Epstein as Voldemort or 'he who must not be named,' "
Farrow wrote.

One day after the story ran, Ito resigned, and MIT's president
called for an independent investigation.

AT THE SAME TIME THAT THE *NEW YORK TIMES* WAS POKING INTO
Epstein's science ties, the *Wall Street Journal* was dissecting Epstein's
financial and personal relationships with some of the wealthiest people in the country, including Leslie Wexner; Leon Black; Jes Staley,
then a top executive at J.P. Morgan; and Glenn Dubin, the cofounder
of Highbridge Capital Management, one of the fastest-growing hedge
fund firms in the 2000s.[10]

J.P. Morgan engaged Dubin's fund to manage assets for clients to
minimize their taxes, and Staley worked at "funneling private banking clients' money directly into Highbridge's growing hedge fund,"
the *Wall Street Journal* reported.

Epstein allegedly earned twenty-nine million dollars from a ten-
million-dollar investment in Highbridge in 1999, according to the
Journal investigation. Highbridge was so successful that J.P. Morgan
eventually paid more than a billion dollars for control of the fund in
2004.[11]

A few days later, *Bloomberg* ran a piece about Epstein's long ties
to what it called "the inner sanctum" of Apollo Global Management
and his association with Black. The story said that Epstein pitched
tax strategies to the investment firm's executives, long after his 2008
sex conviction.[12]

While Epstein knew a lot of Wall Street luminaries from his days
in New York, the article points out that Epstein's ties to Leon Black
stretched longer and "ran deeper" than people at Apollo realized.

The *Bloomberg* piece, as well as others that followed, questioned
why Black, who had vast resources to hire some of the most brilliant

tax minds in the world, would have cultivated such a cozy relationship with Epstein.

Black, who is worth $6.5 billion, according to the Bloomberg Billionaires Index, heads one of the world's largest private equity firms. He is also a philanthropist who formed a number of charities. A review by Apollo concluded that Epstein never worked with the firm, and Black denied that he was aware that Epstein was trafficking girls and women.

Epstein was on the board of Black's family foundation from at least 2001, and his name appeared on government forms until 2012. But a Black spokeswoman claimed that was an error because Epstein was asked to resign in 2007.[13]

Black donated ten million dollars to Gratitude America Ltd., a philanthropic foundation Epstein launched in 2012.[14]

In January 2021, Black stepped down as CEO of Apollo after a company inquiry found he had paid more than $158 million to Epstein from 2012 to 2017. The investigation found no evidence that Black was involved in Epstein's crimes, but nevertheless raised questions about Black's judgment, given that Epstein had long been suspected of sex trafficking.[15]

"Let me be clear," Black said in a statement to investors in October 2020, "there has never been an allegation by anyone that I engaged in any wrongdoing, because I did not. And any suggestion of blackmail or any other connection to Epstein's reprehensible conduct is categorically untrue."[16]

Epstein also tried to secure funding from Microsoft cofounder Bill Gates, whom he met in 2011. Gates, like a lot of other people Epstein associated with, tried to distance himself from Epstein after his arrest. Gates told the *Wall Street Journal* in September 2019, just as questions were being raised in the media about Epstein's relationships with prominent men, that he had no relationship, business or otherwise, with the eccentric sex predator.[17]

But the *New York Times* did some more digging and found that Gates visited Epstein's Manhattan town house at least three times, staying once late into the evening. Others who worked for Gates's foundation also visited Epstein's mansion several times, and Epstein spoke to both Bill and Melinda Gates about a proposed charitable fund that could generate sizable fees for Epstein.[18]

Epstein hoped to attract donations from some of his wealthy friends as part of the venture, seeded with Gates Foundation funds, that would be used for global health causes. Epstein also aimed to personally profit from the project, proposing that he be paid 0.3 percent of whatever money he raised. This meant that if he raised ten billion dollars, he would reap thirty million dollars in fees.

At one meeting with Gates's team, Epstein reportedly mentioned that he had connections to trillions of dollars of his clients' money, a boast that most of the team found incredible. According to the *Times*, Gates met with Epstein and flew on his private jet in 2013 from Teterboro Airport in New Jersey to Palm Beach.[19]

Their philanthropic talks continued, and in October 2014, Gates, at Epstein's behest, gave two million dollars to MIT's Media Lab.[20]

"Over time, Gates and his team realized Epstein's capabilities and ideas were not legitimate and all contact with Epstein was discontinued," Bridgitt Arnold, Gates's spokeswoman, told the *Times*.

"Bill Gates regrets ever meeting with Epstein and recognizes it was an error in judgment to do so. Gates recognizes that entertaining Epstein's ideas related to philanthropy gave Epstein an undeserved platform that was at odds with Gates's personal values and the values of his foundation."[21]

TO THIS DAY, THE ULTRAWEALTHY WHO HELPED FINANCE EPSTEIN'S life of sexual violence maintain that they knew nothing about the deviant behavior exhibited by a man with whom they entrusted billions of dollars.

Universities and research centers, arts institutions, private equity firms, publicly traded companies, and titans of business and government have acknowledged and, in some cases, apologized for associating with Epstein. Usually this repentance coincides with the hiring of a prestigious law firm to conduct an inquiry designed more to mitigate reputational and financial damage than to hold anyone accountable.

chapter 38

IN PLAIN SIGHT

On August 8, 2019, Marie Villafaña resigned from the U.S. Attorney's Office in the Southern District of Florida. Villafaña, who worked as a federal prosecutor for almost twenty years, announced that she was joining the federal Department of Health and Human Services as a lawyer overseeing health care fraud. Her departure came amid the federal investigation into how she and other prosecutors, including Alex Acosta, handled the Epstein case. Two months later, Lanna Belohlavek, the lead prosecutor on the state criminal case against Epstein, was forced out of her post as an assistant state attorney for the Twentieth Judicial Circuit in Fort Myers, Florida, where she transferred after leaving Palm Beach. She would later join a private law firm.

The female lead prosecutors were bearing the brunt of the fallout from the botched case. No one, with the possible exception of Acosta, suffered more damage to their careers than Villafaña and Belohlavek.

The irony of this is that the two female prosecutors probably kept quiet about the case because they thought speaking out about it would undo their careers.

"I think from the very beginning that Assistant U.S. Attorney Marie Villafaña believed, the same as we did, that Epstein was a serial pedophile and should be prosecuted to the full extent of the law," said Michael Reiter, Palm Beach's former police chief. "But unfortunately, she acquiesced to the wishes of her superiors and soft-pedaled the case."

The day after Villafaña's resignation, on August 9, 2019, Maxwell's last-ditch appeal to block the unsealing of documents in her civil defamation suit was rejected by New York's Second Circuit Court of Appeals. I had been up early, working, and was still in my pajamas when the records started hitting the court docket about 9:00 A.M.

The carnage of Epstein and Maxwell's depravity spilled out in the tranche of court records, the largest to be released since the case began. Names of powerful men were mentioned, along with brutal details about Epstein's trafficking of teenage girls in Palm Beach, New York, and overseas, as well as information about Maxwell's role in assisting him with his crimes.

The documents represented only a portion of those that the *Miami Herald* sought, but they were nevertheless damning, raising new questions about whether powerful people pressured federal prosecutors to give Epstein and others a secret immunity deal.

The names of prominent men that Giuffre had accused of sexual abuse were splattered across the pages: Marvin Minsky, the Harvard scientist who has since died; modeling scout Jean-Luc Brunel; former New Mexico governor Bill Richardson; Hyatt hotel magnate Tom Pritzker; and former Maine Democratic senator George Mitchell, who served in the Senate from May 1980 to January 1995.

Also named were hedge fund manager Glenn Dubin, Alan Dershowitz, and Prince Andrew.

When contacted by the *Herald*, each man flatly denied the allegations. Many of them said they had never met Giuffre.

THE DOCUMENTS PROVIDED NEW INSIGHT INTO MAXWELL'S ROLE IN Epstein's life. In one of her unsealed depositions, she said that her primary duties involved running Epstein's various households and hiring assistants, cleaners, butlers, and cooks.

"In the course—and a very small part of my job—was from time to time to find adult professional massage therapists for Jeffrey," Maxwell said in one deposition.

Giuffre's attorney, Sigrid McCawley, grilled Maxwell about where she would find masseuses for Epstein.

"From time to time I would visit professional spas and I would receive a massage, and if the massage was good, I would ask that man or woman if they did home visits."

But when the questioning turned to whether Maxwell ever saw any young girls in Epstein's presence, she became increasingly agitated, evading the questions.

> **MCCAWLEY:** "Have you ever observed a female under the age of eighteen at Jeffrey Epstein's home that was not a friend, a child, one of your friend's children?"
>
> **MAXWELL:** "I have no idea what you are talking about."
>
> **MCCAWLEY:** "You have no idea what I'm talking about in the sense you never observed a female under the age of eighteen at Jeffrey Epstein's home that was not one of your friend's children, is that correct?"
>
> **MAXWELL:** "How could I possibly know how old someone is when they are at his house? You are asking me to do that. I cannot possibly testify to that. As far as I'm concerned, everyone who came to his house was an adult professional person."

Maxwell repeatedly called Virginia a liar, and claimed she had no knowledge of any teenagers who worked in Epstein's homes.

McCawley pointed out that she had already confirmed that Virginia, at seventeen, was working as a massage therapist for Epstein.

Maxwell: "So she was seventeen. At seventeen you are allowed to be a professional masseuse, and as far as I'm concerned, she was a professional masseuse. There is nothing inappropriate or incorrect about her coming at that time to give a massage."

McCawley attempted to force Maxwell to describe how she first met Virginia, and Maxwell became angry.

"No, no! How can you do that, when the basis of this entire horrible story that you have put out is based on this first appalling story that was written," Maxwell shouted while pounding her fists on the table.

BUT PERHAPS THE MOST HARROWING ACCOUNT OF EPSTEIN AND Maxwell's activities was contained in a deposition given by a former chef who worked for Glenn Dubin and his wife, Eva Andersson-Dubin.

Eva met Epstein in 1991, when she was twenty, and they formed "a long and still enduring friendship," according to a bio that Epstein's lawyers gave prosecutors during the criminal investigation in Florida.

Epstein and Eva dated for a time, but when their romantic relationship ended, he continued to help pay Eva's expenses at medical school in Sweden and later, when she continued her studies in California.

Rinaldo Rizzo and his wife worked as chefs for the Dubins, who lived primarily in New York.

Sometime late 2004 or early 2005, he and his wife were in the Dubins' kitchen preparing dinner when Eva Dubin brought in a young girl and told her to sit down.

The girl looked like she had been crying, and she held her head down as if she was ashamed of something she had done.

"She was shaking, I mean literally quivering," Rizzo said in a deposition.

Rizzo uncomfortably introduced himself and his wife. But the girl kept her head down and didn't respond when he asked her if she was okay.

Finally, Rizzo asked the girl about herself.

"What do you do?" Rizzo asked.

"I'm Jeffrey's executive assistant, personal assistant," she said, referring to Epstein.

Thinking she looked too young, Rizzo asked her how she got the job and how old she was.

"And she says to me, point-blank, 'I'm fifteen.' And I said to her, 'You're fifteen years old and you have a position like that?' At that point she just breaks down hysterical, and I feel like I just said something wrong and she will not stop crying," he said.

His wife offered her water and tried to get her to calm down.

Rizzo: "And then in a state of shock, she just lets this rip, and what she told me was unbelievable."

The girl said she had been on Epstein's island, along with Ghislaine Maxwell and Sarah Kellen. Both of them were pressuring her to have sex, she said.

"Sarah took my passport and phone and gave it to Ghislaine," the girl said, weeping. "Ghislaine threatened me. She told me not to discuss this."

Eva Dubin suddenly returned to the kitchen and announced that the girl would be working for her as a nanny.

But about a month later, the girl boarded a flight with the Dubin family. They were headed to Sweden for the summer and Rizzo and his wife were accompanying them.

Rizzo said their plane stopped at an airport en route and the girl got off. He never saw or heard from her again.

Rizzo and his wife left the Dubins' employ in October 2005.

"My wife and I had discussed these incidents and this last one was just, we couldn't deal with it."

The Dubins, through a spokesman, denied that the event Rizzo described ever happened. (A spokeswoman for Kellen also disputed Rizzo's story, saying it was inaccurate.)

"There was never a fifteen-year-old Swedish nanny in the Dubins' home and flight records for the trips to Sweden on the Dubins' plane do not include any minors other than family members," the spokesman said in a statement to the *Herald*.

(The Dubins also say they have flight records that contradict Rizzo's story because their travel to Sweden during that time frame does not show their plane stopping at any other airport enroute to Sweden.)

Earlier, a young woman had reached out to tell me a story about Eva and Epstein.

The woman, who did not want to be identified because she was afraid, said that she lived in Sweden, and in 2003, when she was twenty-one, she answered an ad in a local Swedish newspaper advertising for an au pair. She was interviewed by Eva and hired on the spot. The Dubins provided her plane tickets and instructed her to apply for a tourist visa.

"I was young and adventurous, and I wanted to travel," the woman said.

She flew to New York and was put up in an apartment in the same Upper East Side building where Epstein housed a number of young women and girls, she said.

"One girl was from Israel, she was very pretty. They were all like models but they didn't introduce themselves. They referred to Epstein as a friend and they said that he helped them. I didn't ask any details," she said.

She began working for the Dubins as a nanny. During the course of her work, she said Epstein would come and go from the couple's home in New York.

"I was disturbed by what I saw. I met him a few times and we would be in the kitchen of the Dubins' home, and they had other au pairs. There were times he would grab someone. He would touch you, and he did it in front of the Dubins," she said.

"Their children, they would call him 'Uncle Jeff,' and they told me he was a close family friend," she said. "I think we just all thought he was just a creepy friend of our employer. He would bring young, different women, young girls, a different one each time. I didn't think too much about it at the time. I remember thinking it was kind of weird that he had apartments with young girls staying in them. I assumed that they were not platonic friends, but I didn't ask."

One day another girl arrived from Sweden, saying she had been hired as the Dubins' new assistant. "She told me there was an audition of some sort at a hotel in Sweden. She didn't know what she was supposed to do. This girl said they had been in a hotel to present themselves there, like an audition."

Shortly thereafter, Eva told the nanny that they were letting her go. She called her parents in Sweden and they arranged for her to come home.

The woman said nothing inappropriate had happened. She said she was never propositioned by Epstein or anyone else while she was employed there, which was for only about six months.

When Epstein was still on community control in 2009, the Dubins were invited to Epstein's Palm Beach mansion for Thanksgiving. Eva sent a letter to Epstein's probation officer to obtain permission to allow her children to attend, since Epstein, as a convicted sex offender, was not allowed to be around children.

"I am 100 percent comfortable with Jeffrey Epstein around my children," Eva wrote. All three of her kids were minors at the time, documents show.

Eva, the founder of the Dubin Breast Center of the Tisch Cancer Institute at Mount Sinai's medical school, and her husband, now retired and focusing on private investments, issued a public statement after Epstein's arrest, saying they were shocked by the sex trafficking allegations against Epstein. The couple called Epstein's conduct "vile and unspeakable," adding that had they known, they would have never allowed their children in his presence.[1]

But in the cache of documents released in the Maxwell case, Giuffre alludes to a sexual encounter she had with Glenn Dubin, saying that he was the first client that Maxwell and Epstein directed her to have sex with, when she was seventeen.

Virginia told prosecutors that she was sent by Epstein to give Eva and Glenn a massage at a unit they were staying in at the Breakers in Palm Beach. Virginia had been "in training" for a few months, and Epstein wanted her to try out her "massage skills" on them. At the time, Eva was in the late stages of pregnancy, Virginia recalled, and she was worried about giving a woman in that condition a massage.

Afterward, she was directed by Eva to go into the other room and give Glenn a massage—which ended with oral sex, she said.

Epstein paid her for her services to the Dubins and complimented Virginia on how well she had performed. (The Dubins' lawyer denied that this event ever happened and some flight records and Glenn Dubin's credit card receipts seem to reflect that on certain dates during his wife's pregnancy, he was not in Palm Beach, but in New York. Virginia concedes that her memory of the exact dates of events had faded, but insists the events did occur.)

There was other new material. In one of her depositions, Giuffre described a dinner on the island with Bill Clinton and two brunettes who had flown in to the island from New York. "I'd say they were no older than seventeen, very innocent looking," Virginia said.

"Maybe Jeffrey thought they would entertain Bill, but I saw no evidence that he was interested in them. He and Jeffrey and Ghislaine seemed to have a good relationship. He made me laugh a few times."

She also claimed that she had met Al Gore and his wife, Tipper, and Senator Mitchell, who she said frequented Epstein's New York mansion.

Virginia also brought up then Israeli defense secretary Ehud Barak, who is named in one of her depositions. (Barak, like all of the men Virginia identified, denied that he was involved with Virginia—and said that his relationship with Epstein was all business.)

After the other names of prominent men were released, Virginia's lawyer, David Boies, explained that they decided early on in the civil litigation to focus on exposing Epstein and Maxwell because he believes that they were the masterminds of the sex trafficking operation.

Giuffre admits that she was taking Xanax during much of the time she was with Epstein and that she did not put everything in her memoir that happened to her when she was with Epstein. Thus far, only one other victim, Sarah Ransome, has told a similar story about being trafficked. No other victims or witnesses have come forward publicly to corroborate Virginia's sex trafficking allegations despite the fact that some of the encounters involved multiple girls and women.

Because much of the sexual misconduct alleged against other men happened outside the statute of limitations, it would be impossible to sue them, even if it was proven they were involved, Boies said.

Still, there were enough people around during some of these events who could place Virginia and other victims with Epstein and Maxwell. "I think one of the general points worth making," Boies said, "is how many people knew about this and did nothing and how long it went on right in plain sight. This went on for years, right in front of everybody."

chapter 39

JEFFREY EPSTEIN DIDN'T KILL HIMSELF

The Metropolitan Corrections Center is four blocks from the Brooklyn Bridge, tucked behind the federal courthouse in Lower Manhattan's financial district, a stone's throw from the halls of Wall Street where Epstein began his mysterious financial career.

Epstein's jail was a notoriously inhumane gulag that had been condemned for years by human rights groups. It has housed some of the most notorious criminals of all time, including convicted Ponzi schemer Bernie Madoff, New York mob boss John Gotti, mob hit man Sammy "The Bull" Gravano, and Mexican drug lord Joaquín Guzmán, also known as El Chapo.

Epstein's cell on 9 South, among the jail's most restrictive units, has two men to each unit. He was only allowed to shower every few days.

In July 2019, Epstein was said to still be on suicide watch, facing the isolation that comes with being in a cell with virtually nothing, including bedsheets—which may have been even worse torture for him than sharing a cell with a beefy man accused of killing four people.

Federal prison officials had not released the report of his first alleged suicide attempt, but sources had leaked out that people at the prison were skeptical that Epstein's incident was legitimate and speculated about whether he had staged it to gain special accommodations from the judge handling his case.[1]

Just as he had done in jail in Florida, he paid a squadron of lawyers to babysit him up to twelve hours a day. He had also already paid several inmates for protection by depositing money into their commissary accounts. As a rich pervert who abused children, he would be expected to live in a daily hell, if he wasn't beaten or killed. But Epstein had money, lots of it, so he had the means to buy protection.

He was released from suicide watch and returned to the special housing unit on July 30, where he was bunked with Efrain "Stone" Reyes, a Bronx drug dealer.[2]

Two days later, on August 1, Epstein met with David Schoen, an Atlanta lawyer whom he had known for years. Schoen spent five hours with Epstein preparing a battle plan to help fight the criminal charges and clear his name. Schoen claimed that Epstein wanted him to take over the case and issue rebuttals, including a statement about my series.

"I thought he was getting killed in the media and when he could respond, he should at least explain and respond. There was a miserable failure to do so and his lawyers were dysfunctional," Schoen said.[3]

Schoen, in an email, told me that Epstein had asked him to write an opinion piece about my series, which he felt "mischaracterized" the deal he received from the federal government.

"Jeffrey actually was so hurt by your piece that he drafted a response and asked me to write an op-ed addressing it directly," Schoen said.

Epstein had paid a price for his offenses, Schoen said, and had suffered serious consequences as a result, including lifetime sex offender registration as well as having to pay millions in legal fees and victims' settlements.

Epstein also felt that my stories, as well as other media coverage of the case, failed to examine the motives behind some of the victims' lawyers, who he suggested were more interested in money than justice.

"One lawyer, who said his client only wanted her day in court to confront Mr. Epstein and bring out the truth. Really? I have a letter from that lawyer that some might consider extortion . . . he threatens criminal charges at first and then says he has contacted the media but can call them off if Epstein pays $25 million. Just wanted her day in court?"

ON AUGUST 8, EPSTEIN SIGNED A NEW WILL, SETTING UP WHAT HE called the 1953 Trust, named after the year he was born. He bequeathed all his property and assets to the trustees, but the beneficiaries were not part of the public record. His brother, Mark, was named as his only relative.

His longtime lawyer Darren Indyke and his accountant, Richard Kahn, were designated as executors. The document, filed in St. Thomas, said he was worth $578 million. One of two lawyers who witnessed Epstein's signing of the documents was Mariel Colón Miró, a diminutive twenty-six-year-old who also represented Joaquin "El Chapo" Guzmán. Epstein had briefly been housed three cells down from Guzmán, and soon Miró had been brought onto the Epstein case by another of Guzmán's attorneys, Marc Fernich, whom Epstein also had hired.[4]

EPSTEIN SPENT ALMOST THE ENTIRE DAY OF AUGUST 9 WITH HIS lawyers, who would later report that they had been working diligently on his bail appeal. They believed they had made progress in their goal to prove that the immunity that Epstein received under his 2008 plea deal was a global one—meaning that it covered any crimes he allegedly committed in New York and anywhere in the country.

"No competent defense counsel negotiating in good faith with the prosecutors would have ever agreed to a deal back then that allowed New York prosecutors to indict for precisely the same conduct in the future, which, of course is what happened," Epstein attorney Reid Weingarten said later in court.

Weingarten and Weinberg said that they and their client had confidence they would be able to have the new charges against Epstein in New York dismissed, and in the meantime, an appeal of his bail was set for August 12.

The last time they saw Epstein, they said, "We did not see a despairing, despondent suicidal person."

That same day, Epstein's cellmate, Reyes, was transferred out of the Metropolitan Correctional Center and inexplicably moved to a privately run facility in Queens that houses cooperating witnesses.[5]

As night fell, the two corrections officers assigned to monitor Epstein spent several hours playing and shopping on their computers, allegedly unaware that anything suspicious was happening in Epstein's cell. Both of them then allegedly fell asleep.

THAT SAME NIGHT, AFTER SPENDING ALMOST TWELVE HOURS REVIEWING over two thousand pages of documents in the Maxwell case, I climbed into bed, wearing the same pajamas I'd woken up in that morning.

I had to do a phone interview with National Public Radio about the Maxwell documents first thing in the morning.

After waking up, I called Mike Reiter to talk about the Maxwell case. He is one of the few people that know as much, if not more, about the Epstein case than I. So he was a good sounding board for some of the things that were going through my head.

As we spoke, my phone alerted me that I had another call. I thought it was a bit early for my NPR interview, but I took the call.

"Julie, did you hear? Jeffrey Epstein is dead," the NPR producer said.

"What? It must be some mistake," I said. "It was just another suicide attempt, right?"

"No, we're hearing that he is dead."

"I gotta go."

I hung up and called a source in the federal prosecutor's office in New York.

"I can confirm for you that Jeffrey Epstein was found dead this morning. That's all I can tell you right now," the source answered when I pressed.

My next calls were to Jena-Lisa, Michelle, Courtney, and Virginia.

I think I reached Michelle first. By that time, the news was all over television.

"I just can't believe it," Michelle said. "How the hell could that have happened? I thought he was on suicide watch."

Jena-Lisa wept. I couldn't reach Courtney, but I did reach her mother.

"That bastard, they must have killed him," Eva said.

The conspiracy theories blew up instantly on Twitter.

Attorney General William Barr was quick to try to dispel them, announcing, before any investigation had even been started, that the death was "an apparent suicide."

Epstein had been found unconscious in the special housing unit at the jail at about 6:30 A.M. on Saturday. Medics dispatched to the jail tried unsuccessfully to resuscitate him, then transported him to a local hospital, where he was pronounced dead.

His death was a stunning embarrassment for the federal Bureau of Prisons, in a lockup that had had the reputation of being one of the most secure prisons in the country. Mental health experts say that an inmate like Epstein, who had been on suicide watch, should have been closely monitored, checked at thirty-minute intervals or less.

The conspiracy theories grew louder in the days ahead, and President Trump tweeted an unsubstantiated rumor that Epstein "had information on the Clintons" and as a result "is now dead." When questioned about the tweet later, Trump said that he had "no idea" if Bill Clinton had anything to do with Epstein's death.

Barr announced that a probe into Epstein's death would be handled by the FBI and the Department of Justice's inspector general, Michael Horowitz.

Within days, it was revealed that the two guards failed to check on Epstein for about three hours.[6]

The officers were suspended, and the warden of the prison was reassigned. Barr continued to monitor the investigation closely, as it slowly grew into another scandal among many for the Trump administration.

"Every single person in the Justice Department—from your Main Justice headquarters staff all the way to the night-shift jailer—knew that this man was a suicide risk, and that his dark secrets couldn't be allowed to die with him," Senator Ben Sasse wrote to Barr the day after Epstein's death.

On August 12, just two days after Epstein's death, New York chief medical examiner Barbara Sampson said all signs pointed to suicide, but the investigation was continuing.

Also present at the autopsy was Dr. Michael Baden, a private pathologist hired by Epstein's brother, Mark.

Baden, whom I've interviewed many times over the years, has handled a litany of high-profile deaths. For nearly five decades, he has also been a member of a New York state commission that reviews deaths in state prisons. He knows how camera footage can be corrupted, or death scenes staged behind prison walls.

Baden had previously reviewed a number of controversial Florida prison deaths for me, at no cost, including that of Darren Rainey, an inmate who had died after officers left him in a burning hot shower at Dade Correctional Institution. Baden's examination of the autopsy report, as well as photographs of Rainey's body, led him to conclude that Rainey died of thermal burns over most of his body, which contradicted the Miami-Dade Medical Examiner's conclusion that Rainey's death had been an accident. Baden's findings in that case and others involving the Florida inmates helped lead the Department of Justice to launch an investigation.

ON AUGUST 15, THE *WASHINGTON POST* REPORTED THAT EPSTEIN HAD multiple broken bones in his neck and that the pattern of injuries was usually associated with strangulation rather than with a suicidal hanging. One of the bones was a hyoid bone, which is often broken in older people who die by hanging—but can also be a sign of strangulation.[7]

One day later, Sampson, New York's chief medical examiner, confirmed that Epstein's death was the result of suicide by hanging. Epstein's lawyers immediately denounced the ruling, saying that they intended to sue the government to obtain video of Epstein's cell area at the time of his death.

Soon information leaked out that camera footage of the hallway outside Epstein's cell was corrupted.

Baden said that Epstein's injuries were more consistent with manual strangulation caused by homicide, and that Epstein was likely dead for at least forty-five minutes or more before his body was discovered at six thirty that morning.

"Instead of leaving the cell in the condition it was found, if he had been dead for forty-five minutes or two hours or four hours, there were efforts to move him and, therefore, make it more difficult to reconstruct whether or not he died of suicide or some other cause," said Epstein's lawyer Martin Weinberg.

Baden told me that medics should have never removed Epstein's body, and that the cell should have immediately been treated as a crime scene, even if prison officials suspected Epstein hanged himself. Had it been treated as suspicious, photographs would have been taken—and those images would have provided clues as to how Epstein died, Baden said. However, no pictures were taken of Epstein's body when it was found.

Baden also revealed—for the first time—that the pathologist who actually attended the autopsy, Dr. Kristin Roman, also had difficulty determining at the outset that Epstein had hanged himself.

It is rare for any bones to be broken in a hanging, let alone for multiple bones to be fractured, Baden said.

"Those fractures are extremely unusual in suicidal hangings and could occur much more commonly in homicidal strangulation," he said, adding that there were also hemorrhages in Epstein's eyes that are more common with strangulation.

He described the ligature that Epstein used as a piece of orange bedsheet that was found on the floor of his cell. The officer who discovered him said that Epstein was found on his knees on the floor with the orange ligature around his neck. The other end of the sheet was tied to the top bunk of his cell.

"He was stone-cold dead when they found him," Baden said. "Rigor mortis had already set in."

Photographs taken afterward of Epstein's cell showed what appeared to be an inordinate amount of orange sheets on the bottom bunk and floor of Epstein's cell. The mattress from the top bunk was on the floor, and the higher bunk was filled with toiletries that appeared undisturbed. The photographs also showed a piece of equipment on the floor with wires and cords attached to it, thought to be a sleep apnea machine. It was pointed out that, had Epstein wanted to hang himself, it would have been easier to do it with the cords of the sleep apnea machine than with a ligature made from a bedsheet.

There was also a handwritten note in which Epstein complained that the guards had locked him in a shower stall for an hour. He said one of the officers gave him burned food.

"Giant bugs crawling over my hands, no fun!!" he wrote with a ballpoint pen—another item that a suicidal person should not have access to, Baden pointed out.

Authorities later charged two corrections officers, Tova Noel and Michael Thomas—who were working the night shift—with falsifying documents and conspiracy to defraud the federal government. Authorities said video confirmed that the officers had been asleep.

Baden said that in his forty years of examining prison deaths he has never had a case in which two officers had fallen asleep at the same time. He also said that the photos show multiple nooses in Epstein's cell, tied to the grate of a window and his bunk. Baden said there would not have been enough velocity for Epstein to successfully hang himself from the bunk.

In addition, the ligature wound was in the middle of Epstein's neck, not beneath the jawbone, which would be more common with a suicidal hanging.

Another renowned forensic pathologist, Dr. Cyril Wecht, agreed with Baden's findings. Both of them insisted that Sampson had been premature in her findings, but as a result, no further investigation occurred into how Epstein died.

"Once you decide that it's a suicide, you don't do the same kind of evidence collection that you would if you considered it a suspicious death," said Baden.

Attorney General Barr conceded that, while it was evident it was a suicide, it was "a perfect storm of screw-ups."

But Epstein's brother, Mark, was even more certain his brother didn't kill himself, telling me, "I could see if he got a life sentence,

I could then see him taking himself out. But he had a bail hearing coming up."

He insisted that his brother had reformed after his 2008 arrest, and that his latest arrest was a sham, perpetuated by the media. As you can imagine, I wasn't one of his favorite people.

While not providing details, Mark said that a lot of people wanted his brother dead.

"Jeffrey knew a lot of stuff about a lot of people," he said.

Among those who weren't questioned was Epstein's former cellmate Nick Tartaglione. Tartaglione's attorney, Bruce Barket, told me that there was nothing suspicious about Epstein's death and he had no doubt that he committed suicide.

Brad Edwards, who probably knew Epstein better than most lawyers involved in the case, also believed that Epstein killed himself.

But for me, it's hard to believe that someone who had spent his entire life acting as if he were above the law would give up so easily, so early into his case. He was already busy manipulating the prison system; he was paying off inmates and hiring new lawyers left and right.

I hoped that someone would get to the truth.

In late August, *Rolling Stone* did a story critical of the *Washington Post*, and specifically of Pulitzer Prize–winning journalist Carol Leonnig, one of the few reporters in the U.S. mainstream media willing to entertain the idea that Epstein may not have killed himself.[8]

It made a case that the *Post* and Leonnig were advancing conspiracy theories about Epstein's death. Yes, there was a lot of "feverish speculation," and wildly inaccurate and disturbing stories about Epstein, many of them perpetuated by trolls who know nothing about the case.

But Leonnig's reporting was on target. She was asking questions that deserved to be asked, and she was legitimately reporting that people close to Epstein—including Epstein's own brother—suspected that he was killed.

Leonnig posted a series of tweets, questioning, for example, why authorities had never cleared up the circumstances around Epstein's first alleged "suicide attempt."

"Leonnig's apparent willingness to explore if Epstein had been murdered—or at least her refusal to refrain from directly engaging in that theory—began to seep into the paper's reporting on the story," the *Rolling Stone* story said, offering up the ridiculous notion that she should be removed from covering the story because—well, because she was doing her job.

I didn't have the sources that she and other media with bureaus in New York—where the death happened—had, so I was quietly applauding her for asking the tough questions that all journalists should have been asking.

Isn't our role as journalists to examine things with a critical eye? To ask our government leaders why they did what they did? To hold prosecutors, judges, and sheriffs accountable? Why should we believe Epstein committed suicide without examining the documents, talking to witnesses, and demanding answers?

Yes, the minimal coverage by those journalists (mostly in Britain) who wrote critically about Epstein's death may have fueled far-fetched conspiracy theories. But blaming Leonnig—or any journalist—for this was unfair.

In my mind there was never a full, thorough, and transparent investigation into the death of Epstein—someone who absolutely had enemies, both inside and outside the prison. This doesn't necessarily mean he was murdered. But there are too many questions that authorities—to this day—have failed to answer.

What happened to the jail's tapes? Why was Epstein alone? Why was he released from suicide watch? How would Epstein even know how to hang himself? Why was there a sleep apnea machine in his cell? Who saw him last and when?

Here's a man who was used to having everything done for him, almost down to employing butlers to tie his shoes, yet is able to kill himself so violently that he broke three bones in his neck?

The government has an obligation to investigate this part of the story, if for no other reason than to bring closure for all the women he abused.

Thus far, the FBI and the Justice Department have not persuaded me—or a majority of the public—that Jeffrey Epstein killed himself.

Perhaps with a new administration in the White House someone will finally examine how and why Jeffrey Epstein wound up dead.

chapter 40

THE BOSS

After Epstein's death, it was time for me to turn my attention from my cell phone and computers to taking my son on a road trip and getting him settled at college. Most kids are nervous when they go off to college. In the case of my son, Jake, who had lived through my time working on the Epstein project, he couldn't wait to get to Tallahassee.

He was excited about his new independence and looking forward to living on his own.

But I also entertained the thought that he probably wanted some relief from Bruce Springsteen. Jake had heard me play Springsteen so often during the past year that I feared I instilled in him a disliking of one of the greatest rock and roll artists of all time. Bruce's music, and especially his voice, gave me a sense of comfort and peace. His stories transported me to familiar places that I knew growing up in Philly and from the many summers I'd spent at the Jersey shore. His songs were like compasses that helped me steer my mind to a quieter place. Springsteen's tales about working-class people were the stories of my grandparents and my single mother, of people I knew growing up and the places I longed to visit again someday. Every evening at the end of a long day writing, I would put Springsteen's music on my computer, which is just off my kitchen, and as I cooked dinner, I would listen to his songs and stories. After dinner, I would often keep listening until bedtime. Jake would come in at some point, roll his eyes, eat dinner to Bruce's music, and then, being a teenager, head out to the beach, or retire to his bedroom to escape his mom's obsessions with work and Springsteen. This was my nightly ritual. For me, Bruce's songs were like lullabies that drowned out all the noise in my head. On afternoons when I was exhausted from writing, or reading court transcripts, I would find inspiration from his stories that I needed to keep telling mine. I had come to realize later in life, even though I had always been a fan, that his songs were more than just music; they were chapters of people's lives, delicately woven into larger themes of good vs. evil and heartache vs. joy. I knew I could never write like he did, but I identified with his empathy for the struggles of the common man, and it carried me through difficult times—especially as I was sending my youngest child off into the world.

I would now be alone, though never lonely, because of course, your children never really leave you.

I rented a pickup truck, and Jake and I packed up his worldly belongings, leaving behind only his high school soccer gear and his fishing poles. I kept urging him to take his poles and tackle box ("Jake, you can still go fishing in college," I told him), but his mind was no longer on fishing and soccer; it was on girls and freedom.

With the truck all packed, we set out on the six-hour drive across Florida. We were barely up the interstate when we hit a massive rainstorm and had to park under an overpass and wait for the storm to pass. I don't know why it didn't occur to me that it would rain, since it always rains every afternoon in Florida. Everything got soaked.

The trip took eight hours because of all the weather we hit along the way. But it was probably the longest amount of time I had spent with my son in a while. We recalled funny memories like the time his sister, Amelia, got stuck in the doggie door trying to get into the house after losing her door key. We talked about him meeting new friends and navigating his new college life; he promised me he would call periodically and always take an Uber after drinking.

We spent that weekend browsing thrift stores and consignment shops in Tallahassee. Discoveries like a five-dollar rug and an old abstract oil painting made us feel like we had won the lottery. I helped him unpack his dishes and bedding and filled his refrigerator and pantry.

Then we said our goodbyes—me in tears and Jake just wanting me to leave so no one would see his mom crying.

I was glad I had my work, because I didn't want to think about losing my baby.

Later that same year, to our great joy, Amelia learned she was accepted into veterinary school at the University of Pennsylvania. I surprised her by flying up to Philadelphia that morning, knowing she would hear from the school that day one way or another. It was either going to be the best day ever or the worst, so I figured either way, it was good for me to be there.

With my kids now both away, my house was going to be clean all the time, there would be no dirty dishes in the sink, no underwear in the bathroom. There would be no more "Mom, what's for dinner?" In fact, I didn't have to cook dinner at all.

I got into the rented pickup truck, put Bruce on, and listened to him the whole drive back to South Florida.

About halfway home, I turned on my cell phone.

My other boss had been calling.

Casey had a long list of Epstein stories that still needed to be done.

chapter 41

CONSPIRACIES

One of Palm Beach Sheriff Ric Bradshaw's enemies—and one of the few willing to talk publicly about him—was a so-called whistle-blower named John Mark Dougan, a former PBSO sheriff's deputy who had defected to Russia in 2016.

Prior to leaving the U.S., Dougan had caused a lot of trouble for Bradshaw by starting an internet blog, PBSOtalk.org. The site's central purpose was exposing wrongdoing in his former agency and embarrassing Bradshaw in particular. At times, Dougan was success-ful, like when he published a photo in 2012 of PBSO officers posing with a topless woman at a golf outing—and when he revealed that Bradshaw had spent nearly one thousand dollars taking campaign donors to lunch. There was other dirt, not all of it credible, and some of it outright fake.

All of it was enough to piss Bradshaw off, so the sheriff allegedly assigned a former PBSO deputy, Kenneth "Mark" Lewis, to go after Dougan.

Dougan recorded Lewis admitting that Bradshaw used him to go after people. He warned that if Dougan wasn't careful, he might end up dead.[1]

Dougan reached out to the FBI to ask them to investigate, but when that failed, he became distrustful of the U.S. criminal justice system and began making trips to Russia.

During this time, Dougan figured out a way to use a flaw in Palm Beach County's property database to obtain the home addresses for police officers, federal agents, prosecutors, and other government officials whose information is not public. The personal details were then published on his website.[2]

Dougan blamed the data breach on Russian computer hackers, claiming he had sold PBSOtalk.org to them. But a month later, the FBI raided Dougan's Palm Beach home, armed with search warrants. They seized all his electronic equipment and computers.

Fearing that his arrest was imminent, and that he would land in Bradshaw's county jail, he fled to Russia, leaving behind his ex-wife and children.

Among those whom Florida state senator Lauren Book heard from after she demanded a criminal probe into Bradshaw was Dougan. He contacted her on the same day that she had been receiving threats.

"Be careful," Dougan warned. "Bradshaw has tentacles in high places."

When I finally tracked down Dougan, he compared Bradshaw to a mob boss.

"This guy is like a gangster, and the FBI won't touch him because everybody does favors for everybody in Palm Beach," he said.

Dougan claimed he had evidence in the Epstein case, but I was skeptical.

Now remarried and living in Moscow, Dougan said he had received political asylum in Russia, but had no ties to the Kremlin. He said he owns a technology company and volunteers helping disabled children.

At the same time, a number of British tabloids had reported that England's intelligence services were concerned that Russia had damaging information and videotapes about Prince Andrew's ties to Epstein. That information, they reported, had been given to them by Dougan.[3]

Dougan claimed he had copies of secret videotapes from Epstein's home, and said that the FBI had the originals. Dougan sent me a grainy black-and-white video clip of a young girl having sex with an older man. The man and the girl were unrecognizable, but Dougan insisted he had other videos—and that these tapes had been given to him by the lead detective in the case, Joe Recarey.

The footage was encrypted and could only be unlocked in the event that something sinister happened to Dougan. He said he was revolted by what he saw on the tapes and had no intention of making them public.

It was hard to believe that Recarey would have turned over copies of anything to Dougan. Mike Reiter said that the idea was insane.

But it wouldn't be the first time that someone would try to claim they had Epstein's sex tapes.

AT AROUND THE SAME TIME AS DOUGAN WAS MAKING CLAIMS ABOUT the tapes, another man who claimed to have Epstein's tapes reached out to attorney David Boies and his longtime friend and fellow lawyer Stan Pottinger.

Patrick Kessler, a brawny, hard-drinking hustler, claimed that he had been hired by Epstein in 2012 to set up encrypted servers overseas to archive a decade's worth of his data, including his financial records and sex videos. Kessler said he had stills of the videos, which showed prominent, wealthy men in sex acts with women and girls.

He wanted to expose these men, but he was worried about his safety. He admitted that he was using a false name for security reasons.

I had heard about Kessler's claims, and started poking around to find out about this shadowy figure hawking Epstein's secret videos.

Pottinger's law partner, Brad Edwards, told me he had met with Kessler and instantly decided he was a fraud. But Pottinger wasn't convinced, and asked Boies if he would help him determine whether or not Kessler was legitimate.

At first, Boies thought Kessler might have something.

Kessler produced still photographs of a video that he claimed showed Dershowitz having sex with Virginia Giuffre. Pottinger showed the blurry still to Virginia, which was a partially naked young woman sitting on the lap of a bare-chested older man with black-rimmed glasses.

Virginia felt certain that it was a photograph of her with Dershowitz.

Kessler also claimed to have a trove of other images: Ehud Barak, Prince Andrew, three billionaires, and a CEO.[4]

Pottinger reportedly discussed with Kessler ways to use the sex videos to extract money from some of the men with the intention of donating the settlements to charity. Kessler, however, wanted to make them public, starting with Barak, who was challenging Benjamin Netanyahu for prime minister of Israel. Barak, a frequent visitor to Epstein's homes, had been associated with Epstein for fifteen years.[5]

In mid-September, two *New York Times* reporters were invited by Boies to attend an off-the-record meeting with Kessler, who showed them pixelated stills of the videos on his phone. After the meeting, Kessler arranged to meet separately with the *Times* reporters.[6]

In his meeting with the reporters, Kessler pitched an angle for their story: how the victims' lawyers, namely Pottinger and Boies, were plotting to get payouts from some of the powerful men who were allegedly captured on video.

Kessler furnished the reporters with a flurry of texts and emails showing that Pottinger was entertaining the possibility that Kessler was credible and the videos were real.

When I reached out to Pottinger in early October, however, he, too, had concluded that Kessler was a liar, possibly sent to set the lawyers up.

Boies told me that many of the claims Kessler made turned out to be false, and Kessler refused to turn over the videos to allow them to be authenticated. Boies told me that he reported Kessler to the FBI and federal prosecutors.

Kessler had also contacted Dershowitz. This on its face didn't seem plausible unless he wanted to blackmail him with the images he had shown to the lawyers and reporters.

The *Times* reported that in a conversation that Dershowitz taped, Dershowitz theorized that Boies and Pottinger were plotting against him.[7]

"Did they ask about me?" Dershowitz asked Kessler.

"Of course they asked about you. You know that, sir," Kessler said.

"And you don't have anything on me, right?" Dershowitz said.

"I do not, no," Kessler replied.

"Because I never, I never had sex with anybody," Dershowitz said.

After months of work on the story, the *Times* reporters were unable to confirm any part of Kessler's claims.

Patrick Kessler has never been heard from again.

OVER THE PAST YEAR, PODCASTS HAVE SPRUNG UP ALL OVER THE internet claiming to have "exclusive" information about Epstein's various connections to everything from his work for the Israeli Mossad to pedophile rings in far-flung nations. Some people claimed that he had surgery and is still alive and in hiding. Unfortunately, Epstein's victims have fallen prey to some of these opportunists who enjoy the attention their antics draw on social media. One woman, for example, said she was a shaman who was planning an exorcism ceremony at Epstein's Florida mansion, which had been sold to a developer who planned to raze it. She called some of Epstein's victims and invited them to the demolition, telling them she would supply sledgehammers so they could participate in the "cleansing" event.

At least one of Epstein's victims flew in from out of state at her own expense to participate. The only problem was that the developer didn't even have possession of the property yet, let alone a date for demolition.

The reason that the Epstein story continues to reverberate across social media—and will remain a perfect storm for conspiracy theorists for decades to come—is because what Epstein was able to accomplish, even in death, defies all common sense. He and his associates have flouted the justice system in every way imaginable, creating an alternative reality devoid of facts.

Judges, prosecutors, and law enforcement and prison officials contribute to this maelstrom by condoning the sealing and redaction of public records pertaining to Epstein's crimes on such a large scale.

The FBI files, the Palm Beach grand jury records, witness testimony in civil lawsuits, the Homeland Security plane manifests—even the statement by Epstein's last cellmate—have been sealed or so heavily redacted that the public may never know the truth about what happened in this case.

This only sows mistrust and suspicion and undermines our justice system.

It's one thing to seal records to protect Epstein's victims; it's another to keep them secret to cover up crimes.

Chapter 42

THE RECKONING

The chair in the New York federal courtroom that Jeffrey Epstein had sat in one month earlier was eerily empty as more than two dozen women arrived on August 27, 2019, for a historic hearing that would change the course of how the U.S. criminal justice system treats victims of sexual assault.

The women all had strikingly similar features—in their appearance, their words, and their experiences. They were mostly fair, blond, and petite, with model-like posture; they brought with them similar stories of trauma, outrage, and courage. They sat on one side of the courtroom with their lawyers, with the horde of media and reporters, some of whom had waited in line for hours, on the other side.

The hearing was held to formally dismiss the criminal complaint against Epstein, a routine matter that would not normally trigger such a dramatic public event. But the judge and prosecutors noted that they had reached out to as many women as possible to invite them to speak for the first time about how, as teenagers or women barely out of their teens, they were preyed upon and abused by Epstein, Maxwell, and others who helped them advance their trafficking enterprise.

The opportunity, however, afforded little solace for those, like Courtney Wild, who had been fighting for years to see Epstein go to prison.

"Jeffrey Epstein robbed myself and all the other victims of our day in court to confront him one by one, and for that, he is a coward," she said in court.

"It's a rather stunning turn of events," Judge Richard Berman conceded.

He pointed out that he was bound by the Crime Victims' Rights Act to allow Epstein's victims to finally have their say.

"This is being done here, both as a matter of law and as a measure of respect that we have for the victims' difficult decisions to come forward in this matter," Berman said. ". . . I believe it is the court's responsibility and manifestly within its purview to ensure that the victims in this case are treated fairly and with dignity."

Prosecutor Maurene Comey announced that despite Epstein's death, the dismissal of his indictment would in no way stop the federal investigation into the case—which would now focus on other "co-conspirators."

Epstein's attorneys, however, used the hearing as a platform to urge the judge to launch a judicial inquiry into Epstein's death.

"Your honor, I think it is an understatement of the year to say the world looks and feels differently today than it did the last time I was before you," said Epstein's lead attorney Reid Weingarten.

"I would like to tell you how we see the world and where we are on that subject.

"We start with the Attorney General's statements, public statements, that there were very serious improprieties in the jail. We obviously read the press. We see that the warden has been taken out. We see that the guards on duty at the time have been put on leave.

"We understand guards are refusing to cooperate with the investigation. We have heard allegations that people at the time who had responsibility for protecting our client falsified information. We understand that there were orders out there that Jeffrey Epstein was never to be left alone and that the orders were ignored by many of the employees of the prison.

"So where does this lead?" Weingarten asked. "I think where it leads, Judge, is there are incredibly important questions that remain open. The public interest in this matter is obvious from this courtroom. There are conspiracy theories galore. We are all for finding the truth. We believe this court has an indispensable role to play.

"Whether or not this indictment is dismissed, I think this court has the inherent authority to find out what happened on its watch," Weingarten said.

Defense attorney Martin Weinberg contended that Epstein had no "defeatist attitude" and they had all been confident that they would be able to get him acquitted.

Comey, however, countered that the Justice Department had already convened a special grand jury to investigate Epstein's death—and that a separate team of prosecutors in the Southern District of New York were in charge of that investigation. Beyond that, anything else was irrelevant to the day's proceeding, which should focus on the victims.

"I think we've heard enough," Berman agreed, turning to the women in the courtroom.

"I have in the courtroom today fifteen victims that I represent and have represented over the years," said lawyer Brad Edwards. "There are at least twenty more who didn't make this hearing today for a multitude of reasons, some out of fear of public exposure, others because the way in which this case ended will never bring full justice, and they decided it was best for them not to talk today."

Edwards noted that regardless of the outcome of the case, he appreciated the concerns noted by Weingarten and Weinberg.

"There are a lot of people here today that are very sad by the way that this ended for both Mr. Epstein and the fact that full justice was robbed from them once again."

Then, one by one, the women walked up to the podium.

"In 2004, when I was fifteen years old, I flew on Jeffrey Epstein's plane to Zorro Ranch, where I was sexually molested by him for many hours. . . . I remember feeling so small and powerless," said one woman. "He positioned me by laying on the floor so that I was confronted by all the framed photographs on his dresser of him smiling with wealthy celebrities and politicians.

"I felt powerless, not merely because one man wanted to strip me of my innocence, but because I was the victim of a system that just disenfranchises human beings, making them vulnerable to pedophilic exploitation."

Amid tears, the women, many of them now mothers, spoke of years of self-loathing, shame, suicidal thoughts, and anger.

There was the story of a fifteen-year-old girl from a small Texas town near the New Mexico border who had lost her mother to cancer when she was eleven. She was following her mother's dream that she become a master at playing the violin. At a local mall, she was approached by "a lady" who saw the violin case and asked if she could play, and during the ensuing conversation she asked why the girl was wearing shabby clothing.

The older woman told the girl that she worked for a wealthy man who had a home nearby and he would pay to hear her play the violin. After some hesitation, she agreed.

"This was the beginning of the end of my childhood," she said.

"The man who only identified himself as Jeff had asked if I would give him a massage, and over four visits, eventually progressed to forced oral copulation. The money he gave me placed my young soul into a perverse sense of hell. I was so utterly disgusted with myself and what he did to me that I stopped going to see him. I had documented the events with a Texas rape crisis center about the man I know now as Jeffrey Epstein. . . . His actions placed me, a young girl, into a downward spiral to the point where I purchased a gun and drove myself to an isolated place to end my suffering.

"A voice that could only have been from my mother told me—'I am not the victim, I am the victor, and I dare not pull the trigger.' I returned the gun days later."

THERE WAS A RECKONING THAT DAY, HOWEVER, FAR GREATER THAN the horrific crimes of sexual abuse and the complicity of all those who knew about Epstein's crimes.

That day, in that courtroom, for the first time in their lives, Epstein's victims were not alone. There was a bond, a sisterhood that they were only just beginning to understand.

"It took me years to tell anyone what Epstein did to me because I was so ashamed and embarrassed at what people would say or think of me until I found out there were other victims, girls just like me," said Jennifer Araoz, who was raped by Epstein when she was fifteen.

Said Virginia: "The reckoning must not end. It must continue. He did not act alone and we, the victims, know that. We trust the government is listening, and that the others will be brought to justice."

AFTER THE HEARING, THERE WERE MORE TEARS. I COULD HEAR THE women talking about details of their experiences, comparing the names of recruiters, places they were taken, events that mirrored one another's. In the coming year, they would become friends on social media, they would visit one another and share photographs of their children.

Some of them would mount their own investigations into their recruiters and abusers.

I watched as Virginia, Michelle, Courtney, and Jena-Lisa became close friends and even stronger advocates for victims of sexual abuse.

Emily and I returned to interview them, nearly two years after first meeting them.

They were no longer the same women whom Emily and I had met back then.

Now they are warriors.

EPILOGUE

On July 2, 2020, a convoy of fifteen unmarked police vehicles lined up in the parking lot of the Market Basket, a grocery store in rural Warner, New Hampshire. It was just before dawn in this small village, about eighteen miles northwest of Concord. About a dozen federal agents gathered at the staging site—as aircraft buzzed overhead, portending that something was amiss in the rolling Mink Hills of the Merrimack River Valley.

At about 8:30 A.M., as I was working on this book, FBI agents barreled up the steep gravel road to a million-dollar mountaintop Tudor lodge. It was locked behind metal gates and hidden in the wilderness outside of Bradford, an enclave of 1,680 people.

The agents, armed with bolt cutters, breached the gate and marched to the front door with warrants, demanding that the private security guard inside open up. Through a window, they could see Ghislaine Maxwell disappear into another room and shut the door.

The agents broke down the door, finding her crouched in a back room. She was handcuffed and taken into custody.

It was almost a year to the day after Epstein's arrest.

The FBI and federal prosecutors in New York had been keeping a close eye on the fifty-eight-year-old British socialite as they quietly built a federal sex trafficking case against her in the aftermath of Epstein's death.

While the media speculated incessantly about her whereabouts, the woman accused of procuring underage girls for Epstein had been splitting her time between an oceanfront home in Massachusetts and the luxurious 156-acre spread in the New Hampshire mountains that she purchased with cash in December, prosecutors said.

She went to great lengths to remain in hiding, changing her phone number, registering her account in another name, "G-Max," and ordering packages under several pseudonyms.

Maxwell was now attached to Scott Borgerson, a former coast guard officer turned tech entrepreneur fifteen years her junior. Before fleeing to New Hampshire, she had left her partying life behind, taking on the role of stepmother to Borgerson's children at a $2.3 million estate in Manchester-by-the-Sea, Massachusetts.

Maxwell was charged in an eighteen-page grand jury indictment with six felony counts, including sex trafficking of minors as young as fourteen, as well as perjury. The abuse happened between 1994 and 1997 in New York, Florida, New Mexico, and Maxwell's home in London.

"Maxwell tried to normalize the sexual abuse . . . through a process known as grooming," Acting New York U.S. Attorney Audrey Strauss said at a press conference following Maxwell's arrest.

"Maxwell's presence as an adult woman helped put the minor victims at ease . . . and in some cases, Maxwell participated in the abuse herself."

Bill Sweeney, the assistant director of the FBI's New York bureau, said that agents were well aware that Maxwell was trying to evade them. But they had been keeping tabs on her through her cell phone.

"We recently discovered that she had slithered away to a gorgeous property in New Hampshire," he said.

Indeed, in the months before her arrest, Maxwell lived in the four-bedroom mansion on East Washington Road. The property, called "Tucked Away," had a main residence with a floor-to-ceiling fieldstone fireplace, stone patio, covered porch, and vast windows overlooking the mountains.

Despite the fact that she was one of the world's most-wanted women, a lot of folks in the small town didn't know who she was.

Federal prosecutor Alison Moe said Maxwell toured the New Hampshire home in November 2019, using the alias Janet Marshall and telling the real estate agent that she was a journalist. There was a man with her who identified himself as Scott Marshall. The property was purchased through an anonymous LLC with a Boston mailing address, prosecutors said.

The security guard on the property told authorities that one of Maxwell's brothers had hired former British military members to protect her in New Hampshire, and that she hadn't left the property since moving in.

Maxwell made her first court appearance in the midst of the coronavirus epidemic via video before a federal judge two days after her arrest. A phone number was given for members of the media and public to call in and listen to the hearing. I dialed in early, because I knew there would be a limited number of people able to get access to the call.

As I waited patiently in silence, I heard a woman with a British accent suddenly sobbing on the line. It startled me.

"Why is this happening?" the woman wailed. "I don't understand, I don't understand."

A court officer then interrupted her, telling the attorneys on the line to mute their microphones.

It was clear to me that the woman who had been crying was Maxwell, although her attorney wouldn't confirm my hunch. And when Maxwell did speak during the hearing, she sounded composed, prompting some members of the media to speculate that the woman who had been crying was someone else.

MAXWELL'S NEW DIGS AT THE METROPOLITAN DETENTION CENTER IN Brooklyn were a far cry from her spacious chalet in New Hampshire. She was assigned to an eight-by-ten cell in the federal prison, which is about three miles from the Metropolitan Correctional Center in Lower Manhattan, where Epstein spent his last days.

Attorney General William Barr vowed that federal authorities would not repeat the mistakes made with Epstein.

"We have asked them to tell us specifically the protocols they're following," Barr told ABC News. "And we have a number of systems to monitor the situation."

Maxwell hired criminal defense lawyer Christian Everdell, a former New York prosecutor who helped convict drug kingpin El Chapo; and former federal prosecutor Mark S. Cohen, known for the successful 1992 conviction of Mafia hit man Thomas "Tommy Karate" Pitera, who was suspected of killing more than one hundred people as a soldier in the Bonanno crime family.

Maxwell also had her civil lawyers in Colorado, New York, Britain, and the U.S. Virgin Islands.

Her family later added Miami criminal attorney David Oscar Markus, a protégé of Alan Dershowitz's who was one of the first people to come to the defense of Alexander Acosta after my series ran. Markus wrote an op-ed piece for the *Herald* praising Acosta as a dedicated public servant and tough prosecutor.

In a court filing, federal prosecutors said Maxwell was "an extreme flight risk," citing her wealth and international ties. Over the last three years, she had taken fifteen international trips and had more than two dozen bank accounts through which she transferred more than twenty million dollars, prosecutors said.

She held three passports, as a citizen of England, France, and the U.S., and had no real ties to the United States, except for a husband whom she declined to identify—but whom everyone assumed was Borgerson. U.S. District Judge Alison Nathan denied her bail, and Maxwell remained in prison, awaiting trial.

In the months that followed, Maxwell's lawyers complained about her oppressive jail conditions, including invasive searches, around-the-clock monitoring, and mouth inspections that she said exposed her to the risk of contracting the coronavirus.

In December 2020, her lawyers renewed their bail request, presenting another package, this time for $28.5 million, most of it pledged by her husband, whose name was still redacted from the public court filing. Prosecutors, however, noted that Maxwell was divorcing him, a move that her lawyers insisted she only considered to protect his reputation.

Still, Nathan denied the second request, criticizing Maxwell for giving the court misleading information about her finances and her marriage.

"The defendant now argues that her newly revealed relationship with her spouse signals her deep affective ties in the country, but at the time she was arrested, she was not living with him and claimed to be getting divorced," Nathan wrote.

Maxwell also claimed upon her arrest that she was worth $3.5 million, when in fact she and Borgerson had $22.5 million in assets.

Noting that Maxwell "demonstrated an extraordinary capacity to evade detection," the judge denied her bail request a second time.

IN THE DAYS BEFORE MAXWELL'S ARREST, I HAD BEEN CLOSELY following another dramatic story—the ouster of Geoffrey Berman, the U.S. attorney for the Southern District of New York.

On June 20, 2020, Berman—the prosecutor responsible for Epstein's arrest—was hastily fired by President Trump. His removal led to a public standoff between Berman and Attorney General William Barr, who had initially declared that Berman was resigning. But Berman refused to leave, suggesting that it was a clandestine effort by Trump to delay or disrupt investigations in SDNY's office.

Barr finally agreed to allow Berman's second-in-command, Audrey Strauss, to step in until a replacement could be confirmed by the Senate. Trump had already announced that he intended to nominate Jay Clayton, former head of the U.S. Securities and Exchange Commission, to the post.

During Berman's tenure, his office spearheaded the prosecution of former Trump attorney Michael Cohen and investigated several other Trump associates.

While the Epstein-Maxwell case was never mentioned by Berman, it's telling that Maxwell's arrest came so quickly after Berman was fired. This spawned a series of theories about whether Trump and Barr had pushed Berman out in order to install Clayton, a prosecutor who, like Acosta, would have been more politically friendly, not only to Trump but to others in his orbit, like Maxwell, who were facing criminal investigation.

Two weeks later, Trump had some kind words for his former socialite friend who was now in solitary confinement at the federal jail.

"I wish her well, frankly," Trump said of Maxwell during a White House press conference. And then in a subsequent interview, he questioned his own attorney general's conclusion that Epstein had committed suicide.

"People are still trying to figure out how did it happen? Was it suicide? Was he killed?" Trump asked.

IN NOVEMBER 2019, PRINCE ANDREW, FACING RELENTLESS SCRUTINY from the British press about his ties to Epstein, agreed to do an interview with the BBC. The move was a public relations ploy to address what he felt were misconceptions about his friendship with the pedophile financier—but it backfired spectacularly. Not only did the prince say he didn't regret his friendship with the notorious sex trafficker, but he noted that Epstein had given him "opportunities" that were "very useful." The interview was a royal disaster.

Andrew denied that he was involved in any inappropriate contact with Virginia Giuffre, noting that her description of him sweating and dancing at a London club had to be made up because the prince had a medical condition that impeded his ability to sweat. Later, photographs of him sweating at other events popped up on the internet.

Critics swiftly attacked him for his lack of candor and his failure to show empathy for the girls and women whom Epstein abused and exploited.

The royals have not always been paragons of virtue, but the interview only fanned the flames for critics, and a week after the interview, Andrew, then fifty-nine, announced he was stepping back from all his royal duties.

"I continue to unequivocally regret my ill-judged association with Jeffrey Epstein," he said in a statement announcing his retirement. "His suicide has left many unanswered questions, particularly for his victims, and I deeply sympathize with everyone who has been affected and wants some form of closure. I can only hope that, in time, they will be able to rebuild their lives."

The Epstein fallout in Europe continued, as Parisian authorities in December 2020 arrested Jean-Luc Brunel, the French modeling agent who had long been implicated in Epstein's sex trafficking operation. His arrest was the result of a broader probe into whether Brunel and others had used their modeling connections to procure minors for Epstein and his friends.

For two decades, Brunel, seventy-five, had faced accusations by models—some of them underage—who allege they were raped, drugged, and sexually abused by him. French authorities, however, ignored their allegations until several women went public in the wake of Epstein's arrest in New York. As a result, eight other women and four witnesses gave statements to French prosecutors.

Brunel was taken into custody at Charles de Gaulle airport as he was about to board a flight for Dakar, Senegal. Brunel was formally charged with the rape of minors that occurred during a time frame within the statute of limitations, French authorities said.

Brunel "organized the transportation and hosting of young women on behalf of Jeffrey Epstein," according to the official indictment. France does not extradite its citizens for prosecution abroad, but it's likely that U.S. authorities will try to question him as part of their investigation into other possible Epstein conspirators.

NEW YORK PROSECUTORS CONTINUE TO INVESTIGATE OTHER EPSTEIN associates, including his pilots, assistants, and financial partners.

Two of the co-conspirators in his 2008 plea deal—Sarah Kellen-Vickers and Nadia Marcinkova—claim that they, too, were sexually abused by Epstein. Kellen-Vickers, forty-one, was raised as a Jehovah's Witness and sexually abused at thirteen. She dropped out of school at fifteen, married at seventeen, and moved to Hawaii. Upon her divorce at twenty-one, she was cast out of the Jehovah's Witnesses and shunned by her family. She met Epstein a year later, and went to work for him as an assistant and continued working for him for more than a decade.

Her spokeswoman, Tracy Schmaler, said she was targeted by Epstein and Maxwell at a time when she was struggling financially and emotionally.

"At no time did Sarah recruit anyone on Epstein's or Maxwell's behalf. Sarah continues to struggle with the trauma of her experiences and has chosen not to speak publicly at this time."

Epstein's victims, however, claim in court files that Kellen acted as a lieutenant in Epstein's operation, organizing his sex schedule and helping him recruit new victims.

Epstein told his associates that Marcinkova, thirty-four (who also uses the name Marcinko), was brought to the United States from Slovakia to be his sex slave when she was fifteen. She is now a licensed flight trainer and pilot who owns an aviation company.

A number of Epstein's survivors have said in court documents that Marcinkova was a willing participant in the sexual abuse of minors, helping to facilitate orgies and threesomes with many girls for Epstein's benefit.

Kellen and Marcinkova visited Epstein more than sixty times while he was in the Palm Beach County jail and on work release.

Marcinkova declined to comment for this book. Her attorney, Erica T. Dubno, issued this statement: "Nadia wants to speak out about her victimization and to correct misconceptions about her. She is horrified and ashamed of having been subjected to forced sexual servitude at Epstein's direction. She also wants to help Epstein's other survivors. Unfortunately, Nadia is not yet able to comment publicly. However, she hopes, in time, for an opportunity to be heard and that all of Epstein's victims receive justice." Another co-conspirator in the 2008 immunity deal, Adriana Mucinska-Ross-Salazar, thirty-four, is a former model from Poland who worked for Epstein in 2002. Now a resident of Miami, in 2019 she married Ariel Salazar, a real estate developer. She has not commented publicly about her ties to Epstein and did not respond to requests for a statement for this book.

Lesley Groff, fifty-four, whom Epstein once described as "an extension of my brain," worked as the financier's executive assistant in New York for two decades. Now living in Connecticut, Groff denies that she knew anything about Epstein's crimes, despite claims in court documents from survivors who allege that she was key to helping him facilitate his criminal enterprise.

Groff's attorney, Michael Bachner, said his client worked as Epstein's business associate and had no knowledge or connection to his trafficking enterprise.

"Prosecutors have indicated in multiple conversations with me that based on the evidence they have so far uncovered during the course of their lengthy investigation, they do not intend to bring criminal charges against Lesley Groff," he said.

Alan Dershowitz, eighty-two, continues to be shadowed by his association with Epstein and his ongoing legal wars with attorney David Boies and Virginia Giuffre, who is suing him for defamation. As of this writing, a date has not been set for the trial, which Dershowitz vows will prove that he was never involved with Giuffre. His legal maneuvering, however, has dragged other high-profile men back into the spotlight, including Victoria's Secret owner Les Wexner and former Israeli prime minister Ehud Barak. The trial could reveal more about their connections to Epstein.

Dershowitz remains professor emeritus at Harvard Law School, where he taught for fifty years. He now is a frequent pundit on Fox News, has a podcast, and wrote a book in which he disputes the sexual abuse allegations that have been leveled against him. Lawyers representing Ghislaine Maxwell did not respond to requests for comment for this book.

IN DECEMBER 2020, DOUG BAND, ONCE A TOP ADVISER TO AND CONFIDANT of former president Bill Clinton, gave an interview to *Vanity Fair* magazine claiming that Clinton had indeed visited Epstein's "Orgy Island," despite the former president's repeated insistence that he had never set foot on Little St. James.[1]

ALSO IN 2020, THE ATTORNEY GENERAL OF THE U.S. VIRGIN ISLANDS, Denise George, brought a multicount indictment and civil enforcement action against Epstein's estate; his longtime attorney, Darren Indyke; and his accountant, Richard D. Kahn.

George is seeking the return of Epstein's islands, worth more than eighty million dollars. She alleges that Epstein used his islands as a home base for his sex trafficking operation and that the financial structure he created in USVI helped conceal his illegal activities. Some of the evidence she collected suggests that Epstein continued to abuse girls and young women in 2018—a full decade after he was given federal immunity. "Indyke and Kahn participated with Epstein in coercing his sex trafficking victims, in at least three cases, to enter into arranged and forced marriages in order to obtain immigration status for the foreign women so that they could continue to be available to Epstein for his abuse—a doubly deep assault on their will and dignity," according to court documents filed in the U.S. Virgin Islands.

George has also issued subpeonas to hedge fund manager Glenn Dubin; his former company, Highbridge Capital; and his wife, Eva Andersson.

IN DECEMBER 2020, THE U.S. DEPARTMENT OF JUSTICE'S OFFICE OF Professional Responsibility closed its investigation into the prosecutors involved in Epstein's 2007–08 criminal case in Florida. They concluded that while U.S. Attorney Alex Acosta executed "poor judgment" when he failed to prosecute Epstein, he committed no legal, professional, or ethical wrongdoing.

"OPR did not find evidence that his decision was based on corruption or other impermissible considerations, such as Epstein's wealth, status, or associations," the report said.

"Letting a well-connected billionaire get away with child rape and international sex trafficking isn't 'poor judgment'—it's a disgusting failure," Nebraska senator Ben Sasse responded after reading the report.

OPR said it reviewed hundreds of records, including emails, letters, memos, and investigative materials; the office also interviewed more than sixty people.

The report painted some of Acosta's top prosecutors in unflattering terms but stopped short of calling their actions improper. The Justice Department also debunked any suggestion that Epstein was an intelligence asset—or that someone in Washington pulled strings to help him obtain federal immunity. The 350-page report does, however, detail how the determined efforts of the lead federal prosecutor, Marie Villafaña, were repeatedly thwarted by Epstein's defense team—as well as her own bosses in the U.S. Attorney's Office, who made it clear that she was not to file any charges against the high-flying financier.

"Ms. Villafaña believes the injustice in this case is a direct result of implicit biases based on gender and socioeconomic status—biases that allowed Mr. Epstein's defense team unparalleled access to the decision-makers at the Justice Department, while the victims, Ms. Villafaña, and the FBI agents working the case were silenced," Villafaña's lawyer, Ty Kelly, said in a statement after the OPR's report was released.

While Villafaña had clear recall, as well as documentation, pertaining to her role in the case, Acosta told OPR he had no recollection of many of the events in question, including the secret breakfast meeting with Epstein's attorney Jay Lefkowitz.

Probably the most interesting factoid in the report is contained in a mysterious, small footnote, in which OPR investigators said that a sizable chunk of Acosta's emails during the critical time when the deal was being negotiated had been lost due to a "technical glitch."

THE CRIMINAL INVESTIGATION BY THE FLORIDA DEPARTMENT OF LAW Enforcement into former Palm Beach state attorney Barry Krischer's and Sheriff Ric Bradshaw's handling of the Epstein case remains ongoing. Justice Department investigators, in the December OPR report, said Acosta should not have ceded the Epstein case back to Krischer—who had already shown that he had been unduly influenced by Epstein and his lawyers. An email written in 2007 showed that federal prosecutors suspected that Krischer had possibly sabotaged the case so that the grand jury didn't get all the evidence that Palm Beach police had accumulated against Epstein.

"The state intentionally torpedoed it in the grand jury so it was brought to us," wrote one of Villafaña's supervisors in the email.

Bradshaw, meanwhile, was reelected in November 2020 to his fifth term as Palm Beach sheriff. In a preelection interview with the *South Florida Sun-Sentinel*'s editorial board, Bradshaw expressed confidence that Florida Department of Law Enforcement's criminal inquiry would clear him of any wrongdoing.

When I sought Bradshaw's comment for this book, his spokeswoman, Teri Barbera, maintained that the allegations against him were unsubstantiated.

IN APRIL 2020, A FEDERAL APPEALS COURT, IN A 2-1 DECISION, overturned Judge Marra's ruling that Epstein's plea deal was illegally executed by prosecutors in violation of the federal Crime Victims' Rights Act.

The 11th Circuit Court of Appeals in Atlanta ruled that because prosecutors never brought federal charges against Epstein, his victims weren't entitled to seek redress under the Crime Victims' Rights Act.

The plaintiff, Courtney Wild, won a rehearing before the full U.S. Court of Appeals for the 11th Circuit in December 2020. The court's decision was still pending when this book was published.

AS OF THIS WRITING, A BIPARTISAN BILL—NAMED THE COURTNEY Wild Crime Victims' Rights Reform Act—is being considered by Congress. The act provides tough penalties for prosecutors who violate victims' rights under federal law. The bill, if passed, will also fund victim assistance programs and provide monetary compensation for victims.

"We have fought for twelve years, and as I've said before, no matter how many obstacles pile up, we will never give up fighting for what's right," Wild said.

AFTER EPSTEIN'S DEATH, THE EXECUTORS OF HIS ESTATE SET UP A victims' compensation fund. As of March 2021, at least 175 women have filed claims and more than 67 million dollars has been paid to his sexual assault survivors.

ACKNOWLEDGMENTS

I have many people to thank for supporting me in this project and others I've tackled throughout my career. First and foremost: Casey Frank, the investigations editor at the *Miami Herald*, without whom I would not have been able to do this story and so many others exposing the cruelties and injustices in Florida's criminal justice system. His relentless passion for journalism and his empathy for the common man and woman have made him the quiet force behind stories that have helped countless vulnerable people and held corrupt and negligent leaders accountable.

I also could not have done this book without the support of our former CEO at McClatchy, Craig Forman; our former executive editor and publisher, Mindy Marqués González; McClatchy's vice president of news, Kristin Roberts; our managing editor, Rick Hirsch; and our lawyers, Sandy Bohrer, Scott Ponce, and Steve Burns. Thanks also to McClatchy's Jeanne Segal and Melanie Jensen.

I am grateful to the brilliant team of graphic artists, copy editors, and journalism magicians who helped me with my *Miami Herald* series on Epstein: Aaron Albright, Eddie Alvarez, Mary Behne, Marta Oliver-Craviotto, Jessica Gilbert, Noel Gonzalez, Monika Leal, Brittany Peterson, Pedro Portal, and Adrian Ruhi.

Thanks to my former *Herald* colleagues who lifted my spirits, let me cry on their shoulders, and made me believe I could do it: Michael Sallah, Audra D. S. Burch, and Sergio Bustos.

I would be remiss if I didn't recognize the countless other talented journalists from all over the world who covered aspects of the Epstein story over the past decade, many of whom are cited in this book. In particular, I want to acknowledge the work of Michele Dargan of the *Palm Beach Daily News*, investigative journalist Vicky Ward, and Fred Grimm, whose columns in the *Miami Herald* inspired me to reexamine this case.

There have been other relentless reporters who contributed to the *Miami Herald*'s coverage of this case over the past two years, including Nick Nehamas, Sarah Blaskey, Jay Weaver, and Linda Robertson, as well as McClatchy's Ben Wieder and Kevin G. Hall.

A long list of people gave generously of their time to help further my understanding of this case. They sat for interviews, took my phone calls, and pointed me in the right direction. Among them: Michael Reiter, Sigrid McCawley, Brad Edwards, Jack Scarola, Paul Cassel, David Boies, Marci Hamilton, Francey Hakes, Jose Lambiet, Kenneth Lanning, Jessica Arbour, Adam Horowitz, Spencer Kuvin, Bob Josefsberg, Bill Berger, Kevin D'Amour, Dr. Michael Baden, Sloane Veshinski, and Jennifer Recarey.

To Geoffrey Berman, Maurene Comey, and Alex Rossmiller: thank you for having the courage to do what weaker prosecutors would not.

Thanks to all my former colleagues at the *Philadelphia Daily News* who made me the reporter I am today. I've been fortunate to have editors who believed in me over the years: Patricia Andrews,

Manny Garcia, Brian Toolan, Michael Days, Kurt Heine, Jack Morrison, and Tony Rhodin.

Special thanks to Carol McKenna for not kicking the kids and me out of our home when I couldn't pay the rent.

Thanks to Eileen Soler and Lynn Occhiuzzo for their help with the book cover.

I am most grateful to my agent, Laurie Liss, who saw this book as a story of triumph over evil and helped shield me from all the slings and arrows that I faced writing it. To my editor at Dey Street Books, Carrie Thornton: thank you for your steady hand and patience. Thanks also to my copy editor, Greg Villepique; my lawyer, George Sheanshang; my assistant, Chandler Plante; my accountant, Isabel Lago; and my life coach and dear friend, Lois Kirn.

Telling the Jeffrey Epstein story would not have been possible without the fierce determination of my friend and collaborator, the great visual journalist Emily Michot, who kept me sane, delivered me from the Epstein darkness, and captured in photographs and video what I could never do in words.

Lastly, I would not have been able to navigate the challenges I've faced without the three loves of my life—my children, Amelia and Jake, and my best friend of forty years, Nancy Morgan.

NOTES

CHAPTER 1: JOE

1. Mike Clary, "Royal Palm Beach Mourns Again; School Copes with 4th Death in Four Years," *South Florida Sun-Sentinel*, November 14, 2004.

CHAPTER 2: FINDING JANE DOE

1. Amy Driscoll, "Cuban American from Miami Leads Attack on Slavery," *Miami Herald*, June 14, 2004.
2. Ibid.
3. Ibid.
4. Charlie Savage, "Report Shows How Bush White House Sought Jobs for Allies," *New York Times*, July 31, 2008.
5. Adam Serwer, "The Scandal That May Haunt the New Nominee for Labor Secretary," *The Atlantic*, February 16, 2017.
6. Josh Gerstein, "Trump's Labor Nominee Oversaw 'Sweetheart Plea Deal' in Billionaire's Underage Sex Case," *Politico*, February 16, 2017.

CHAPTER 4: EPPY

1. Landon Thomas Jr., "Jeffrey Epstein: International Moneyman of Mystery," *New York*, October 28, 2002.

2. "Bill, Stars Enjoy African Trek," *New York Post*, September 25, 2002.

3. Landon Thomas Jr., "Jeffrey Epstein: International Moneyman of Mystery," *New York*, October 28, 2002.

4. Ibid.

5. Landon Thomas Jr., "Financier Starts Sentence in Prostitution Case," *New York Times*, July 1, 2008.

6. Ibid.

7. David Folkenflik, "The *New York Times*, the Unreliable Source and the Exposé That Missed the Mark," NPR, March 12, 2020.

8. "Investigation and Study of the Works Progress Administration," Hearings of the Subcommittee of the Committee on Appropriations, House of Representatives, 76th Congress, First Session, 1939.

9. Ibid.

10. James Patterson, John Connolly, and Tim Malloy, *Filthy Rich: A Powerful Billionaire, the Sex Scandal That Undid Him, and All the Justice That Money Can Buy: The Shocking True Story of Jeffrey Epstein* (New York: Grand Central Publishing, 2016), p. 86.

11. Thomas Volscho, "Jeffrey Epstein Dodged Questions About Sex with His Dalton Students," *Daily Beast*, July 12, 2019.

12. Elisabeth Bumiller, "Headmaster at Dalton Resigns Under Pressure," *New York Times*, March 13, 1997.

13. Donald Barr, *Space Relations* (New York: Fawcett/Crest, 1974).

14. Mike Baker and Amy Julia Harris, "Jeffrey Epstein Taught at Dalton. His Behavior Was Noticed," *New York Times*, July 12, 2019.

15. Ibid.

16. Linda Robertson and Aaron Brezel, "Poor, Smart and Desperate to Be Rich: How Epstein Went from Teaching to Wall Street," *Miami Herald*, July 21, 2019.

17. Gregory Zuckerman and Khadeeja Safdar, "Epstein Flourished as He Forged Bond with Retail Billionaire," *Wall Street Journal*, July 12, 2019.

18. Hannah Gold, "Jeffrey Epstein Was Once *Cosmopolitan*'s 'Bachelor of the Month,'" *The Cut*, July 29, 2019.

19. Sharon Churcher, "Epstein's Girl Friday 'Fixer': Dead Tycoon's Daughter Ghislaine Maxwell and the Girls She Hired for Paedophile's Stable," *Daily Mail*, March 7, 2011.

20. Vicky Ward, "The Talented Mr. Epstein," *Vanity Fair*, March 2003.

21. Ibid.

22. Ibid.

23. Matt Stieb, "Jeffrey Epstein Used a Bullet and a Dead Cat to Intimidate *Vanity Fair* Editor Graydon Carter: Report," *New York*, August 23, 2019.

24. Vicky Ward, "I Tried to Warn You About Sleazy Billionaire Jeffrey Epstein in 2003," *Daily Beast*, January 6, 2015.

CHAPTER 6: DEAD ENDS

1. Ronan Farrow, "The *National Enquirer*, a Trump Rumor, and Another Secret Payment to Buy Silence," *The New Yorker*, April 12, 2018.

CHAPTER 7: THE FIRST DEAL

1. William Kelly, "Attack Ads Begin in Mayoral Campaign," *Palm Beach Daily News*, February 12, 2009.

2. Randy Loftis, "Magic Words: Groucho Can Stay," *Miami Herald*, July 7, 1983.

CHAPTER 8: MUSIC CITY

1. Jose Lambiet, "Exclusive: 'She Suffered Tremendously—and It Started with Jeffrey Epstein,' " *Daily Mail*, July 15, 2019.

2. Ibid.

CHAPTER 11: FOLLOW THE MONEY

1. Adam Davidson, host, "In the Shadow of the Towers," *Broken: Jeffrey Epstein* (podcast), September 26, 2019.

2. Ibid.

3. Ibid.

4. Marc Fisher and Jonathan O'Connell, "Final Evasion: For 30 Years, Prosecutors and Victims Tried to Hold Jeffrey Epstein to Account. At Every Turn, He Slipped Away," *Washington Post*, August 10, 2019.

5. Associated Press, "The Forbes 400: Walton Tops List of Richest Americans," *Los Angeles Times*, October 15, 1985.

6. Emily Steel, Steve Eder, Sapna Maheshwari, and Matthew Goldstein, "How Jeffrey Epstein Used the Billionaire Behind Victoria's Secret for Wealth and Women," *New York Times*, July 25, 2019.

7. Ibid.

8. Ibid.

9. Vicky Ward, "The Talented Mr. Epstein," *Vanity Fair*, March 2003.

10. Brian E. Crowley and Meg James, "Clinton Heads for Haiti to Watch U.N. Takeover," *Palm Beach Post*, March 31, 1995.

11. Ben Davis, "The Artist Who Painted Jeffrey Epstein's Portrait of Bill Clinton in a Dress Tells Us Why She Made It, and What It Means," ArtNetNews, August 20, 2019, news.artnet.com/art-world/artist-epstein-clinton-painting -1628953.

12. Associated Press, "Customs Agent Accompanying Clinton Dies of Boat Injuries," *Chicago Tribune*, January 7, 1998.

CHAPTER 12: FOREVER CHANGED

1. Larry Keller, "Epstein Camp Calls Female Accusers Liars," *Palm Beach Post*, August 8, 2006.

CHAPTER 13: OPERATION LEAP YEAR

1. Susan Page and Kevin Johnson, "As Gonzales Exits, Battles Looming for White House," *USA Today*, August 28, 2007.

CHAPTER 17: VIRGINIA

1. Elliot Kleinberg, "A Shadow in the Land," *Palm Beach Post*, August 19, 2017.

CHAPTER 20: MADAM GHISLAINE

1. Martha M. Hamilton, "Robert Maxwell's Death at Sea Gives Birth to a Big Mystery," *Washington Post*, December 23, 1991.

2. Ibid.

3. Nick Sommerlad, "Ghislaine Maxwell Ordered Shredding of Crooked Dad's Paperwork Hours After He Drowned," *Mirror*, August 2, 2020.

4. "Board of Bankrupt *Daily News* Meets with Kevin Maxwell," United Press International, December 19, 1991.

5. "What Robert Maxwell Left His Sons," *Financial Times*, June 18, 1992.

6. Craig R. Whitney, "Robert Maxwell, 68: From Refugee to the Ruthless Builder of a Publishing Empire," *New York Times*, November 6, 1991.

7. Elisabeth Maxwell, *A Mind of My Own* (New York: HarperCollins, 1994), pp. 256, 346–50.

8. Craig R. Whitney, "Robert Maxwell, 68: From Refugee to the Ruthless Builder of a Publishing Empire," *New York Times*, November 6, 1991.

9. Elisabeth Maxwell, *A Mind of My Own* (New York: HarperCollins, 1994), p. 379.

10. Roger Cohen, "Maxwell's Empire: How It Grew, How It Fell, Charming the Big Bankers Out of Millions," *New York Times*, December 20, 1991.

11. Ibid.

12. Elisabeth Maxwell, *A Mind of My Own* (New York: HarperCollins, 1994), p. 469.

13. Eleanor Berry, *My Unique Relationship with Robert Maxwell: The Truth at Last* (East Sussex: Book Guild Publishing, 2019), p. 38.

14. Elisabeth Maxwell, *A Mind of My Own* (New York: HarperCollins, 1994), pp. 376–77.

15. Tom Poster and Phil Roura, "N.Y. Overnight," *St. Louis Post-Dispatch*, May 17, 1989.

16. Alessandra Stanley, "Daily News Becomes the Fief of an Often Imperious Master," *New York Times*, March 17, 1991.

17. Craig Whitley, "The Media Business: Public Stock Offering Set by Maxwell," *New York Times*, May 1, 1991.

18. Alex Jones, "The Media Business: Press Notes; Maxwell Fights Murdoch on New Front: Coupons," *New York Times*, June 10, 1991.

19. Martha M. Hamilton, "Robert Maxwell's Death at Sea Gives Birth to a Big Mystery," *Washington Post*, December 23, 1991.

20. Ibid.

21. Richard Lorant, "Family Prepares to Leave Canary Islands with Maxwell's Body," Associated Press, November 7, 1991.

22. Carolyn Davies, "The Murky Life and Death of Robert Maxwell," *Guardian*, August 22, 2019.

23. "Shamir Describes Maxwell as Friend of Israel," Associated Press, November 5, 1991.

24. Ibid.

25. Gordon Thomas and Martin Dillon, *The Assassination of Robert Maxwell: Israel's Superspy* (London: Chrysalis Books Group, 2003), p. 8.

26. John Barry, Daniel Pedersen, Tony Clifton, Tom Morganthau, and Theodore Stanger, "One Man, Many Tales," *Newsweek*, November 4, 1991.

27. Ibid.

28. Elisabeth Maxwell, *A Mind of My Own* (New York: HarperCollins, 1994), pp. 513–16.

29. Ibid, p. 521.

30. Ibid, p. 529.

31. Ibid.

32. Michael Robotham, "The Mystery of Ghislaine Maxwell's Secret Love," *Daily Mail*, November 15, 1992.

CHAPTER 21: THE PRINCE AND THE PIPER

1. "Mirror Group Claims Ian and Kevin Maxwell Diverted Funds," Associated Press, December 19, 1991.

2. Tony Maguire, "Life's Still Sweet for Maxwell Girls," *Evening Standard*, June 29, 1992.

3. Nigel Rosser, "Andrew's Fixer: She's the Daughter of Robert Maxwell and She's Manipulating His Jetset Lifestyle," *Evening Standard*, January 22, 2001.

4. Marcus Scriven, "The Return of Ghislaine," *Evening Standard*, April 24, 1997.

5. Alan D. Abbey, "Isabel Maxwell Fights Back," *Jerusalem Post*, December 12, 2003.

6. Louise Oswald, "Fury over High Flying Maxwell," *Herald Sun,* November 11, 1992.

7. Michael Robotham, "The Mystery of Ghislaine Maxwell's Secret Love," *Daily Mail,* November 15, 1992.

8. "Randy Andy's Hush-Hush Visit," *New York Post,* April 21, 1999.

9. "Lawsuit Evolves over Woman's Dinner with Prince Andrew in Hawaii," Associated Press, August 6, 1999.

10. Nick Sommerlad, "Sordid High Life of Paedo Billionaire Who Became Prince's Pal," *Daily Mirror,* January 5, 2015.

11. Karen Rockett, "Andrew's 20,000-Pound Fling for Ghislaine," *Sunday Mirror,* December 10, 2000.

12. Jon Clarke and Caroline Graham, "Prince Andrew, a Blonde Model Who Runs a Sex Aid Company and the Flights on Donald Trump," *Daily Mail,* January 7, 2001.

13. Gita Mendis and John Sturgis, "Girls, Girls, Girls," *Evening Standard,* January 4, 2001.

14. Emily Maitliss, "Prince Andrew and the Epstein Scandal," *BBC Newsnight,* November 15, 2019.

15. Sharon Churcher, "Can Lynn Rescue Andrew's Image?," *Mail on Sunday,* May 6, 2001.

16. "The Top Ten Naughty Heiresses," *Evening Standard,* March 5, 2004.

17. George Gurley, "Vikran Chatwal, Turban Cowboy," *New York Observer,* November 18, 2002.

18. Catherine Ostler, "Andrew, Young Girls, and the Very Unsavory Life of Captain Bov's Daughter," *Daily Mail,* March 5, 2011.

CHAPTER 23: BAIT AND SWITCH

1. Larry Keller, "Plea Deal Denied for Dad Accused of Killing Baby," *Palm Beach Post,* November 20, 2007.

2. Nancy Othon, "Judge Rejects Plea Deal in Crash That Killed Two," *South Florida Sun-Sentinel,* October 13, 2007.

3. Susan Spencer-Wendel, "Man Pleads Guilty in Crash," *Palm Beach Post,* March 31, 2007.

CHAPTER 24: THE GET OUT OF JAIL FREE CARD

1. Sarah Blaskey and Nicholas Nehamas, "Why Was Jeffrey Epstein Allowed to Purchase Small Women's Panties from the Palm Beach Jail?" *Miami Herald,* August 19, 2019.

2. Michele Dargan, "PB Sex Offender in Work-Release," *Palm Beach Daily News,* December 11, 2008.

CHAPTER 25: SHOE-LEATHER REPORTING

1. Francisco Alvarado, "Big-Name Founders of Miami's U.S. Century Bank in Big-Money Fight with Bank's Board," *Florida Bulldog*, December 12, 2018.
2. Brian Bandell, "Former U.S. Century Bank Director Barreto Defends Loan Modification Targeted in Lawsuit," *South Florida Business Journal*, December 11, 2012.

CHAPTER 28: AFTERSHOCKS

1. Benjamin Weiser, Ben Protess, Matthew Goldstein, and William K. Rashbaum, "Preet Bharara Shunned Politics. His End Was Tinged by Them," *New York Times*, March 12, 2017.

CHAPTER 32: KATIE JOHNSON

1. Jacob Bernstein, "Whatever Happened to Ghislaine Maxwell's Plan to Save the Oceans?," *New York Times*, August 14, 2019.
2. Michael Rothfeld and Joe Palazzolo, "Trump Lawyer Arranged $130,000 Payment for Adult-Film Star's Silence," *Wall Street Journal*, January 12, 2018.
3. Michael Cohen, *Disloyal: A Memoir* (New York: Skyhorse Publishing, 2020), pp. 331–55.
4. Lester Holt, "A Video 27 Years Ago That Offers a Glimpse into the Past Relationship Between Trump and Jeffrey Epstein," NBC News, July 17, 2019.
5. Beth Reinhard, Rosalind S. Helderman, and Marc Fisher, "Donald Trump and Jeffrey Epstein Partied Together. Then an Oceanfront Palm Beach Mansion Came Between Them," *Washington Post*, July 31, 2019.
6. Ava Van de Water, "Palm Beach Estate Sells for $12 Million," *Palm Beach Post*, December 2, 1994.
7. Jeff Ostrowski, "Russian Fertilizer Mogul Scoops Up Trump Property," *Palm Beach Post*, June 24, 2008.
8. Ibid.
9. Michael Gross, "Inside Donald Trump's One-Stop Parties: Attendees Recall Cocaine and Very Young Models," *Daily Beast*, October 24, 2016.
10. Lisa Bloom, "Why the New Child Rape Case Filed Against Donald Trump Should Not Be Ignored," *Huffington Post*, June 29, 2016.
11. David Fahrenthold, "Trump Recorded Having Extremely Lewd Conversation About Women in 2005," *Washington Post*, October 8, 2016.

CHAPTER 33: FIREWORKS

1. Meghan Morris, "We Found Jeffrey Epstein's Social-Media Accounts. On Spotify, His Tastes Ranged from Louis C.K. to Songs Like 'Before You Accuse Me' and 'Hot for Teacher,'" *Business Insider*, August 22, 2019.
2. Pervaiz Shallwani, Kate Briquelet, and Harry Siegel, "Jeffrey Epstein Arrested for Sex Trafficking of Minors," *Daily Beast*, July 6, 2019.

CHAPTER 34: NO APOLOGIES, NO REGRETS

1. Mimi Rocah, Jennifer Rodgers, and Berit Berger, "Acosta's Epstein Excuses Are Nonsensical and Self-Serving," *Daily Beast*, July 11, 2019.
2. Kate Bolduan, "Labor Secretary Acosta Resigns amid Furor over Epstein Case," CNN, July 12, 2019.

CHAPTER 35: INMATE 76318-054

1. "Hon. Richard M. Berman." Practising Law Institute.
2. Elizabeth Rosner, Tina Moore, Larry Celona, and Bruce Golding, "NYPD Let Convicted Pedophile Jeffrey Epstein Skip Judge-Ordered Check-ins," *New York Post*, July 10, 2019.
3. Ibid.

CHAPTER 36: PEDOPHILE ISLAND

1. Holly Aguirre, " 'The Girls Were Just So Young': The Horrors of Jeffrey Epstein's Private Island," *Vanity Fair*, July 20, 2019.
2. Suzanne Carlson, "Contractor Recalls 6 Years on Epstein's Island," *Virgin Islands Daily News*, July 22, 2019.
3. Suzanne Carlson, "Maxwell Not Facing Criminal Charges in Virgin Islands, AG Says," *Virgin Islands Daily News*, July 3, 2020.
4. Allison Quinn, Harry Siegel, and Pervaiz Shallwani, "Jeffrey Epstein Found Injured in Manhattan Jail Cell," *Daily Beast*, July 24, 2019.
5. Hunter McFerrin, "Why Causes of Poverty in Virgin Islands Are Likely to Fester," *Borgen Magazine*, October 15, 2017.

CHAPTER 37: HARVARD, MIT, AND THE BILLIONAIRES CLUB

1. Tim Stewart, "Stephen Hawking Pictured on Jeffrey Epstein's 'Island of Sin,' " *Telegraph*, January 12, 2015.
2. Peter Aldhous, "How Jeffrey Epstein Bought His Way into an Exclusive Intellectual Boys Club," *BuzzFeed*, September 26, 2019.
3. James B. Stewart, Matthew Goldstein, and Jessica Silver-Greenberg, "Jeffrey Epstein Hoped to Seed Human Race with His DNA," *New York Times*, July 31, 2019.

4. Ibid.
5. Diane E. Lopez, "Report Regarding Jeffrey Epstein's Connections to Harvard," Harvard University, May 1, 2020.
6. Ibid.
7. Ibid.
8. Sonali Basak, Heather Perlberg, and Sabrina Willmer, "Jeffrey Epstein Had a Door into Apollo: His Deep Ties with Leon Black," *Bloomberg*, July 31, 2019.
9. Ronan Farrow, "How an Élite University Research Center Concealed Its Relationship with Jeffrey Epstein," *The New Yorker*, September 7, 2019.
10. Khadeeja Safdar, Rebecca Davis O'Brien, Gregory Zuckerman, and Jenny Strasburg, "Jeffrey Epstein Burrowed into the Lives of the Rich and Made a Fortune," *Wall Street Journal*, July 25, 2019.
11. Ibid.
12. Sonali Basak, Heather Perlberg, and Sabrina Willmer, "Jeffrey Epstein Had a Door into Apollo: His Deep Ties with Leon Black," *Bloomberg*, July 31, 2019.
13. Ibid.
14. Kate Briquelet, "REVEALED: We Found Billionaire Pedophile Jeffrey Epstein's Secret Charity," *Daily Beast*, April 16, 2019.
15. Matthew Goldstein and Katherine Rosman, "Apollo CEO to Step Down After Firm Finds More Payments to Jeffrey Epstein," *New York Times*, January 25, 2021.
16. Matthew Goldstein, "Leon Black Calls Relationship with Jeffrey Epstein a 'Terrible Mistake,'" *New York Times*, October 20, 2020.
17. John Jurgensen, "In Bill Gates's Mind, a Life of Processing," *Wall Street Journal*, September 10, 2019.
18. Emily Flitter and James B. Stewart, "Bill Gates Met with Jeffrey Epstein Many Times, Despite His Past," *New York Times*, October 12, 2019.
19. Ibid.
20. Ronan Farrow, "How an Élite University Research Center Concealed Its Relationship with Jeffrey Epstein," *The New Yorker*, September 7, 2019.
21. Emily Flitter and James B. Stewart, "Bill Gates Met with Jeffrey Epstein Many Times, Despite His Past," *New York Times*, October 12, 2019.

CHAPTER 38: IN PLAIN SIGHT

1. William D. Cohan, "For Billionaire Glenn Dubin, the Epstein Saga Isn't Over," *Vanity Fair*, September 4, 2019.

CHAPTER 39: JEFFREY EPSTEIN DIDN'T KILL HIMSELF

1. Ali Watkins, Danielle Ivory, and Christina Goldbaum, "Inmate 76318-054: The Last Days of Jeffrey Epstein," *New York Times*, August 17, 2019.

2. Stephen Rex Brown, "AG Quizzed Celli, Barr 'Livid' After Perv's Suicide," *Daily News* (New York), January 5, 2021.
3. Dan Bates, "EXCLUSIVE: 'It Was a Homicide—but I Don't Know Who Killed Him,' " *Daily Mail*, May 26, 2020.
4. James D. Walsh, "The 26-Year-Old Defense Attorney Whose First Two Clients Were El Chapo and Jeffrey Epstein," *New York*, August 29, 2019.
5. Stephen Rex Brown, "AG Quizzed Celli, Barr 'Livid' after Perv's Suicide," *Daily News* (New York), January 5, 2021.
6. Andrea Salcedo, "What We Know About Jeffrey Epstein's Death," *New York Times*, August 15, 2019.
7. Carol D. Leonnig and Aaron C. Davis, "Autopsy Finds Broken Bones in Jeffrey Epstein's Neck, Deepening Questions Around His Death," *Washington Post*, August 15, 2019.
8. E. J. Dickson, "*Washington Post* Doubles Down amid Epstein Conspiracy Theory Controversy," *Rolling Stone*, August 21, 2019.

CHAPTER 41: CONSPIRACIES

1. Lawrence Mower, "Deputy Who Said He Went After Bradshaw's Enemies Investigated by PBSO," *Palm Beach Post*, August 27, 2015.
2. Jess Swanson, "Hackers Post Confidential Records of 4,000 Palm Beach County Cops, Prosecutors, and Judges," *Broward-Palm Beach New Times*, February 16, 2016.
3. Paul Thompson, "Exclusive—Revealed: Ex-Cop Who MI6 Fears Has Leaked Files on Prince Andrew's Friendship with Jeffrey Epstein to Russia Breaks Silence to Say He's Got Hours of Footage Taken from Inside Paedophile's Florida Mansion," *Daily Mail*, September 24, 2019.
4. Jessica Silver-Greenberg, Emily Steel, Jacob Bernstein, and David Enrich, "Jeffrey Epstein, Blackmail and a Lucrative 'Hot List,' " *New York Times*, November 30, 2019.
5. Isabel Kershner, "Epstein's Ties to Former Israeli Leader Shake Up Election Campaign," *New York Times*, July 16, 2019.
6. David Folkenflik, "The *New York Times*, the Unreliable Source and the Exposé That Missed the Mark," NPR, March 12, 2020.
7. Jessica Silver-Greenberg, Emily Steel, Jacob Bernstein, and David Enrich, "Jeffrey Epstein, Blackmail and a Lucrative 'Hot List,' " *New York Times*, November 30, 2019.

EPILOGUE

1. Gabriel Sherman, "Confessions of a Clintonworld Exile," *Vanity Fair*, December 2, 2020.

ABOUT THE AUTHOR

Julie K. Brown is an investigative reporter with the *Miami Herald*. During her forty-year career, she has worked for a number of newspapers, focusing on crime, justice, and human rights issues. As a member of the *Herald*'s Investigative Team, she has won dozens of awards, including two George Polk Awards, a Robert F. Kennedy Journalism Award, and the Hillman Prize for Journalism in the Common Good. In 2020, she was named as one of *Time* magazine's 100 Most Influential People of the Year. Her 2018 *Miami Herald* series "Perversion of Justice" led to the arrest of Jeffrey Epstein and his former partner Ghislaine Maxwell; the resignation of President Trump's labor secretary Alex Acosta; two federal investigations; a compensation fund for Epstein's victims; and national reforms in the way victims are treated by the criminal justice system.

Brown previously won acclaim for a series of stories about abuses and corruption in Florida prisons. The stories led to the resignations of top agency officials, firings of corrupt corrections officers, and an overhaul of the treatment of women prisoners and inmates with mental and physical disabilities. Born in Glenside, Pennsylvania, she grew up in the Philadelphia suburbs and graduated with a bachelor's degree in journalism from Temple University. She lives in Hollywood, Florida.